THE PROBLEM OF PRISONS

Publication of this book would not have been possible without the generous support of the New Zealand Law Foundation. This support is gratefully acknowledged by the author and publisher.

The
Problem of Prisons

CORRECTIONS REFORM IN NEW ZEALAND SINCE 1840

GREG NEWBOLD

dp

This book is dedicated to (the late) Gerry Orchard

© 2007 Greg Newbold

Published in 2007 by

Dunmore Publishing Ltd
PO Box 25080
Wellington
books@dunmore.co.nz

National Library of New Zealand Cataloguing-in-Publication Data

Newbold, Greg.
The problem of prisons : corrections reform in New Zealand
since 1840 / Greg Newbold.
Includes bibliographical references and index.
ISBN 978-1-877399-21-3
1. Corrections—New Zealand—History. 2. Criminal justice,
Administration of—New Zealand—History. 3. Prison
administration—New Zealand—History. I. Title.
364.60993—dc 22

Text: Warnock Pro 10.5 / 12.75
Printer: Keeling and Mundy, Palmerston North
Typesetting & design: Matthew Bartlett, Wellington
Cover design: Central Media, Wellington
Front cover photograph: Grant Hunter

*The support of the New Zealand Law Foundation
and the Ministry of Justice is gratefully acknowledged.*

CONTENTS

FOREWORD

Shortly before he left office in 1960, Sam Barnett, Secretary for Justice for the previous 11 years, declared that New Zealand had no national penal policy. "We are imitators," he wrote in the Justice Department's annual report for 1959. "We have to be convinced by experiment and experience in other countries before we will venture. New Zealand has a reputation for independent thought and courageous initiative in the social field. That is certainly not true in the penal field."

Nearly 50 years later, it is interesting to ask whether a distinctive national penal policy has emerged in this country. Clearly, we have been strongly influenced by dominant overseas models, principally those of the United Kingdom and the United States of America. The national prison system established by Arthur Hume in the 1890s was closely based on the British system of that time. Subsequent reforms during the first two thirds of the last century were clearly influenced by movements in both Britain and America. More recently, aspects of the Canadian correctional system have been very influential. In broad terms, the criminal justice systems in western-style democracies tend to have more similarities than differences. In a sense, the most distinctive feature of the New Zealand system has been our relatively high imprisonment rate – compared to countries such as Australia, Canada and the United Kingdom – which has persisted over many decades. Our imprisonment rate is currently the fourth highest of the OECD countries. At the same time, our criminal justice system has generally been more liberal than many of our fellows – we rejected capital punishment earlier than most comparable countries and have been progressive in the use of community-based sentences for less serious offenders, the introduction of a world-leading youth justice system and initiatives in restorative justice. And our prison system has largely been free of the egregious abuses that have plagued other countries.

Barnett's rather pessimistic comments were doubtless influenced by his own unhappy experience as driver of penal policy. He had a powerful colourful personality and was acknowledged as one of the outstanding public servants of his era. Barnett harboured great ambitions for what could be achieved in the penal field in a small, young country like New Zealand. He was the prime mover in the comprehensive reform of the sentencing framework in the Criminal Justice Act 1954, which ushered in a suite of indeterminate sentences that, broadly speaking, divided offenders into those who were considered reformable and those who were not. Barnett also gained government approval for establishing a national prison centre at Waikeria, near Te Awamutu in the Waikato, which would transform the prison system.

By 1960, Barnett had frankly acknowledged the failure of both of these initiatives. Indeterminate sentences were now seen as adding to offenders' instability and insecurity and two of the new sentences introduced in 1954, corrective training and preventive detention, had virtually fallen into disuse. A sharp increase in the prison population – the number of inmates increased by 45 per cent between 1955 and 1959 – put paid to the idea of housing most of the nation's prisoners on a single site.

The Barnett era is instructive in that it illustrates a recurring theme in the history of corrections in this country. New systems are introduced with great fanfare and high hopes of achieving unprecedented reductions in criminal offending only to be watered down and ultimately abandoned, if not expressly rejected, in the years that follow. Periods of reform and high ambition tend to be followed by those with little change. The Barnett philosophy had a comparatively short shelf-life, having burst onto the scene and virtually burnt itself out in less than a decade. Indeed, Barnett acknowledged the failure of his major strategies during his own term of office.

A comprehensive history of New Zealand's correctional system is overdue. The story now extends to nearly 200 years and it is one that includes many fascinating developments and tales. Up until now, the story has been told in a very piecemeal fashion and there has been no full account. In particular, there is no authoritative description of the significant changes that have occurred since the late 1980s. This period has included a major structural change with the establishment of the Department of Corrections as a dedicated government department. Previously, prisons, probation and psychological services were all part of the old Department of Justice, which was also responsible for a wide range of other government activities, including the administration of the courts and the conduct of general elections.

Too many of the published works that are available on this subject have come from official sources. For example, Dr John Robson, Barnett's successor as Secretary for Justice (and founding director of the Institute of Criminology at Victoria University of Wellington), wrote a number of substantial articles on various topics as well as a comprehensive history of policy development in the Justice Department up until 1970 (*Sacred Cows and Rogue Elephants: Policy Development in the New Zealand Justice Department*. Wellington, NZ: Government Printing Office Publishing, 1987). Official documents and the writings of government officials are an important part of the tapestry, but it is important that we have a full account by an independent commentator. There is no one better qualified for this task than the author of this book. I have known Greg Newbold since the early 1980s and shared many enjoyable, wide-ranging discussions about the criminal justice system and prison history. Greg has produced a formidable list of published works on various topics relating to the history of corrections in this country over the last 20 years – including capital punishment, the maximum-security prison, private prisons, and female prison officers in male prisons. He also has the more unusual qualification of having experienced imprisonment first-hand during the 1970s, after which he wrote New Zealand's leading prison memoir, *The Big Huey*.

I commend this book to all of those with an interest in our criminal justice system (or even a general interest in New Zealand history). Recent decades have seen responses to crime take a much more prominent position in the political scene and the news media. This book provides an excellent resource for discussions on this subject in setting out in a clear and readable style the history of our corrections system up to this point.

John Meek
Principal Adviser, Ministry of Justice, Wellington

PREFACE

Early in August 2002 I went to see Gerry Orchard at his home in Merivale, Christchurch. Gerry was a highly distinguished Professor and Dean of Law at Canterbury University who in 1987 had supported my appointment to the sociology department and had always been happy to advise me about my academic career. As an ex-criminal who had served sentences of periodic detention and detention in a detention centre as a teenager, followed by a seven-and-a-half-year prison term as a young adult, I was a contentious candidate and I know that Gerry had been one of the strongest voices on Staffing Committee in favour of giving me a chance. The application was accepted and I was signed on as a lecturer in February 1988.

On this last occasion I went to see him about a bid I was about to make for promotion to the relatively senior position of Associate Professor. Gerry's advice was practical and sound and I was successful. But Gerry was in pain. His shoulder was giving him hell and he was going to see the doctor about it. Sounded like arthritis or something. But it was much worse. Gerry had an aggressive and inoperable brain tumour. Within a few weeks his arm was paralysed; by October he was in a wheelchair. He died on 19 January 2003 at the age of 58.

In spite of the terminal diagnosis and his rapidly deteriorating condition, and against the imprecations of his colleagues, Gerry insisted on finishing his year's teaching so that students would not be disadvantaged. On 24 October 2002 a farewell function was held in the Law Faculty at Canterbury University, attended by eminent scholars from all over the country. From his wheelchair, when I arrived Gerry clasped my hand warmly and said how good it was to see me. A few minutes later, at the head of the room, he hauled himself out of his seat, stood unsteadily on his feet and began to speak. He thanked everyone for coming, recalled the richness and fulfilment of his life, dwelt on the wonderful times and friends he'd made while working at the University of Canterbury and finally, he bade us a fond farewell. He spoke for about 30 minutes and it was one of the most powerful, passionate and moving addresses I've ever heard. After he finished, the room was silent for about five minutes.

It was at Gerry's send-off that the idea for this book came about. In conversation with Professors Warren Brookbanks from Auckland and Geoff Hall from Otago, I mentioned the paucity of published material in New Zealand about corrections and the criminal justice process. They agreed that a full treatment of the subject was well overdue. This made my mind up and the next day I began preparing a chapter breakdown. When I returned from summer leave in January 2003 I started chapter drafts and, between teaching and other commitments, I have worked continuously on the book ever since. The final piece is a result of four years of writing, backed by 30 years' experience of, and research in, the criminal justice system.

The objective has been to create a book which looks comprehensively at the historical evolution of New Zealand corrections and analyses contemporary developments in this light. Some of the material draws upon information I collected for my MA thesis, which I wrote while I was in maximum security at Paremoremo, and for my doctoral dissertation on correctional history, which I commenced after I got out of jail at the end of 1980. The book is informed not only by my personal observations and research, but also by my involvement with numerous governmental advisory committees and policy groups over subsequent years. This has resulted in a book which I hope is not only historically informed, but which provides a depth of insight based on decades of experience on both sides of the law.

A confusing feature of corrections administration over the years has been its propensity to change the names of its prisons. Rimutaka was once called Wi Tako; Hautu and Rangipo have at times been administered separately and at other times together under the title Tongariro. The prison at Mt Eden used to be called Auckland prison. Now it's called Mt Eden and Paremoremo is Auckland prison. For this reason, throughout most of the book, I have preferred to stick to popularly recognised terminology. Thus, Auckland prison is referred to as Paremoremo, Hawke's Bay prison is called Mangaroa, Manawatu prison is called Linton, Christchurch prison is called Paparua.

A book of this type has required the assistance of many who have given support and advice, or looked at drafts and contributed generally to the quality of the finished product. Jeremy Finn, Celia Lashlie, Barry Matthews, Phil McCarthy, Michelle Nicholson, Scott Optican, Jenny Torr and Bridget White all took time to read preliminary drafts of some chapters, or provided advice and feedback. At the Department of Corrections, Ben Peck and Heather Woods gave kind assistance with the production of photographs and Grant Hunter took the cover shot. John Meek, former Secretary of the parole board and now principal advisor at the Ministry of Justice, who is one of the most knowledgeable people I know on the subject of prison history and who has become a frequent consultant and friend, read the entire draft and has done me the honour of writing the Foreword. Joanna Morton and Susan Williams, editors with Dunmore Publishing, did a magnificent job tightening the script up, pointing out possible ambiguities, and identifying points of repetition.

A book of this type and size, complete with photographs and figures, is expensive to produce and with New Zealand's limited market is difficult to sell to a publisher. In that respect I want to thank Sharmian Firth, Publisher at Dunmore, for putting her faith in the book and for being so easy and pleasant to work with. That said, without financial support, the book would still never have got off the ground. Thus I am deeply indebted to the New Zealand Law Foundation for their generous grant to assist with production costs and to Andrew Bridgman of the Ministry of Justice, who took a personal interest in the project and very kindly arranged a top-up. Without the first grant, the book would not have been published; without the second, the graphs and pictures would have been unaffordable.

Finally, I want to return to the fellow who helped start it all. Gerry Orchard was not only an eminent authority in criminal law he was also a terrific friend, advocate, occasional drinking mate, and a thoroughly nice guy. He is one of a number of people over the years who have helped significantly in my progress from imprisonment to professorship and I wish he was here to see this product of it. From the very start it was my intention to complete the project in honour of Gerry's memory and, accordingly, it's to him that I have the pleasure of dedicating the book.

Greg Newbold, January 2007

INTRODUCTION

T he problem of what to do with offenders has been central to criminology ever since the discipline was created almost 250 years ago. Driven by the philosophies of 18th-century social reformists, criminology was initially conceived as a philanthropic attempt to rid the world of felonious evils. This gave rise to general dissatisfaction with some of the barbaric criminal justice methods of the day and to a search for a humane alternative. The answer came with the measured punishment of the penitentiary. Although prisons, dungeons and other forms of confinement had been around for centuries, they were normally reserved for short-term or pre-trial detention and lacked any systematic philosophy or design. Since the 16th century prison workhouses and 'houses of correction' had existed in Europe, but the widespread use of imprisonment as a primary means of treating offenders was not established until more than 200 years later.

The nation that led the world in the development of the penitentiary system in the late 18th century was the newly independent republic of the United States. Once organised penitentiary systems had commenced in America they attracted such interest that by the mid 19th century every country in Europe had followed suit. England was a relatively late starter and did not create its own comprehensive prison programme until 1839. New Zealand, as a colony of Britain, followed her example, but its prison administration was largely ad hoc until it was consolidated in 1880.

The penitentiary, of course, never managed to fulfil its promise, but has remained the mainstay of world correctional systems. However, the general failure of incarceration as a reformative agent has not occurred without significant effort being invested into trying to make it work. In fact, controversy over how best to produce salutary change in a prisoner under lock-up has existed from the outset. The birth of the penitentiary itself was marked by heated debate over the relative merits of two versions of the same idea: complete isolation versus a degree of social mingling, albeit without communication. Overcrowding soon resolved this issue and experimentation began with systems of progressive privilege and early release for good behaviour, and the provision of training and education, particularly for younger offenders. By the late 20th century, use of probation had also appeared as an intermediate alternative to fining and imprisonment, and since then a number of other non-custodial remedies have been introduced as well.

As a small nation New Zealand, possibly more than other countries, has taken its lead from correctional developments overseas. In fact, apart from the innovations of probation in 1886 and periodic detention in 1962, correctional change here has followed international trends. England has been the greatest influence, but the United States was increasingly so over the 20th century. Numerous examples of New Zealand's tendency to imitate can be seen in the forthcoming chapters.

After New Zealand centralised its prison administration in 1880 it embraced the punitive ethic of England until an era of reformism commenced in 1910. Since that time, the history of corrections in this country has seen a succession of attempts to stop criminals from reoffending through various forms of treatment. The efforts have been manifold and have involved a range of sentence variations: reformative, deterrent, short, long, determinate, indefinite, fully custodial, semi-custodial and non-custodial. These variations have been accompanied by a series of experiments in treatment strategies, release systems, forms of supervision and a wide variety of other intermediate sanctions. The innovations typically have been introduced in a flush of enthusiasm without proper research or planning, have been misunderstood by sentencing judges, misapplied by correctional authorities and, most importantly, have had almost no measurable effect on recidivism. Successively, after years of failure, the various experiments have usually been abandoned but have just as often been remodelled at a later date by administrators with little knowledge of the past. The old adage that the history of corrections is a 'graveyard of abandoned fads' is as true for New Zealand as anywhere. This country's lack of success in the field is evidenced in the fact that today, despite over 120 years of systematic correctional enterprise, 86 per cent of New Zealand's inmates are reconvicted within five years of release, and more than half are re-incarcerated.

Little has been published about the history of corrections in New Zealand, and even less about the circumstances behind it. Administrators have therefore generally had only a vague appreciation of the past. Knowledge of what has gone before and what may or may not succeed is essential to architects of social policy, and provides the primary rationale for this book. The text is divided into two parts in order to give historical context as well as information about specific topic areas. Part I briefly introduces the birth of the penitentiary before looking at the chronological unfolding of New Zealand's correctional system over the last 160 years or so. There is particular focus on recent developments and on some of the principal drivers of change, as well as a critique of contemporary policy. Part II is also quasi-historical, and focuses on certain aspects of corrections in New Zealand: the current prison system, the maximum-security prison, women's prisons, private prisons, capital punishment and other sentencing variations. Throughout, the book deals not only with shifts in law and penal policy but also with sentence administration itself, discussing some of the major social and political influences behind the changes.

Many years of correctional experiment and innovation have failed to produce a programme that 'works' consistently in terms of significantly reducing recidivism, and New Zealand is not alone in this situation. The task of reforming criminals has proven far more difficult than generally imagined. Advocates of correctionalism anticipate only a 10 to 15 per cent improvement in recidivist rates – contingent on an accurate assessment of individual client needs and followed by tailor-made therapeutic programmes delivered by highly trained personnel. In the harsh and fiscally straitened world of the prison, such requirements can rarely be met.

The concluding chapter attempts to explain why rehabilitating criminals is so difficult. This chapter examines the major variables behind offending and argues that, since most of them relate to circumstances – historical and present – beyond the prison walls, or to factors close to the heart of the human condition itself, the chances of bringing metamorphic change in the majority of criminals are slim. But this is not to deny the value of programmes which are fundamental to good prison management. The primary value of mainstream programmes lies in the humanising influence they have on inmates and staff, the potential they have for allowing determined inmates to improve themselves, and the essential role they play in maintaining morale so that prisons can operate on an even keel.

PART I

The Historical Development of Corrections in New Zealand

CHAPTER 1
BIRTH OF THE PRISON

The use of imprisonment as a primary means of dealing with criminals is relatively recent, and was rare before the early 19th century. Before this a variety of punitive methods was employed. As shown in chapter 11, capital punishment was a popular sanction until the 1830s, but other methods (for example, torture, pillories and flogging) were also favoured in 16th- and 17th-century Europe. From about 1500 in France, Spain and most Italian states, galley servitude became common. Compulsory public work was another alternative. Countries such as France, Russia and England transported some of their convicts. England used transportation most often, and between 1787 and 1847 this was the mainstay of the English penal system.[1] This country introduced transportation in 1615 but it was not used extensively until 1718, with convicts sent first to America (until it was stopped by the American Revolution in 1776) and then to Australia. When transportation was abolished in 1867 some 50,000 British convicts had been shipped to America, another 187,000 to Australia and a smaller number to Norfolk Island.[2]

But the most enduring penal development in the 16th century was imprisonment. During medieval and Tudor times imprisonment was used rarely, being generally reserved for the temporary detention in dungeons or towers of those awaiting trial or execution, or those owing money for fines. In England, statutory provision for the establishment of common jails had been made in 1403 but these too were a short-term measure. However, in 16th-century Europe, prisons and prison workhouses began to appear.[3] Britain was a leader in this area, with 'houses of correction' – or bridewells – developed in London in 1553 to combat the growing problem of vagrancy. Other English towns followed, so that by the early 17th century about 170 houses of correction had been opened around the country. A number of other European countries developed purpose-built prisons in the 17th century as well.[4]

The growing crime rate that occurred as cities expanded caused prisons to become rapidly overcrowded and that, accompanied by the sudden cessation of transportation to America in 1775, begged a rapid solution. Thus in 1776 the first 'convict prison', operated by central government, was opened in England.[5] That same year, old ship hulks moored in the Thames and other estuaries were used to confine prisoners. Although pressure on the prisons was alleviated somewhat by transportation of convicts to Australia between 1787 and 1867, the use of hulks continued until 1857.[6]

From the late 17th century the evolution of criminological thinking and practice was increasingly influenced by the intellectual advances of the Enlightenment. The Enlightenment was a general intellectual movement that swept through Europe – principally France and Britain – questioning the authority of the Church and the monarchic state, and arguing that legitimate laws and governments are dependent on the consent of the governed. In addition, the Enlightenment (sometimes known as the Age of Reason) produced a set of theses based on rationalism, which held that human beings are fundamentally logical and capable of intelligent self-determination. This set the intellectual foundation for democracy and was directly responsible for the revolutions that broke out in America in 1775 and France in 1789.

Out of the Enlightenment came a new way of looking at crime and punishment. Where, in medieval times, punishment of crime was seen as retribution for sins against God and King, Enlightenment theorists saw punishment as a practical means of protecting social harmony. They believed that laws were created for the greater good of society and that law breakers were *non-rational* because they threatened the integrity of the social fabric. The enforcement of law was thus a pragmatic, not a moral, exercise. The writer who brought these 'utilitarian' principles to law enforcement was Cesare Beccaria, an Italian Jesuit scholar whose essay *On Crimes and Punishments* (1963/1764) established him as the world's first criminologist. Beccaria attempted to analyse criminal offending in a pragmatic light and, opposing both corporal and capital punishment, argued that punishment should be no more severe than necessary to deter criminals and protect public security.

Being the only work of its kind, Beccaria's essay significantly impacted on the development of philosophical criminology. One who was deeply influenced by it was John Howard, Sheriff of Bedfordshire and a former prisoner of war of the French, who toured the prisons of England and Wales and published his famous *The State of the Prisons in England and Wales*, in 1777. This book sharply criticised prison conditions as well as transportation, and called for the establishment of imprisonment with solitary confinement, labour and religious instruction.[7] As a result of this pressure, the first penitentiaries were legislated for in the Penitentiary Act 1779.

The other major English influence on prison reform in the 18th century was Jeremy Bentham. Also influenced by Beccaria, Bentham was the first utilitarian philosopher to focus his attention on criminology. Believing that crime was caused in part by bad social influences, one of Bentham's primary goals was to reform criminals through deterrence, discipline and exposure to salutary influences. To this end, in 1791 he developed the 'panopticon', a model prison which he hoped would reproduce the best aspects of a healthy society. The panopticon was a multi-storeyed circular prison with cells around the perimeter and a central observation tower. A prisoner would be kept strictly isolated from other inmates and observed from the tower at all times during his sentence. Prison administrators as well as the general public would have access to the tower. This would not only ensure that the staff did their jobs properly, but would also demonstrate to the inmate that his actions were constantly under observation. In this way it was hoped this experience would instil self-control and honest habits that would be continued after release.[8]

Partly because steam power and steel production were still in their infancy in the late 18th century, making the mass production of large, multi-tiered buildings difficult and expensive, the panopticon never achieved the amplitude it might have. Also, Bentham was unable to convince the English Government to back his project.[9] However, as steam power and steel became increasingly available in the early 19th century, a number of panopticons were constructed in various parts of the world.

The Penitentiary System

Apart from limited technology, another reason the panopticon did not take off was that a competing system began to take form in the United States. This became known as the penitentiary system, which eventually spread to every nation in the West.

The term 'penitentiary' had first been used in the English Penitentiary Act 1779 but, as with the panopticon, technological, financial and political difficulties prevented any large-scale penitentiaries from actually being built in England until Millbank commenced construction in 1813.[10] Instead it was in the US state of Pennsylvania, dominated by the Quakers, where the new experiment commenced. Quaker philosophy held that man is basically good, and becomes bad through bad associations. If a bad man could be removed from his contaminating influences, it was believed his natural goodness would flourish.

A century before Millbank, a prison of a similar style to the English houses of correction had been constructed in Philadelphia by the Quaker William Penn, but this ceased to function after his death in 1718. Then, in 1787, a philanthropic group that came to be known as the Philadelphia Prison Society, attempted to devise a rational and humane way of reforming criminals, and in 1790, at the 17-year-old Walnut St Jail in Philadelphia, the first American penitentiary was opened. From the start penitentiaries differed from short-term workhouses and jails, as they offered a long-term, state-run system of incarceration for felons who would otherwise have been flogged or executed.[11]

Strongly influenced by the writings of Beccaria and Howard, the penitentiary was designed as a humanitarian alternative to the barbaric methods of the day. At Walnut St minor offenders worked together while serious or violent criminals were kept in strict isolation with little to read but the Bible. In 1818 the system was expanded with the passage of the Pennsylvania Statute, which legislated the construction of penitentiaries in that state. Western Penitentiary at Pittsburgh, built according to Bentham's panopticon design, opened the same year and in 1829 Eastern Penitentiary at Cherry Hill was established. Cherry Hill had 400 single cells with individual exercise yards, and was constructed with its cellblocks radiating off a central hub. It was at Cherry Hill that the so-called 'Pennsylvania system', also known as the 'separate system', whereby inmates could be kept separated for the whole of their sentences, came into full fruition.[12] The 'radial' prison became synonymous with this system, but the only American state to follow Pennsylvania's example was New Jersey, which had a radial prison built at Trenton in 1833.[13]

As we shall see, the idea of isolating prisoners from one another gained more support from European than American observers. The solitary system attracted strong opposition from the Boston Prison Discipline Society, which considered isolation to be inhumane and unhealthy. Thus, at Auburn prison, New York, in 1823 and at Ossining (Sing Sing), New York, two years later, a competing system was devised. In what became known variously as the 'Auburn', the 'New York', the 'congregate' or the 'silent' system, prisoners were kept alone at night but released during the day to work together in rigorously enforced silence. Inmates were prohibited from looking at one another and when being moved in squads were forced to march in lockstep – chest-to-back with heads turned to the side – to prevent the possibility of communication. The Auburn system, which used large internally constructed cell blocks known as 'big houses', received high approval in the United States, and by 1835 ten more American states had similar systems.[14]

Although in retrospect both systems appear crude, the ideology behind them was a progressive reaction to some of the barbaric methods in use at the time. In Pennsylvania the religious preoccupations of the Quakers had led them to view criminality as a result of frivolous living, inadequate discipline and bad influences. The enforced solitude and austerity of the penitentiary was designed to allow the convict a chance to reflect upon, repent of and renounce his previous ways, while at the same time teaching the habits of orderly asceticism that were essential to his redemption. While the method employed at New York was slightly different, the principles of both were largely the same. The penitentiary experiment became heralded as the saviour of the American union, and there was a firm belief that the penitentiary held the key to solving the moral and social problems of the day. The idea spread quickly, and by 1835 the first genuine and systematic penal system in the world had established itself in the United States.

The two new systems being developed in America were watched with interest by European observers. Guy de Beaumont and Alexis de Toqueville from France, Nicholas Julius and Friedrich Demetz from Prussia, and William Crawford from England all visited the United States in the 1830s and 1840s and were particularly impressed. Following his visit in 1832 Crawford favoured the separate system, and with his support the 1839 Prison Act specifically legislated for prisons with solitary confinement in England. Accordingly, in 1842, Pentonville, England's first penitentiary modelled on the radial design at Cherry Hill, was opened and became the blueprint for 54 new English prisons. The solitary system was subsequently also adopted by Germany, France, Belgium, Holland, Denmark, Norway and Sweden.[15]

Enthusiasm was relatively short-lived. After visiting the Eastern Penitentiary in 1842, English novelist Charles Dickens severely criticised it for its inhumanity, and the prediction of many that long-term solitary confinement would upset men's minds was borne out.[16] Within a few years 'jail sickness' or 'prison psychosis' had been identified and reached climactic levels. Moreover, locking inmates in solitary confinement proved extremely expensive, and overcrowding necessitated a doubling-up in cell accommodation. In America, England and elsewhere the ideals of the penitentiary system therefore soon were replaced by a code that permitted (at least) limited social intercourse. The previous imperative of preventing 'cross-contamination' of convicts was destroyed, and by 1850 the central premise upon which both the separate and silent systems had been founded had been abandoned.

With the corruption of the penitentiary's original ideals, a search for alternatives commenced. Around the world numerous experiments now began, with treatment programmes designed to stop criminals from reoffending and improve their chances of social reintegration. In 1840, at the English penal colony of Norfolk Island, Alexander Maconochie established a system of marks for good behaviour which, as they accumulated, could earn a prisoner greater freedoms within the colony.[17] Four years later and influenced by Maconochie, Sir Walter Crofton, chairman of the Irish Board of Directors of Convict Prisons, established a graduated system also based on marks, whereby well-behaved prisoners could pass through three 'stages' during their sentences before being discharged. The first stage was purely punitive, but in stages two and three conditions became progressively better and freedom was more liberal. Once stage three had been successfully completed, a prisoner could be given a 'ticket of leave', which granted early, supervised release.[18]

The systems established by Maconochie and Crofton became the template for numerous developments in corrections throughout the Western world. America's first parole system at Elmira Reformatory in 1876 was a direct consequence, as was the borstal system that England legislated in 1908. New Zealand was profoundly and similarly affected because when this country began to forge its own prison system after 1840, developments in England, many of which had originated in the United States, strongly influenced the course of correctional policy. The interesting and varied manner in which certain international developments drove penological evolution in New Zealand will become clear in the ensuing chapters.

Notes

1 Rose, 1961: 3, 11.
2 Ekirch, 1987; Hirst, 1995; Spierenburg, 1995: 67–68.
3 Fox, 1952.
4 Grunhut, 1972; Johnson, 1988: 160–162; McGowen, 1995: 80–85; Spierenburg, 1995: 72–76.
5 Newbold, 1999.
6 Garcia, 2005:420; McGowen, 1995: 84–85.
7 Howard, 1929/1777: 60; Johnson and Wolfe, 1996: 129–132.
8 Jones, 1986: 68–73.
9 Semple, 1993.
10 Colvin, 1997: 47–48; Grunhut, 1972: 55; Johnston, 2000: 62.
11 Colvin, 1997: 42–57.
12 Rothman, 1973; Johnson, 1974: 405–409.
13 Grunhut, 1972: 43–48.
14 Grunhut, 1972: 48.
15 Grunhut, 1972: 43–63.
16 Teeters, 1937: 219–229.
17 Bosworth, 2005.
18 Heffernan, 2005.

References

Beccaria, Cesare (1963/1764) *On Crimes and Punishments*. (Tr. Henry Paolucci). New York: Macmillan.

Bosworth, Michael (2005) 'Maconochie, Alexander'. In Mary Bosworth (ed), *Encyclopedia of Prisons and Correctional Facilities*. Thousand Oaks, CA: Sage.

Colvin, Mark (1997) *Penitentiaries, Reformatories, and Chain Gangs: Social Theory and the History of Punishment in Nineteenth-Century America*. New York: St Martin's Press.

Ekirch, Roger (1987) *Bound for America: The Transportation of British Convicts to the Colonies 1718–1775*. Oxford: Clarendon Press.

Forsythe, William (1987) *The Reform of Prisoners 1830–1890*. New York: St Martin's Press.

Fox, Lionel (1952) *The English Prison and Borstal Systems*. London: Routledge and Kegan Paul.

Garcia, Venessa (2005) 'History of Prisons'. In Mary Bosworth (ed), *Encyclopedia of Prisons and Correctional Facilities*. Thousand Oaks, CA: Sage.

Grunhut, Max (1972) *Penal Reform: A Comparative Study*. Montclair, NJ: Patterson Smith.

Heffernan, Esther (2005) 'Irish (or Crofton) System'. In Mary Bosworth (ed), *Encyclopedia of Prisons and Correctional Facilities*. Thousand Oaks, CA: Sage.

Hirst, John (1995) 'The Australian Experience: The Convict Colony'. In Norval Morris and David Rothman (eds), *The Oxford History of the Prison*. New York: Oxford University Press.

Hood, Roger (1965) *Borstal Re-assessed*. London: Heinemann.

Howard, John (1929/1777) *The State of the Prisons in England and Wales*. London: John Dent.

Johnson, Elmer H. (1974) *Crime, Correction and Society*. Illinois: Dorsey.

Johnson, Herbert (1988) *History of Criminal Justice*. Cincinnati: Anderson.

Johnson, Herbert and Wolfe, Nancy Travis (1996) *History of Criminal Justice*. Cincinnati: Anderson.

Johnston, Norman H. (2000) *Forms of Constraint: A History of Prison Architecture*, Urbana, IL: University of Illinois Press.

Jones, David A. (1986) *History of Criminology: A Philosophical Perspective*. New York: Greenwood.

McGowen, Randall (1995) 'The Well-Ordered Prison'. In Norval Morris and David Rothman (eds), *The Oxford History of the Prison*. New York: Oxford University Press.

Newbold, Greg (1999) 'A Chronology of Correctional History'. *Journal of Criminal Justice Education* v.10(1): 87–100.

Owens, J.M.R. (1992) 'New Zealand Before Annexation'. In Geoffrey W. Rice (ed). *The Oxford History of New Zealand*. Auckland: Oxford University Press.

Rose, Lionel (1961) *The Struggle for Penal Reform: The Howard League and its Predecessors*. London: Steven and Sons.

Rothman, David J. (1973) 'The Invention of the Penitentiary'. In Leonard Orland (ed), *Justice, Punishment, Treatment*. New York: Free Press.

Schmalleger, Frank (2001) *Criminal Justice Today*. Upper Saddle River, NJ: Prentice-Hall.

Semple, Janet (1993) *Bentham's Panopticon: A Study of the Panopticon Penitentiary*. Oxford: Clarendon Press.

Spierenburg, Pieter (1995) 'The Body and the State: Early Modern Europe'. In Norval Morris and David Rothman (eds), *The Oxford History of the Prison*. New York: Oxford University Press.

Teeters, Negley (1937) *They Were in Prison: A History of the Pennsylvania Prison Society 1787–1937*. Chicago: John C. Winston.

CHAPTER 2
THE DEVELOPMENT OF CORRECTIONAL POLICY IN NEW ZEALAND: 1814–1949

From the start, prison development in New Zealand was deeply influenced by early 19th-century European trends, particularly those in England. The first European settlers, in the form of runaways, castaways, sealers, whalers and escaped convicts from the penal colonies in Australia, began arriving in New Zealand in the late 18th century. They were followed by the missionaries – Samuel Marsden and Thomas Kendall – who came to the Bay of Islands in 1814 where Kendall, appointed by Governor Macquarie of New South Wales and supported by three Maori chiefs, was installed as Resident Magistrate. He was followed by Rev. John Butler in 1819. Representing the Crown, James Busby became British Resident in 1833, with the duty of attempting to regulate the trade and conduct of British subjects and apprehend escaped convicts. None of these functionaries had legal power or any military backing, nor, for that matter, any real influence in regulating the young colony.[1]

In 1817 the Imperial Parliament in England emphasised that it did not consider New Zealand a part of its domain, but the Murders Abroad Act 1817 gave it the right to treat homicides committed by British subjects in New Zealand and other undeveloped countries as if they had been committed on the high seas.[2] From December 1813 onward a number of English ordinances gave New South Wales increasing jurisdiction over Europeans in New Zealand, and it was on this basis that in 1837 Edward Doyle was hanged in Sydney for robbery and attempted murder committed in the Bay of Islands.[3] Until 1854 the worst criminals were transported to Australia, but after New Zealand began administering its own legal system in 1841, New Zealand courts were empowered to sentence offenders to imprisonment with hard labour in local prisons.

Generally, however, law enforcement in early New Zealand was carried out without legal sanction. Settlers regulated their own communities. In 1833 Kororareka in the Bay of Islands drew up a set of self-policing rules, and in May 1838 the Kororareka Association established a code of justice with punishments consisting of fines, tarring and feathering, and confinement in an old sea-chest ventilated with gimlet holes.[4]

Pre-Centralisation

By proclamation of Sir George Gipps, Governor of New South Wales, New Zealand became a British possession as an appendage to New South Wales on 14 January 1840. It remained subject to the laws of New South Wales until 1842 when a legislative council was established. From this time New Zealand's first governor, Captain William Hobson, was responsible for the administration of law, overseen by the Colonial Office in London.[5] In 1840 prisons and lockups were already in existence in various settlements and that year the first official prisons were proclaimed in Okiato and Kororareka. Akaroa, Petone and Hokianga had *de facto* jails, and Auckland's first lockup opened in 1841. Jails were usually makeshift structures of wood, raupo and toetoe, and so insecure that prisoners had to be restrained in irons much of the time. In 1838 two Maori who had killed a settler in Hokianga were tried in an impromptu court presided over by Busby, and one of them, Kati, was subsequently executed by tribal chiefs. But the procedure was *ad hoc* and lacked due process,[6] and the new colony did not have its first true judicial execution until 1843. That year Wiremu Maketu, the son of a Ngapuhi chief, was hanged in Auckland for the 1841 murders of four people in the Bay of Islands.

The law and its enforcement were ramshackle for the most part. Unlike Australia, areas of which had served as a penal colony between 1788 and 1867, New Zealand had never operated a penal colony, and the only convicts transported there were 98 boys aged 11–20 who arrived from Parkhurst prison in 1842–1843. The move was extremely unpopular due to the boys' ongoing delinquency, and the experiment was never repeated. In the meantime, more local prisons, hulks and jails were established, receiving their first statutory regulation in an Ordinance for the Regulation of Prisons in 1846, which attempted to bring some administrative uniformity. The ordinance gave the governor the power to declare buildings to be jails and laid down some basic rules for prison administration and discipline.[7]

Under the New Zealand Constitution Act 1852 New Zealand became self-governing, but English law was followed until it was gradually replaced by New Zealand ordinances and statutes. English criminal law, for example, had been inherited almost in its entirety and, although often inappropriate for a new colony, remained in place until the passage of the Criminal Code Act 1893. Penal law was different, however, and local administration began much earlier.[8] The first significant step was the Secondary Punishment Act 1854, which replaced transportation with penal servitude. Penal servitude required prisoners to be kept in irons at hard labour (often on public works) for the duration of their sentences, with the exception of reprieved murderers who until 1863, were to be kept separate from other prisoners and in close confinement at hard labour for the rest of their lives. How penal servitude differed from imprisonment with hard labour is unclear, since the requirements of each were practically identical.

The Secondary Punishment Act forced the government to take full account of its growing convict population, which by then exceeded 70. Moreover, consequent to the New Zealand Constitution Act 1852 a system of provincial administration was established, dividing the country into six (and later 10) regions, each responsible for the running its own affairs, including prisons. Because provinces were often short of money, prison upkeep took a low priority and prisons soon fell into indiscipline and general disorder.

As the colony matured and the poor state of the prisons grew more obvious, penal institutions received increasing criticism from letters to newspapers, visiting justices, politicians and judges. In 1858 the question of remedying the situation by unifying the prison system was discussed in parliament, and that year the Department of Justice was created as a separate entity to oversee prison administration. At the same time, confirming existing practice, the Gaolers Act 1858 handed official responsibility for prison administration to provincial superintendents. This move boosted the ongoing decentralisation of prison administration, which many recognised as a major reason for prisons underperforming.

In 1861, with the disgraceful condition of the prisons unimproved, Chief Justice Arney, supported by his fellow judges and the grand jurors of Auckland, took the unusual step of writing a letter to the governor, complaining at length about the atrocious conditions at the Mt Eden Stockade and at the Auckland gaol in Victoria St, and recommending centralised control.[9] On the basis of this advice, a Penal Establishments Committee was set up in 1866, but this committee finally refused to recommend centralisation of the country's 10 prisons because it believed it would be uneconomic.[10] Two years later a Royal Commission on Prisons reported on 11 major jails and 19 lockups about the country. The 11 jails at that time held a total of 601 inmates, and all of the facilities were vastly overcrowded and/or provided insufficient accommodation. The commission, highly critical of the overcrowding and conditions in prisons generally, made a number of proposals, including the abolition of inmates working in public, the provision of single cell accommodation in all prisons and, once more, centralisation of prison administration.[11]

Despite the clear and unequivocal tone of the 1868 commission's advice, the government still dithered. In 1873 the Prisons Act was passed, repealing the ordinance of 1846 and defining the law relating to the administration of prisons. That year parliamentary authority was granted to build a central prison for New Zealand, but the matter was not acted on. Three years later, however, provincial government was abolished, simplifying the prison unification process, and the matter of centralisation was again raised in parliament. A decision was made to appoint an officer to manage the nation's prisons, but as no money was set aside for his salary the matter was again left on the table. Finally, in 1878, the position was advertised in England,[12] and attracted 37 applicants. The successful candidate was Captain Arthur Hume (40), a career soldier who had left the army in 1874 and had worked as deputy governor at the English prisons of Millbank, Portland, Dartmoor and Wormwood Scrubs. Hume and his family arrived and he commenced duty as New Zealand Inspector of Prisons in July 1880.[13]

The Hume Era: 1880–1909

Hume had worked under Edmund du Cane, the notoriously harsh chairman of the English Prison Commission, and ran England's jails between 1863 and 1895. Against mounting local opposition, it was this method, based on the solitary system, which Hume attempted to import to New Zealand. Hume's first report of 1881 clearly reflected his English experience, recommending: the abolition of inmate education beyond basic reading and writing; a reduction in ration scales; a prohibition on smoking; the removal of sentence remission for good behaviour (in place since 1875); and the introduction of birching for indiscipline.[14] Association and communication between prisoners was to be highly restricted, and Hume (himself an Irishman) introduced a graduated privilege regime among penal servitude inmates similar to the four-stage system of Irish penal reformer Sir Walter Crofton. In Hume's version, subject to good conduct and industry, an inmate would serve a probationary period of one year or one-quarter of sentence, then be promoted through a series of third, second and first classes. Classes were to be kept separate from one another and demarcated by different coloured badges and facings.[15] This system was incorporated in the regulations of 1883, and although spatial constraints prevented its full operation it remained nominally in place until 1920.

Although not all of Hume's recommendations were acted on and he modified his views with the passage of time, English disciplinarianism remained his primary reference point. In 1892 he wrote, "The English system is the best system and is, as far as practicable, being carried out in New Zealand prisons".[16]

Arthur Hume, Inspector-General of Prisons 1880–1909.

In 1882 parliament passed a new Prisons Act, which was not particularly different from its 1873 predecessor except it established the legal basis for a national prison system under Hume's control. The following year, under new Prison Regulations and an amendment to the Prisons Act – and against Hume's wishes – flogging for prison rule infractions was abolished, as was also confinement in a dark cell (in place since 1873). In line with Hume's recommendation, the 1882 regulations prohibited prisoners from smoking; however, from 1902, hard-labour prisoners sentenced to at least three months were issued with an ounce (28gm) of tobacco a week, and a tobacco allowance was specifically provided for in the 1925 regulations.[17]

In 1878, just before Hume's appointment, there were four major prisons – at Auckland, Wellington, Lyttelton and Dunedin – catering for 641 inmates, plus 30 minor jails

Staff of Lyttelton gaol about 1900.

DEPARTMENT OF CORRECTIONS

Exercise yards at Mt Eden prison, designed under Hume, showing the 'bull rings' around which inmates marched in silence.

holding 343 inmates and 70 more inmates in lockups: a total of 1,054 at a time when the population of New Zealand was about 415,000 (about 250 prisoners per 100,000 population).[18] Hume believed that in order to enhance the prison's reformative potential, penal servitude and long-sentence hard-labour prisoners should be separated from the rest. Accordingly, in 1883 he established two classes of prisons: first-class prisons at Auckland, Wellington, Lyttelton and Dunedin for hardened criminals, and second-class prisons at New Plymouth, Napier, Wanganui, Nelson, Addington, Westport, Timaru, Hokitika and Invercargill, for the remainder. Hume considered repeat offenders to be non-redeemable, but held out hope for the young and inexperienced. In order to prevent the proliferation of criminal ideas, he prohibited all communication between redeemable inmates. A general rule of silence had in fact been in place since 1875, but overcrowding prevented silence from ever being properly imposed. For it to work, all inmates would have required separate cells, and silence was totally impractical in the tree-planting camps that appeared from 1901. Nonetheless, the control of communication endured. The 1925 regulations continued to stipulate silence at certain times (such as in cells and while marching to and from work) and communicating without authority remained an offence until 1961.

In an attempt to provide secure accommodation for seasoned offenders, one of the first things Hume did on arrival was to order new prisons for Auckland, Wellington and Dunedin. Lyttelton had been built in 1860 and a new jail on an existing site at Dunedin was commenced in 1895.[19] But the Wellington institution reflected Hume's English experience more than any other. Designed as a classic radial prison on an

Dunedin prison, opened in 1898 and still operating.

existing site at Mt Cook commencing 1882, the Wellington jail had five wings radiating from a central hub and was originally intended to be the primary penal institution for New Zealand. Continuing controversy and opposition from local residents forced its closure in 1900, however, and it was converted into a military barracks (which was demolished in 1924 to make way for the new Dominion Museum).[20]

The Auckland institution proved far more enduring. A walled lockup known as The Stockade had existed at Mt Eden since 1856 and had been scathingly rebuked – by the judges in 1861, by a committee of inquiry into the prison in 1866, by the Royal Commission of Inquiry in 1868 and by an Auckland Gaol Commissioners' report to parliament in 1877. According to the 1877 report, conditions at the jail were appalling. Consisting at the time of a series of wooden buildings surrounded by a six-metre rock wall, the lockup had no workshops worthy of the name and only one cold bath for its 160-odd prisoners. Toilet facilities consisted of open wooden troughs in the yard.[21]

Mt Cook prison, soon after its completion in 1897.

Mt Eden prison, designed in 1882 and still operating.

The stark interior of Mt Eden prison.

DEPARTMENT OF CORRECTIONS

The Terrace gaol, Wellington, demolished 1928. Site of the present Te Aro School.

Hume set about relieving this situation immediately. By 1882 plans were ready for an English-style radial-type prison to be constructed within the walls of The Stockade, and the new buildings began to receive prisoners six years later in 1888. Built by convict labour from bluestone quarried on the site, the prison was fully completed in 1917. So it was that Mt Eden, with an eventual capacity of over 300, served as the country's principal lockup until a riot wrecked it in 1965.

Hume was chief executive of New Zealand's prison system until 1909, and his regime is not remembered for its progressiveness. Like du Cane, Hume's rationale for punishment was 'reformative deterrence' based on three principles: hard physical labour, control over association to reduce cross-contamination, and severe discipline under austere conditions. He believed that, in order to deter effectively, prisons should offer a standard of living lower than that normally experienced in the free community.[22]

During his time in office Hume moderated his punitive stance as he came to accept that some offenders could be diverted from future offending. The first departure from the old philosophy came with the First Offenders Probation Act 1886. Under this legislation, supported by Hume, the world's first national probation system was created.[23] Passed in the same year as the New Zealand Police Force was established – with Arthur Hume becoming its second commissioner in 1890 – probation was intended as an alternative to imprisonment and was administered by appointed probation officers, who were normally policemen.

Four years after the introduction of probation came another experiment. In December 1890, 45 prisoners and six officers sailed from Wellington to Milford Sound, where they were ordered to build a prison camp (called Humeville prison) and construct a five-metre-wide carriageway through to Te Anau. For 18 months prisoners and staff struggled with persistent rain, mud, sandflies, rotten food, inadequate equipment, sickness and rebellion, and still the carriageway was not completed. Finally, in June 1892, the project was scrapped and the camp abandoned.[24] The concept survived, however, and in the wake of Milford, five more camps were set up. In 1901 a tree-planting camp was established at Waiotapu (closed 1913), followed by others at Hanmer (1903–1913), Dumgree (1904–1908), Waipa Valley (1904–1916) and Kaingaroa (1913–1920). By 1920, when the last camp, Kaingaroa, was handed over to the Forestry Department, nearly 41 million trees had been planted over a total of almost 6,500 hectares.[25] These early attempts at open incarceration prefaced an expansion in prison camps that occurred after Hume's retirement and eventually became a mainstay of New Zealand's correctional system.

Under Hume, imprisonment in the hulks of old ships was abolished in 1891, and he had more new prisons built at Napier, New Plymouth, Greymouth, Wanganui, Invercargill and Gisborne. In the field of criminal justice, the Criminal Code Act 1893 abolished the Penal Servitude Act 1854 and replaced penal servitude with imprisonment (with or without hard labour). A widening raft of criminal and criminal justice law was finally consolidated in the Crimes Act 1908.

Early release

When prisons were first established in New Zealand after 1840 there were no formal provisions for early release. Before 1864 governors used their Letters Patent to release prisoners early for various purposes. Apart from this, unless a Royal Prerogative of Mercy was issued, a prisoner could expect to serve all of his or her sentence. In 1864 the government drafted a set of rules to govern the granting of the prerogative on the grounds of good behaviour, but a formal system of remission was not established until 1875. At this time, following the initiative by of Alexander Maconochie on Norfolk Island in the 1840s, inmates serving sentences of hard labour or penal servitude qualified, after three months, to accumulate marks that might earn them up to one-quarter off their sentences during the time the marks were awarded.[26] There was no time off for prisoners serving sentences without hard labour and this, together with better rations for hard-labour prisoners, encouraged many non-hard-labour convicts to volunteer for the hard labour alternative.

Maconochie established a system of positive and negative conduct marks which, when reaching a certain total, could qualify an inmate for early release.[27] A version of this idea was applied in the 1850s by Sir Walter Crofton in Ireland, establishing the rudiments of a parole system, to allow deserving convicts release on a 'ticket of leave', with freedom dependent on continuing good behaviour.

Both systems were known in New Zealand by the late 19th century, but of more direct relevance to this country was the Elmira Reformatory in New York. Elmira, established in 1876 and directly influenced by the ideas of Walter Crofton, was the first experiment in what is known as the reformatory era, where an attempt was made to rehabilitate criminals aged 16–30 with salutary influences such as trade instruction, education, religion, and healthy living. Inmates at Elmira passed through a system of earned privilege, before receiving conditional release on parole.[28] Although for a variety of reasons the Elmira experiment failed, and was abandoned in 1910, it received glowing comment in the New Zealand House of Representatives.[29] As a direct result, and with the support of Arthur Hume, the government created the first indeterminate sentence under the Habitual Criminals and Offenders Act in 1906.[30]

While the reformatory was dedicated to the redemption of young criminals, the Habitual Criminals and Offenders Act 1906 was aimed at custodial deterrence of hardened offenders. The similarity of the two ideas was in their use of parole. Under the act, someone convicted for a third time of the same class of offence could be declared a habitual criminal and detained indefinitely pending his supposed reformation. Initially release was on a judge's recommendation to the governor but, under an amendment to the Crimes Act in 1910, it passed to a newly formed authority known as the prisons board. The Habitual Criminals Act also specified that habitual criminals could be required to report to a probation officer for up to two years after release and be subject to recall for non-compliance. Thus, in 1906, the first provision for post-release supervision was created.

Corporal Punishment

Corporal punishment was practised for exactly 100 years after New Zealand formed a Legislative Council in 1841 and began administering its own laws. Corporal punishment in the form of whipping and flogging was one of England's oldest penalties[31] and was a tradition inherited by England's colonies. In New Zealand corporal punishment was administered in two separate areas: as a punishment in prisons for disciplinary infractions, and as a sentence in its own right, ordered by the courts for criminal transgression. As in England at the time, there were two forms of corporal punishment: whipping across the buttocks with a birch (normally inflicted upon boys under the age of 16), and flogging with the cat-o'-nine-tails for adult men. Women in New Zealand have never been subjected to corporal punishment.

When New Zealand was first annexed to the British Crown in 1840, it lacked any laws of its own and was administered initially by New South Wales and until 1893 by English common law. Under this framework, public flogging of criminals was established at the outset, although it is unknown how often this took place. The first legislative recognition of corporal punishment occurred in the 1846 Ordinance for the Regulation of Prisons where, along with punishments such as solitary confinement and limiting rations to bread and water, visiting justices were empowered to order unspecified amounts of 'personal correction' – that is, flogging – on inmates guilty of serious or persistent misconduct. Repeating this, section 10 of the Secondary Punishment Act 1854 allowed the governor or his representative to enforce prison discipline by the use of solitary confinement, placement in irons or "by such other discipline as may be prescribed in that behalf" – which would certainly have included corporal punishment.

These early acts were extremely vague, permitting considerable license to sheriffs and gaolers which, given the cavalier nature of prison administration at the time, very likely led to brutality and abuse. Not until 1863 did an amendment to the Secondary Punishment Act place any limit on the amount of personal correction a prisoner could receive: in this case 50 lashes.

In 1867 the Offences Against the Person Act, closely following the wording of an English act of the same name, was the first to allow the whipping and flogging of criminals convicted by the courts. The highly specific nature of crimes to which these punishments applied strongly suggests that flogging under common law seldom took place in New Zealand. To begin with, boys under 16 could be privately whipped for three types of offence only: injuring with explosives, interfering with railway tracks and stealing children. No maximum number of strokes was set, with the amount of punishment up to the court. Men, on the other hand, could be whipped for just one crime: choking people in order to commit an indictable offence. The very next year an amendment added whipping for any person committing a sex offence on a female. In the case of adult men only, a maximum of 50 strokes could be administered at a time on each of three occasions over a six-month period. The amount of whipping boys could receive remained open.

In the Prisons Acts of 1867 and 1882, flogging of up to 50 lashes for prison disciplinary offences was repeated, although Arthur Hume personally favoured the birch which, he felt, would be more humiliating to prisoners. But flogging prisoners seems generally to have been unpopular among prison staff,[32] and no sooner had the Prisons Act 1882 been passed than, against Hume's wishes, the penalty was abolished. From 1883 corporal punishment remained available only as a court-ordered punishment for criminal offending.

An amendment to the Offences Against the Person Act in 1874 extended the range of offences punishable by flogging and whipping, and they were expanded further in the Criminal Code Act 1893. Now flogging and whipping became available for a variety of offences, including eight types of sexual offence and three other crimes – disabling in order to commit a crime, aggravated robbery and assault with intent to rob. However, flogging was restricted to men over the age of 16, and now only one set of up to 50 lashes was allowed. Boys aged 16 and under could receive a maximum 25 strokes of a rod. These limits were repeated in a major consolidation of the criminal law that came with the Crimes Act 1908.

By 1936 flogging could be imposed for 13 types of offence, and whipping of children and young persons was available for 20 offences; however, that year corporal punishment for all young offenders dealt with in children's courts was abolished. Corporal punishment effectively remained for adult men only although, according to former Secretary for Justice Eric Missen,[33] it was never actually carried out after 1937. In the Crimes Amendment Act 1941, flogging and whipping were both struck out entirely. Corporal punishment in the form of caning or strapping on the hand or the buttocks remained available to schoolteachers until 1990. [34]

According to Bert Dallard,[35] Controller General of Prisons between 1925 and 1949, birching during his time was normally applied by a policeman or a child welfare officer with a rod. Floggings were carried out in a prison, with the victim strapped to a triangle, his legs apart and fastened to the base; his hands together above his head and bound to the apex. Each cat-o'-nine-tails had to be approved by the Minister of Justice and consisted of nine lengths of whipcord fastened to a handle. The length of the handle, the lengths of the whipcord and the weight of all the components were all precisely specified and, in New Zealand at least, the ends of the whipcord were not knotted or weighted in any way. The victim was screened by canvas sheeting so he could not see the person administering the flogging, and he wore thick leather straps around his neck and loins to protect him from any misdirected strokes. A medical officer was on

Figure 2.1: Whippings Ordered (Juveniles)

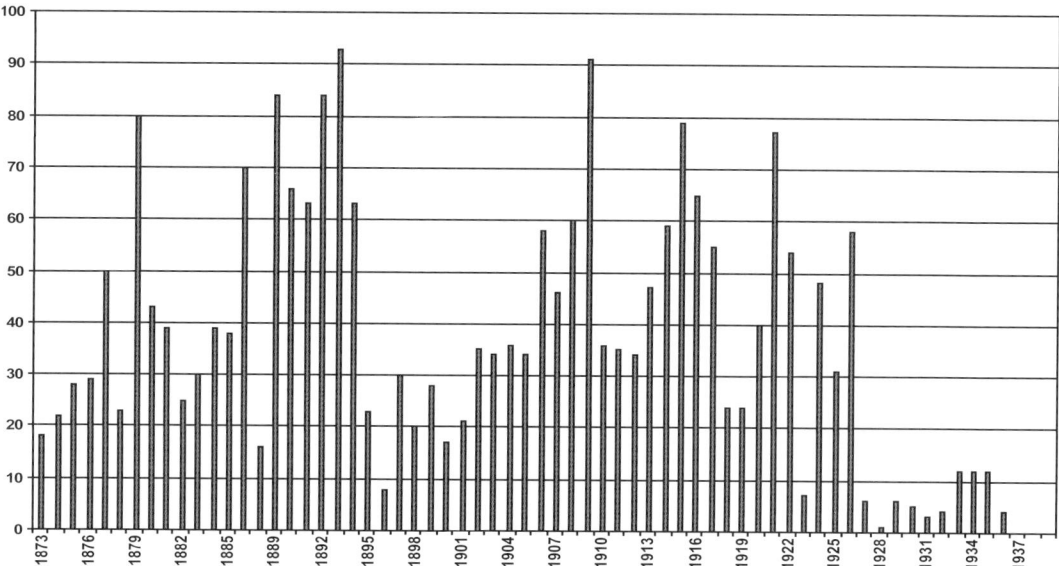

hand to apply ointment to injuries and to stay proceedings if he saw fit.

Details of floggings and whippings in the early 19th century are sketchy, and there are no reliable records of the number of floggings meted out as part of prison discipline. Between 1919 and 1935, however, 17 men were flogged for criminal (primarily sexual) offences, all receiving sentences of between 10 and 15 lashes.[36] Yearbook entries for the later 19th and early 20th centuries show that the judicial whipping of boys under aged 16 was relatively common until the mid-1920s. In the last six years of the 19th century an average of 25 whippings were ordered per year, followed by about 45 each year between 1900 and 1926. After that came a sudden drop, so that between 1927 and the last year whippings were ordered (1936), there averaged only 6.4 per year – mostly for property offences. The victims received between four and 12 strokes across the buttocks with a birch or some other instrument such as a leather strap.[37]

Why sentences of whipping dropped so dramatically after 1926 is unclear, but it may have been influenced by the Child Welfare Act 1925, which created the Child Welfare Branch within the Education Department. This act was an attempt to provide for the control, protection and care of neglected,

Flogging apparatus, about 1930.

indigent or delinquent children under the age of 17, rather than simply subjecting them to chastisement. In addition, the new sentence of borstal detention, a highly popular reformatory measure introduced in 1924 for boys aged 15–21, was another attempt to provide training rather than punishment for youth at risk. Thus, an ethic of paternal benevolence replaced punitive castigation in the treatment of young offenders from about the mid-1920s onward.

As has been noted, floggings, considered more severe than whippings, were far less common. According to the Yearbooks, there were two floggings ordered in 1932, three in 1934 and one in 1935, the year Labour became government for the first time. Another was ordered in 1939 but it was not carried out.[38] The decision to abolish flogging occurred as a result of an incident at Mt Eden in October 1940, when an inmate called RRD Smith and three accomplices escaped from the prison, severely injuring an officer in the process. The four were quickly recaptured and in February 1941 were sentenced to 12 years' hard labour each and 20 lashes of the cat. Embarrassed at having to carry out a penalty it considered barbaric, the Labour Government moved quickly to have both whipping and flogging abolished before the year was out. Thus, the 1940 sentences were never applied.[39]

The New Method: 1909–1924

In 1909, after 29 years in office, Hume retired. A controversial appointment from the start, he had succeeded in bringing order to a system in chaos. Although he had moderated his views with time, his enduring commitment to punitive discipline had been regularly criticised and it was with some relief that his resignation was accepted. That year nine lockup prisons existed: at Auckland, New Plymouth, Wanganui, Napier, Wellington, Lyttelton (closed 1920), Hokitika (closed 1909) and Dunedin. Auckland, Wellington and Lyttelton were the only institutions holding more than 100

Figure 2.2: Prison Musters 1873–1925

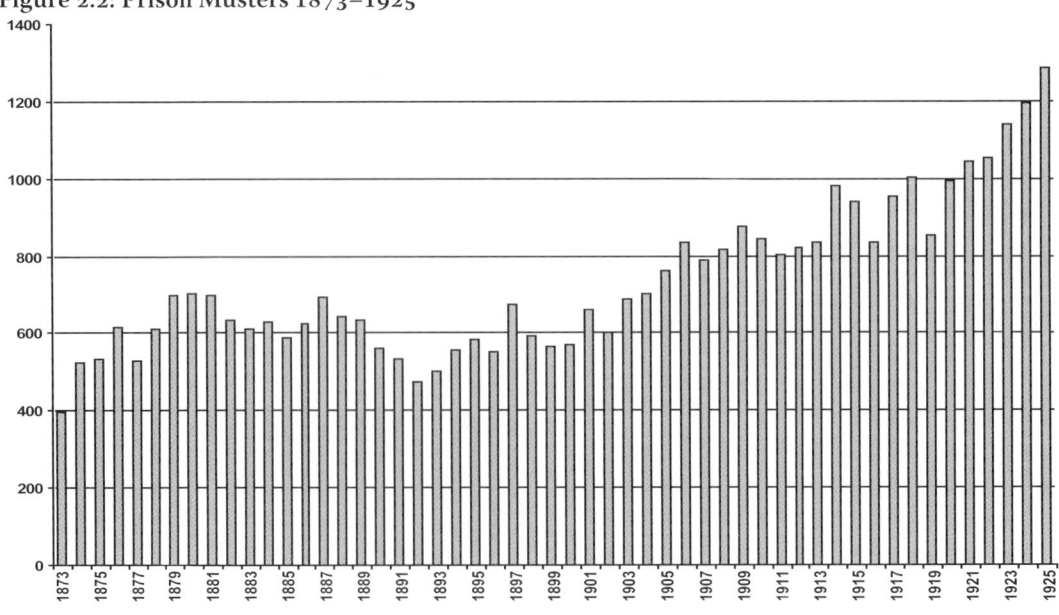

inmates. Small forestry camps for up to 35 existed at Hanmer, Waiotapu and Waipa.[40] Prison populations, which in 1881 had stood at 726 (including remands), declined during Hume's time to a low of 457 in 1893. Thereafter they had risen, and at the time of his retirement the muster was 915.

When Hume stood down, control of the Prisons Department was taken over by Dr Frank Hay, but it was Minister of Justice Dr (later, Sir) John Findlay, a highly intelligent lawyer and former academic, who was most active in modernising the correctional system. As part of this, in 1910 New Plymouth prison was designated a criminal asylum for the detention of mental defectives and 'sexual perverts' who, it was thought, also suffered from mental infirmity.[41] But Findlay's main reformative tool was the Crimes Amendment Act 1910. In parliament, as well as in the public service, there was a flush of enthusiasm, led by Findlay, for ridding the system of its punitive emphasis and replacing it with correctional training. Using Elmira as an example, Findlay announced that the use of reformative principles in prisons could have a real impact on recidivism. In a formula that would become the basis of corrections philosophy thereafter, the three components of what he called 'the new method' were: to restore self-respect in criminals; to identify the precipitating causes of an offence; and to prescribe a treatment that would stop reoffending. "When this Bill becomes law," he announced, "we will have a prison system as efficient as any existing anywhere in the world."[42]

No sooner was the legislation passed than Findlay lost his seat in the general election of 1911. Six months later a confidence vote led to the dissolution of parliament. The Liberal Government was ousted and the Reform Party sworn in. Early in 1914, under the Reformists, the energy of prison administration returned to the public

Sir John Findlay, Minister of Justice 1909–1912.

Charles Matthews, Controller-General of Prisons 1912–1924.

Inmate huts and bunkhouse at Hautu prison farm in the 1920s.

service and Charles Matthews, formerly Findlay's under-secretary, became Inspector of Prisons.

Although more conservative than Findlay, Matthews had a similar vision. He was scathingly critical of Hume's repressive regime, arguing that it brutalised inmates and led to savage attacks on staff. Matthews believed that violent outbreaks could be eliminated by treating inmates as responsible human beings. "Men are punished by being sent to prison," he wrote, "they are not punished while in prison."[43] The reform of prisoners was paramount and he believed this could best be achieved by supplying prisoners with healthy outdoor work. When Hume retired, the bulk of work done by inmates consisted of boot and clothing manufacture, brick making, road making, tree planting, land reclamation and quarrying.[44] The basis of Reform Party support was the small North Island dairy herder and accordingly, farming and agriculture now became the linchpin of prison industry. In 1910 an institution at Invercargill prison opened on land reclaimed from the Waihopai estuary and after this, as a consequence of the new policy, more prisons were established on a total of 11,000 hectares that was developed at Waikeria (1912), Paparua (1914), Wi Tako (1919), Hautu (1921), and Rangipo (1925). Prison farms were established on these sites as well as a roading camp and a saw mill at Erua/Waikune in 1920. Through these projects and by what Matthews[45] called, "the gospel of hard work", the reformation of prisoners was pursued. Matthews believed that if handled properly, 75 per cent of prisoners could be managed like ordinary people. Thus, between 1910 and 1923, the number of prisoners employed in outside work schemes grew from eight per cent to 70 per cent, and by 1919, 53 per cent of all inmates were engaged in farming or land development.[46]

The first major piece of correctional legislation during this period was the sentence of reformative detention as part of the Crimes Amendment Act 1910. Introducing the legislation the minister, apparently unaware of the serious difficulty Elmira was in, referred constantly to the reformatory that this legislation was based on.

The new sentence, founded on correctional principles, provided for a convicted felon to be given a non-determinate sentence of reformative detention for up to three

DEPARTMENT OF CORRECTIONS

Early prison farming at Waikeria, 1919.

years by the Magistrates Court or up to 10 years by the Supreme Court. The sentence could commence either immediately or following completion of a fixed term, with final discharge determined by a prisons board. The board, which had to review each case at least once a year, was given similar powers in relation to habitual criminals. Although the sentences would be served in conventional prisons, reformative

The old prison at Napier about 1920.

detainees were supposed to be subjected to special programmes. Once released, under the 1910 amendment, both reformative detainees and habitual criminals would be on probationary licence for up to two years and subject to recall for serious misconduct, or up to three months imprisonment and/or a fine.[47]

The flaws in the new legislation soon began to show. The courts were inconsistent and often arbitrary in awarding reformative detention, and many detainees were indistinguishable from hard-labour prisoners. Moreover, several of the old jails – such as Dunedin, Lyttelton and Napier – were completely unsuited to reformative programmes so that in fact reformative detainees often got the same treatment as ordinary convicts. It was in recognition of the artificial differences between reformative detainees and other convicts that in 1917 the Statute Law Amendment Act brought prisons board jurisdiction to the majority of prisoners. In addition to its powers regarding reformative detainees and habituals, the act made inmates serving fixed sentences of more than two years eligible for parole at half sentence, or after eight years in the case of 'lifers'.[48]

Remission operates essentially as a reward incentive for good behaviour in prison. Parole systems, on the other hand, are based on predictions about behaviour after release – that is, they allow early release for those judged to have 'reformed' and who thus are predicted to be unlikely to reoffend. During the Matthews era it was confidence in the ability of prisons to reform that led to the favouring of parole over remission. Accordingly, in 1920 parole provisions were liberalised further. Now lifers became parole-eligible after five years and all inmates could be paroled at half sentence, after they had served at least six months. Fixed remission was abolished.

Another innovation during Matthews' time was borstal detention. The term 'borstal' recognised the town of Borstal, in Kent, where one of the first British youth reformatories was established in 1900. Influenced directly by the reformatory experiment at Elmira, the first English borstal was designed for offenders aged 16–21 and received statutory recognition in England in the Prevention of Crime Act 1908.[49] New Zealand established Invercargill as a reformatory for youth under the age of 25 in 1910 and gazetted it as a 'borstal' in 1917. In 1924 legislation came with the Prevention of Crime (Borstal Institutions Establishment) Act. Under this law, rather like reformative detention, young offenders aged between 15 and 21 could be given an indefinite term of one to three years' borstal detention if sentenced by the Magistrates'

New Zealand prison classification 1917

- **Mt Eden** (Auckland): just completed and the largest prison in the country, reserved for habitual criminals, hardened offenders and security risks.
- **New Plymouth**: sex offenders (until 1952).
- **Waikeria**: reformative detainees and reformable hard-labour men.
- **Wellington**: a reception centre and short-termers' prison.
- **Napier**: short termers.
- **Paparua** (Christchurch): a general prison for the South Island.
- **Addington**: females.
- **Lyttelton**: short termers (closed in 1920).
- **Invercargill**: a borstal for young offenders up to age 25.
- **Kaingaroa**: military defaulters (closed in 1920).
- **Rotoaira**: previously used for habituals and converted for military defaulters (transferred to Erua/Waikune in 1920).
- **Wanganui**: a short-term prison (used from 1924 for geriatric inmates).

The quarry at Mt Eden prison.

Court, and two to five years by the Supreme Court. Release was at the discretion of the prisons board. Once released, borstal detainees were on probation until 12 months after expiry of the full term. During this period they could be recalled to borstal for up to six months.[50]

In 1917 Matthews classified the country's 12 prisons to allow them to provide specialised treatment for certain types of criminal. For a time the classification system was quite successful and remained largely in place until the 1950s.[51]

Charles Matthews died in 1924, the same year that borstals gained statutory recognition. Prison populations, which had totalled 915 when Hume retired, had risen only slightly in the following 15 years to 1,196.[52] But by the time of Matthews' death, a radical transformation had taken place. The agrarian programme was in full swing and more than two-thirds of inmates were employed in productive outside labour. Even at Mt Eden, 15.5 per cent of the inmate workforce was now working in the quarry. In 1914 the first schoolteacher was appointed to Mt Eden and from 1921 inmates were able to earn a modest wage to assist their dependants. Prison lighting was improved, lighting hours were extended, education became generalised and libraries were enlarged. The emphasis on security was relaxed. Broad arrow markings were removed from prisoners' clothing after 1913 and by 1918 the general issue of firearms to prison officers had ceased.[53] Until the 1960s the uniform for inmates consisted of white moleskin trousers, jacket and cap, with boots for outside work and leather slippers inside. The atmosphere within prisons was more relaxed and serious assaults on prison officers, which had been common during Hume's time, had virtually ceased.[54] Beyond prisons, the probation system had been expanded to apply to all offenders, not just probationers. Fourteen years of unremitting effort had resulted in a revolution whereby Hume's regimen of punitive confinement had been replaced by one where custody and reformation stood side by side.

The Dallard Era: 1925–1949

Enthusiasm for the new order was not shared by all. Some thought Matthews had gone too far and that criminals were being mollycoddled. Moreover, several of Matthews' ventures had been expensive failures. The post-WWI economy was erratic and many felt tighter control of prison spending was required.[55] These conditions affected the choice of Matthews' replacement.

Bert Dallard, Controller-General of Prisons 1925–1949.

From 1919 the permanent head of prisons was known as the Controller General of Prisons, and the person chosen for the new position reflected a perceived need for retrenchment that arrived in the early 1920s. Berkeley 'Bert' Dallard was an accountant and a career public servant with a conservative and somewhat authoritarian approach to his job. At the time of his appointment in 1925 he was Public Service Commission Inspector and as soon as he took over as Controllor General of Prisons he toured the prisons to familiarise himself with them. Sensing that the agricultural programme was performing below par, he sought to revitalise it using modern farming methods and developing the land projects at Hautu and Rangipo into fully operational farms. It was due to the success of this scheme that the economy of the jails during the Depression suffered less than it might have, and conditions in the borstals – where particular interest was taken – were probably better than in many sectors of the free community.

Dallard appointed the first full-time probation officers in 1926 and oversaw with some enthusiasm the application of the new borstal sentence, which had been legislated in 1924. But the advancement of the agricultural programme was his most important contribution to criminal justice. Although his objective of self-sufficiency was never achieved, by 1933 prisons were producing 40 per cent of the cost of their own rations.[56] He enhanced sanitation in prisons by improving bathing facilities, ordering carbolic soap for all inmates and requiring prisoners to be issued with bed sheets. He had air vents and floorboards fitted to some cells, improved educational programmes, put radios in all institutions and improved classification. In 1927 he reinforced New Plymouth's role as a sex offenders' jail by transferring all sex offenders there. But Dallard was also deeply conservative in his beliefs. With the election of the first Labour Government in 1935, for example, against Dallard's wishes capital punishment was placed in abeyance and all death sentences automatically commuted to life imprisonment. Six

Figure 2.3: Prison Musters 1920–1950

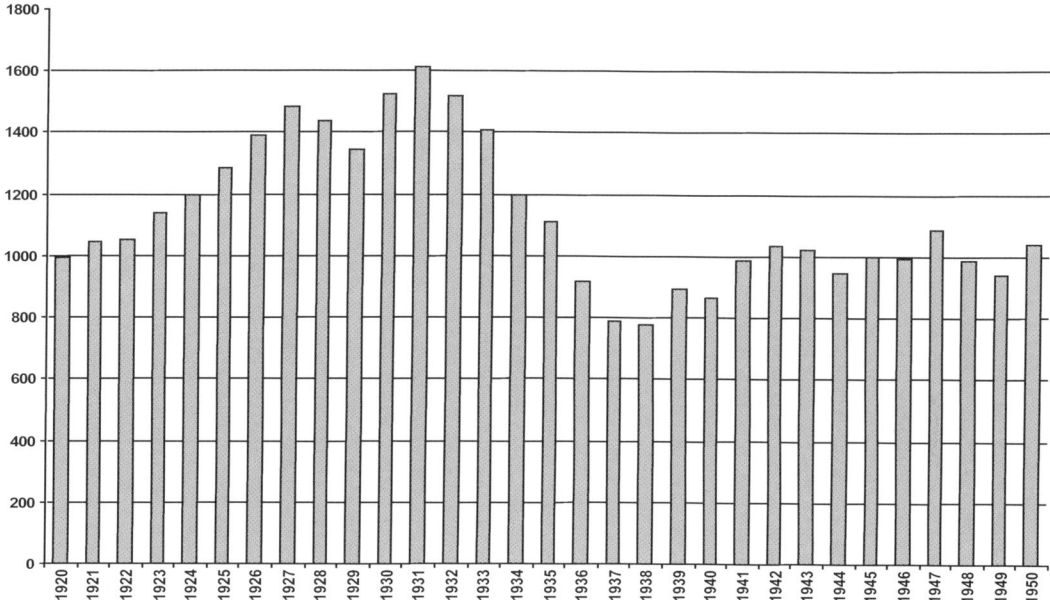

years later, also against his wishes, capital punishment for murder and sentences of flogging were statutorily abolished.

During most of his time, Dallard was in charge of 13 prisons, three state reformatories and three borstals. Prison populations, which had been fairly stable at 1,200 in 1924, rose to 1,600 at the height of the Depression in 1931, but fell to less than 800 by 1938.

Dallard's overall impact on prisons was minor and his 24-year tenure is remembered more than anything else for its austerity, conservatism and uneventfulness. Annual prison expenditure, for example, dropped from an average of £73.1 per head in 1920–1924 to £58.9 in 1925–1929.[57] Dallard was domineering and autocratic, and delegated little. He had a strong influence on his ministers; this was one reason why, when Labour created the welfare state in its 1935–1949 term, almost nothing was done for penal reform. Only one new prison was built during his time – Arohata Girls' Borstal (now Arohata prison) which opened in 1944. Even this was forced upon Dallard, after it was pointed out to him that the existing women's prison at Point Halswell in Wellington was located next to a wartime ammunition dump.[58] Dallard's parsimony had, however, endeared him to his employers in the first place, and it is significant that in 1933, at the height of the Depression, Dallard was put in charge of the Department of Justice as well as of prisons.

Dallard was also a man with limited vision and stereotypical values. He believed in corporal punishment for sex offenders and felt that hanging was an appropriate penalty for murder. He opposed the abolition of both in 1941. As part of what he called a shift from custody in prisons to a philosophy of 'reclamation', he ordered that prisoners march to and from their places of work and stand to attention and salute whenever addressed by officers or visitors. Familiarity between staff and inmates was discouraged. Dallard said that he did not want prisons to become comfortable places

Cell interior, Mt Eden prison.

Ormond Burton, former soldier turned pacifist and 1940s prison reform campaigner.

and wished no reforms that would detract from the fear of imprisonment.[59]

Due to the collapse of the economy during the Depression in the early 1930s followed by the Second World War, interest in prisons during Dallard's time was minimal. Inmate expectations were low and prisons were relatively quiet. In 1936 there was a strike at Mt Eden and a group escape from Waikune. In a sensational event in July 1944, prisoners using gelignite smuggled from the quarry blasted a hole in the perimeter wall of Mt Eden's exercise yard, allowing two habitual criminals to escape. Both were later recaptured.[60] But troubles of this type were rare. As the war came to a close, however, military defaulters, the most difficult of whom were held in the nation's prisons (as opposed to defaulter camps), began to clamour for release. This drew public attention to the prisons, and in 1945 their profile was enhanced by the publication of a book called *In Prison* by the renowned pacifist Ormond Burton.

As a young soldier in the First World War Burton had been wounded twice and decorated for bravery. He subsequently became a Methodist minister and an opponent of war. A personal friend of Prime Minister Peter Fraser (himself a former pacifist), Burton was arrested and jailed five times during the Second World War for anti-war activities, serving a total of 23 months in custody. He was already a published writer, and disgusted by the conditions he found in prison he wrote *In Prison* as a stinging, satirical attack on Dallard and the prisons he ran. The book was humorous and effective and although Dallard quite characteristically mounted a spirited defence, support for Burton grew stronger. Eventually the tide of public opinion turned against Dallard and it became generally accepted that wide deficiencies existed in the prisons he ran.

Inmates, aware of the changing tide of opinion, responded to the prospect of better conditions by protesting, and in 1947 and 1948 there were a number of demonstrations against food and other conditions. Previously ignored by the press, these protests now became highly topical and increased the demand for reform. In spite of the rising opposition to his methods Dallard refused to budge, but his age of public service retirement was approaching and it was with some relief that in 1949, at the age of 60, the government received his resignation.

Notes

1 Hill, 1986: 35–41; Missen, 1971; Owens. 1992: 42; Ringer, 1991: 17–18; Sinclair, 1988: 50–55.

2 Missen, 1971: 1.

3 Hill, 1986: 77–78.

4 Dallard, 1980: 28–33; Department of Justice, 1969: 4; Hill, 1986: 85–86; Lingard, 1936: 7.

5 Ringer, 1991: 18; Joseph, 2001: 36–38.

6 See Hill, 1986: 84.

7 Burnett, 1995: 24; 43; Mayhew, 1959: 8–14.

8 Spiller, Finn and Boast, 1995: 102–103.

9 AJHR D–2 A.6, 1861.

10 AJHR A–G F.14, 1866.

11 AJHR A.12, 1868; see also Pratt, 1992: 123–130.

12 AJHR I.14, 1878.

13 AJHR A.12, 1868; see also Pratt, 1992: 123–130.

14 AJHR H.4, 1881.

15 AJHR H.4, 1881: App. A.

16 Cited in Ritchie, 1984: 31.

17 Webb, 1982: 91–92.

18 Lingard, 1936: 11–12; 32.

19 Gee, 1975; Martin, 1998.

20 Burnett, 1995: 103; Crawford, 1993.

21 AJHR H.30, 1877.

22 Missen, 1971: 7.

23 Campbell, 1954: 267; Webb, 1982: 161.

24 Mayhew, 1959: 83–88.

25 Lingard, 1936: 15; 22.

26 Webb, 1982: 133–136.

27 Forsythe, 1987: 81–88.

28 Schmalleger, 2001: 448–449.

29 See NZPD v.132, 1905: 555–6; v.137, 1906: 163.

30 Webb, 1982: 17, 26.

31 Scott, 1996.

32 See Mayhew, 1959: 61–62.

33 Missen, 1971: 25.

34 See McGeorge, 1993.

35 Dallard, 1980: 112.

36 Department of Justice, 1974: 224–225.

37 Department of Justice, 1974: 224.

38 Missen, 1971.

39 Newbold, 1990: 158.

40 NZPD v.150, 1910: 353; Mayhew, 1959: 101.

41 Boston, 1995.

42 Missen, 1971; NZPD v.150, 1910: 360.

43 Matthews, 1923: 4.

44 Lingard, 1936: 16.

45 Matthews, 1923: 8.

46 Newbold, 1989: 3–4.

47 Mayhew, 1959: 115–123; Webb, 1982: 25–32.

48 Matthews, 1923; Webb, 1982: 32–37.

49 Hood, 1965: 19–20.

50 Department of Justice, 1968; Webb, 1982: 37–43.

51 Andrews and van Zoggel, 2001; Gee, 1975; Mayhew, 1959: 102.

52 Lingard, 1936: 43.

53 Ritchie, 1984: 112.

54 Matthews, 1923: 13–14.

55 Dallard, 1980: 47.

56 Ritchie, 1984: 119–136.

57 Lingard, 1936: 60.

58 Dallard, 1976.

59 Newbold, 1998.

60 Morris, 1975.

References

Andrews, Mike and van Zoggel, Peter (2001) *Addington: The Prison*. Whitecliffs: Purple Barn Conspiracy.

Boston, Peter (1995) *'A Heaven for Homosexuals': A Brief History of the New Plymouth Prison 1910–1952*. Unpublished paper presented to the 1995 NZPGSA Conference, Wellington.

Burnett, R.I.M. (1995) *'Hard Labour, Hard Fare, and a Hard Bed': New Zealand's Search for its Own Penal Philosophy*. Wellington: National Archives of New Zealand.

Burton, Ormond (1945) *In Prison*. Wellington: Reed.

Campbell, I.D. (1954) 'Criminal Law'. In J.L. Robson (ed), *New Zealand: The Development of its Laws and Constitution*. London: Stevens and Sons.

Crawford, J.A.B. (1993) 'Hume, Arthur 1838–41?–1918'. In Claudia Orange (ed) *Dictionary of New Zealand Biography Vol. II: 1870–1900*. Wellington: Bridget Williams Books/Department of Internal Affairs.

Dallard, Berkeley (1976) *Recorded Interview with Margaret Long, NZ Department of Justice*. (Unpublished).

Dallard, Berkeley (1980) *Fettered Freedom: A Symbiotic Society or Anarchy?* Wellington: Department of Justice.

Department of Justice (1968) *Review of Borstal Policy in New Zealand*. Wellington: Government Printer.

Department of Justice (1969) *Information About the Department of Justice*. Wellington: Government Printer.

Forsythe, William (1987) *The Reform of Prisoners 1830–1890*. New York: St Martin's Press.

Gee, David (1975) *The Devil's Own Brigade: A History of the Lyttelton Gaol 1860–1920*. Wellington: Millwood Press.

Hill, Richard S. (1986) *Policing the Colonial Frontier: The Theory and Practice of Coercive Social and Racial Control in New Zealand, 1767–1867, Part 1*. Wellington: Government Printer.

Hood, Roger (1965) *Borstal Re-assessed*. London: Heinemann.

Joseph, Philip (2001) *Constitutional and Administrative Law in New Zealand*. Wellington: Brookers.

Lingard, Frank (1936) *Prison Labour in New Zealand: A Historical, Statistical and Analytical Survey*. Wellington: Government Printer.

Martin, Bill (1998) *Dunedin Gaol: A Community Prison since 1851*. Dunedin: Bill Martin.

Matthews, Charles (1923) *The Evolution of the New Zealand Prison System*. Wellington: Government Printer.

Mayhew, Peter (1959) *The Penal System of New Zealand 1840–1924*. Wellington: Department of Justice.

McGeorge, Colin (1993) 'Corporal Punishment in New Zealand Primary Schools in the Late Nineteenth and Early Twentieth Centuries. *Journal of Educational Administration and History*, v.25 (2): 122–137.

Missen, Eric (1971) 'The History of New Zealand Penal Policy', a seminar given to the *Changes in Attitudes to Punishment* conference, Victoria University of Wellington, Sept 3–4, 1971. Wellington: Victoria University of Wellington Department of University Extension.

Morris, Bruce (1975) *Jailbreak: Violent Episodes in New Zealand*. Auckland: Wilson and Horton.

Newbold, Greg (1989) *Punishment and Politics: The Maximum Security Prison in New Zealand*. Auckland: Oxford University Press.

Newbold, Greg (1990) 'Capital Punishment in New Zealand: An Experiment that Failed'. *Deviant Behavior*, v.11: 155–174.

Newbold, Greg (1998) 'Dallard, Berkeley Lionel Scudamore'. In Claudia Orange (ed), *Dictionary of New Zealand Biography, v.4: 1921–1940*. Wellington: Auckland University Press/Department of Internal Affairs.

Owens, J.M.R. (1992) 'New Zealand Before Annexation'. In Geoffrey W. Rice (ed). *The Oxford History of New Zealand*. Auckland: Oxford University Press.

Pratt, John (1992) *Punishment in a Perfect Society: The New Zealand Prison System 1840–1939)*. Wellington: Victoria University Press.

Ringer, James B. (1991) *An Introduction to New Zealand Government: A Guide to Finding Out About Government in New Zealand, its Institutions, Structures and Activities*. Christchurch: Hazard Press.

Ritchie, Brian (1984) *Prison Industries in New Zealand*. Unpublished manuscript, Wellington: Department of Justice.

Schmalleger, Frank (2001) *Criminal Justice Today*. Upper Saddle River, NJ: Prentice-Hall.

Scott, George (1996) *The History of Corporal Punishment*. London: Senate.

Sinclair, Keith (1988) *A History of New Zealand*. Auckland: Penguin.

Spiller, Peter; Finn, Jeremy and Boast, Richard (1995) *A New Zealand Legal History*. Wellington: Brookers.

Webb, Patricia, (1982) *A History of Custodial and Related Penalties in New Zealand*. Wellington: Government Printer.

CHAPTER 3

TWO DECADES OF REFORM: 1949–1970

T he officer selected to replace Dallard as Secretary for Justice was, not surprisingly, a man of an entirely different feather. Sam Barnett was a controversial personality who had served the government for more than 30 of his 48 years. As a career public servant equipped with an LLB, Barnett was well acquainted with the vagaries of law and departmental politics, and at the time of his assignment he had been Dallard's deputy in Prisons and Justice for a year. Although the appointment was opposed by the Labour Minister of Justice Rex Mason, it is likely that the Public Service Commission, which confirmed Barnett as Dallard's successor six months before the latter retired, had had Barnett tagged for the job for some time.

The Barnett Era: 1949–1960

Barnett had already shown himself to be innovative and unafraid of experimentation. He was a strong and confident manager who prided himself on the efficiency of his administration, qualities that made him the ideal replacement for Dallard and marked him as a potential prison reformer.

Apart from Mason, another who was less than enthusiastic about Barnett was the new Minister of Justice, Clif Webb, who had become minister on the crushing defeat of Labour by the National Party in 1949. Webb who, like Mason and Barnett, was a lawyer, was a conservative man whose first self-appointed task was to reintroduce capital punishment for murder, abolished by Labour just eight years before. As a result, between 1952 and 1957, eight men were hanged (see chapter 11). Barnett was adamantly opposed to the death penalty, while Webb saw little point in vigorous penal reform.[1] So the association between the two was polite but sometimes strained and Barnett's hopes for sweeping legislative change were moderated.

Much of what Barnett did in office was effected in his early years and was of administrative rather than legal significance. After Dallard left, the departments of Prisons and Justice were buzzing with optimism, reflected in the bold and somewhat uncontrolled developments that punctuated the first half of the decade. Barnett went overseas for eight months in 1950 and by

Sam Barnett, Secretary for Justice 1949–1960.

the time he returned the first changes had commenced. Staff uniforms were improved; the old khaki 'bandsman's tunic' was replaced by a navy open-fronted jacket with navy pants, white shirt and a black tie. 'Prison warders' became 'prison officers', and to underline the new professionalism a staff training school was established which all recruits had to attend for four weeks. Pay levels were revised in 1951 and prison officers' duties were diversified.

Conditions for prisoners also got better. At Mt Eden a part-time welfare officer who had started in 1949 was given full-time status in 1950. In December 1949 Barnett directed that all inmates considered likely to benefit from some form of education should be encouraged to apply for enrolment. Where possible, trade training was also introduced. This was followed in March 1950 with the appointment of full-time school teachers in some institutions and a full-time supervisor of education in Wellington. Daily newspapers, previously prohibited, were now allowed and inmate discussion groups were arranged. Protestant churches were encouraged to second full-time chaplains to every penal institution, and the first psychologists were appointed. In 1952 new classification boards were established to assess inmates on entry and decide which institution would best suit their temperaments and needs.

Leisure was improved. Prison recreational and sporting teams were formed, with equipment paid for by the government. Special attention was given to the maximum security jail of Mt Eden, where concerts and shows were organised and feature-length movies screened every six weeks. At this institution the retirement of the tough old disciplinary superintendent, John Lauder, in 1951 opened the way for a man of more liberal persuasion. The successful applicant was Horace Haywood, an imaginative and compassionate officer from Christchurch who had been marked for promotion since Barnett took over. Under Haywood, recreation committees were permitted – elected from among the inmates – and a debating team established. Nationwide, ration scales were improved, inmate canteens introduced and visiting liberalised. In 1952 an elected Prisoners' Council was created at Mt Eden to communicate inmate interests to the superintendent.[2]

Senior staff, Mt Eden prison, 1950. Left to right: John Lauder, Superintendent; Horace Haywood, Deputy Superintendent; F.T. 'Scarface' McKenzie, Chief Warder; Capt. Stanley Banyard, Welfare Officer.

The National Penal Centre

The focal point of Barnett's crime control strategy in the 1950s was the establishment of a specialised national correctional centre. Plans to close Mt Eden and relocate to Waikeria were declared in 1950, and in his annual report of 1951 Barnett announced a desire to concentrate New Zealand's penal services at a National Penal Centre at Waikeria. This would allow for better deployment of correctional resources and maximisation of treatment efficiency. However, no sooner had the announcement been made than prison populations, which had been stable since the mid-1930s, suddenly escalated. Between 1953 and 1960 musters grew by 60 per cent, placing huge stress on existing accommodation and making radical reworking of the system difficult. In 1953 the Minister of Justice announced that plans to close Mt Eden were being postponed, and although planning for the National Penal Centre continued, there was little attempt to put it into effect.

Barnett remained committed to the centralisation idea but not everyone agreed. Within the Justice department several senior officials, among them Barnett's own deputy John Robson, felt that smaller regional prisons were preferable to large complexes. There was scepticism in parliament as well. In 1957 the proposed size of the centre (now renamed the National Prison Centre) was cut from 1,200 inmates to 1,000. Two years later, overwhelmed by rising opposition and continuing population pressure, the secretary conceded that the idea was no longer viable and would be abandoned. The National Prison Centre would become a National Youth Penal Centre for 935, devoted solely to the treatment of borstal and corrective trainees.[3]

The Criminal Justice Act 1954

When Clif Webb became Minister of Justice, just three months after Barnett's appointment, the secretary wrote to his new minister describing a series of legislative reforms that he felt were needed. Webb concurred that change was essential and he worked with Barnett in drafting the new laws. The English Criminal Justice Act 1948 was of significant influence, as was Pat Mayhew who arrived from the English probation service in 1951 to be Regional Probation Officer for Auckland. Mayhew moved to Wellington as Chief Probation Officer in 1954, and between 1956 and 1960 served as Director of the Penal Division. He was in a strong position to advise the department on English developments, and before he retired he wrote a detailed monograph of New Zealand's early penal history in which both reformative detention and habitual criminals' declarations were severely criticised.[4]

Barnett was, of course, also active; in a memo to Webb in December 1949 he attacked the treatment of reformative detainees as being indistinguishable from that of other prisoners. He argued that all sentences should be reformative. Likewise, the distinction between imprisonment with or without hard labour had not existed for many years. As a result of his efforts both provisions were abolished.

Corrective Training

Reformative detention was replaced by corrective training (CT), an indefinite sentence of 0–3 years, which was similar to the borstal sentence except it was intended for an older age group. The age range for CT was 21–30 years, or 35 in special circumstances.

Corrective trainees were kept separate from other prisoners at first, but with rising musters in the 1950s and associated accommodation problems this soon became impossible. In addition, for some reason which Barnett could not explain, corrective training was not favoured by the courts. These circumstances resulted in the repeal of CT in 1963.[5]

Borstal Training

Borstal detention was changed too. The sentence created in 1924 was renamed 'borstal training' and the lower age limit was lifted from 15 years to 17 with an upper limit of 20. The length of the sentence (previously 1–3 years, or 2–5 years depending on the sentencing court), was now set at 0–3 years and became known as 'BT' or 'nought-to-three'. Released borstal trainees were to be on probation for 12 months from their date of release.

Detention in a Detention Centre

The other provision designed for young offenders and enacted in 1954 was the detention centre. Modelled on the English legislation of 1948, the New Zealand concept was designed to provide a short deterrent regime for young first offenders. Similar to the 'boot camps' established in the United States from 1983, this 'shock incarceration' was to steer young offenders away from a life of crime by giving them a painful introduction to the world of lockup.

Originally detention in a detention centre was aimed at persons aged 17–23 who had never been incarcerated. The sentence – initially a fixed term of four months with one month off for good behaviour – though legislated, was not put into effect until 1961 when the first detention centre was established at Waikeria.

Preventive Detention

Although some form of indeterminate sentence for persistent offenders was thought necessary, the Habitual Criminals Act 1906, which allowed indefinite confinement of three-time felons (in much the same way as the American 'Three Strikes' laws operate today) was deemed too harsh and by the early 1950s was seldom used by the courts. Moreover, as Barnett pointed out to Webb in his memo of December 1949, persons declared to be habitual criminals were usually released within one or two years of expiry of their initial sentence.[6] It is primarily for these reasons that the penalty was struck out in 1954. In its place came preventive detention for offenders aged 25 and over who qualified on one of three tests. This is discussed more fully in chapter 13.

The term of preventive detention was 3–14 years generally, and 3–life in the case of child sexual offenders. This brought the sentence closer to that of life imprisonment, for which parole eligibility after five years had been in existence since 1920. Once released, detainees were on probation until expiry of their full terms.

Sentence Remission

While the legislation of the early 1950s enhanced the power of parole in some areas, the Criminal Justice Act 1954 reduced the scope of the prisons board (now renamed the parole board), confining its jurisdiction to borstal training, corrective training, preventive detention and life imprisonment. Automatic remission, which had been abolished in 1920, was reintroduced. Fixed terms of imprisonment were removed entirely from parole board discretion and, under the Penal Institutions Act 1954 early release was determined by remission at three-quarters of sentence, subject to "good conduct and industry". Thus the early release system of 1954 reverted to something similar to what had been in place between 1875 and 1920. Additionally, all offenders imprisoned for fixed terms carrying maximums of a year or more would have a year's probationary supervision after their release.

The Penal Institutions Act 1954

The other major piece of criminal justice legislation passed in 1954 was the Penal Institutions Act. The objective of this act essentially was to consolidate a range of legislation that had amended the Prisons Act since 1908. Apart from introducing fixed remission, the act provided a statutory basis for the establishment of inmate classification committees. Following English precedent, it also legislated for the temporary release of inmates on parole for special purposes. This measure had considerable significance because through it the legal foundations of later initiatives such as home leave were laid down. In terms of punishments for inmate transgressions, punitive confinement in irons was specifically outlawed. Section 19 of the act stated that no inmate was to be placed under mechanical restraint unless necessary – such as when being escorted outside the institution.

The System in Progress

The legislation of 1954, while not revolutionary in its content, was significant and progressive, modernising a prison system that had effectively stagnated for three decades. Clif Webb, a principal architect of the changes, retired from politics in 1954 and went to London as New Zealand High Commissioner. His replacement was John (later, Sir) Marshall, another lawyer, who had acted as Webb's understudy. Like Webb, 'Gentleman Jack' Marshall was a supporter of capital punishment, known for his firm Christian beliefs, his conservatism and his sense of honour and decency.[7]

The departments of Prisons and Justice, which had effectively been operating together since 1933, were formally united in 1954 but Marshall's impact was not great. Marshall simply administered the new laws, oversaw the operation of capital punishment and left Barnett fairly much to run his own show. During the next four years, therefore, in spite of the orthodoxy of the minister, the secretary's liberal initiatives continued. In the prisons inmate–staff discussion groups commenced and a full-time psychologist was appointed to Mt Eden. Divisional officers, reporting directly to the superintendent, were appointed to run sections of some

Sir Jack Marshall, Minister of Justice 1954–1957.

prisons with the purpose of creating greater hands-on management. In 1955 a prison library fund was established and inmates at Mt Eden were accepted for extramural degree courses by Auckland University. From this point, prison education continued to expand, with full-time teachers appointed to several institutions in the late 1950s. Additionally, in 1957 a decision was made to establish a research unit within the Department of Justice, and in 1955, under the temporary parole provisions contained within the 1954 Penal Institutions Act, the first inmates were released for short-term home leave with their families.

These innovations in prisons took place quietly and without much publicity. However, some also occurred in the absence of proper planning, oversight or regulation, and it was this which caused a series of crises that eventually crippled the reform programme. The first, occurring at the end 1955, involved the escape of a dangerous prisoner called Edward Raymond Horton.

The Horton Escape

The Horton affair was the first sign of endemic procedural flaws in some of the radical moves that been made in the early 1950s. Just as Barnett had been given loose rein in running his department, so had superintendents been allowed latitude in operating their prisons. At Mt Eden, under a programme known as 'reformative recreation', Superintendent Haywood had allowed sports teams to travel outside the institution to participate in competitions, and inmates had been given a relatively free hand in organising their own recreational activities. Moreover, staff and money shortages meant there were few resources available to provide appropriate monitoring for the groups of maximum-security prisoners who now went regularly on outside excursions.

It was in this context that on the evening of 6 December 1955 a group of 17 inmates, escorted by just three officers and the prison psychologist, left the institution to take part in a monthly bowls tournament at the Hibernian Society hall in Mt Albert. The team had been selected by one of the prison's lifers, and it consisted of a number of high-profiled and extremely dangerous convicts. A dozen of them were doing life for murder. Among them was Edward 'Slim' Horton, a compulsive rapist whose brutal sex-slaying of widow Kitty Cranston in Wellington late in 1948 had been a principal factor in the decision to restore capital punishment in 1950.

Soon after arriving at the Hibernian hall, while the bowls were in progress, Horton slipped out unseen. When his disappearance was discovered, the gravity of the situation was immediately apparent. Recollection of the Cranston murder caused panic throughout the city and a massive manhunt commenced. In Auckland all police leave was cancelled and reinforcements were flown in from Wellington and Christchurch. Horton was found hiding in a wooded copse by the Whau Creek and was captured without fuss two days later, but the incident seriously rattled the Department of Justice. The reformative recreation programme was cancelled and was later replaced by one that was far more restrictive. In addition, on 20 August 1957, Marshall presented *The New Penal Policy (The Second Phase)* to the House of Representatives, part of which involved a tightening down of prison management practices.[8]

The Second Labour Government

In the national elections of 1957 Labour defeated National with a single seat majority, and Rex Mason, who had been Minister of Justice in the first Labour Government (1935–1949), again took the Justice portfolio. Immediately, as in the late 1930s, *de facto* abolition of capital punishment for murder was reinstated, with all death sentences automatically commuted to life imprisonment. Partly due to his party's slender majority and partly to his own indifference towards penal reform, Mason did little else of significance in his three years of office. Moreover, his administration was marred by a scandal perhaps even more serious than the Horton incident. In June 1958, just six months into Mason's term, it was discovered that dangerous inmates had been escaping from Mt Eden prison at night, committing crimes in Auckland city and re-entering the institution before daylight.

The Escapades of 'Maori Mac'

The lax management practices that had allowed the Horton fiasco were again evident in a series of escapes that took place in 1968. Since 1952 Mt Eden prison had had an inmate orchestra, which gave live public concerts from time to time to packed houses in the prison visiting room. The band was the brainchild of Superintendent Haywood's wife Ettie, who not only trained the bandsmen but adopted a highly protective, maternalistic attitude towards 'her boys' in the band. Thus these men got privileges and freedoms that other inmates were denied. Twelve of the bandsmen were permitted to live together in Association Cell A in the basement of the East Wing, and in order to avoid upsetting his wife, Horace Haywood tacitly accepted that this cell did not need to be regularly searched.

Under these conditions some bandsmen, led by a notorious preventive detainee called Richard Dick McDonald (known as 'Maori Mac'), were able to surreptitiously cut through the bars of the cell and hold them in place with a mixture of plasticine and quarry dust, without being discovered. They also made a makeshift ladder, which they used to climb the perimeter wall, and hid it in pieces under their floorboards. Thus equipped, a total of four men were able to escape on five occasions from Association Cell A and commit crimes at large. Stolen contraband, including clothing, cigarettes, alcohol and a kettle drum, found its way back into the prison and was secreted beneath the floor of the cell. On a more serious note, one evening during this time three men fitting the description of some of the prison band inmates brutally raped a trainee nurse in Cornwall Park.

Association Cell A, Mt Eden prison.

An anonymous tip-off eventually alerted the superintendent to the escape scheme and a massive cover-up occurred. If the truth had come out both Haywood and Barnett would have lost their jobs. As it happened the contraband found in the cell was quietly destroyed and McDonald admitted to breaking out just once from the cell, on his own. Having pleaded guilty to escaping and two charges of breaking and entering, he received a term of two years to run concurrently with his existing sentence of preventive detention (3–14 years). In what was seen largely as a reward for helping the department avert a ruinous scandal he was granted parole just three years later.[9]

Thus Haywood and Barnett retained their posts, although Barnett was forced to relinquish his position as Commissioner of Police, which he had held since 1955. In addition there was a further inquiry and another clamp on security and procedures at Mt Eden. The band virtually ceased to function and a close watch was kept on Haywood.

Prison Populations

Overcrowding, a major concern, was held partly responsible for the problems that had occurred. Throughout the 1940s the prison population had remained relatively stable at just over 1,000. However, in the 1950s, due partly to a boom in youth offending and a tendency toward longer sentences, the prison population exploded – from an average of about 1,000 inmates up to 1953 to over 1,700 seven years later.

First noted in the department's annual report of 1954, overcrowding placed immense pressure on prison administration and was commented on by Barnett with increasing desperation every year until his retirement. By 1956 the prisons were filled to capacity, with particular pressure on youth institutions. Invercargill borstal was so packed that a special wing at Wi Tako had to be converted to take the overflow.

Figure 3.1: Prison Musters 1945–1975

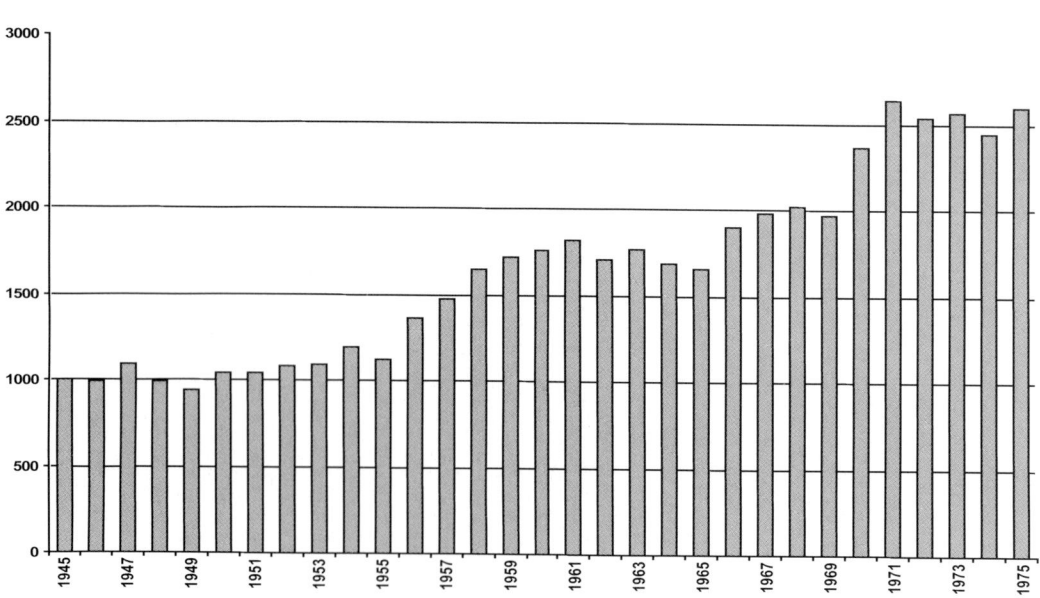

In other institutions men were sleeping on the floors of the wings or in assembly halls. Some cells contained three inmates, and classrooms, libraries and dining halls were converted to dormitories.[10] In 1959, in his penultimate report before retirement, Barnett revealed the depth of his despondency:

> In truth, this country has no national policy. We are imitators. We have to be convinced by experience in other countries before we will venture. New Zealand has a reputation for independent thought and courageous initiative in the social field. That is certainly not true in the penal field, although we have singular opportunities to develop our own practices and policy.
>
> We do not command international attention in the penal field. Few nations would come to learn from us. True, we have made advances in recent years, but few could be said to be characteristic of a young country exercising its own national attitude toward crime and criminal offenders.[11]

Maori Prisoners

A significant feature of this period was the increasing ratios of Maori prisoners. Between 1950 and 1970 the number of Maori inmates received into prisons, relative to all prisoners, doubled. In the 19th century the ratio of Maori inmates had fluctuated at between 1.5 and 3 per cent of all receptions, rising to 4.6 per cent in 1918. This figure stayed relatively stable until the post-Depression economic recovery, growing to 11 per cent in 1936. During the Second World War urban drift caused Maori receptions almost to double (21%) by 1945.

Maori receptions stabilised once more before jumping again to 25 per cent in 1960. By then the Department of Justice realised that New Zealand had a 'Maori crime problem', which continued as urbanisation increased. By 1971, 40 per cent of all receptions were Maori and by 1980 had reached their current level of 50 per cent. To

Figure 3.2: Maori Received into Prisons as % of Total Received

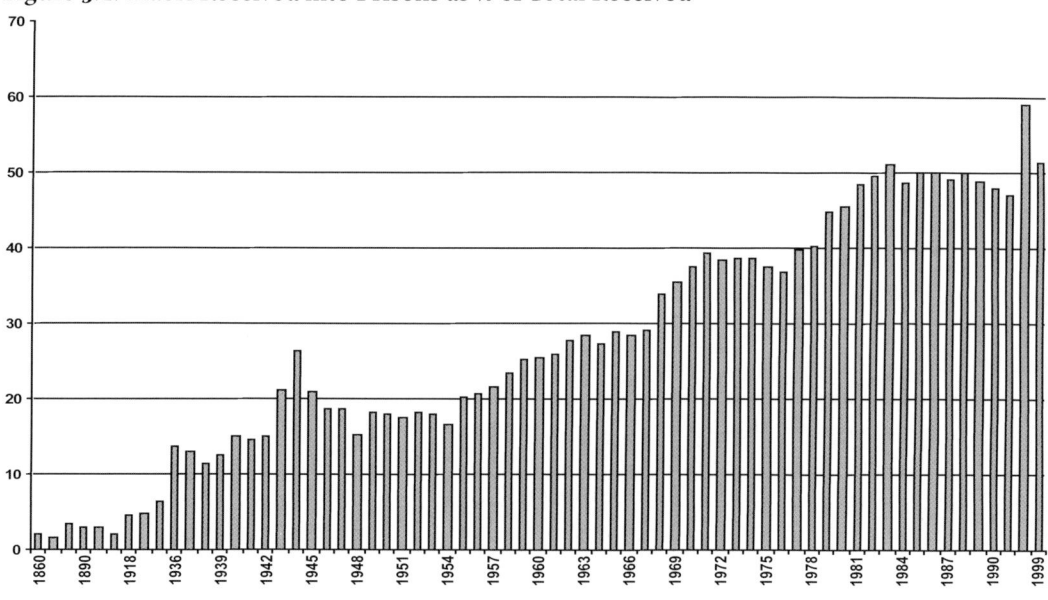

place this in context, the Maori population of New Zealand was about five per cent in 1910. It rose to nine per cent in 1966 and is currently about 15 per cent of the total population.

Seeking Solutions

Crime was rocketing. After the war reported crime had been stable at about 35,000 offences per year, but by 1960 this had almost tripled and showed no sign of abating. Crime, of course, impacted on prison receptions, and as it became clear that prison populations would continue to grow the Secretary for Justice wrote a series of desperate letters to his minister, pleading for relief. A frantic search for quick solutions commenced. In 1957 the Rolleston barracks south of Christchurch were taken over from the army and reopened as Rolleston prison the following year. In 1958 the North Extension (women's) wing at Mt Eden was taken for use by men. The women were sent temporarily to Arohata, near Wellington, until more permanent accommodation was ready. Later in the year the new facility for women in a converted section of a Dunedin building sequestered from the Defence department began receiving inmates. The following year a decision was made to construct a purpose-built prison for women in Christchurch. However, it would be another 15 years before this was achieved.

In 1959 Addington prison, which had served as an army detention barracks since 1949, was reopened for use by the Department of Justice, and a new 60-bed minimum security dormitory was established at Waikeria. By now a major prison-building programme had been announced and, with the scrapping of the idea of a National Prison Centre, new prisons would be dispersed around the country. Soon after, in 1960, a decision was made to build a new maximum-security prison in Auckland.

That year Barnett retired, his final report a bitter review of the past 10 years combined with a pessimistic outlook on the future. In spite of all efforts, he noted, prison populations continued to rise, a third of all inmates were Maori, prisons were overcrowded and insufficiently staffed and nearly all of New Zealand's existing penal institutions were archaic. Borstals did not seem to be working and the youth crime rate was growing faster than ever. The efforts he and his department had put into controlling the country's crime problem had achieved little.

Nineteen-sixty was election year and one of the major planks of National's campaign was law and order. Labour had only been in power since 1957 but this period had seen rapid rises in crime. Between 1956 and 1960 the number of charges heard in Magistrates' Courts grew from 96,600 to 124,800 – a jump of 29 per cent, while Children's Court charges rose even more, from 6,000 to over 10,000. As a result, throughout 1960 National hammered rising crime – particularly youth crime – blaming the Labour Government for ineffective crime control policies. The most significant event in this regard was the Hastings Blossom Festival of September 1960 when large numbers of young people began drinking, fighting and destroying property in the small town of Hastings. This mass drunken youth revelry was the first of its type and it made headlines in newspapers throughout the nation. With events deliberately exaggerated by both the press and the National Party it became a major feature of the election campaign. Capitalising on public fears, National decried 'hooliganism' and delinquency and pledged, if elected, to make serious efforts to control it. Although its tactics were venal, the National opposition won the 1960 election in a landslide and immediately set about fulfilling its promise. Much of the criminal justice legislation of the early 1960s was directed at attempting to control the problem the new government had identified.

The Hanan–Robson Era: 1960–1970

Sam Barnett's replacement as Secretary for Justice was John Robson, a career public servant with a PhD in law who had served as Assistant Secretary for Justice since 1951. Later that year, with the ousting of Labour in the 1960 General Election, Rex Mason also lost his job. His place was taken by Ralph Hanan, who became Minister of Justice with the incoming National Government.

Dr John Robson, Secretary for Justice 1960–1970.

For the next 10 years Hanan and Robson had the helm of the Department of Justice. Ralph Hanan, a man of compassion and intelligence, was an experienced policy-maker and one of the most respected men in politics at the time. Robson, his permanent head, was an organised thinker with a wealth of innovative ideas. He and Hanan agreed on most things, and it has often been said the two exemplified the ideal relationship that can exist between a politician and a senior public servant. Certainly, this unique combination made the 1960s the most progressive decade ever in the history of New Zealand corrections.

Hanan was a passionate opponent of capital punishment and one of his first actions as minister was to draft a section abolishing the death penalty for murder, in the Crimes Act 1961. Capital punishment for murder had originally been put into abeyance by the Labour Government in 1935. Formally struck out in 1941, it was reintroduced by National in 1950 but put in recess once more when Labour took over in 1957. Now it was scotched again, by a free vote in the House of Representatives. At the same time the maximum penalty for rape was reduced from life to 14 years. To better signify the gravity of murder, however,

Ralph Hanan, Minister of Justice 1960–1969.

an amendment to the Criminal Justice Act in 1962 raised the non-parole period for murderers from the five years set in 1920, to 10 years. Other lifers remained parole eligible at five years.

The Detention Centre

One of National's first moves was to put into effect the detention centre legislation of 1954. Under an amendment in 1960 the original sentence had been altered, with the age range now 16–21 and the term cut from four to three months, with one month still remittable for good behaviour. The sentence was followed by 12 months' supervision.

The first detention centre (DC) opened on the site of Waikeria borstal in June 1961, and was followed by centres at Tongariro prison farm in the central North Island and at Rolleston south of Christchurch. Modelled on the military boot camp, the objective of the DC was to crush the rebelliousness of young first offenders by subjecting them to a regime of strict and uncompromising discipline combined with fast tempo, hard work and austerity. The active ingredient of the detention centre was disciplinary deterrence. At the Waikeria DC, for example, to which this author was sentenced in March 1970, inmates had their heads shaven upon entry and all personal effects, including watches, were removed. Training in parade drill started on reception and from then on all group movement was in squad formation. Talking was prohibited most of the time, including after lockup, and was a chargeable offence. Prisoners were abused, sworn at, cuffed and kicked by staff on a regular basis.

Routine involved work six days a week, with no recreation, and lockup at 7 pm. Every cell was inspected rigorously each morning to ensure bedrolls were properly made up and of the correct configuration, and that items such as toothpaste, toothbrushes and combs were laid out according to a set pattern. Work was conducted in gangs of about eight men each, supervised by an officer, and consisted mostly of manual farm detail such as ditch-digging, scrub-cutting and wood-chopping. On Sunday morning detainees went for a run over a military-style confidence course. Visits were allowed on Sunday afternoon. Rations were the bare minimum and hunger was constant. There were six privilege levels, and only those who had achieved the top levels were allowed second helpings at meal times. Any prisoner who escaped was normally beaten on recapture before being placed in solitary confinement, and a new sentence of borstal training was almost automatic. In spite of the severity of this sanction escapes were not uncommon.

The effect of the regime was to produce a cowed and submissive inmate, but the effects were short-lived. About 60 per cent of DC trainees were reconvicted within one year of release and 70 per cent reconvicted within three years.[12] As a lasting deterrent, therefore, the sentence was a failure, and it was replaced in 1981 by a similar but altered sentence known (somewhat confusingly) as 'corrective training' – although with no similarity to its 1954–1963 namesake.

Waipiata Borstal

Another attempt to deal with young offenders was Waipiata borstal. Located in Central Otago and opened in 1961, Waipiata was an open borstal in a former Health department sanatorium, designed for the treatment of hand-picked 'reformable' inmates. Emphasis at the institution was unobtrusive security and trust, with trainees given ample opportunity to interact with the free world and work on community projects. In this way it was hoped a sense of personal and social responsibility would be fostered. Although the experiment was ultimately a failure, with Waipiata's reconviction rate of about 70 per cent within three years proving no different from borstal trainees overall,[13] the attempt was typical of the optimism of the time. Growing scepticism about the effectiveness of borstals led to under-use of Waipiata in its latter years and the institution closed in 1979, two years before borstal training was abolished.

Modernising Corrections

However, in the early 1960s confidence in the potential of borstals was still strong. In 1962, in the belief that long terms of incarceration were bad for young offenders, the upper limit for borstal training was reduced from three years to two, and in January 1963 summer work camps for borstal trainees were established at Invercargill. In 1962 special parole boards – distinct from the national prisons parole board and known as borstal parole boards – were established, with a board assigned to each borstal. There were rehabilitative initiatives in adult prisons as well. Established in 1920, Waikune prison near Ohakune was rebuilt in 1963, and the next year a major forestry planting scheme commenced. In 1964 the 45-year-old Wi Tako prison was established as a special treatment centre for adult first offenders, along with the country's first fully-fledged adult classification programme. A showpiece of reformative corrections the whole prison was rebuilt in 1967. In 1964 the first adult pre-release work hostel was opened in Christchurch.

Remission and Home Leave

In 1964, in an amendment to the Penal Institutions Act, an extra one-twelfth remission was legislated for exemplary service or conduct, thus increasing the maximum remission from a quarter to a third. Over time awarding the 'third' became more

DEPARTMENT OF CORRECTIONS

Wi Tako prison, rebuilt as a model first offenders' facility in 1964.

relaxed and by 1975 had become standardised for all inmates in minimum-security camps (known as 'camp remission') and available to all other prisoners on application to the Secretary for Justice. In addition, in March 1965 the special parole provisions of the Criminal Justice Act 1954 were activated in the form of an organised scheme of home leave. Initially the scheme allowed married first offenders with minimum-security status to apply for 72 hours at home with their families every four months.[14] In 1974 the programme was made available to all minimum-security prisoners and in 1975 the time between leaves was reduced to two months.

Periodic Detention

Another set of initiatives aimed to divert young people convicted of non-serious criminal offences away from prison altogether. In an amendment to the Criminal Justice Act periodic detention (PD) was created in 1962. Originally aimed at the juvenile first offender aged 15–21, periodic detention involved replacing short sentences of imprisonment with weekend detention. The maximum term available was 12 months. The advantage of PD was that it avoided the stigma and disruption of jail and helped to relieve prison populations. Initially PD was residential and took place in hostels. Detainees would report to the hostel on Friday evening, work all day Saturday and be released on Sunday morning. Usually attendance at a Wednesday evening lecture was required as well.

The first juvenile PD centre was established in an old homestead in the upper-class suburb of Parnell, Auckland, in July 1963. By 1966 there were three more centres, in Lower Hutt, Christchurch and Invercargill. PD was extended to adults the same year and the first centre for adults opened in Auckland in 1967. Unlike juvenile PD centres the adult centres were not residential and required attendance one day a week only. Non-residential juvenile centres also began to appear and the more expensive residential centres went into decline. By the early 1980s, residential PD had ceased to exist.[15]

Periodic detention was highly successful. The numbers sentenced to PD grew from 288 in 1969 to 3,010 in 1974, resulting in a proliferation of PD centres in the early 1970s. All of these were for males; the first centre for females aged 16 and over was not established until 1974 in Auckland. Periodic detention was the most successful intermediate sanction ever used in New Zealand, and it continued until 2002 when it was replaced by a similar sentence called community work.

Work Parole

Work parole was legislated through an amendment to the Penal Institutions Act in 1961, which allowed inmates nearing the end of their terms to be given daytime release to work in the community. This was followed soon after by the opening of a pre-release hostel in Invercargill for borstal trainees on work parole. Work parole for adults started in 1962, initially operating from prisons only. But in 1964 a hostel for adult work parolees opened in Christchurch, followed by a second one in Auckland five years later. Work parole hostels closed during the 1980s when they became too expensive to run efficiently and today all release to work takes place from prisons or as a part of home detention.

Restricted Diets

Within prisons there were some minor changes too. In 1961 the Penal Institutions Regulations were rewritten and the punishment of bread and water, first legislated in the Ordinance of 1846, was done away with. In its place came two forms of restricted diets known as No.1 diet and No.2 diet. 'Number One' (accompanied by solitary confinement) consisted of bread, potatoes, milk and dripping for up to 15 days, with full rations every fourth day. 'Number Two' (also with solitary confinement), which could continue for 15 days straight, consisted of bread, oatmeal, potatoes, salt, sugar, milk, cheese and dripping. In practice, No.2 diet was seldom used and No.1 diet was rarely awarded for more than a week. Both diets effectively ceased from 1975 and were abolished in 1981.

Penal Grade

Another institutional penalty introduced in the 1961 regulations was penal grade. Inmates who had been convicted of three serious acts of prison indiscipline could be transferred to penal grade for up to three months. Penal-grade inmates lost most of their privileges, lived in a special section of an institution, had to be kept separate from other prisoners most of the time and wore distinctive clothing: usually normal prison kit with a black stripe on the leg. As time went on, penal grade was imposed with decreasing frequency – part of the problem was the inability to restrict contact between penal-grade inmates and other prisoners in a system that was chronically overcrowded. Use of the penalty stopped when it was struck out of the Penal Institutions Act in 1975, although the law did not formally take effect until 1981.

Continuing Problems

In the early 1960s rapid rises in the prison population, and the resultant overcrowding, were alleviated. Daily average prison populations stabilised at about 1,900 in 1961 and trended downward over the next five years. Musters then began to grow again, but not as quickly as in the 1950s. Between 1965 and 1970 prison populations grew by another 43 per cent, to 2,365.

One consequence of the rising musters and overcrowding was an apparent increase in escapes and disorder. Apart from the Horton incident and the issue over the prison band, and notwithstanding the security measures that ensued, there were numerous other problems. In 1959 a procession of serious assaults on staff took place at Mt Eden, including an attack on the deputy superintendent. In November 1959, soon after it was taken over by women, there was a riot at Dunedin prison, and in December came a rebellion at Invercargill. Overcrowding, poor conditions and associated administrative difficulties were held to blame. In 1960 there were more strikes, attacks on staff and group rebellions at Mt Eden, often followed by retaliatory assaults by staff on inmates.

A further tightening of security and administration after Robson took over in 1960 led to a drop in escapes nationwide, but overcrowding at Mt Eden, combined with poor administration, caused this institution to buck the trend. Whereas between 1950 and 1958 there had been only 12 breakouts from Mt Eden, in the next five years there were 17. Many of these were high-profile incidents that caused acute humiliation to the department. In April 1960, for example, in a highly-publicised scandal, Sicilian lifer Angelo La Mattina, the first man sentenced to death, and reprieved after Labour became government in 1957, disappeared and was assumed to have escaped. A week later he was discovered hiding in the attic of the West Wing. In January 1962 La Mattina, now a recognised security risk, pulled off a real escape when he hacksawed through the bars of his cell and got over the perimeter wall, accompanied by an inmate called Eddie Tell. They were recaptured after two days, but just six months later, using a homemade rope, La Mattina scaled the wall again, and was caught on the other side with a broken foot. These incidents were extremely embarrassing for the administration and were put down to overcrowding and continuing laxness in procedures.

Mt Eden was becoming an administrator's nightmare, with one crisis after another. Early in 1961 Trevor Nash, serving seven years for a £19,875 payroll heist (at the time, New Zealand's largest-ever theft), escaped from the prison engineering shop and was at large for 158 days before being recaptured in Australia. A few months later, a shot of gelignite from the quarry blasted a 16-kilogram rock 200 metres into the air and through the roof of a classroom at Auckland Grammar School. Fortunately the room was empty, but the incident forced closure of the quarry and put a quarter of the prison's population out of work. Resulting idleness aggravated unrest, with further assaults on staff and other problems. On 1 October 1962 an attempted escape by four prisoners was detected and foiled. More security measures were announced, but just three weeks later Frank Matich, a trusted inmate serving four-and-a-half years for violence and property offences, disappeared from an outside work party. Recaptured within 36 hours and now classified as a security risk, Matich's escapades were not yet over.

A friend of Matich's, and the most famous escapee of the 1960s, was George Wilder. In May 1962 Wilder, serving four years for burglary, escaped from New Plymouth prison. The escape itself was insignificant, but the hunt attracted wide publicity. Often living in bush huts, Wilder captured the spirit of the Kiwi 'man alone' and managed to evade police for a full 65 days. Sentenced to another three years for the escape and crimes committed while on the run, Wilder was returned to Mt Eden prison where he was confined in the East Wing basement along with Frank Matich and others who were security risks.

Determined to break out again, in January 1963 Wilder chiselled his way out of his cell and, equipped with a homemade key, unlocked Matich and two other former escapees, Patrick Wiwarina and Reuben Awa. They then surprised a prison officer, knocked him unconscious and took his keys. With these they got into the old hanging yard and scaled the wall using a knotted sheet. Although spotted by a sentry and fired at with buckshot, the four men made good their escape. Matich, Wiwarina and Awa were recaptured quite quickly. Wilder, however, was an experienced bushman and managed to elude police for 173 days before being caught in a bush hut near Taupo. He was returned to prison with six more years on his seven-year term.

From the time he had taken over Justice in 1960 Robson had been unhappy about the way Mt Eden was being run, and the series of escapes and disturbances of the early

1960s convinced him that Haywood was no longer up to the task. In the 12 months before May 1963 there had been another nine escapes from the maximum-security prison. Fires, assaults and strikes had continued. Haywood's health was deteriorating and in May, with Wilder still at large on his second escape, he was shifted to a sinecure in Christchurch. He died 10 months later.

Haywood's replacement was Eddie Buckley, a rigid, rule-book man from Christchurch who had been working in prisons for 26 years. Buckley was chosen for his approach to governance, which was uncompromising and orthodox and had a strong emphasis on discipline. However, 'Black Buckley', as he was known, was a poor manager of men and his bombastic outbursts soon alienated not only the inmates but also many of his own staff. It was not long, therefore, before trouble at Mt Eden exploded.

The 1965 Hostage Incident

On return from his escape in 1963 George Wilder was placed back in the security division in the basement of Mt Eden's East Wing. Here conditions were even worse than before and men were locked in solitary confinement for most of the day. Some security-division men, however, were allowed out of their cells to work; one of these was Leonard Evans, serving 11 years for escape and burglary. On the afternoon of 4 February Evans, who had just returned from court, told an officer he was feeling sick and asked to be locked up. He was escorted back to the security wing with his coat draped over his shoulder. Underneath the coat was a loaded, sawn-off shotgun, which he had presumably obtained at court that morning.

At about the same time John Gillies, a lifer in the security division who had been jailed with co-offender Ron Jorgensen for an infamous double slaying in 1963, complained of diarrhoea and requested to be unlocked to go to the toilet. He then went into the ablutions section and sat down. Minutes later Evans entered the security area and walked directly into the ablutions. He handed his gun to Gillies, who ordered five officers at gunpoint to get into Evans' cell where they were locked in. George Wilder was then let out and, taking Second Officer Dan Cavanagh as a hostage, the men forced him to open the grilles and

Prison officer Dan Cavanagh, taken hostage by 'Dirk' Gillies, Len Evans and George Wilder in 1965.

doors leading to the outside. There a truck was commandeered and the three inmates, with their hostage, crashed through a barrier and raced off down the road followed by a load of buckshot from No.1 sentry tower. Realising their chances of getting away were slim, the men drove only about a kilometre before charging into a house in Horoeka Avenue and taking the two occupants hostage.

Within minutes the house was surrounded by regular police and members of the newly formed Armed Offenders Squad, and a standoff commenced. The escapees' position was clearly hopeless and at 6 pm, having negotiated a bottle of whisky in a surrender agreement, the men threw out their weapon and were taken back into custody. Each received five years' imprisonment for his role in the escape. How the gun got into the prison was never determined with certainty, but in his report on the incident Magistrate Mr A.A. Coates underlined the inadequacy of the prison for maximum-custody purposes and urged the construction of a new separates division as soon as possible.

The Department of Justice at this time was beset with an acute staffing crisis. Annual staff turnover was 16 per cent and there was difficulty getting replacements. At Mt Eden the situation was worse than anywhere. Morale was low and between December 1962 and September 1964 half its complement resigned. By mid-1965 the prison was 24 men short of its establishment of 177 officers and instructors and many existing staff were inexperienced recruits. After the February hostage crisis Buckley tightened security even further, so morale among inmates was as poor as it was among the officers. The ample ingredients for serious trouble provided the recipe for the worst prison riot in New Zealand history.[16]

The Mt Eden Riot

In July 1965 a .22-calibre Beretta revolver was smuggled into Mt Eden prison, possibly by a corrupt officer, and given to a remand inmate called Jon Sadaraka. Also in the remand section was an intelligent but psychotic desperado called Daniel McMillan, awaiting trial for a £15,000 bank robbery – then the largest robbery ever committed in New Zealand. From the day he entered Mt Eden McMillan planned to break out, and having befriended Sadaraka the two conspired to use the gun in a bid for freedom. Homemade keys that could open the primitive locks on the old jail's cell doors were easy to procure in the 1960s and it was one of these that opened the cell doors of McMillan and Sadaraka on the evening of 19 July 1965. Once out, a patrolling officer called Marchant was ambushed, bashed to the ground with an iron bar and his keys taken. A second officer, rushing to investigate Marchant's screams, was taken hostage and a warning shot was fired from the pistol. When the men found their keys would not unlock the final grille leading out of the prison they fired more shots at a fleeing officer and took two more hostages.

Meanwhile the alarm had been raised and it was obvious the escape attempt had failed. Instead, the two would-be escapees began releasing inmates with their key. Among the first were the men in the security division, including John Gillies, Len Evans and George Wilder, who had been in close confinement for 22 hours a day since the hostage incident almost six months before. Gillies began smashing the prison's administrative centre with the iron bar, and the prison was set alight. Although made of stone, the prison walls were covered in thick oil-based paint and the dry sarking in the ceilings burned fiercely. Fire-fighters trying to douse the flames were attacked and repelled, but prison officers who entered to release inmates trapped in their cells were permitted to proceed. With the jail perimeter surrounded by armed police and soldiers and the hostages released, no attempt was made to force a surrender, and it was three days before the last of the men, cold and dispirited, gave themselves up.

Mt Eden was now temporarily uninhabitable and accommodation for its 293 inmates had to be found elsewhere. Most were sent to other institutions around the country – some of whom assaulted staff at Mt Crawford prison on their arrival. At Invercargill borstal a copycat plan burn the prison down was discovered, and at Paparua men transferred from Mt Eden organised another rebellion, taking over the chapel, setting fire to the East Wing and fighting with officers.

The most dangerous convicts went to Waikeria borstal where the East Block was taken over and converted to maximum security. Conditions at Waikeria were austere in the extreme, and it remained home to about 90 men until a new prison was built at Paremoremo, 30km north of Auckland.[17]

Paremoremo Prison

The need for a new maximum-security prison had been obvious for some time, and for years Justice ministers had declared they were going to pull Mt Eden down and replace it. Webb had pledged this as one of his primary objectives in 1950 and 1951, Marshall had promised to demolish Mt Eden and re-site it in 1957, and Hanan had promised repeatedly to do the same from 1960 onward. Hanan had taken some steps but, partly due to opposition from within caucus, progress had been slow. Land for a new prison had been purchased at Paremoremo, north of Auckland in 1962, but by the time of the riot in July 1965 earthworks had not

Minister of Justice Ralph Hanan inspects damage caused by the 1965 Mt Eden riot.

Damage caused by the riot at Paparua in 1965.

yet commenced. Plans were still incomplete and there were, in fact, moves within Treasury to have the whole project scrapped.

The riot made provision of a new facility an absolute priority. For the next four years the construction of Paremoremo was the primary focus of the Department of Justice. Delayed by bad weather, particularly in its early phases, the prison opened in early 1969. Built on the 'telegraph pole' plan, with its five cell blocks leading off a central corridor, the prison incorporated some of the latest developments in European and American design and technology. Most closely, however, Paremoremo resembled the United States Penitentiary in Marion, Illinois. Opened in 1964, Marion was, at the time, the smallest and most secure prison in the American Federal system.

As a smaller and more modern version of Marion, Paremoremo in 1969 was among the most technologically advanced and secure penal institutions in the world. Its working population of 200 inmates was housed in self-contained single cells with tool-proof manganese steel bars. The internal location of cells made it impossible to break out of them directly to the outside. Cellblock windows were made of armour-plated glass and protected by thick reinforced-concrete mullions. Cells were opened remotely from a locked steel cabinet outside the housing section, and sally ports throughout the prison were electronically controlled and monitored from a secure central control unit. Critical areas in the institution such as sally ports, the visiting room and the gym could be watched 24 hours a day by closed-circuit television. Exercise yards had concrete floors and were surrounded by seven-metre-high grapple-proof concrete walls with electronic trip wires on the top, and the whole institution was surrounded by a double close-mesh fence topped with barbed wire. With inmates never allowed outside the confines of the cell blocks or the small exercise yards adjacent to them, escaping from Paremoremo would be extremely difficult.[18]

The End of the Sixties

Paremoremo began receiving inmates in March 1969, and its opening marked the start of a new era in New Zealand corrections. Based on an American concept as it was, Paremoremo was an early departure from the traditional reliance on English correctional models. From about this time, the department began looking wider afield in its search for new ideas and it also became more methodical and scientific in its methods. After the 1965 riot, however, little significant progress in corrections took place as the Department of Justice focused on building the new prison. The only moves came as adjustments to existing practice. Organised home leave started in 1965 and there were changes to parole. A Criminal Justice amendment in 1967 brought parole for all offenders serving at least six years, after they had completed three-and-a-half years. Preventive detention was changed. Originally involving two sentences (3–14 years or 3–life), it now became restricted to repeat sexual offenders and standardised at 7–life.

Finally, recognising that short sentences of imprisonment have little reformative value, the 1967 amendment placed a general restriction on sentences of less than six months. Accordingly, as an alternative to short-term imprisonment, periodic detention was extended to adults on a non-residential basis. The first centre for adults opened in Auckland in April 1967.

In July 1969, only a few months after Paremoremo opened its doors, Ralph Hanan suddenly died. Less than a year later, in March 1970, John Robson retired. Thus ended the Hanan–Robson era, a decade remembered for its energy, innovation and experiment. During the 20 years after 1950 the corrections system of New Zealand had grown from the archaic to the modern. In the wake of this metamorphosis came five years of conservatism where changing administrators, rising prison populations and serious prison unrest dominated Department of Justice concerns.

Notes

1 See Belshaw, 1979.
2 Unfortunately this quickly became dominated by powerful prisoners acting in their own interests, and was soon disbanded. Newbold, 1989: 36–37.
3 See Newbold, 1989: 35–69.
4 Mayhew, 1959.
5 Webb, 1982: 57–66.
6 Newbold, 1989: 43; Webb, 1982: 68.
7 See, e.g., Marshall, 1957; 1983.
8 For a full treatment of the Horton affair, see Newbold, 1989: 48–57.
9 For a full treatment of the MacDonald affair see Newbold, 1989: ch.7.
10 Newbold, 1989: 63–67.
11 AJHR H.20, 1959: 5
12 Walker and Brown, 1983: 40.
13 Department of Justice, 1971: 9.
14 AJHR H.20, 1966: 13; Department of Justice, 1970: 11.
15 Webb, 1982: 183–190.
16 See Newbold, 1989: 137–142, for full coverage of these events.
17 The Mt Eden riot is fully covered in Newbold, 1989: 149–163.
18 The building of Paremoremo maximum-security prison is fully covered in Newbold, 1989: 175–185.

References

Belshaw, Sheila (1979) *Man of Integrity: A Biography of Sir Clifton Webb*. Palmerston North: Dunmore Press.

Dallard, Berkeley (1976) *Recorded Interview with Margaret Long, Department of Justice*. (Unpublished).

Dallard, Berkeley (1980) *Fettered Freedom: A Symbiotic Society or Anarchy?* Wellington: Department of Justice.

Department of Justice (1969a) *Information About the Department of Justice*. Wellington: Government Printer.

Department of Justice (1969b) *Review of Borstal Policy in New Zealand*. Wellington: Government Printer.

Department of Justice (1970) *Penal Policy in New Zealand*. Wellington: Government Printer.

Department of Justice (1971) *Waipiata: A Study of Trainees in an Open Borstal Institution*. Wellington: Government Printer.

Marshall, John (1957) *The New Penal Policy (The Second Phase)*. Wellington: Mt Crawford Prison Press.

Marshall, John (1983) *Memoirs, Volume One: 1912–1960*. Auckland: Collins.

Matthews, Charles (1923) *The Evolution of the New Zealand Prison System*. Wellington: Government Printer.

Newbold, Greg (1989) *Punishment and Politics: The Maximum Security Prison in New Zealand*. Auckland: Oxford University Press.

Walker, Walton and Brown, Robert (1983) *Corrective Training: An Evaluation*. Wellington: NZ Department of Justice.

Webb, Patricia (1982) *A History of Custodial and Related Penalties in New Zealand*. Wellington: Government Printer.

CHAPTER 4
MODERNISING THE SYSTEM: 1970–1985

When Ralph Hanan died in 1969 his portfolio was taken over by Dan Riddiford, a lawyer from a prominent Wairarapa farming family, with old-school values, a short attention span due to a chronic heart condition and no particular interest in prisons. Soon after accepting the post Riddiford announced that penal reform had gone far enough.[1] He remained in office for just over two years, and when illness forced him to relinquish his portfolio in 1972 his replacement was the incumbent Speaker of the House, Sir Roy Jack, who remained until the National Government was defeated later that year. Jack had become a Minister of the Crown reluctantly, and only at the specific request of the Prime Minister, Sir Jack Marshall. One of the few qualified lawyers in parliament, Jack, like Riddiford, was a man of cultured tastes who also had little interest in, nor aptitude for, the running of prisons.

The chief executive of Justice at this time was Eric Missen, a career public servant who had been Assistant Secretary then Deputy Secretary for Justice under John Robson. Thus, although fully conversant with contemporary policy, he was handicapped by two successive ministers who were not interested in further reform.

The first few years after Robson's retirement were beset by overcrowding and tension in the nation's prisons. The prison population which had been stable during the early 1960s increased between 1966 and 1972 as it had in the 1950s, with the national muster growing by a third during that period. Between 1970 and 1971 alone, the rise was 11 per cent. Such growth in so short a period of time placed further stress on prison accommodation and programmes, contributing toward unrest which triggered a spate of riots and other disturbances.

The 1970s Riots – An International Phenomenon

Politics of the times also fanned the fires of inmate discontent.

Sir Roy Jack, Minister of Justice 1972.

Dan Riddiford, Minister of Justice 1969–1972.

Paremoremo maximum-security prison, opened in 1969.

In 1964 the United States had decided to send combatant troops to assist democratic South Vietnam in its war with the communist North, and New Zealand announced an intention to do the same in 1965. The Vietnam War became an issue of major international debate, and civil protests against it spread worldwide, peaking in 1968. In New Zealand, regular demonstrations began in 1967 and continued until America finally pulled its troops in 1973. In the meantime other human rights issues came into focus. Movements for workers' rights, minority rights, indigenous rights, women's rights and gay rights were all born or boosted during the 1960s and 1970s. In addition, movements in support of or opposed to political situations, such as apartheid in South Africa, British policy in Northern Ireland and the Cultural Revolution in China, also flourished. In New Zealand the seat of these protests was the universities, where enrolments had almost doubled between 1959 and 1969.[2]

On the heels of civil unrest and growing political awareness in the free community came disturbances in prisons. Starting in North America, prisoners, many of them black, began to see themselves as victims of state oppression, a feeling enhanced by the beatings and arrests of political agitators. This awareness was accompanied by a spate of prison riots, many of them organised by state and national prisoners' unions. In 1968 there were five prison riots in America, rising to 27 in 1970 and including a three-week strike at Folsom prison in California. The following year 37 riots were recorded and a riot at Attica, New York, resulted in the fatal shootings of 39 inmates and hostages by state police. In 1970 and 1971 prison activists Jon and George Jackson were gunned down in custody in California, and their attorney, civil rights leader Angela Davis, was arrested and charged with supplying weapons to Jon Jackson. In

1972 there were 48 riots, more than in any other year in American history.[3]

A similar pattern appeared in the UK. In 1969 one of the most serious riots in history broke out at Parkhurst prison on the Isle of Wight. From there the level of tension rose, reaching a climax in 1972. Between January and May 1972 some 50 collective inmate protests were recorded in Britain, and on 11 May a prisoners' union called 'Preservation of the Rights of Prisoners' (PROP) was born. PROP's activities prompted a 'national strike' at over 30 English prisons on 4 August 1972. This was followed by disturbances at more than 20 British institutions, including Albany, Dartmoor, Parkhurst and Peterhead.[4]

Many of the rebellions that afflicted New Zealand prisons between 1969 and 1975 must be seen in this context. Prison inmates were aware of the civil protests and riots overseas, and of the writings of prison activists. Many, particularly the men at Paremoremo, identified with and were directly motivated by left-wing American political figures.[5] Others were simply influenced by the turbulent mood of the times.

Accordingly, almost as soon as Paremoremo opened in 1969 there was trouble. The first escorts were from Waikeria where maximum-security inmates had been contained in conditions almost devoid of recreation and without adequate facilities since the Mt Eden riot four years before. Embittered by lengthy deprivation and poor treatment and unified by a sense of collective martyrdom, many of these men rebelled almost upon arrival at Paremoremo where Eddie Buckley, appointed superintendent and still smarting from the Mt Eden riot, had decided to keep a tight rein. Vocal protests, strikes, fires, cell flood-outs and serious assaults on staff started in March and continued throughout 1969. In November a toy pistol modified to fire .22-calibre ammunition was discovered in A Block, along with several .22 cartridges concealed on a woman visitor. That same month, in the intractables' unit of D Block, two staff were hospitalised and a surveillance camera smashed during a confrontation with two prisoners who refused to obey an order.

The pattern of violence continued. In 1969 ten serious attacks on staff were reported. Over the next 10 months there were at least 15 more, including one where two officers were concussed and one hospitalised with fractures to the face and jaw. This was followed some months later by a take-over in D Block, in which staff were beaten and seriously injured and four were taken hostage and threatened with death. Strikes, floods, fires and assaults occurred elsewhere in the prison. These problems continued in 1971 and 1972 with fights between inmates and staff, destruction of equipment, strikes and floods happening on a regular basis.

The publicity generated by these events sparked similar action elsewhere. In 1970 serious assaults took place at Mt Eden and Christchurch (Paparua) prisons, resulting in criminal charges and transfers to Paremoremo. The next year there was a riot and a strike at the severely overcrowded institution at Mt Eden, which ended when staff opened fire with pistols, wounding an inmate in the leg. There were riots also at Mt Crawford and Paparua prisons. Intense pressure from the media and the prison officers' union finally forced the government's hand and in December 1971 an Ombudsman's inquiry was ordered. An immediate result of the report, submitted early in 1972, was the sidelining of Paremoremo superintendent Eddie Buckley. His replacement was the affable and capable Jack Hobson, fresh from putting down the recent riot at Mt Eden.

In 1971 a lobby group known as Project Paremoremo had formed in support of the inmates' cause. Led by peace and human rights activist Maynie Thompson, Project Paremoremo campaigned for a second inquiry. Ordered late in 1972 and much larger than the first, this report recommended a number of changes but gave overall support to Hobson's regime.[6] Although Hobson continued to face difficulties, they became less frequent and by 1975 the prison was quiet. Developments in maximum security are dealt with more specifically in chapter 8.

Other Changes

Due to these problems, the previous two decades of reform and the lack of ministerial interest, other developments in the early 1970s were few. Major changes involved the provision of more beds to deal with the increasing numbers: fortunately intakes stabilised during the 1970s with a slow but erratic increase only over the next 15 years. Musters did not grow sharply again until 1986. Existing pressures remained, however, so as soon as Paremoremo maximum was occupied plans began for a medium-security prison next door. This was followed in 1970 by a 10-year building plan.[7] A new borstal at Kaitoke had been commissioned in 1969, and in 1971 an old miners' hostel at Ohura was purchased, to become a minimum-security prison for men the next year. In 1971 areas of Mt Eden that had been unused since the 1965 riot were re-roofed and re-commissioned. New detention centres were opened at Tongariro in 1971 and at Rolleston the following year.

The Third Labour Government: 1972–1975

The general election in November 1972 buried the National Government, which had been in power in 1960, in a Labour landslide. The new prime minister was the

charismatic 'Big Norm' Norman Kirk, and his Minister of Justice was a legal scholar and intellectual who openly loathed the idea of maximum security and tended to sympathise with the underdog. Dr Martyn Finlay had a PhD in law and had been an early campaigner for a solution to problems at Paremoremo. His liberal tendencies – which although based on fine principles were often quite impractical – made him immediately unpopular with prison officers and eventually alienated him from his own executive.

Youth Sentences

One of Finlay's lasting decisions, broadly supported by his department, was the abolition of the two youth sentences: borstal training and detention in a detention

Dr Martyn Finlay, Minister of Justice 1972–1975.

centre (DC). Scepticism about the effectiveness of both had intensified as a result of studies in the late 1960s. The detention centre had been legislated in 1954 but had not commenced until 1961. Its objective was to deter young first offenders from further crime through rigorous work and discipline. As early as 1966, however, it was known that two-thirds of DC releases were reconvicted within two years, and subsequent studies showed no improvement.[8] In 1968 the Department of Justice annual report published research showing that only 20 per cent of DC trainees released between 1961 and 1963 had not re-offended by the end of 1966. More than 50 per cent had been convicted of major offences.[9] It was clear that the deterrent impact of the sentence was ephemeral.

Borstal training told a similar story. Unlike DC, the objective of borstal was long-term training for young offenders, specifically to: detain youths and prevent them from further crime; develop good moral standards, vocational skills, work habits and hygiene; and train youths to live as responsible citizens.[10] It too was a failure. As early as 1962 a British study of youth recidivism found that reformative programmes in borstals produced results no different from those of youth prisons, where few programmes existed.[11] In 1968 a Department of Justice study found that recidivism among borstal trainees in New Zealand was very high, with 71 per cent reconvicted within three years of release[12]. It noted, however, that most trainees were seasoned offenders and were a hard group to deal with.[13]

If this was the case, then the 'open' borstal at Waipiata, the former sanatorium in Central Otago acquired from the Department of Health in 1961, should have produced better results. This centre was designed specifically for boys who had been identified as good prospects for reform. They were extracted from the main borstals after sentencing and sent to Waipiata, where they were housed in well-equipped buildings on a 1,200-acre farm. Unfortunately, the results from Waipiata showed an almost identical reconviction rate to other borstals, of 70 per cent.[14] A review of borstal training in 1969 recommended significant changes, but they brought no improvement.

The failure of youth programmes was a matter to which Finlay and his department gave immediate attention in 1973, and a replacement for the detention centre, to be known as corrective training but bearing no resemblance to its 1954 namesake, was announced. Accordingly, in 1975, borstal training was legally abolished in favour of ordinary imprisonment, and corrective training (or CT) replaced the detention centre. Due to expense and logistical problems, however, this legislation was not actually implemented until 1981.

Other Measures

Eric Missen retired in March 1974 and his place as permanent head of Justice was taken by Gordon Orr, a lawyer and former chairman of the State Services Commission who specialised in administrative law. Orr remained in office until 1978, when he took a law professorship at Victoria University, and it was during his first two years under Minister of Justice Martyn Finlay that the most important changes were made.

Finlay began his programme in 1973 by announcing that from 1974 the home-leave scheme would be extended to all minimum- and some medium-security inmates,

Former Secretaries for Justice: Gordon Orr 1974–1978; Jim Callahan 1982–1986;
John Robson 1960–1970; and Eric Missen 1970–1974.

and would not be restricted to first offenders. In 1975 the period between leaves was reduced from four to two months. As a result the number of home leaves approved grew from 174 in 1973 to 526 in 1974 and 747 the following year. The system suffered a setback when, on 24 December 1974, an inmate from Wi Tako who had been granted leave for Christmas shot his wife then committed suicide. This, along with other breaches and abscondings, led to a tightening of home-leave applications and a 10 per cent reduction in approvals in 1976.

In 1974 mail censorship was relaxed, and from May 1975 minimum-security inmates were allowed regular telephone calls. Access to one-third remission was extended in 1975 so that most low-custody inmates automatically qualified. Moreover, part or all of this extra one-twelfth was also made available, on application to the Secretary for Justice, to inmates in more secure establishments.

Like most of Finlay's early changes, the substance of these alterations was administrative and was hardly affected by statute. However, since 1972 Finlay had been working on law changes, and in September 1975 two amendments with implications for prisoners went through parliament. First, by amendment to the Criminal Justice Act, the non-parole period for murderers was reduced from ten to seven years and the minimum parole eligibility for finite sentences was cut from six to five years. Instead of having to serve at least three-and-a-half years before qualifying for parole, a candidate now only had to serve half his sentence or three-and-a-half years, whichever was the shortest, before making a board appearance. In the same amendment was the abolition of borstals and detention centres.

The other relevant piece of justice legislation in 1975 was the Penal Institutions Amendment Act, relating to restricted diets. Finlay had ordered the cessation of such diets in 1973 but the instruction had been ignored by some superintendents. Now discontinuance was put on a legal footing, and at the same time the punishment known as penal grade was abolished. Like the abolition of BT and DC, however, much of this legislation did not take immediate effect. Not until 1981, for example, was authority for restricted diets and penal grade formally removed by Amendment No.3 (1981) of the Penal Institutions Regulations 1961.

Penal grade had allowed the punitive separation of troublesome inmates for up to three months, similar to the administrative segregation used in Paremoremo's D Block. Both of the Ombudsmen's reports into maximum security had endorsed the use of D Block, and in 1975 the idea of long-term segregation for administrative purposes was made general for all prisons. The measure could be applied summarily for up to 14 days, and because its function was administrative rather than punitive it could continue indefinitely with head-office approval, subject to three-monthly reviews by the Secretary for Justice.

Perhaps Finlay's most controversial decision, in September 1973, was to allow inmates to write uncensored letters to him. According to Finlay[15] this action, more than any other, incensed staff and convinced them that he was siding with prisoners. Their fears seemed to be confirmed when a letter he had written to an inmate was published in the *Sunday Herald* on 5 October 1975 and in the *New Zealand Herald* and the *Auckland Star* the following day. Starting "Dear Les", the letter was written to Les Vercoe, a solicitor serving six years at Mt Eden for almost half a million dollars in fraud. The minister had done little more than express his dissatisfaction with the general state of the prison system, but the media made a feast of it, inflicting severe damage upon Finlay's credibility. The prisons' inmates worsened things by goading staff and threatening to write to "Uncle Martyn" unless they got their way. By 1975, Finlay told this author he was so unpopular with staff that he sometimes felt he needed protection when visiting an institution. His popularity was not enhanced by one of his last legislative moves, an amendment to the Electoral Act, which gave prisoners the vote. Inmates of course welcomed their enfranchisement, but the gesture became a powerful tool for the opposition to hammer the message that Labour was 'soft' on criminals.

Nineteen seventy-five was election year and these events, coming just months before the poll, were bad news for the government. Rampant inflation and billowing overseas debt as a result of a series of sharp oil price rises in the 1970s, the death of Prime Minister Norman Kirk in 1974, unpopular criminal justice policy and withering attacks from opposition leader Robert Muldoon, all undermined Labour's popularity and contributed to its crushing defeat in the November election.[16] The ascendance of National ended the single term of the third Labour Government and finished the ministerial career of one of the most compassionate justice ministers the country has known. In spite of his errors and ebbing popularity, Many of Finlay's reforms had a lasting impact on correctional policy, and the spoor of his passing remains visible today.

National Resumes Office

The new Minister of Justice under the National Government was David Thomson, a conservative 63-year-old former prisoner of war with a background in farming. No

David Thomson, Minister of Justice 1975–1978.

Jim McLay, Minister of Justice 1978–1984.

fan of pandering to criminals, he endeared himself to prison officers and the general population almost as soon as he took office in December 1975 by withdrawing the right of prisoners to write to him. He also promised to disenfranchise prisoners once more and in 1977 inmate voting rights were removed.

Like Riddiford and Jack, Thomson's time as minister was largely inactive, if not reactionary. Although Finlay had reduced the non-parole period for lifers to seven years, Thomson vowed that while he was minister no lifer would get out in less than ten. Additionally, Finlay's parole changes for finite sentences were hardly effective. In practice, as this author observed between 1975 and 1980 and as the Penal Policy Review Committee confirmed in 1981,[17] parole-eligible, finite-term inmates were normally kept in prison until within one or two months of their dates for automatic release on remission.

Thomson lost his place in a cabinet reshuffle in 1978. His term marked the end of an era where the permanent heads of the Justice department had an obvious effect on penal developments. His replacement was Jim McLay, a comparatively liberal lawyer who, at 34, was the youngest member of the Muldoon cabinet. McLay's youth and energy had already marked him as a potential high-flyer in politics. In 1977 he had brought a private member's bill that successfully restricted unfair cross-examination of complainants in rape trials about their sexual histories. Two years later McLay presided over the reorganisation of the courts system. Thus from 1979 the Magistrates' Court became the District Court, and Stipendiary Magistrates in these courts had

Figure 4.1: Prison Musters 1965–1985

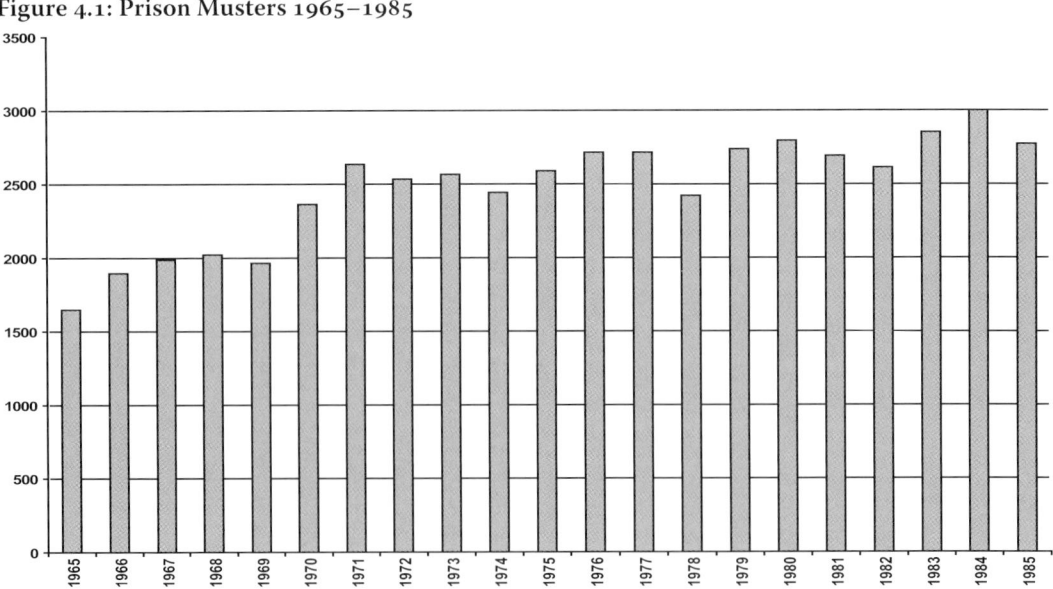

Ohura prison, a former miners' hospital converted into a prison in 1972 and closed in 2005.

their status elevated to District Court Judges, who wore gowns on the bench. From 1981 lower court judges were empowered to preside over trials by jury. At the same time, the Supreme Court was renamed the High Court.

Prison populations rose gradually in the early 1970s, peaking at 2,880 in 1976 – a 29 per cent rise over 1970. They then stabilised for another 10 years. Nonetheless, the building plan announced at the end of 1970 began to bear fruit. In 1971 C Block, the only block at Paremoremo still empty, received its first inmates, bringing the prison into full commission. A new detention centre was established at Tongariro prison farm. Another opened at Rolleston in 1972 and the former miners' hostel at Ohura began receiving inmates. In 1974 the old women's prison at Dunedin was converted for use by men and a new prison for women opened at Christchurch, now the country's main institution for female inmates. In 1975 a new cell complex was built at Rangipo prison, and the first periodic detention centre for women opened in Epsom, Auckland, the same year. In 1978 a new medium-security prison was opened at Kaitoke near Wanganui, and in 1979 Linton prison in the Manawatu, intended initially as a youth institution, received its first inmates. In 1981 Linton became a reception and classification centre for all lower North Island prisoners under the age of 20. At Invercargill in 1980 a new remand facility was opened and finally, in 1981, the new medium-security complex at Paremoremo, which had been planned in 1969, began receiving prisoners.

Legislation

Jim McLay's period as Justice minister (1978–84) saw some significant legal developments. In 1980 the non-parole period for those sentenced to life imprisonment for crimes other than murder (for example, manslaughter), which had been set at five years in 1920, was raised to seven years, bringing it in line with preventive detention and life imprisonment for murder. In 1981 the legislation relating to youth institutions, which Finlay had enacted in 1975, finally came into effect. From this time borstals ceased legally to exist and became known as 'youth prisons'. Detention centres were also abolished and replaced by corrective training centres. Initially this new form of corrective training (not to be confused with its namesake of 1954–1963) was intended to involve two alternative sentences – three and six months – but in 1980 it was confined to three months. Designed to remedy the deficiencies of the detention centre, corrective training #2 was, in fact, both in operation and in definition, almost identical to it. The primary difference was that CT was not reserved for first offenders and so could be served more than once. Another difference was that CT was available to females. Both sentences were based on deterrent discipline, and CTs were located in old detention centre units: at Tongariro prison farm (Hautu), Rangipo prison farm, and Rolleston and Invercargill prisons. The female CT centre, a wing at Arohata women's prison,[18] never received enough inmates to be viable.

Considering its close similarity to DC, it is not surprising that CT proved no more effective. In fact, given that CT took recidivists, it might have been predicted that its failure rate would be even worse — which it was. In 1983 a Department of Justice study found that 71 per cent of corrective trainees were reconvicted within a single year of release, compared with 50–60 per cent of detention centre trainees.[19] Although it was thus known and conceded from the start that the new sentence was an even greater failure than its predecessor, corrective training was not abolished for another 19 years.

Changes were made to non-custodial options as well. In 1980 a new community-based sentence known as 'community service' was created as another alternative to imprisonment. Designed to complement periodic detention, community service was aimed at the more sophisticated offender. Whereas periodic detention required weekly attendance at a centre from which parties were despatched for labour on public projects, community service involved a fixed number of hours — up to 200 over a 12-month period — in an approved, specialised area. Community service did not require attendance at a centre and supervision was provided by community agencies. Community service was normally given to low-risk offenders with specific skills — for example, art and music — that could be made use of by public bodies. At the same time, in 1980, residential periodic detention, which had remained available for young offenders, was phased out entirely.

The Penal Policy Review Committee 1981

In 1977 the Ombudsman's annual report had criticised the prison system in New Zealand, recommending an extensive review of the penal programme.[20] The call was rejected by David Thomson, but less than four years later, at the instigation of his successor Jim McLay and permanent head John Robertson, a high-powered committee of eight criminal justice professionals was set up to examine, report on and make recommendations about corrections in New Zealand. Known as the Penal Policy Review Committee, it took public submissions, visited prisons and finally tabled a 232-page report in December 1981.

At the time the report was the largest and fullest review of its type ever conducted in New Zealand, with 73 major recommendations. Perhaps its most significant statement was that prisons cannot rehabilitate and cannot be expected to do so.[21] It recommended restricting imprisonment as much as possible and expanding alternatives to incarceration. This comment, which was central to the tenor of the report as a whole, had significant impact on the Criminal Justice Act when it was rewritten in 1985. However, as is common with such exercises, a number of the recommendations were set aside by government. For example, part of recommendation 7, that parole should be restricted to indeterminate sentences (life and PD) was ignored — in fact, from 1985 parole was broadened. Disregarded also was recommendation 8, that the mandatory life sentence for murder be replaced by life as a maximum. Another part of recommendation 7, that the non-parole minimum for life should remain at seven years, was observed temporarily, until 1987, when the minimum was raised to 10 years. Recommendation 10, that preventive detention be abolished, was ignored; in fact, from 1987 PD was strengthened. Recommendation 21, that prisoners should be entitled to vote, was rejected as well.

And so it went. A few small concessions were made. Corrective training (recommendation 24) was evaluated and found to be virtually worthless. Periodic detention facilities were made more accessible to women (recommendation 42). The terms 'Regional Prisons' (recommendation 15) and 'Throughcare' (recommendation 11) were adopted and became departmental jargon, but really changed nothing. The 'Regional Prisons' concept, which began in 1983, simply confirmed the practice initiated by Robson in 1960 of placing prisoners as close to family or support groups as possible. 'Throughcare' just meant, in broad terms, attempting to rehabilitate inmates and maintain links between them and the community. This objective had been central to departmental policy since 1910.

At the time of the report New Zealand had one maximum security facility, seven medium security, seven minimum, three youth institutions catering for young inmates and corrective trainees, and two institutions for females.[22] For the moment prison populations were stable and existing institutions satisfied current needs. As a result, in 1982 the maximum security 'Separates Division' at Mt Eden, which had been constructed after the escapes of Evans, Gillies and Wilder in February 1965, shut its doors – albeit temporarily. Likewise, in anticipation of the 1983 report, there was a gradual winding down of corrective training with the closure of the Rolleston centre in 1982.

Problems in Prisons

Drugs

In the late 1960s a 'drug problem' was identified in New Zealand, and police-reported drug crimes increased from 400 in 1970 to nearly 10,000 a decade later. A great deal of publicity was attached to the phenomenon, with several measures taken in a vain attempt to contain it.[23] A large number of offenders were imprisoned. When the first prison census was taken in 1972, 49 of the country's 2,522 sentenced prisoners (1.9%) were doing time for drugs.[24] By the time of the second departmental census in 1987 prisons contained 241 drug offenders, which was nine per cent of the sentenced muster.[25] Stiff penalties were awarded for producing and trafficking drugs, and terms in excess of five years were not uncommon. The longest drug sentence in the 1970s was 13 years, given to Wayne Beri in 1975 for importing heroin. Many drug offenders continued to use drugs in prison and introduced other inmates to them, so that by mid-1975 when this author was jailed for selling heroin, drugs were freely available in penal institutions about the country.

Although superintendents took rigorous steps to stop the flow, the problem of drugs in jails went largely unnoticed by the press until May 1977 when a series of articles about the issue appeared in newspapers. Concern deepened in August, when an inmate died from an overdose at Addington prison in Christchurch, and again the following year, when counsel for a drug addict facing burglary charges claimed his client had been able to maintain his opiate habit during previous sentences at Paremoremo maximum-security prison.[26] Throughout 1979 there was a splurge of publicity about drugs in prisons. The government was forced to act. Searches by drug dogs first made their appearance that year, and an amendment to the Penal Institutions Act gave superintendents the right to order finger swabs and sputum and urine samples from inmates thought to be under the influence of drugs. In addition, that year a general prohibition on gifts of food and other items to inmates came into effect.

Prison Violence

The other emerging problem in the 1980s was prison gangs and associated violence. As seen previously, the early 1970s witnessed a surge in organised prison protests, which came on the heels of the worldwide protest movement. In the late 1970s violence returned, but its form was different. Violence now tended to be more explosive and individualised, much of it gang related. Gang activity became increasingly prominent, and police-estimated gang membership doubled between 1980 and 1988, to 4,400.[27] A 1983 survey estimated that 21 per cent of male inmates were gang members,[28] and a later one in 1987 found that gang members represented 15 per cent of the sentenced inmate population.[29]

Some of these changes reflected soaring levels of violence in the community at large. Between 1970 and 1980 convictions for crimes of violence grew by 89 per cent. They rose by another third in the next five years. The greatest jumps were in serious violence. During the same two time frames, for example (1970–1980 and 1980–1985), convictions for crimes such as homicide grew by 130 per cent and then by another 60 per cent; serious assaults grew by 290 per cent and then 30 per cent; rape by 240 per cent and then 50 per cent; while robbery convictions grew eleven-fold between 1970 and 1980 and by another 30 per cent in the next five years.[30]

These dramatic leaps inevitably affected the prison population and hence the culture of penal institutions. Between 1979 and 1985 the number of violent offenders sent to prison each year grew by 53 per cent.[31] By 1987, 42 per cent of all prison inmates were doing time for a crime of violence.[32] The pressure was first felt at Paremoremo maximum, where the country's most dangerous inmates were held. Here, in a race-based confrontation in late 1975, an inmate was stabbed almost to death, and in 1979 child sex killer Keith Hall died after having his throat cut in A Block. Cedric James, a member of the Head Hunters Motorcycle Club, was charged with the murder but acquitted. Hall's was the prison's first homicide; in fact it appears to have been the first jail homicide recorded in New Zealand. There have been another nine inmate homicides in New Zealand since.

In 1980 several more serious assaults were reported at Paremoremo. Between 1978 and 1984, despite a low and stable incidence of violence against staff, assaults among prisoners grew almost three-fold. Reciprocally, the numbers of prisoners segregated – either at their own request or at the superintendent's direction – more than doubled. At the end of 1980, as a result of a serious attack on a sex offender in December, a landing in the classification block was set aside for protective custody.

Soon after, the whole block was taken over for protection and classification services were transferred to Mt Eden. As will be seen in chapter 8, tensions at the prison continued to build during the 1980s, with a leap in suicides and a major gang fight between the Head Hunters and the Mongrel Mob in the gymnasium on Christmas Eve 1984. This resulted in a number of stab wounds and head injuries to Mob members, and necessitated a complete reorganisation of the prison's routine.[33]

The problems at Paremoremo were reflected elsewhere. There had been disturbances at Addington, New Plymouth and Waikeria prisons in 1976 and 1977, although the department's annual report for 1978 noted it was a quiet year, with a slight decline in prison populations. A further muster decline in 1979 led to an optimistic report, but the 1980 report noted that populations had begun to rise again and commented on the increasing problem of drugs, the homicide at Paremoremo and violent incidents elsewhere. Gang strife was experienced at a number of institutions, one of which happened in January 1979 when a brawl between rival gangs broke out among remand inmates at Mt Eden. Later that year a Paremoremo prison officer was slashed in the face by an inmate. In 1982 at Mt Crawford, a bomb was lobbed into a remand cell containing eight suspects in a gang killing (they managed to eject it just before it exploded), and there was a strike at Paremoremo medium. The following year there was a three-day strike at Waikune; 70 DC inmates rioted at Invercargill, stabbing officers in the process; six remand inmates broke out of Mt Eden in March followed by another five in September; an inmate was stabbed at Paremoremo medium; and an inmate had both his legs broken in a gang-related incident at Mt Eden. As a result of these problems, and a short but sharp rise in musters between 1982 and 1984, the separates division at Mt Eden, which had closed its doors in September 1982, reopened just 13 months later.

In 1985 there was a second prison murder, this time at Mt Eden, when an inmate called Darcy Te Hira had his skull fractured after being hit with a long-handled porridge stirrer, allegedly over a drug debt. Tensions created by the rising violence were reflected in suicides. Before 1980 prison suicides were comparatively rare, but they became a persistent problem as a result of a Committee of Inquiry into malpractice at Oakley Hospital in 1983, which stopped the routine transfer of psychiatrically disturbed inmates to mental hospitals. Instead, disturbed inmates had to remain in the prisons, which had neither the expertise nor the facilities to treat them. Thus, at Paremoremo maximum, which prior to 1980 had had only one suicide since opening in 1969, there were 14 suicides between 1980 and 1987. Five of these occurred in the years 1984–85. Nationwide the pattern was similar: of the 29 prison suicides recorded between 1971 and 1985, more than half took place in the last two of these years.

By this stage a new administration had taken over in Wellington. In June 1984, after nine years in government, the Prime Minister Robert Muldoon dissolved parliament and called a snap election. The sudden announcement caught everyone unawares – not the least his own caucus – and was an apparent attempt to catch the opposition off guard at a time when the government was flagging in the polls. The gamble failed and National suffered a crippling defeat. Labour now took control of the Treasury with a majority of 17 seats, and a powerful mandate for change.

Notes

1 Newbold, 1989: 199.
2 Newbold, 1989: 217.
3 Newbold, 1989: 218–219; Useem and Kimball, 1991: 9–18.
4 Fitzgerald, 1977: 136–158.
5 Newbold, 1989: 218–219.
6 AJHR A.6 vol.1, 1973.
7 *NZ Herald*, 30 Dec, 1970.
8 Walker and Brown, 1983: 40.
9 AJHR H.20, 1968.
10 Department of Justice, 1969: 5.
11 Little, 1963.
12 Department of Justice, 1971: 9
13 AJHR H.20, 1969.
14 Department of Justice, 1971: 35.
15 Pers. comm.
16 See Bassett, 1976; Levine and Robinson, 1976.
17 At p. 56.
18 Walker and Brown 1983: 5–6.
19 Walker and Brown, 1983: 40.
20 AJHR A3, 1977: 8–9.
21 At p.62.
22 *Report of the Penal Policy Review Committee*, 1981: 177-180.
23 See Newbold, 2000: ch 6; 2004.
24 Department of Justice, 1975: 7.
25 Braybrook and O'Neill, 1988: 41.
26 *NZ Herald*, 26 May, 1978.
27 Dennehey and Newbold, 2001: 169–183.
28 *NZ Herald*, 29 Feb, 1984.
29 Braybrook and O'Neill, 1988: 62.
30 Department of Justice, 1986: 48.
31 Department of Justice, 1986: 62.
32 Department of Justice, 1988: 41.
33 Meek, 1986: 33–40; Newbold, 1989: 290–293.

References

Bassett, Michael (1976) *The Third Labour Government: A Personal History*. Palmerston North: Dunmore.

Braybrook, Bev and O'Neill, Rose (1988) *A Census of Prison Inmates*. Wellington: Department of Justice.

Committee of Inquiry into Procedures at Oakley Hospital and Related Matters (1983) *Report*. Chair: R.G. Gallen. Wellington: Government Printer.

Department of Justice (1969) *Review of Borstal Policy in New Zealand*. Wellington: Government Printer.

Department of Justice (1971) *Waipiata: A Study of Trainees in an Open Borstal Institution*. Wellington: Government Printer.

Department of Justice (1975) *Justice Department Penal Census*. Wellington: Department of Justice.

Department of Justice (1986) *Submission to the Committee of Inquiry into Violence*. Wellington: Department of Justice.

Fitzgerald, Mike (1977) *Prisoners in Revolt*. Middlesex: Penguin.

Levine, Stephen and Robinson, Alan (1976) *The New Zealand Voter: A Survey of Electoral Opinion and Electoral Behaviour*. Wellington: Price-Milburn.

Little, Alan (1963) 'Penal Theory, Penal Reform and Borstal Practice'. *British Journal of Criminology* v.3: 257–275.

Meek, John (1986) *Paremoremo: New Zealand's Maximum Security Prison*. Wellington: Department of Justice.

Newbold, Greg (1989) *Punishment and Politics: The Maximum Security Prison in New Zealand*. Auckland: Oxford University Press.

Newbold, Greg (2000) *Crime in New Zealand*. Palmerston North: Dunmore.

Newbold, Greg (2004) 'The Control of Drugs in New Zealand'. In R. Hil and G. Tait (eds) *Hard Lessons: Reflections on Governance and Crime Control in Late Modernity*. Hants: Ashgate.

Report of the Committee of Inquiry into Procedures at Oakley Hospital and Related Matters. (1983) Chair: R.G. Gallen, QC. Wellington: Government Printer.

Report of the Penal Policy Review Committee 1981 (1981) Chair: Justice Sir Maurice Casey. Wellington: Government Printer.

Report by Sir Guy Powles and Mr L.G.H. Sinclair into Various Matters Pertaining to Paremoremo Prison 1972. (1972) Wellington: Officer of the Ombudsman.

Useem, Bert and Kimball, Peter (1991) *States of Siege: US Prison Riots 1971–1986*. New York: Oxford University Press.

Walker, Walton, and Brown, Robert (1983) *Corrective Training: An Evaluation*. Wellington: Department of Justice.

CHAPTER 5
LATER DEVELOPMENTS: 1985–1995

When Labour took office from National late in July 1984 it faced problems in Justice with which the previous minister had just begun to grapple. The correctional philosophies of the two governments were similar, with Labour and National's views on criminal justice closer than in probably any other area. Although Jim McLay had represented a conservative party, he was nonetheless a liberal where justice was concerned and had been supported by his Prime Minister. As a young parliamentarian in 1961, Robert Muldoon had been one of only 10 National Party politicians to cross the floor and vote with Labour against capital punishment, and he had debated against Mt Eden's prison team as a member of the Young Nationals in 1953. The new Prime Minister David Lange was a former criminal lawyer who had worked in Auckland at the same time as McLay. A practising Methodist and an accomplished orator, Lange had a reputation as friend of the oppressed and frequently represented clients without charging them. The man Lange chose as his Minister of Justice was a quiet law professor named Geoffrey Palmer, who had only been in parliament since 1979. He, too, was a man of strong liberal persuasion.

Difficulties Facing the Minister

The department Palmer inherited in 1984 was troubled and restless. Between 1982 and 1984 prison populations had risen by 15 per cent, creating accommodation problems and threats of industrial action from staff. Inmate–inmate violence was increasing, suicides were soaring and the question of psychiatric placement was still unresolved. The seven prison suicides reported in the period 1969–1979 jumped to 47 – all but one of them male – between 1980 and 1990. The peak year was 1985, when eight men committed suicide.[1] In March 1985 two inmates at the Waikeria Youth Centre drank weed killer, one of whom died, and in April a schizophrenic inmate at Mt Eden gouged his eyes out. In June a prisoner in the newly established psychiatric unit at Paremoremo cut his own throat with a razor blade. Another did the same in June and tried again in July. Both men survived, but the acts underlined the inadequacy of prisons' makeshift psychiatric services. In fact, between the time Oakley

Geoffrey Palmer, Minister of Justice 1984–1989.

Hospital ceased taking prison admissions in 1983, and December 1986, the Justice department recorded 126 self-mutilations (in addition to 20 suicides) in New Zealand prisons.[2]

In response to these conditions, eight inmates – most of them at Paremoremo – independently went on prolonged hunger strikes between November 1983 and February 1985. In April and May 1985, 25 D Block men went on strike and two others refused to eat, over the administration's failure to deal effectively with the prison's suicide problem. Noting there had been 12 suicides since March 1983, Palmer promised an immediate boost to prison psychiatric services.[3] But the problem remained, with two more suicides at the end of June. In response Palmer promised improvements to psychiatric facilities at Paremoremo.[4] But the slow progress failed to satisfy inmates. Of the 47 inmates who took their lives between 1980 and 1990, 17 (more than a third) were at Paremoremo maximum, which housed only about five per cent of the nation's

Figure 5.1: Prison Suicides as % of Total Muster

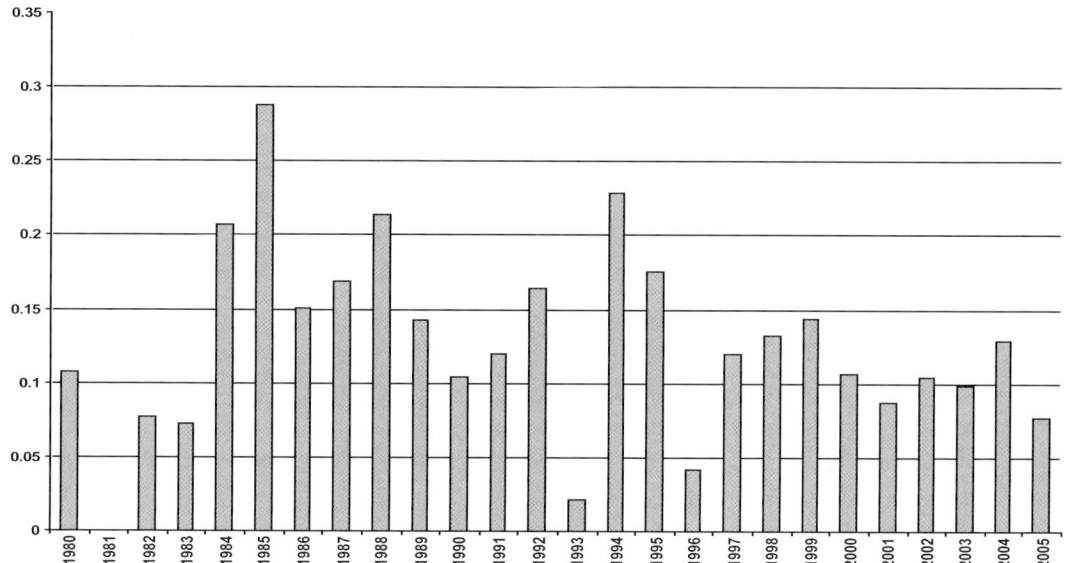

inmates. In August 1985 another three began a protest fast, and in the next 28 months seven more of Paremoremo's 200 prisoners committed suicide.

Violence continued as well. As noted, there was a serious gang brawl at Paremoremo in December 1984, and in January 1985 the Te Hira homicide at Mt Eden. The next day a multiple stabbing at Paremoremo resulted in an inmate being hospitalised. Three months later another was admitted to hospital after a stabbing at Paremoremo medium, and at Mt Eden a fight between 35 members of the Mongrel Mob and Black Power gangs caused numerous injuries and hospitalisations.

The Criminal Justice Act 1985

Palmer's primary response to these challenges was to replace the Criminal Justice Act 1954 with an entirely new act, which came into effect on 1 October 1985.

This consolidated some of the post-1954 amendments, but it also contained a number of measures taken in the light of the 1981 Penal Policy Review Committee recommendations. It also aimed to reduce overcrowding. Of the legislation, former Deputy Secretary for Justice Charlotte Williams[5] commented that it marked a high point in the liberal, rehabilitative school of thinking and had probably already been overtaken by retributive public opinion by the time of its passing. The fact that it was extensively amended in 1987, 1993 and 2002 certainly supports this view.

The principal components of the Criminal Justice Act were that, first, in an attempt to address the problem of rising violence, it mandated imprisonment for offenders convicted of violent offences carrying minimums at least five years' imprisonment. However, in a concession to the Penal Policy Review Committee comment that prisons cannot rehabilitate, the new law stated that property offenders convicted of crimes punishable by seven years or less should not be sent to prison other than in exceptional circumstances. The sentence of probation was renamed 'supervision', compensation was renamed 'reparation' (both with some variations on their predecessors) and a new community sentence called 'community care' was created. Community care required the consent of the offender and allowed the court to direct him or her to attend a community programme for up to 12 months, at least six months of which could be residential. Examples included Maori culture or marae-based programmes, alcohol and drug addiction programmes, recreational programmes and halfway houses. The adaptability of the sentence was demonstrated a few months later when, under a sentence of community care, a 27-year-old disqualified driver with a drink problem was sentenced to complete 36 parachute jumps.[6]

One of the lasting components of the Criminal Justice Act 1985 related to parole. Under the Finlay administration, parole had been made available at half sentence or seven years, whichever was the shorter, but applied only to sentences of five years and above. Lifers and preventive detainees also had to serve at least seven years. Now parole was made available to all inmates serving finite terms, at half sentence or seven years, whichever was the shorter. A number of local district prisons boards were created to hear cases involving sentences of less than seven years, while those of seven years or more were heard by a national parole board. Prisoners released on parole from finite terms were subject to supervision and conditions for six months. Lifers and preventive detainees remained on licence for the rest of their lives. For inmates denied parole, 'automatic' release on remission was now set at two-thirds of sentence, with conditions for six months in the case of all those sentenced to a year or more. Because of this, many doing less than a year elected to serve their full two thirds rather than accept parole and face six months supervision. Thus in 1989 an amendment removed parole eligibility for inmates serving sentences of less than a year, who were now released automatically at half sentence.

The impact of the 1985 act was a sudden exodus from prisons as the parole board and district prisons boards, quite indiscriminately, ordered the release of large numbers of prisoners who had served half or more of their sentences. Between September 1985 when the act came into effect and March 1986, more than 1,000 inmates – a third of the entire prison muster at the time – were released early under the terms of the new act. National prison populations plummeted, dropping 11 per cent between 1984 and 1986. The 1986 muster of 2,662 was the lowest figure recorded since 1975, and the year's nadir of 2,217 recorded in February was the lowest muster since 1970. As a result, a delighted minister announced in May 1986 that two prisons – Wanganui and Waikune – would close as they were no longer needed. The department hoped to reduce its expenditure in 1986 by $20 million as a result of lower running costs and profits from the sale of surplus land.[7] Recouping was less than anticipated, however, and five years later with jails once again full to bursting Waikune prison, originally valued at $2.5 million but now dilapidated and useless, remained unsold. The 499-hectare site was finally purchased in 2003 by the Office of Treaty Settlements.

So, as may have been predicted, the Minister's optimism proved premature. The exodus of inmates did little more than shorten the recidivism cycle and prisons soon began to fill again. By May 1986 the department reported that, of the 1,750 inmates released on parole or on their two-thirds remission dates since the previous September, 300 had already re-offended.[8] Within two years inmate numbers were back to 1984 levels and they continued a steep and unremitting ascent. By 1990 there were nearly 4,000 inmates and by 1995 there were 4,553 – 69 per cent more than a decade before. The experience of 1985 showed that there are no cheap or easy answers to the problem of rising prison musters.

Figure 5.2: Prison Musters 1970–2000

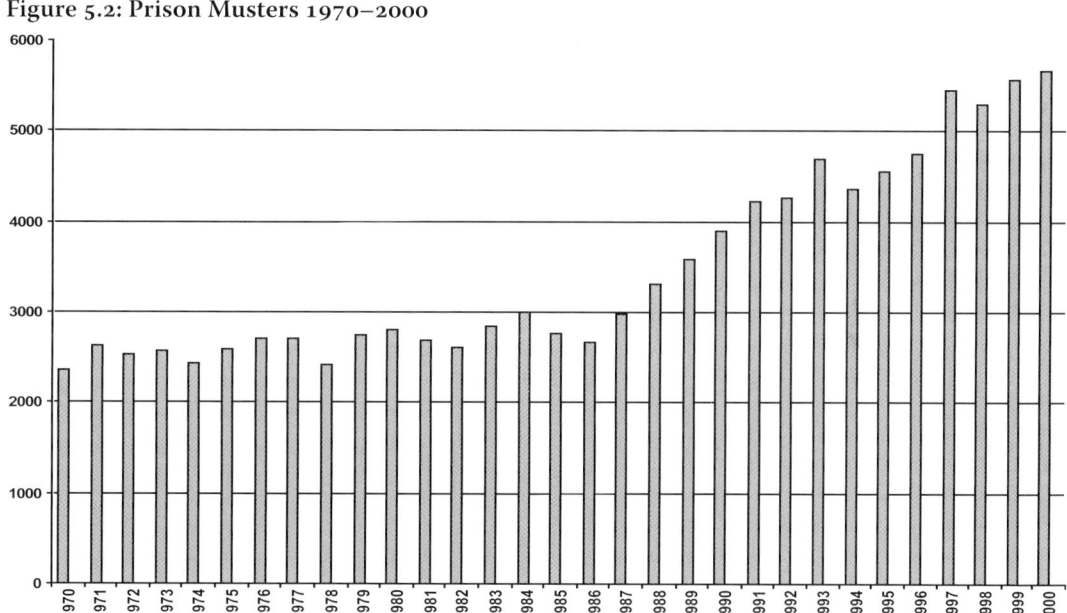

Violence and Serious Crime after 1985

The intention of the 1985 act to reduce violent offending by mandating prison sentences for violent crime also failed. This was not surprising, given that the socioeconomic factors behind the changes in offending patterns remained the same.[9] Between 1984 and 1987 the percentage of violent offenders sentenced to prison rose only slightly, since before the act most serious violent offenders had been jailed anyhow. There was, however, a 26 per cent increase in the average length of prison sentences, but this may merely have reflected the fact that more crimes of serious violence were being committed. Between 1984 and 1987 convictions for violence grew by 16 per cent, and violence as a percentage of other crimes also grew. The largest leaps were in crimes of a serious nature: injuring or wounding – up by a third; aggravated robbery – up 22 per cent; rape – up 37 per cent; indecent assault – up 73 per cent; and homicide – which doubled.[10] More important, however, was that from 1985 rising levels of crime, particularly violent crime, occupied considerable media attention, and alarmist police commentary – such as they were "losing the battle" with crime[11] – exaggerated the problem in the eyes of the public.

A number of crime issues captured attention during this period. First, there was concern about organised drug trafficking. Drugs had first been identified as a problem in New Zealand in the late 1960s, and in the 1970s a gang later known as the 'Mr Asia' gang created a brief flurry – with Police Commissioner Ken Burnside talking about a 'Mr Big' who was taking over New Zealand crime[12] – before moving offshore and finally being busted in the UK in 1979. The demand for drugs remained, however. In 1979 Brian Curtis was convicted of importing three kilograms of heroin and sentenced to life imprisonment. This was the first life term imposed under a 1978 amendment to the Misuse of Drugs Act 1975, although the sentence was later commuted to 16 years. The influx of heroin then abated somewhat but in November 1985 Wayne Beri, who had been paroled from a 13-year term for importing heroin just 15 months before, got life for possessing $300,000 worth of the drug for supply. A number of other well known New Zealand crime figures were convicted in this case as well. That same year Peter Fulcher, formerly an associate of the Mr Asia syndicate, got 14 years for importing heroin.[13]

Another high-profile issue in 1986 and 1987 was the 'gang problem'. Gangs were first recognised as a social issue in the 1950s, and have continued to stimulate the collective imagination since. In the mid-1980s there was considerable publicity about gang activity, in particular gang abuse of government work schemes and the large amounts of money some gangs had managed to accumulate as a result. In the middle of this furore, in December 1986 at an officially sanctioned Mongrel Mob convention at Ambury Park in Auckland, a woman passer-by was pack-raped and brutalised. A number of members landed heavy prison terms as a result of this incident, gang access to work schemes soon ceased and calls for harsher measures to control the gangs intensified.[14]

Drugs, gangs and general concern about rising violence were all important catalysts to hardening attitudes towards crime in the 1980s. But it was a number of tragic sex-related murders which amplified calls for an end to liberalism in criminal justice more than anything else. One involved a serial violent offender called Rufus Junior Marsh. In 1975, while on parole for robbery, Marsh (19) and co-offender Dennis Luke (15) kicked an elderly man to death in Wellington. Luke was convicted of murder, while Marsh got manslaughter and seven years' imprisonment. Soon after his release for this offence in 1983, Marsh was jailed for two years for attempted rape, followed soon after by a year in prison for another robbery. In November 1986, shortly after release from his last jail term, Marsh entered the house of 32-year-old Diane Miller, tormenting her for at least 20 minutes before bashing her skull in with a brick and slashing her throat. He was sentenced to life imprisonment.

In October 1986, just a month before the horror of the Miller killing, six-year-old Louisa Damodran was abducted as she walked home from school in Christchurch. Taken to a remote spot where she was presumably sexually assaulted, she was tied up and gagged and thrown into the Waimakariri River where she drowned. Her killer, Peter Joseph Holdem, had previous sex offences against young girls and was on parole at the time.[15] This particular matter, coming so soon after Miller's death, prompted Geoffrey Palmer to draft important amendments to the Criminal Justice Act, only a year after it had come into effect. But before the amendments were made another incident reinforced the need for change. In June 1987 Teresa Cormack, also aged six, disappeared under similar circumstances to Damodran as she walked to school in Napier. Her body was later found amid debris on Whirinaki Beach. Like Holdem, Cormack's killer Jules Mikus had a history of sex crimes (although this was unknown at the time). Mikus remained undetected until being identified by DNA, and was convicted in 2002. Both crimes prompted deep community revulsion, and after the Cormack murder there were nationwide calls for a return to capital punishment.

Nineteen eighty seven was an election year, and already under pressure to respond to public demands, Palmer took two important initiatives. First, in 1986 he ordered a committee of inquiry into violence. Chaired by retired High Court Judge Sir Clinton Roper, the report, presented in March 1987, recommended (at p. 126) tougher parole conditions for violent offenders and an increase in the non-parole period of lifers from seven years to ten.

The 1987 Amendments

Palmer's other response was the first of the previously mentioned changes to the Criminal Justice Act which appeared as Amendments No. 2 and No. 3 in 1987. The overall intention of these amendments was to make penalties for violence even more stringent than before.

The principal effects of the 1987 amendments, which came into force only weeks after the Cormack killing in June and the sentencing of Holdem in July, were to increase the likelihood of a violent offender being sent to prison and extend the time serious violent offenders spent locked up. This occurred by lengthening the non-parole periods of preventive detention and life imprisonment, and removing parole eligibility for specified violence offenders serving finite terms. In the six years between 1987 and 1993, the likelihood of a convicted violent offender being sentenced to imprisonment remained about the same – 25 per cent – but the number imprisoned grew by 45 per cent. The average sentence length for violence overall grew by only 10 per cent but for serious violence the increases were greater: 16 per cent in the cases of manslaughter and wounding or injuring, and 24 per cent for aggravated robbery.[16] As noted, the proportion of sentences served was also greater.

Impact of the Legislation

As before, the legislation had little apparent effect on violent crime. Between 1987 and 1993 convictions for violence grew by 50 per cent, while convictions for other forms of offending rose by only 11 per cent. As before, the biggest hikes were in the

The 1987 Criminal Justice Act Amendment

- The minimum non-parole period for life and preventive detention was raised from seven years to 10 years.
- The age of eligibility for preventive detention was reduced from 25 to 21. The sentence became available to all offenders aged 21 and over who had committed a serious sexual offence, having previously committed such an offence since reaching the age of 17. Although in 1985 Palmer had considered abolishing preventive detention, he now strengthened it.
- The threshold at which the presumption of imprisonment applied to violent offenders was reduced from crimes punishable by at least five years, to those punishable by at least two years, provided that the offender used serious violence or endangered somebody, or had been convicted at least once before of a violent crime punishable by at least two years imprisonment.
- Parole eligibility for violent offenders sentenced to finite terms of more than two years for certain 'specified' violent offences was removed. The list of specified offences included crimes of serious personal violence, plus robbery and sexual violation. Thereafter, however, although no longer eligible for parole, these offenders, like all others, still qualified for automatic release after serving two thirds of their sentences.
- A proviso to early release provisions was added under s.107A, which was that if it was believed that, after release on remission, a specified violence offender was likely to commit another specified crime of violence before his sentence had expired, the Secretary for Justice could order that he be kept in prison to serve his full term. This was a highly controversial matter, because it effectively meant that violent offenders (and violent offenders only) could be punished for crimes they had not committed, on the assumption that they would probably commit them in the future.

area specifically targeted by the new law: serious violence. In that six-year period, convictions for aggravated robbery grew by 66 per cent – although simple robbery remained static. Convictions for threatening to kill or cause grievous bodily harm grew by 86 per cent. And, partly as a result of rising public awareness, there were major jumps in convictions for sexual offences and sexual violence, with convictions for rape up 74 per cent, attempted sexual violation up 83 per cent, and indecent assault up 139 per cent. In addition, partly due to a tougher police approach to domestic violence after 1987, convictions for 'male assaults female' grew by a staggering 246 per cent between then and 1993.[17]

Inevitably these shifts in crime rates and sentencing policy affected prison populations. Musters rocketed after 1985 and when the first major census was done in November 1987, the incarcerated population was over 3,000 (including 120 women). About 44 per cent of inmates were Maori and 43 per cent were incarcerated for a crime of violence as their major offence. The Criminal Justice Act restriction on imprisoning property offenders notwithstanding, the next largest group was property offenders (31 per cent). About 15 per cent were gang members. In 1987, nine per cent of male inmates (244) were in protective custody.[18]

In 1989 there was another prison census[19] and a further one in November 1991.[20] By 1991 the muster had risen to over 4,200, with nearly all of the increase due to more males being imprisoned. Now over half of all inmates were doing time for violence, and 428 men – 12 per cent of all men – were in protective custody (there were no women). At the maximum-security prison Paremoremo, more than a quarter of all prisoners were 'on protection'. There were 310 patched gang members in prison (7 per cent), a decrease from 1989 numbers because 'gang associates' were no longer included in the category. At Paremoremo maximum more than a quarter of inmates were gang members, with Black Power and the Mongrel Mob by far the largest.

Problems in Prisons

The problem of inmate violence and disturbances was aggravated by the gang factor, and also by the chronic overcrowding and the concentrations of violent inmates. As noted, 1986 and 1987 saw seven more suicides in the maximum-security prison. In 1987 a three-man Department of Justice team investigated the problems, and in March it made a number of recommendations. That very month three men took their lives at Paremoremo maximum. A Ministerial Inquiry into psychiatric hospitals and services was then set up, and heard that the opening of a cell block in 1987 to complement the 1985 psychiatric unit at the prison seemed to have solved the problem.[21] These units were geared to provide assessment for acutely disturbed inmates and long-term care where necessary, and were proving effective. Although one man took his life in December 1987, there were only two more up to March 1991. In addition, in 1988 a special psychiatric unit for remand inmates was established at Mt Eden.[22]

At Paremoremo maximum there was ongoing trouble with the Mongrel Mob, which mounted a spontaneous and co-ordinated attack on staff in B Block in November 1985. A similar incident occurred 11 months later. At Mt Eden in 1986 there was a series of assaults, escapes and escape attempts, with two inmates climbing onto the roof of the remand wing in protest at remand conditions, several abscondings over the wall and an attack by two remandees who fractured an officer's leg in three places with an iron pipe and injured two others in an attempt to break out. At Waikeria in October 1986, more than 50 inmates barricaded themselves in an exercise yard in a protest against conditions. Ten officers and 25 inmates were injured when staff entered the yard to force a surrender. Twelve months later five more men got out of Mt Eden, and in October 1988 a police search of six women visitors for drugs led to a riot at Addington prison in Christchurch. Early in 1989 a search of cells at Paremoremo maximum found three bottles of Tia Maria and 400 grams of cannabis.

A lot of these problems were put down to overcrowding. At Mt Eden, which in April 1987 held 100 more than its recommended maximum of 366, staff refused any more inmate receptions because of a fear that prisoners would riot. According to the chairman of the prison officers' subgroup of the Public Service Association, some cells now contained eight inmates with only two 'piss pots' between them. "The prison is in a state of controlled chaos," he said. "There is potential there at any time for a totally uncontrolled situation."[23] In the end the prison officers' union forced standardised wage increases of up to 15 per cent when musters exceeded certain agreed levels, and threatened to strike if numbers rose too far above those levels. Prison officers were soon receiving between $6 million and $7 million a year in penalty payouts. Vigorous efforts to provide more accommodation followed, but increases continue to outstrip available bed space. The penalty arrangement continued until August 1993 when, with prisons 7.5 per cent over capacity, staff threatening to strike and armed services standing by to fill in, the government bought out the contracted 'muster allowance' in a one-off payout of $6,000 per officer.

In the meantime, threats of industrial action at Paremoremo continued throughout 1986 over management's inability to deal effectively with the jail's intensifying gang problem. In 1987, after 37 assaults on officers, the prison's superintendent was removed and replaced. Problems at the institution declined, although a four-month Mongrel Mob protest outside the prison in 1988 again had officers threatening action. A separate industrial issue at this time involved female officers, who had been working at other male institutions since 1985. On the grounds that women would not be able to deal with violent men and would compromise the safety of male staff, officers at Paremoremo maximum threatened to strike if any women were deployed there. This standoff continued until 1991 when three females commenced frontline duties.[24]

Administrative Responses

In order to deal with the crisis at Mt Eden, mass inmate transfers commenced in 1986 and 21 police stations were gazetted as jails. But then the police started to refuse to deal with inmates as well. Desperate for a solution, Palmer announced that 100 more staff would be hired for the nation's penal establishments and a special psychiatric wing at the prison was planned by Christmas. Meanwhile, moves began for the building of more prisons to ease accommodation pressure. As a result, capital expenditure on prison construction ballooned from $5.4 million in 1986–87 to $27.6 million in 1987 and 1988.[25] Another idea discussed in 1987 was home detention, whereby some inmates might serve their time at home, their movements controlled by electronic monitoring. Although nothing transpired at the time, this opened a discussion that would re-emerge frequently. By 1989 Palmer had made firm plans for the introduction of home detention, and these were taken up in 1991 by Doug Graham, Minister of Justice under a new National Government. A pilot home detention scheme finally began in Auckland in April 1995 (see chapter 12).

As noted, 1987 was election year and these issues became fodder for opposition forces. In the lead-up to the poll, Leader of the Opposition Jim Bolger went on the offensive over rising levels of violence, which he accused Labour of failing to address. The sex-killings of Louisa Damodran in October 1986 and Teresa Cormack eight months later had led to public calls for the restoration of the death penalty. Bolger promised a referendum on capital punishment if National won the election and blamed Labour for letting Damodran's killer, Peter Holdem, out of prison early on a previous charge.[26] In response, on 24 July 1987 Labour's MP for Roskill, Phil Goff, sent a letter to constituents, highlighting the tougher measures brought by the 1987 Criminal Justice Act amendments, and Labour's strengthening of police numbers. Further action was promised.

In the end National's campaign failed and Labour held on for another term. Early in March 1988 drugs again became a major issue, and after a meeting with superintendents Palmer proposed a number of measures, including tighter screening of visitors, more use of drug dogs and higher security in visiting rooms. But action was slow. In May and July 1988 two inmates fatally overdosed – making ten drug deaths recorded since 1968. As we have seen, an amendment to the Penal Institutions Act in 1979 had allowed for compulsory drug testing of inmates, but systematic testing did not begin until 1998. In 1991 a pilot drug-dog scheme was launched, but searching remained haphazard until 1996 when organised teams of prison drug dogs and handlers began to operate.

The 1989 Prison Review

Prison numbers continued to rise, increasing by over 900 between 1987 and 1990. By mid-1988 men were being temporarily housed in secure sections at Christchurch women's prison to ease the pressure in male facilities. At this stage, another inquiry into prisons was in progress. Only seven years before the Penal Policy Review Committee had presented its substantial report to National's Minister of Justice. Now Labour wanted another report, and a five-person Committee of Inquiry was commissioned in August 1987. For a body charged with giving informed advice on the future of penal policy, the composition of the committee was odd. Chaired by retired High Court Judge Sir Clinton Roper, other members of the committee were a management consultant, a former nurse, and a Maori tribal representative and executive of the Ringatu Church. The only party with any professional experience in corrections was Bill Garrett, a former prison superintendent and retired inspector of prisons. This committee, notwithstanding its unfamiliarity with its assignment, conducted investigations throughout 1988 and presented a report in April 1989.

Predictably, the report, known as the *Prison Review*, reflected the naivety of its composers. Its central recommendation, contained in Part II of the 287-page document, was for a 'new way' in corrections which would involve dismantling the traditional prison system and replacing it with a series of small 'habilitation centres', the focus of which would be to provide specialist treatment to specific types of offenders. Without citing any studies, the report confidently declared, "There is now sufficient research to suggest that with a more intensive and extensive therapeutic approach, it is possible to reduce the rate of offending of some individuals or turn them from crime altogether."[27] No indication of how many criminals might be thus diverted was offered, but on this basis the review proposed a system similar to that envisaged by Irish prison reformer Sir Walter Crofton in the late 19th century. Under what was termed 'Te Ara Hou' (The New Way), inmates would commence their sentences in local medium-security prisons housing no more than 100 inmates each, where they would be assessed before being sent to designated 'habilitation centres' and subjected to therapeutic programmes organised by psychologists according to identified needs. Although security would be low at such centres, the committee believed that abscondings would be rare because habilitation centres would be nicer places than prisons and supervision would be close. Release would occur automatically at half sentence.

For the minority who failed to respond at habilitation centres or who absconded from them a few prisons would remain. These prisoners would receive work and education but no therapy, and would be released at two-thirds of sentence. Although the system would cost a lot of money to set up (no estimates were offered), the review predicted significant savings in the longer term as fewer inmates would be returning to prison. Initial set-up costs would be offset by selling the nation's prison farms, which would no longer be needed under the new system.

This breathtaking proposal, which formed the committee's central thrust, was a reformer's reverie and an administrator's nightmare. Had it been adopted it would have cost hundreds of millions to set up, been impossible to run, and there was no guarantee at all that recidivist rates would be significantly altered. The Minister of Justice, who had commissioned the report, saw immediately that the inordinate costs of what would effectively amount to a complete reconstruction of the country's prison system made it unthinkable. Moreover, no doubt with the effects of the 1985 Criminal Justice Act fresh in his mind, he must have known there was no reason to be confident that Te Ara Hou would generate lower recidivist rates. In an apparent bid to extricate himself from the report, therefore, almost as soon as it was released Palmer commissioned this author to write a counter report on the proposal's viability.

In all, including the habilitation centre proposal, the committee made 205 separate recommendations, nearly all of which were ignored by the government. However, habilitation centres were legislated in 1993, and four pilot centres were eventually set up to deal with offenders after they had been released from prison. The first contract was awarded in 1996 to the Salisbury Street Foundation in Christchurch. This contract proved highly successful, but it was unique in that respect (see chapter 10), and the habilitation centre concept was largely a failure. In July 2002 the centres ceased to exist as legal entities.

He Ara Hou

Some of the basic concepts within Te Ara Hou did not go unnoticed within Corrections, however. In 1989 former policeman and public service executive Kim Workman became Assistant Secretary Penal Institutions, under Secretary for Justice David Oughton. Convinced that something could be done to improve the effectiveness of prisons, and inspired by the *Prison Review*, Workman set about devising some radical changes in the way correctional facilities were run. His new programme was conceived in May 1989, but was not made public until July the next year.[28] It was projected to become fully operational in all institutions by June 1992. In recognition of its relationship with Te Ara Hou, Workman called the new system '*He* Ara Hou' (*A* New Way). With a strong emphasis on rehabilitation, He Ara Hou created a significant – albeit short-lived – revolution in New Zealand corrections. A New Way aspired to provide better programmes for inmates and attempted to force a dramatic shift in the working philosophy of prisons, from one dominated by discipline, custody and punishment to one of co-operation, treatment and training.

Such ideals had long been central to departmental doctrine, which since the Prisons Regulations of 1913 had accepted the dual role of the prison officer as both a custodian and an agent of convict reform. The principle had been repeated many times since,[29] but Workman's objective was to put the ideal into true effect, for example by requiring prison officers to become directly involved with the welfare and programmes of inmates. It commenced in 1990.

David Oughton, Secretary for Justice 1986–1994.

The task of administering He Ara Hou to a body of often cynical prison officers was difficult and created its own problems. Resistance from some quarters and administrative errors impeded the changeover process, but by mid-1993 both unit management and case management had been fully implemented. As part of the scheme, senior management positions were redefined and staff had to reapply for them in terms of new job descriptions. Not all reapplied or were reappointed. One general manager was taken from outside the penal division, a pattern that has been repeated since. In the case of some positions, inmates were informally consulted in the selection process. More women were hired. Women have worked in male facilities since 1985 and by 2001 they comprised 26 per cent of the employment complement of public prisons.

Kim Workman, Assistant Secretary Penal Institutions 1989–1993 and architect of He Ara Hou.

The early results of He Ara Hou were encouraging. In its first year there was a reported threefold increase in the number of inmates completing educational courses.[30] By 1991 more than a quarter of prisoners were engaged in academic study.[31] In addition, there was a reported 75 per cent reduction in annual misconduct reports and escapes declined from 5.5 per hundred inmates in 1986 to 1.2 per cent in 1993.[32]

Although suicide numbers were unaffected, there was a reported nationwide total of only 34 assaults by inmates on staff in 1992–93 (but no previous comparison was

The Major Components of He Ara Hou

- The objective of rehabilitation was upgraded to give it equal status to security. Programmes managers were appointed to all institutions to work alongside custody managers.
- The old military-style prison organisation, with five ranking officer levels headed by a prison superintendent, was abolished and replaced with three management levels headed by a general manager. The wearing of rank insignia by officers was discouraged, and inmates no longer had to wear uniforms.
- A formal system of unit management was installed in all institutions. Unit management involved dividing prisons into small administrative bodies of about 60. Creativity was encouraged. Managers were given considerable discretion in the way they ran their units and they made the bulk of day-to-day decisions. This decentralisation was designed to encourage teamwork and delegation of authority and allow greater line-level participation in operational processes.
- Case management was formalised. Line staff were encouraged, in addition to maintaining security, to become involved with inmates and their programmes. Many staff volunteered to act as case managers, signing contracts with individual prisoners to assist in the setting and attainment of goals. As a result, some officers took a personal interest in prisoners and even signed them out for excursions on their days off. Staff and inmates sometimes played together on the same sports teams, organised plays and concerts together and were often on first-name or nickname terms.
- There was a major shift in expectations from inmates. Prisoners were actively discouraged from simply 'doing their lags' while incarcerated. They were confronted with the implications of their crimes and urged to participate in correctional activities.

Figure 5.3: All Escapes as % of Total Muster

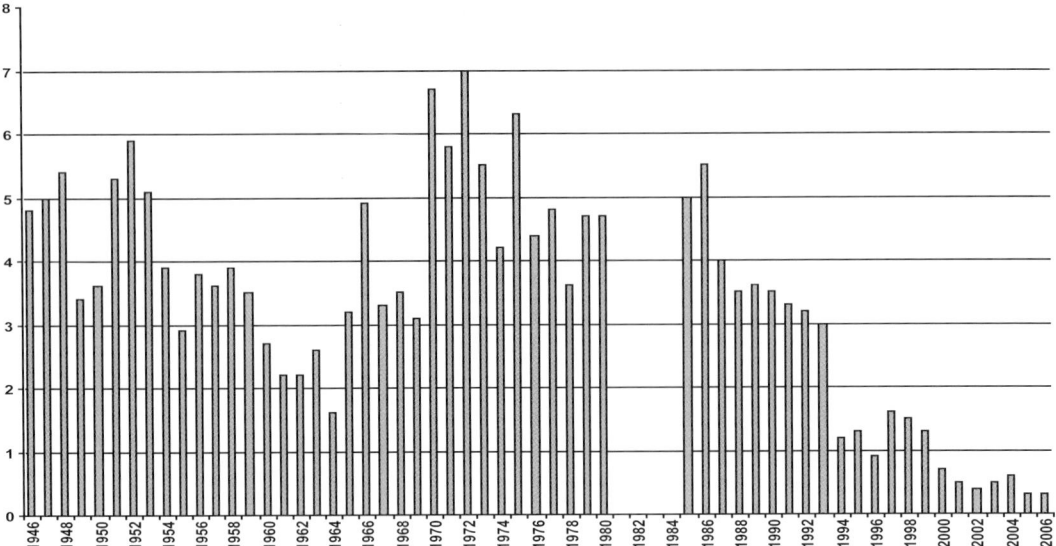

offered).[33] From 1989 and into the 1990s, 'harmony units' were created, carrying extra freedoms for inmates prepared to sign 'good behaviour bonds'. Inmate governing councils were formed, segregation units were desegregated and club activities, many involving outside participants, rose dramatically.

According to most staff and inmates spoken to by this author at the time, He Ara Hou reduced prison tension and improved overall morale. Traditional antagonisms between keepers and the kept declined, and at Mt Crawford prison in Wellington staff and inmates even played together on the same football team in the local competition. However, the effects of He Ara Hou were never systematically analysed and its objective achievements were lower than the department's publicity plugs suggested. Within the department there was concern about increasing licence and departures from proper procedure. Heedless of warnings, the determined Workman pressed on, but the early 1990s brought a number of embarrassing scandals which exposed the limitations of the regime.

In 1991 Dean Wickliffe, a high-profile lifer at Paremoremo maximum, escaped from the top-security unit of D Block, ascending two inner walls and two high perimeter fences before taking a service worker hostage and forcing him to drive off in his car. It was Wickliffe's second breakout from maximum security, and although he had been recaptured quickly on the first occasion (in 1976), this time he remained at large, with attendant publicity, for a whole month. Early the following year, at Kaitoke prison near Wanganui, six inmates escaped in one month, including an incident involving three prisoners who beat an officer up and stabbed him before taking his keys. The prison officers' union alleged that the jail's superintendent had been told about the planned escape, but had not informed his frontline staff.[34] Although escapes overall were falling, it was announced in the 1992 annual report that there had been a 28 per cent increase in 'walkaways' over the previous year, the majority occurring from sporting and recreational groups.[35] In addition, late in 1992 another chink in the new system was created when the manager of Mt Crawford – one of Workman's showpiece prisons – was relieved of his post after questions were raised about his staff's penal payments.

Some of these problems are unavoidable in any prison system, but their intensity suggested fundamental problems and raised questions about whether He Ara Hou had seriously changed anything. However, the damage at this stage was nascent and it was not until 1993 that the fatal blows to the 'new way' concept were delivered.

The most destructive scandal began at Hawkes Bay (Mangaroa) prison in 1992. Mangaroa, the department's first new prison since 1981, had opened in October 1989 soon after He Ara Hou commenced. Trouble began almost immediately, with deficiencies in recruiting, training, supervision and overall management. A blurring of prison officers' roles between custody and treatment caused by the changes of He Ara Hou was also a factor in the faults that emerged. Staff were encouraged to develop personal relationships with prisoners while maintaining control and discipline. Most of Mangaora's staff were recruited locally and, with 70 per cent of them completely inexperienced and improperly trained, it was easy for roles to become confused. This led to a series of minor breaches of professional conduct which, left unchecked, very quickly developed into major problems. The consequence was that, from November 1989, Mangaroa was beset by a stream of incidents involving staff corruption, theft of inmate and departmental property, drug dealing, illegal trading with inmates and inappropriate relations (including sexual relations) between inmates and staff. As well there were allegations of beatings, humiliation, intimidation and degradation of inmates by staff, and neglect of the suicidal. In one of the worst incidents, a squad of Mangaroa prison officers systematically attacked a group of prisoners over a period of three days in January 1993, and left some of them outside overnight, stripped and without medical attention. As a result of this and other incidents, 12 officers were sacked, and in 2000 four inmates won a reported $325,000 settlement from the Crown to compensate them for mistreatment. It was later disclosed that the civil suit had only proceeded after the police had declined criminal prosecutions against the officers concerned.[36]

Early in 1993 a ministerial inquiry into the prison was ordered, chaired by ANZ Banking Group director Basil Logan, who presented his 92-page report in July that year. While the overall concept of He Ara Hou was accepted, it was also clear that it contained systemic faults. Of the 60 recommendations in the report, almost all of which the Minister of Justice ordered implemented, 46 related to actions to be taken by the officer in charge of prisons. In its wake a tightening of procedures commenced, but continued problems over the next year led to even greater criticism of the 'new way'. Just a month after the report was released two inmates – Brian Curtis (60) serving 18 years for importing LSD, and Michael Bullock (26) serving life imprisonment for murder – escaped from Paremoremo maximum-security prison. Like Wickliffe they scaled a tall concrete exercise wall and negotiated two high perimeter fences before disappearing. Undiscovered for several hours, they got clean away. Bullock was not recaptured until 1999, in Wellington, while Curtis remained free until 2001 when he was discovered living in Manila. This second escape from Paremoremo in just two years showed serious, uncorrected flaws in security procedure. As the officer in charge of prisons, Kim Workman took ultimate responsibility, and critics of He Ara Hou used it further to denigrate his approach. Later that same month an independent inquiry into Mt Crawford prison found a "breakdown in internal discipline" at the institution, with six officers suspended for beating inmates who had sometimes been handcuffed at the time. Other staff had stood by and watched without doing anything.[37]

The pressure on Workman over these scandals proved intolerable and at the end of 1993 he resigned. But problems at Mangaroa remained. In February 1994 Mongrel mobster John Gillies, jailed for stabbing police officer Nigel Hendrikse in the spine and partially paralysing him in 1993, sawed through his bars and absconded. It was the prison's 20th escape in just two years. During the inquiry into the escape it was found that Gillies, already an identified high-security risk, had been permitted an unauthorised visit to his girlfriend in December 1993 while on temporary escort to Paremoremo. A scathing report on the matter led to public criticism by the Minister of Justice, and a few days later Secretary for Justice David Oughton fell on his sword as well. From there on the project Workman had battled so hard to create was doomed. It had survived only four years. Although many of the innovations Workman had fostered – such as unit management – remained, security and procedure gradually tightened from 1994 onward.

One positive result of the 1993 Logan inquiry was a recommendation for the establishment of an authority to hear complaints by inmates. A panel was established in 1993 to examine this possibility and eventuated, in 1995, in a special agency within the Ombudsman's office dedicated to the investigation of prisoners' grievances.

A Change of Government

After National had taken over from Labour in November 1990, the new Justice minister, Doug Graham, served for the rest of the decade. A lawyer by profession, Graham came from an Auckland upper-class background and, like McLay and Palmer, was a man of liberal sympathy and humanitarian principles. Determined to be an active minister who 'made a difference', early in 1991 he formed a three-man 'think-tank' (of which this author was a member) to advise him on possible directions in prison reform. A

number of options were considered and accepted, including private prisons (which the Justice department had opposed in 1989) and home detention. Both of these initiatives were actioned during Doug Graham's term.

The continually rising prison population was an overriding concern for government. Graham initially hoped to solve this through a 'Three-Phase System' (which, like Te Ara Hou, was similar to the 19th-century Crofton model), which he hoped would reform prisoners while at the same time relieving muster pressures by letting inmates out early. Phase One, lasting perhaps a quarter of sentence, would be retributive, involving a period of 'hard porridge' during which inmates would have few privileges and would

Doug Graham, Minister of Justice 1990–1999.

be punished for their crimes. Phase Two, lasting up to a quarter of sentence, would be reformative and would allow inmates full access to industries and rehabilitation services. Co-operative inmates would be entitled to remission of up to half sentence. Finally, during Phase Three, in the last six months of their terms, inmates would work in the community on day leave.

Somewhat surprisingly, after two meetings with his think-tank, the enthusiastic minister publicly announced his plan in May 1991.[38] Following further discussion about the extremely complicated and expensive practical problems the system would produce – including the issue of accommodating different sentence lengths, age categories, sex categories, offending groups and security levels, within a fixed programme – the idea was quietly dropped and so did Graham's desire for radical reform. Once again, soaring prison populations demanded immediate action. Between 1986 and 1990 the department had spent $150 million upgrading prison facilities and holding capacities. In Graham's nine years musters jumped 42 per cent and the unresolved problem of overcrowding dogged his entire administration. Within eight months of taking over, Graham pledged another $20 million worth of expansions for the next financial year, and by December 1991 he acknowledged that 1,000 new cells would soon be needed, at a cost of $75 million.[39]

The Criminal Justice Amendment Act 1993

Two major factors caused Graham to decide in 1992 that further amendments to the Criminal Justice Act were necessary. The first was parole, the second overcrowding.

At the beginning of 1991 it was publicly revealed that a serial rapist called Mark Stephens was about to be released on parole.[40] A violent sex offender, Stephens, known popularly as the 'Parnell Panther', had attacked and severely beaten well-known television producer Robin Scholes in 1984. He was sentenced to nine years for this and a number of other sexual assaults, and the horror of the Scholes' attack resulted in the formation of neighbourhood support groups throughout New Zealand. In 1985, while Stephens was in prison for the Scholes incident, he received a further 12 years for the rape and torture of a Parnell woman in 1983.

Because Stephens had been sentenced before the 1987 law change he was eligible for parole, but when it was announced in late January 1992 that he was to be freed after serving a little more than half of his 12-year sentence, a wave of anger swept the country. Facing pressure from within his own caucus, Graham intervened and Stephens' parole was cancelled, just days before his discharge date. He was granted parole again in August 1992 but was returned to prison five months later for breaching his conditions. Stephens was finally released on remission in February 1993.

Another significant crime that hardened attitudes was the rape and murder of 15-year-old South Otago schoolgirl Kylie Smith by Paul Bailey in 1991. Bailey, who was already on bail for attempted rape at the time, had accosted Smith while she was out horse riding and forced her into his car at gunpoint. Bailey drove her to a remote spot, forced her to undress, sexually violated her and then shot her several times in the head. As a result a petition containing 265,000 signatures calling for heavier penalties was presented to parliament in 1993.

This was an election year and a government committee consisting of Police minister

John Banks, Attorney General Paul East and Minister of Justice Doug Graham was set up to consider further changes to parole laws, particularly relating to recall. Under the 1985 Criminal Justice Act parole could only be cancelled after a hearing before a judge, and for a number of years the parole board had been seeking to streamline the process. The board had first called for greater powers in 1989 when Joseph Boyd Parker, a serial child-rapist who had been released from preventive detention in 1986, proceeded to rape and molest at least six girls while on parole in Northland. It had been argued at the time that the board should not have to wait for an offender to commit another serious crime before being recalled, when he had already been identified as at risk.[41] The board got what it wanted with an amendment to the Criminal Justice Act in September 1993.

The 1993 Criminal Justice Act Amendment

- All offenders, whether discharged on parole or remission, were subject to conditions up until the termination of their full sentences. Prisoners released before their full time could be recalled directly by the parole board or by a district prisons board if they breached their conditions. Those serving finite terms, however, could not be recalled during the last three months of their sentences.

- Section 107A of the 1987 amendment, allowing inmates imprisoned for specified offences to be held in prison for their full terms if it was believed they were likely to reoffend, now became s105. Under s105 a similar condition applied, except that the list of 'specified offences' was widened to include a range of sexual offences in addition to violent crimes and sexual violation. Offenders subject to a section 105 order now had to be released three months before sentence expiry, to allow the imposition of release conditions.

- The maximum penalty for rape was increased from 14 years to 20 years.

- Preventive detention was widened. It became available on a first offence to all serious sex offenders aged at least 21, and also now applied to crimes of serious violence on a second offence since age 17.

- In the case of life and preventive detention, courts were enabled to impose non-parole periods that exceeded the statutory minimum of 10 years. The first such sentence was a 13-year minimum, awarded to Turoa Hapi in July 1994 for the rape and murder of a Hawkes Bay woman.

- Violent offenders serving 15 years or more became eligible for parole after 10 years, except that as with lifers and preventive detainees, a longer non-parole minimum could now be set by the court. Violent offenders serving less than 15 years were still ineligible for parole.

- In order to help relieve the extra strain that the above provisions might produce, parole became available to non-specified offenders at one-third of sentence instead of at one-half. All offenders serving 12 months or more remained generally eligible for automatic release at two-thirds of sentence. As noted, since 1989 those doing less than 12 months had been ineligible for parole, but were released at half sentence.

- The 1993 amendment legislated the setting up of post-release, privately-run habilitation centres, with the first pilot centres being contracted in 1996.

- The sentence of community care, created in 1985, now became called 'community programme'.

- Home detention, which had been under official discussion since at least 1987, was legislated. Although a two-year pilot home detention programme started in Auckland in 1995, the scheme did not commence in full until 1999 (see chapter 12).

The amendment made a number of changes to the law which strengthened the supervision of released offenders, streamlined the recall process, and increased the power of courts to award lengthy prison terms for acts of violence or sexual predation. It also increased the courts' options for non-custodial sanctions.

Impact of the 1993 Amendment

Predictably the 1993 amendment, with its further measures against violent crime, affected sentencing policy and placed more pressure on custodial services. Between 1991 and 2000 average sentence length for violence grew by 22 per cent. Again, the greatest jumps were in crimes at the more serious end of the scale, with sentence lengths for manslaughter growing by 38 per cent, attempted murder by 31 per cent, rape by 37 per cent, unlawful sexual connection by 46 per cent, grievous assault by 36 per cent and aggravated burglary by 145 per cent.[42] Correspondingly, between 1992 and 2000 inmate numbers grew by a third, to 5,661. Prison populations also reflected the trends, with the percentage of inmates doing time for violence growing from 51 per cent in 1991 to 62 per cent in 1999.[43] According to the 1999 prison census, 16 per cent of prisoners were gang members or affiliates, eight per cent of whom were patched members. The Mongrel Mob and Black Power gangs accounted for 68 per cent of all prison gang membership

The changing profile of the prison population intensified the problem of prison violence. The number of inmates requiring protective custody grew from 244 (nine per cent) in 1987 to 989 (19 per cent) in 2003. Another measure of prison tension is suicides. Whereas in the 1980s there had been an average of 4.2 suicides per year, over the next 10 years there were 5.8.

The 1990s also saw the appearance of regular fatal violence. Of the ten prison homicides on record, eight occurred after 1990, with three homicides in the 1990s and another five since 2000 (see appendix 4).

Interestingly, after 1993 the rises in violent crime which New Zealand had been battling since the 1950s began to level off or decline. Overall, the number of violent crimes reported to the police peaked in 1996, and reported murders peaked in 1993 at 73. Better data are available for convictions (which we can assume generally occur six to 12 months after the event). This reveals a similar pattern, with convictions for assaults peaking in 1995 and those for sexual violation and attempted sexual violation peaking in 1996 (many of these cases were historic). Robberies and aggravated burglary peaked later, in 1997. Some of the subsequent drop may have been due to tougher sentencing regimes, but a variety of factors was doubtless at work. Convictions for property offences, for example, peaked early, in 1992 and drug crimes peaked later, in 1998. Traffic offences declined throughout the decade. But not all offence types fell. Crimes against the administration of justice, for example, and against good order, increased during the 1990s.[44] The reasons for these trends – which were not restricted to New Zealand – are manifold and complex.

An improvement in the economy, with a fall in unemployment from a peak of 11 per cent in the early 1990s to less than half of this from the mid-1990s, is one broad factor in the drops. Apart from this, different conditions have affected different crimes. For example: use of electronic credit systems and better home and vehicle security have caused thefts and burglaries to drop; better bank and business security has caused robberies to drop; higher levels of rape consciousness, long sentences, and an exhaustion of historic abuse cases have caused sexual violations to decline; and more rigorous gun control with better first-aid services have caused homicides to fall. A decline in per capital alcohol consumption as a result of vigorous drink-drive campaigns is a partial cause of the overall drops in violent crime. A fall in reported marijuana offences has been caused partly by higher police attention towards methamphetamines.[45]

These are some of the reasons why the 1990s was a time when crime generally was in regression.

Other Developments

After the 1993 amendment several other important initiatives were taken in justice and corrections. In 1993 draft legislation for New Zealand's first private prison was prepared. As noted, discussion about private prisons had begun in 1988, and Doug Graham had been considering them favourably since coming to office in 1990. In 1995, by amendment to the Penal Institutions Act 1994, private prisons were legislated. Tenders were called in 1995 but the four-man committee appointed to evaluate the tenders was unable to find a suitable proposal. Due to political opposition after the 1996 election the matter was then dropped, but it was resurrected with the calling for tenders in 1998. In 1999 a five-year management contract was awarded to Australasian Correctional Management, and the country's first private facility, for 251 remand prisoners, finally opened in Auckland in May 2000 (see chapter 10).

In 1994, immediately after the departure of Workman, and influenced by recommendations in the Logan report on Mangaroa, the corrections division within the Department of Justice was restructured and plans also began for the restructuring of justice administration as a whole. Thus from October 1995 the Department of Justice was split into three administrative entities – the Ministry of Justice, the Department of Corrections, and the Department for Courts. The chief executive of the new Department of Corrections was Mark Byers, who had been Deputy Secretary in charge of Corporate Services to the Treasury. The arrival of Byers and the programmes he underwrote signalled a major change in the direction taken by corrections in New Zealand. From this point attempts at rehabilitating inmates wore a distinctively scientific mantle, but at the same time tightening budgets, continuing population pressure and a renewed emphasis on security from the late 1990s created problems in themselves and moderated the achievements that the new approach envisioned.

Notes

1 Department of Justice, 1991.
2 Department of Justice, 1991; *Sun*, 6 November 1987.
3 *NZ Herald*, 12 April 1985.
4 *NZ Herald*, 28 June 1985.
5 Williams, 2001: 41.
6 *NZ Herald*, 5 Dec 1985.
7 *NZ Herald*, 22 May 1986.
8 *NZ Herald*, 13 May 1985.
9 See Newbold, 2000: ch 5.
10 Spier and Luketina, 1988: 34.
11 *NZ Herald*, 11 September 1986.
12 *Auckland Star*, 14 October 1976.
13 See Newbold, 2004: 57–58.
14 See Dennehey and Newbold, 2001: appendix.
15 See Coddington, 2004: 132.
16 Spier, 1995: 63.
17 Newbold, 2000: 127; Spier, 1995: 28.
18 Braybrook and O'Neill, 1988: Part A.
19 Braybrook, 1990.
20 Braybrook and Southey, 1992.
21 *NZ Herald*, 12 November 1987.
22 Department of Justice, 1991; He Ara Hou no.13, Feb. 1993: 3; Simpson *et al.* 1999: 9–10.
23 *NZ Herald*, 4 April 1987; 6 April 1987.
24 See Newbold, 2005.
25 Ministerial Inquiry, 1989: 249.
26 *NZ Herald*, 3 July 1987; 12 & 13 August 1987; *Sunday Star-Times*, 5 July 1987.
27 At p.35.
28 *The Dominion*, 7 July 1990.
29 See, e.g., Department of Justice 1954; 1964; 1968; 1969; Penal Institutions Regulations 1961 s.62.
30 He Ara Hou no.10, August 1992: 8.
31 Braybrook and Southey, 1992: 87.
32 McLellan, Newbold and Saville-Smith, 1996: 7, appendix 1.
33 *Corrections Operations*, December 1993.
34 *The Dominion*, 10 April 1992.
35 AJHR E.5, 1992: 26; *The Dominion*, 17 October 1992.
36 *NZ Herald*, 25 September 2004.
37 *NZ Herald*, 25 August 1993.
38 *The Dominion*, 2 May 1991.
39 *NZ Herald*, 7 December 1991.
40 *The Dominion*, 27 January 1992.
41 *The Dominion*, 9 February 1992.
42 Spier, 2001: 43.
43 Braybrook and Southey, 1992: 49; Rich, 2000: 18.
44 Spier, 2001: 8.
45 Newbold, 2000.

References

Braybrook, Beverley (1990) *Census of Prison Inmates 1989*. Wellington: Department of Justice.

Braybrook, Beverley and O'Neill, Rose (1988) *A Census of Prison Inmates*. Wellington: Ministry of Justice.

Braybrook, Beverley and Southey, Pamela (1992) *Census of Prison Inmates 1991*. Wellington: Department of Justice.

Coddington, Deborah (2004) *The New Zealand Paedophile and Sex Offender Index*. Auckland: Alister Taylor.

Committee of Inquiry into the Prisons System (1989) *Prison Review: Te Ara Hou: The New Way*. Chair: Sir Clinton Roper J. Wellington: Government Printer.

Committee of Inquiry into Violence (1987) *Report*. Chair: Sir Clinton Roper J. Wellington: Government Printer.

Department of Justice (1954) *A Penal Policy for New Zealand*. Wellington: Government Printer.

Department of Justice (1964) *Crime and the Community*. Wellington: Government Printer.

Department of Justice (1968) *Penal Policy in New Zealand*. Wellington: Government Printer.

Department of Justice (1969) *Information about the Department of Justice*. Wellington: Government Printer.

Department of Justice (1991) *Inmate Deaths in Custody*. Wellington: Department of Justice. Unpublished.

Dennehy, Glennis and Newbold, Greg (2001) *The Girls in the Gang*. Auckland: Reed.

McLellan Velma; Newbold, Greg; and Saville-Smith, Kay (1996) *Escape Pressures: Inside Views of the Reasons for Escapes*. Wellington: Ministry of Justice.

Ministerial Inquiry into Management Practices at Mangaroa Prison (1993) *Report*. Chair: Basil Logan. Wellington: Department of Justice.

Newbold, Greg (2000) *Crime in New Zealand*. Dunmore: Palmerston North.

Newbold, Greg (2004) 'The Control of Drugs in New Zealand'. In Richard Hil and Gordon Tait (eds), *Hard Lessons: Reflections on Governance and Crime in Late Modernity*. Hants, UK: Ashgate.

Newbold, Greg (2005) 'Women Officers Working in Men's Prisons'. *Social Policy Journal of New Zealand*, issue 25: 105–117.

Impson, A.I.F., Brinded, P.M.J, Laidlaw, T.M., Fairley, Nigel, and Malcolm, Fiona (1999) *The National Study of Psychiatric Morbidity in New Zealand Prisons*. Wellington: Department of Corrections.

Spier, Philip (1995) *Conviction and Sentencing of Offenders in New Zealand, 1985–1994*. Wellington: Ministry of Justice.

Spier, Philip (2001) *Conviction and Sentencing of Offenders in New Zealand: 1991–2000*. Wellington: Ministry of Justice.

Spier, Philip and Luketina, Francis (1988) *The Impact on Sentencing of the Criminal Justice Act 1985* Wellington: Department of Justice.

Rich, Michael (2000) *Census of Prison Inmates 1999*. Wellington: Department of Corrections.

Williams, Charlotte (2001) *The Too Hard Basket: Maori and Criminal Justice Since 1980*. Wellington: Institute of Policy Studies, Victoria University of Wellington.

CHAPTER 6
CONTEMPORARY CORRECTIONS: 1995–2006

The department that Mark Byers took over in October 1995 was still reeling from the shock of the Mangaroa debacle and the resignations of two of Justice's top executives. In his annual report of 2003 Byers wrote, "In 1995, the Department of Corrections inherited an organisation that was lacking in effective processes, systems, sufficient management capability and adequate infrastructure".[1] For example, according to prisons general manager Phil McCarthy:

> There was no business platform to speak of; no email outside of national office, virtually no integration of service delivery … and absolutely no traction on anything organisational. There were also significant deficits in property and security.[2]

As a professional manager Byers determined to remedy this, which led to a comprehensive overhaul of operational management and human resource systems. Thirty million dollars was spent upgrading email and computer processes and providing a completely new business platform for the department. But Byers was also keen to continue the rehabilitative approach embraced by Workman, albeit on a more methodical footing. Like Workman, Byers became committed to the therapeutic ideal and the system he sponsored, which is unmistakeably associated with his 10 years in office, is known as Integrated Offender Management.

The Rehabilitation Debate: Does Anything Work?

In the 1950s, after a century and a half of searching for therapeutic solutions to the problem of recidivism, scepticism began to grow about the ability of programmes to achieve reform in criminals. In the famous Cambridge-Somerville study published in 1951, for example, two matched samples of 325 delinquent boys in Boston were created, with one group receiving intensive counselling and treatment for an average of almost five years, the other receiving no treatment. Little difference was found in the reoffending rates of the treated and untreated groups.[3] Several authorities later in the 1950s raised similar doubts about the efficacy of treatment,[4] and this train of scepticism continued into the 1960s. In 1966 an evaluation of 100 surveys

Mark Byers, Chief Executive of the Department of Corrections 1995–2005 and sponsor of Integrated Offender Management.

DOMINION POST

of correctional outcomes discovered a variety of methods – and a large number of studies – of questionable rigour. Moreover, positive results were identified in only half of the cases cited.[5] Debate about the effectiveness of corrections continued[6] but seemed to have been settled in 1974 when, following an evaluation of 231 experimental programmes published in the English language between 1945 and 1965, American researcher Robert Martinson[7] concluded, '*With few and isolated exceptions, the rehabilitative efforts that have been reported so far have had no appreciable effect on recidivism*' (Martinson's emphasis).

The Martinson paper confirmed a great deal of popular thinking.[8] Its apparently conclusive finding that 'nothing works', while no surprise to some, did not end the matter but simply revived an old debate. Before long, intense critical bombardment caused Martinson to recant,[9] while others continued to affirm his findings. In 1977, for example, Greenberg updated the Martinson research and concluded, "the blanket assertion that 'nothing works' is an exaggeration, but not by very much".[10] Later studies based on reviews of rehabilitation work in juvenile settings had similar results: there was little evidence that treatment programmes were effective in reducing recidivism.[11]

But at the same time studies began to appear asserting that rehabilitation can work. Palmer[12] was one of the first, and he was followed by droves of researchers who were and are committed to the idea that some rehabilitation programmes can and do produce positive results. Today most of these rely on an approach known as 'meta-analysis', which involves using multiple regression techniques and other statistical instruments in an attempt to objectively synthesise the results of studies which may vary considerably in terms of treatment methods, treatment objectives, study design, sample composition, sample sizes and so on. Meta-analytical techniques have been around since the early 19th century at least, but the term itself was not coined until 1976.[13] The approach became increasingly popular during the 1980s and is now the primary method of research synthesis.[14]

Since the 1970s a huge number of publications, many of them using meta-analysis, have asserted that treatment interventions can work if they are applied appropriately.[15] As early as 1987 Paul Gendreau and Robert Ross, two of the most energetic advocates of meta-analysis, stated categorically that "it is downright ridiculous to say 'nothing works'".[16] Paul Gendreau, a Canadian psychologist and probably the most well-known and prolific advocate, with scores of publications to his name, is an ardent proselyte of the meta-analytic method.

Not all meta-analytical studies have produced such positive results. A large meta-analytical review of 50 controlled delinquency studies published between 1975 and 1984 found treatment to be ineffective.[17] American psychologist Mark Lipsey's review of studies that have used meta-analysis in delinquency projects found a wide variety of outcomes, ranging from highly effective to ineffective. He concluded

> The pattern of the general results presented here throws some light on the chequered history of research reviews in delinquency treatment. The grand mean effect is perilously close to zero. While not so close as to justifying the 'nothing works' rhetoric of the 1970s, convincing positive effects would be difficult to discern in any sample from this literature.[18]

Part of the problem lies in the inevitable subjectivity of meta-analysis itself. In 1981 Gene Glass, creator of the term 'meta-analysis', co-authored a book in which the weaknesses of the approach were traversed. Although still supporting the method, Glass and his associates noted the unaccountable variability of results that meta-analysis has produced. Subtle differences in the way data are collected and organised, and unconscious biases among those collecting the data, for example, may affect the results of meta-analysis in ways that are difficult to discern.[19] Lipsey has made similar comments, attributing variations in findings to the wide variety of approaches used and the extreme complexity of the method itself. He writes, "the different approaches and restrictions adopted by the various meta-analysts make it difficult to compare their results or find interpretable patterns across them";[20] "there must be some circumstances in which studies yield large effects and others in which they yield small effects";[21] and "wide variability in effects found [in the delinquency literature] means that different reviews that sampled portions of it could come, quite legitimately, to different conclusions".[22]

Contemporary researchers observe that the different approaches used by meta-analysts make it difficult to compare or make sense of their varying results.[23] Lipsey[24] notes cynically that studies where the researcher has personal involvement with a programme tend to produce better results that those where the researcher is independent.

The debate over 'effectiveness', what it means, how to achieve it and the most appropriate means of testing it, continues. It may well be that some rehabilitation programmes can, in fact, produce changes in some offenders. However, exactly what works, on whom and how well is still not clear.[25] Moreover, reliance on official recidivist statistics gives a fairly narrow and crude measure of success. One of the major problems is that many treatment programmes are simply not administered properly.[26] In 1990, a group of Canadian and United States researchers[27] commented, "The effectiveness of correctional treatment is dependent on what is delivered to whom in particular settings", and they noted that inappropriate programmes can have negative effects, particularly in residential contexts such as prisons.[28] A review of the copious literature on this subject makes it clear that if anything works at all, success is dependent on dedicated, skilled and trained practitioners applying programmes that are carefully tailored to meet the needs of individual offenders. Successful programmes are properly administered and well resourced. Those that are not have little chance of success and may even have deleterious effects[29]. These principles will be recalled later in the chapter, as we review New Zealand's latest experiment in prison rehabilitation.

New Zealand Experiments

In New Zealand in the late 1970s, following international trends, scepticism about the effectiveness of correctional treatment increased. With the failure of the borstal and detention-centre experiments becoming clear, the ability of a correctional system to deliver generally applicable programmes to an inmate population of wide diversity in terms of age, ethnicity, criminal experience, intelligence, education, mental stability, vocational training and social background, was in doubt. Reflecting this view in 1981 the Penal Policy Review Committee stated:

We think a mistaken belief that prison can rehabilitate has influenced whatever policy and planning has been developed over the past 40 years, and is still a major factor in penal thinking, in spite of all the evidence to the contrary.[30]

The committee rejected the notion that rehabilitation could or even should be a central goal for prisons, because of the difficulty in achieving significant success. Prisons, instead, should be places that deliver punishment in a fair and measured way. The committee continued:

> The purpose of imprisonment can therefore be seen as the containment of individuals who are being punished by the loss of their liberty under humane, fair and restrained conditions, inflicting the least possible physical, mental and social harm, in the hope that the prisoner will at least leave the institution no worse than when he entered it.[31]

This observation was one of many the government subsequently ignored and which was lost in the flush of excitement that followed the 1989 *Prison Review*. In 1989 the Children, Young Persons and their Families Act introduced family group conferences to deal with offenders under the age of 17. Based on a 'restorative justice' model,[32] the primary objective of the family group conference was to divert juveniles from more formal criminal justice processes by confronting them and their families with the consequences of their offending and effecting a reconciliation between them and their victims. By treating young offenders in this way it was hoped that family and community bonds would be strengthened and offending behaviour would cease.[33]

In the end family group conferences fell short of their primary objectives,[34] but they were fuelled by a similar type of idealism that had driven Kim Workman in his He Ara Hou programme. In 1992, at the height of He Ara Hou, Kaye McLaren of the Department of Justice had published a monograph which examined the effectiveness of various correctional 'interventions' – that is, programmes directed at reducing recidivism. Basing her findings primarily on overseas research, McLaren concluded that some interventions can work, if they are delivered appropriately and to the right categories of inmates. These findings were repeated in a conference paper she presented in 1996.

For McLaren, a clear example of a treatable offender group was the paedophile, a specific class of offender for whom tailor-made programmes do seem to produce measurable improvements. In September 1989 a dedicated 60-bed child-sex offender unit called 'Kia Marama' (Behold the Light) opened at Rolleston prison in Canterbury, offering specialised therapy to inmates convicted of child sexual abuse. Dealing only with volunteer candidates who admitted their guilt, the programme soon boasted success rates two to three times those of the untreated.[35] As a consequence a second unit, 'Te Piriti' (The Bridge), was opened in Auckland in 1994.

In 1994, in the months leading up to Byers' appointment, buoyed by the success of Kia Marama, the Justice Department was touting the use of psycho-social techniques as a general solution to offending. In June that year preliminary results of a major study by Bakker and Riley of the department's Psychological Services Division found that giving offenders psychological treatment in prison dramatically reduced both reconviction frequency (by 55%) and seriousness of offending (by 40%).[36] Later that year, influenced by Canadian psychologists,[37] the department's Corrections Operations Group resurrected one of McLaren's 1992 findings that, if a person's criminogenic motivators can be identified, these may be treated to reduce reoffending.[38] *About Time*, a departmental policy document published in 2001 which Cabinet at the time adopted "in its entirety",[39] declared the 'nothing works' philosophy to be outdated, and agreed with Gendreau and others in the somewhat loose assertion that, "some rehabilitation programmes are successful with some offenders in some settings when applied by some staff".[40]

In 1994 McLaren was working as Advisory Officer Corrections Development within the Corrections Operations Group – the group that was to form the basis of the new Department of Corrections in October 1995. The model McLaren favoured was a medical-psychotherapeutic one, based on the assumption that criminality is caused by some deficiency.[41] McLaren used the same reasoning and terminology employed by Gendreau and others – offending-related deficiencies were 'criminogenic needs', or CRN, effective diagnosis of which requires a sophisticated data collection system that gives therapists critical information about an inmate. From this information risks of reoffending and criminogenic needs can be identified and a tailor-made intervention programme delivered.

When Mark Byers took over on 1 October 1995 his senior advisers were already committed to this psycho-therapeutic approach. Not surprisingly, therefore, within a year the new chief executive announced in the department's newsletter an entirely new scheme that was to drive the Department of Corrections into the 21st century. The new scheme, which constituted a revolutionary change in the policy and operations of corrections in New Zealand, was to be called 'Integrated Offender Management'.[42]

Integrated Offender Management

By the time Integrated Offender Management (IOM) was announced in 1996, aspects of it were already underway, along with an associated patois of acronyms. The first, announced at the same time as IOM, was Structured Decision Making (SDM). Structured Decision Making was an American concept and had been suggested by the parole board's previous chairman, Justice Tom Thorp, after sabbatical leave to the United States in 1994. Formal planning began in March 1995, seven months before Byers took office. The concept relates to the operation of the parole board and is an objective attempt to assess an inmate's likelihood of reoffending.

IOM itself was part of an integrated crime-prevention strategy announced by the Ministry of Justice in 1996. The strategy was a multi-pronged attempt to reduce offending by combining the efforts of police, justice and welfare agencies. Improvements in the interventions provided by Corrections (such as IOM), and facilitating inmate reintegration after release, were part of this process.[43] The effectiveness of SDM and IOM would thus be central to the success of the crime-prevention strategy (later known as the Responses to Crime Strategy).

From the beginning IOM occupied significant departmental time and, in addition to regular updates in *Corrections News*, the department published a large number of glossy monographs dealing with its various aspects. IOM was brought in in four phases and was scheduled to be fully operational by 2002.[44]

Critical to both IOM and SDM was the development of a computer database designed to hold the information upon which intervention programmes and SDM determinations could be made, and to be a platform to support the Corrections department's operational and business processes. This detailed database, from an American design, was named the Integrated Offender Management System (IOMS). Cabling for the new system began in 1997 and was completed in June 1999. Once in place the installation of IOM itself could begin.

IOM was put into operation in April 2000 but did not become fully functional until June 2002. Part of the problem facing the department was to convince cynical prison officers, most of who were still dazed by the cyclonic introduction and subsequent sidelining of He Ara Hou, that this complicated new programme would actually work. A massive training programme was launched, involving 3,000 staff in a total of 22,500 training days over a two-year period.

Staff introduced to IOM had first to understand a growing lexicon of IOM-related terminology, consisting of terms such as: SME (Subject Matter Expert); LES (Law Enforcement System); CNI (Criminogenic Needs Inventory); OCN (Offending period Criminogenic Needs); PCN (Pre-disposing period Criminogenic Needs); LNA (Living Needs Assessment); IEEA (Inmate Education Employment Assessment); RNA (Reintegrative Needs Assessment); M-PRO (Multiple needs Program); RoC/RoI (pronounced, 'Rock-Roy') (Risk of Reconviction/Risk of Imprisonment); RI (Recidivism Index); RQ (Rehabilitation Quotient); MODS (Making Our Drivers Safe); DOT (Driver Offender Treatment); RYOP (Reducing Youth Offending Programme); MST (Multi-Systemic Therapy); MaCRNs (Maori Culture-Related Needs); FReMo (Framework for Reducing Maori Offending) and BTM (Bi-cultural Therapy Model).

The IOM procedure that used these strategies was designed to apply to all offenders, short- or long-term, sentenced to imprisonment or supervision. Although there are variations in practice, the ideal process is described: after conviction but before sentencing the offender is interviewed and a RoC/RoI assessment made. Those with a higher risk of offending have an initial CNI taken by a probation officer to determine the needs connected to their offending. This forms the Offending period Criminogenic Needs assessment', or OCN, which is made available to the sentencing judge, along with a sentencing recommendation.

After sentencing – whether to imprisonment or supervision – an offender's rights and obligations are explained at an induction interview. Another assessment using the above information is then made. For prison inmates this involves a security classification based on an accumulated points system, which uses factors such as sentence length, escape risk, motivation, prison discipline and risk to the community. There are four security classifications: maximum, high–medium, low–medium and minimum.

Separate from the security classification but related to it in terms of sentence management, is the rating of an offender's reintegrative needs. Those

Computing SDM

SDM is based on statistical risk assessment using computerised criminal history information, combined with a needs analysis questionnaire (NAQ) which collects information about the programmes and interventions taken by an offender while they are in prison. A psychopathy checklist (PCL) supplements the above information by identifying personality defects that may predispose individuals to serious and persistent offending. In summary, information gleaned from the risk assessment instrument, the NAQ and the PCL allows the parole board to perform SDM.

serving less than 26 weeks receive brief living needs and reintegrative needs assessments soon after arrival. Longer-term inmates get a needs assessment based on motivation, OCN, education level and so on. If they are assessed as highly likely to re-offend, the second part of the CNI is carried out, which is known as a 'Predisposing period Criminogenic Needs assessment' (PCN). Information from this complicated process is used to create an offender-management profile and sentence plan for each offender, and the offender is allocated to one of seven treatment categories (these are listed in the shaded box on p.112).

Those sentenced to probation or released on parole go through a similar process under the administration of the Community Probation Service.

Security Classifications
- **Maximum**: High risk of escape; high risk of public harm or internal risk. Intensive supervision and separation from the mainstream.
- **High Medium**: High risk of escape; moderate-to-high risk to public or internal discipline. High level of supervision.
- **Low Medium**: Low escape risk; low level of internal risk; but may endanger public safety. Moderate level of supervision.
- **Minimum**: Low escape risk; low risk to public or internal discipline. Low level of supervision.

The objective of the sentence plan is to create a programme that matches an offender's status, needs and motivation. Once the plan has been developed an offender leaves the assessment unit and is appointed a case manager who manages the plan. The plan is reviewed every six months and updated toward the end of an sentence to prepare the inmate for reintegration into the community. A range of programmes is available, including violence prevention, straight thinking (logical decision making), substance abuse prevention, drink-drive prevention, NCES (basic education), M-PRO (a generic programme for multiple needs inmates and smaller institutions) and special, focused programmes for young offenders and Maori. An apparent effect of this policy was visible in figures on the percentage of inmates enrolled in programmes, which grew from 46 per cent in 1997 to 85 per cent in 2001. Since then, however, muster blowouts and budget overruns have seen significant cutbacks in prison programmes.

The Focus on Maori

Although attention to Maori cultural needs has been a component of correctional practice since at least the 1970s, the concept of cultural appropriateness became a central feature during the period of He Ara Hou and further under IOM. It is well known that Maori are heavily overrepresented in criminal justice statistics, particularly for violent offending, and although they make up only about 12 per cent of the population aged 15 and over, they constitute about half of those in prison. Today the department's Maori initiatives are based on the popular but unproven theory that high levels of Maori offending are due largely to cultural dislocation in a Pakeha-dominated world. This belief was stated unequivocally in the Department of Justice's submission to the *Prison Review* in 1988[45] and has been at the apex of Maori criminal justice policy since the Department of Corrections was founded. There is also an abiding credo in Corrections that reintroducing Maori to their tikanga (cultural principles) will restore their sense of mana (prestige) and thus reduce their offending.

Notwithstanding the extremely shaky basis upon which such assumptions have been made,[46] the Department of Corrections has been at great pains to identify,

Treatment Categories

- **Remand**: Remandees with more than seven weeks in custody are given an interim sentence plan.
- **Short-Serving**: Inmates serving less than 26 weeks receive basic Living Needs, and Reintegrative Needs Assessments.
- **Maintenance**: Those with a statistical low risk of reoffending according to the RoC/RoI are deemed ineligible for programmes.
- **Functional Support**: Provided to inmates with severe behavioural problems or disabilities.
- **Motivation**: Inmates assessed with low motivation to address offending behaviour and not suitable for most programmes. *Motivation* inmates are, however, prioritised for motivational 'straight thinking' and tikanga schemes.
- **Intervention**: Inmates assessed to have a willingness to address offending behaviour, and to be suitable for programmes.
- **Youth**: Inmates under the age of 20, who are isolated and treated separately from the mainstream.

address and advertise what it sees as 'Maori needs' in terms of 'Maori perspectives'.[47] As early as 1996, in fact, a (Maori) cultural perspectives unit was established in the Ministry of Justice with the specific purpose of "[helping] the Ministry to interpret the Maori mind" and create strategies to reduce Maori offending.[48] In 1998 $469,000 was allocated over a three-year period to develop a 'bicultural therapy model' within the Department of Corrections. Early in 1999, as the installation of IOM neared completion, a cultural advisory team was established to monitor IOM and its application to Maori (and also Pacific peoples). Then, in November 2001, Mark Byers announced his intention to establish a treaty relationships manager, with the purpose of "strengthening [Corrections'] efforts in relating to Maori communities of all types". Hoping to improve communication with Maori, he wrote, "The Maori community has much to offer in better informing what we are trying to do and also has a crucial contribution to make in the reintegration of offenders".[49] At the same time, in October 2001, work began on a 'Maori Communications Strategy', to get a better understanding of Maori needs and "improve communications with Maori communities".[50]

IOM, both as it was initially conceived and as it matured, includes a highly contestable assumption that there is such a thing as a 'Maori community', a 'Maori mind' and a 'Maori way of thinking', and that Maori as a category have 'needs' that are significantly different from non-Maori. This is why there has been a concentration on developing programmes thought to be of specific value to this group.

Thus from 1999, as an integral part of IOM, the department developed separate needs-assessment procedures for Maori (MaCRNs) and an analytical framework tool to guide the development of policy for reducing Maori offending (FReMO). These were supplemented by the establishment in 1996 of a Maori focus group within the Ministry of Justice; the opening of the first of five prison Maori focus units at Mangaroa in Hawkes Bay in December 1997; the allocation of $500,000 over three years for the appointment of Maori tohunga (experts) and other services in prisons;[51] the commencement of a marae-based non-custodial programme for Maori as an alternative to periodic detention in 2000; the employment of Maori cultural advisers within the Public Prisons Service (PPS); and the establishment of a 'kaiwhakamana' (leadership by example) policy in May 2002, giving Maori kaumatua (elders) privileged access to Maori inmates. Since the late 1980s, in fact, prison-related ceremonies – such as conferences and the opening of new facilities – have had a predominantly

Maori focus, typically commencing with a karanga (call to enter), a wero (challenge), a haka (war dance) and a powhiri (welcome) followed by whaikorero (speeches), waiata (songs), karakia (prayers), whakapaingia (blessings) and a hongi line (nose-pressing greeting). Proceedings are conducted largely in Maori and are often followed by a hangi.

Any person entering Corrections today must therefore very quickly become familiar with marae protocols and develop rudimentary Maori language skills in order to avoid embarrassing *faux pas* in the course of their work. To assist this, in September 2004 desktop resource kits were distributed to frontline Corrections staff, containing handy words and phrases in Maori. The department's Senior Human Resources Adviser (Responsiveness) said the purpose of the kits was to provide better responsiveness to Maori and to "support and encourage staff to use Te Reo [Maori language] in the workplace".[52]

Maori language resource kits used by Department of Corrections staff.

Costs

The expenses associated with IOM are difficult to assess. The capital costs of IT developments following the establishment of the Department of Corrections were $30 million. The bill for IOMS was $13.8 million of this. It cost another $4.1 million to adapt the system to changes brought by the Parole Act 2002 and the Sentencing Act 2002. Training staff to use IOM took 22,000 worker days. Running expenses are easier to see. Published figures show that in the financial year 2002–2003 the department spent about $514 million in total; $288 million of which was allocated to running prisons. Of the total Corrections budget, $42 million was spent on rehabilitative programmes (most of which fell under IOM), and $20.5 million of this specifically on trying to reduce Maori reoffending.[53]

Many costs have never been publicly detailed, but since IOM was first announced, progress reports have occupied increasing space in the department's monthly newsletter, *Corrections News*. With rising zeal the department trumpeted the changes the system would bring, proclaiming bravely in its February 2000 edition "Corrections is trialling a new system of managing offenders that is proven to break the reoffending cycle".[54] In May 2000 this author was invited to Wellington for a day-long briefing on IOM by Mark Byers and Ann Clark, General Manager Community Probation Service. At that point it was hoped IOM would produce at least a 10 per cent reduction in reconviction percentages – that is, a minimum 25 per cent improvement in overall correctional efficacy. At the end of the day the author's response was that he thought the concept would be too complex for many staff to understand and operate, that large numbers of staff would be cynical and have little interest in it, that it would be too complicated and expensive to apply to all eligible inmates or even to a majority of them, and that even if it could be applied properly there was no guarantee it would work.

Two years later, observing that it had not been possible to apply programmes to all eligible inmates as originally hoped, Byers clarified his position on IOM's effectiveness. He said the system aimed to achieve a predicted minimum 10 per cent reduction in reconviction percentages *among those subjected to programmes*. Results to that point had shown no reductions, although he hoped in time that figures would improve. As originally planned, IOM was prioritised for Maori and other high-risk groups. Low or zero priority was given to short-termers, young offenders, low-risk offenders and maximum-security inmates. Prisoners identified with low motivation were also largely excluded, but they were considered high priority for motivational programmes such as 'straight thinking' and tikanga Maori.[55]

According to the departmental publication *About Time*, integrated offender management programmes in 2001 were funded to apply to 18 per cent of eligible offenders only – even though it predicted the programmes could generate reductions as high as 15 per cent (that is, a one-third improvement in efficiency). It was estimated that increasing the applicability of IOM to include half of all eligible offenders would cost an extra $26 million.[56] Thus the applicability of IOM was reduced dramatically before it had even become fully operational. As will be seen, by 2003 the functionality of the system was being seriously questioned as well.

Rising Corrections Populations

Integrated Offender Management was a major aspect of Corrections business after 1995, but it was not the only concern. At the same time as Corrections rationalised its treatment strategy, it also attempted to improve security and deal with the eternal problem of rising prison numbers. In the final five years of the decade community corrections numbers remained stable, but prison populations grew by 24 per cent, to 5,661 in 2000. To help accommodate this expansion 1,500 new cells were built between

Figure 6.1: Prison Musters 1980–2006

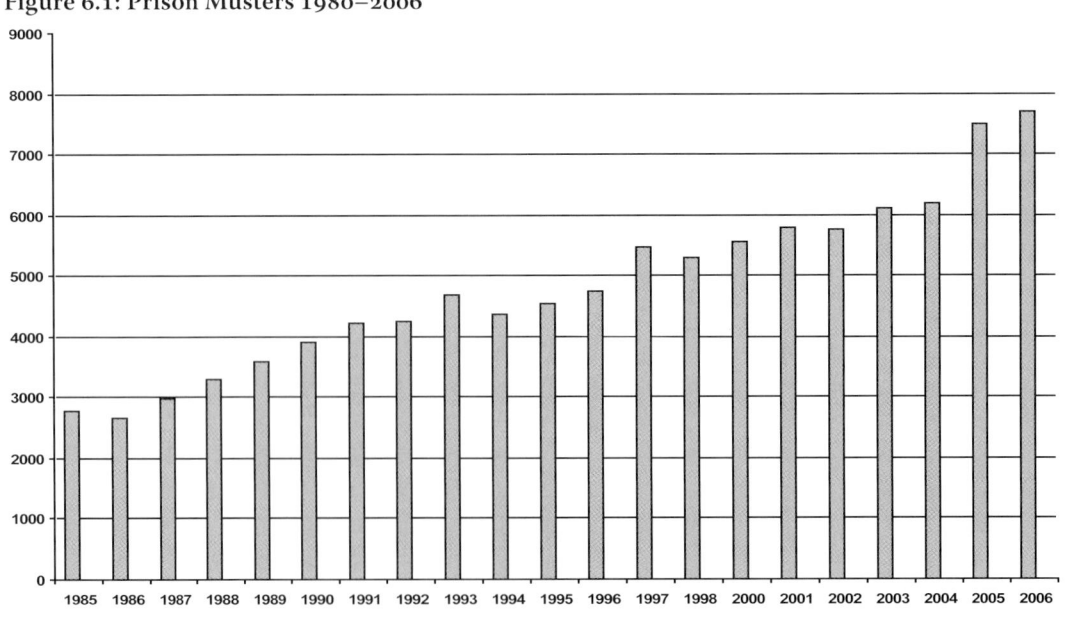

1995 and 2003.[57] The decision to call for tenders for a private prison, the establishment of the first habilitation centres and the pilot home-detention programme, all occurring in 1995–96, were other attempts to deflect costs associated with rising musters. One of the clear appeals of IOM – had it been able to hit its targeted 10–15 per cent reduction in reoffending – was that it would also reduce pressure on correctional services.

Security Problems

As well as trying to deal with problems associated with prison crowding and reoffending, the late 1990s was also a time of attention to security. In February 1996, Carl Rolander, a 28-year-old neo-fascist gang member serving seven and a half years for kidnapping and assault, cut a hole in a fence at Paparua prison and escaped. Two weeks later, surrounded by armed police in a Christchurch house, he shot himself. Later that year, in December, serial offender Barry Johansen (28) serving 10 years for aggravated robbery, and Joel Sutton (16) doing nine-and-a-half years for rape, escaped from Paparua's security wing after stabbing three prison officers with a bayonet and taking one hostage. They were captured the next day after robbing a bank of $13,000. The following month three more dangerous prisoners broke through a grille in the gymnasium. In December 1996 and January 1997, in fact, nine prisoners escaped from Paparua prison.

An inquiry after the Rolander escape led, in May 1996, to Canterbury being announced as the first stage in a national review of prisons. This involved a reorganisation of management with Paul Monk, recruited from Canterbury Health, taking the newly established position of Regional Manager Canterbury Prisons in September 1996. In 1998 this administrative model was applied nationally, with the country divided up into nine separate regions, each overseen by a regional manager. The Canterbury region covered the two Paparua sites (Christchurch Men's and Christchurch Women's), plus Rolleston and Addington. Included in Canterbury's remedial package was a $200,000 security revamp.

Before this was completed, however, there was the Johansen/Sutton escape in December 1996 and seven more escapes from Paparua in the ensuing seven weeks. In September 1997 explosives were found in the grounds of the prison. The following month five inmates, four of them serving life terms for murder, led by lifer Rex Haig (49), took six officers hostage in protest at the murder convictions of Haig and another inmate, Michael Wayne October. After a 26-hour siege, the hostages were released unharmed. Another security review took place, with more improvements pledged. Four million dollars would now be spent on erecting a tall, razor-wire-topped fence right around the Christchurch men's complex. This was finished in 2000.

In March 1998, while the Corrections minister Nick Smith was visiting Paparua to announce the proposed security measures, a gang fight broke out between armed members of Black Power and Highway 61. Some inmates were injured. The same month, reminiscent of the adventures of Maori Mac at Mt Eden in 1958, it was discovered that inmates had been escaping overnight from the 123-year-old remand prison at Addington and returning next morning. A few weeks later it was announced that Addington would close. New remand units at Paparua opened between July and December 1999, allowing Addington finally to shut its doors in December 1999.

In the late 1990s Paparua was a site of particular difficulty, but problems at other prisons also contributed to the introduction of new security measures towards the end of the decade. Tensions continued and the number of inmates in protective custody peaked at 20 per cent in 1995. In 1993 there had been a homicide at Paremoremo, when double murderer Steve Matchitt (22) was stabbed to death in A Block. His 32-year-old assailant was acquitted on the ground of self-defence. This was only the third prison homicide in the country's history but before the decade ended there were two more: in March 1997 James Tyson (52) was beaten to death in an exercise yard at Manawatu prison after asking an inmate to turn his radio down. His 23-year-old killer, serving six and a half years for armed robbery, was convicted of manslaughter and given another seven years. Then in September the next year Nga Trego (35) died from burns after two men doused him in accelerant and set him alight in his cell at Tongariro prison. One of his attackers was convicted of murder, the other of manslaughter.

In August 1997 Mongrel Mobster Chris Lemalie, convicted in January 1997 of killing bank teller Bill Brown during a robbery, was stabbed through the lung at Paremoremo maximum-security prison. He was transferred to North Shore Hospital under guard. The next month an inquiry was launched when hospital staff reported that guards had failed to act when Lemalie's visitors broke a number of hospital rules, even allowing him to have sex with his girlfriend in the ward. That same month an officer at Paremoremo maximum was stabbed in the stomach, hands and legs by a lifer. At Rimutaka, where a number of serious assaults on staff had taken place, inmates got drunk in October 1997 and rioted, wrecking equipment and injuring an officer. Immediately after that came the Paparua hostage incident, resulting in the prison's second security review of the year.

The Security Clamp

The November 1996 General Election resulted in a National-led government in coalition with New Zealand First. In the portfolio allocations after the election, Paul East QC, National's previous Corrections minister, was replaced by Nick Smith. Smith was a conservative 33-year-old with a PhD in civil engineering who had firm ideas about prison security and discipline. As soon as he took over he began working with senior department staff to make important changes to the way prisons were run.

IOM was still in its infancy at this stage, and while Smith did not interfere with this, there was a renewed emphasis on security. A security review of all prisons was completed, resulting in an extra $22.5 million in the 1998 budget for security improvements.[58] Included in this was provision for the construction of high fences around the perimeters of a number of prisons that did not already have them.

Drug Control

One of the first things Smith did was to oversee a departmental initiative for a more proactive drug control policy. Drugs in

Nick Smith, Minister of Corrections 1997–1999.

*Entrance to a medium-security unit at Rimutaka prison, showing use of
close-mesh fencing and razor wire.*

prisons had continued to receive publicity since first coming to notice in the late
1970s. In the 1990s a number of piecemeal steps had been taken to control them; for
example, in 1991 a drug and crime intelligence scheme was piloted at Paparua and
became a national programme the next year; and in 1992 drug dogs, initially trained
by the Royal New Zealand Air Force and later by the police, were officially piloted in
New Zealand prisons and commenced full deployment in 1996.

Publicity about drug use continued to embarrass the department, and it was
revealed that between 1990 and 1996 a total of 4,000 drugs charges had been laid
internally against prison inmates. As the jail population then totalled about 4,500 this
was considered extremely high, but it was still obviously a conservative indication of
drug use in prisons. A prisoner in 1996 estimated that about 90 per cent of inmates
used marijuana in prison and noted that staff often overlooked it.[59] This was certainly
the current author's experience in the late 1970s. When the first habilitation centre
contracts were signed in 1996, a component of the government requirement was for
mandatory drug testing of residents. Contractors soon complained that most inmates
were submitting positive tests on arrival at habilitation centres, and that if Corrections
wanted the centres to be drug free it should put its own house in order first. Pressure
of this type in 1997 resulted in an amendment to the Penal Institutions Act which
mandated random drug testing by requiring that each prison conduct random urine
tests on a fixed proportion of inmates every month. The law came into effect soon
after Smith took over, in February 1998, and a year later a comprehensive drug control
strategy began.

In January 1998 Smith had promised to "win the war on drugs". After the testing
policy became effective a brief period of amnesty took place, following which
rigorous national penalties applied. Since then, prisoners caught with drugs, or who

had submitted dirty urine samples or refused to supply urine or blood samples have generally been given a short term of solitary confinement followed by loss of privileges for 27 days and placement on Identified Drug User (IDU) status for a year. IDU inmates are now prohibited contact visits, restricted in their movements and therefore their employment, are drug tested more often and are more likely to be denied parole. Penalties increase with subsequent detections.

In addition, in 2000 new visiting standards were introduced, requiring all visitors to apply for written official approval before seeing any inmate. Thus, today, visitors with criminal convictions or charges pending are normally denied access. In addition police and/or prison staff conduct random searches of visitors and their vehicles, and if contraband is found criminal prosecution normally follows. This procedure has proven effective in reducing the drug influx. In the year before July 1998, for example, there were 700 successful interceptions of attempts to smuggle drugs into prisons.

The consequences of the policy have been quite dramatic. When compulsory drug testing started in June 1998 approximately 35 per cent of all samples returned positive. Within five months it had dropped to 21 per cent, although it later rose to about 25 per cent before stabilising at 16–18 per cent. A downside to the policy has been that visits have declined. Because of the hurdles placed before potential visitors, there has been an approximate 25 per cent drop in the volume of visitors since the new measures were introduced.

General Security

In order to make it harder to hide drugs, knives, mobile phones and other contraband, national cell standards were set dictating what each inmate could have in his cell. In February 1998 these standards were phased in with prisoners, for example, restricted in the number and type of books they could have. Pets, such as budgies and goldfish, which for years had been permitted because of their pacifying effect, were now banned completely. At Paremoremo maximum the changes were particularly severe. Because most maximum-security prisoners are inside for many years, from the early 1970s the Paremoremo men had been allowed budgies, goldfish, pot plants, wall hangings, hobby materials and so on, which served to make their cells feel like home and kept them settled. The quality of food was also high, reputedly the best in the country.

Smith felt that the maximum-security prisoners were being mollycoddled and he wanted them brought in line with other prisoners. Cooked breakfasts therefore ceased and cell contents were reduced to meet the new standards. Hours of lockup were extended by four-and-a-half hours a day, bringing daily lockup to 15 hours. Visits were cut back. Nick Smith's arrival extinguished the last flicker of Workman's policy of indulgence in the treatment of inmates.

Consequences of the Regime

In most prisons the new restrictions were applied quite painlessly, but in maximum security the men rebelled against what was a significant erosion of their quality of life. On 26 March 1998, on the eve of the introduction of the new rules, inmates in A Unit took over the block and set about trying to demolish it, breaking down concrete block walls and setting fire to anything flammable. By the time they agreed to surrender five hours later, much of the unit was unserviceable and 12 of its 48 residents had to be moved to Mt Eden. This most destructive riot in the prison's history was followed by a regime far harsher than Smith had proposed. Initially, inmates were locked down for 24 hours a day and guards in riot gear patrolled the corridors, addressing prisoners as "inmate" rather than by their own names and refusing to converse with them. This was a procedure quite foreign to the men in this small institution; indeed it was new to the corrections system as a whole.

In fact the 1998 riot only activated plans that prison managers had been working on for some time, and justified bringing tougher measures immediately into effect. Two staff had been severely stabbed in the year or so preceding the riot, and national prisons manager Phil McCarthy felt that safety and security were at stake. Initially a sentence management system (SMS) consisting of six phases was introduced into Paremoremo. Inmates would normally commence at Phase 1, in D Block, where privileges were almost non-existent, and would have to reach level four to be admitted to the standard units (A, B, and C). Phase 6 in A Unit had the greatest privileges, but lockup hours were now generally very long and association between inmates was highly restricted. Opportunities for sport and recreation were minimal.

Due to numerous practical difficulties the sentence management system did not last in Paremoremo, and within 12 months it had been replaced by a new regime called the behaviour management regime (BMR). Unlike the sentence management system, the new regime was for incorrigibles. Eventually it operated only in D Unit and had four phases, but freedom was very restricted at all levels. By 2006, the three standard units had become fairly uniform, but prisoners were locked up for about 19 hours a day with little work, education or recreation. Association was highly controlled within the different units. Paremoremo maximum is an entirely different institution to the one the author experienced in the late 1970s.[60]

As will be seen chapter 8, the experiment with behaviour management regime was a partial success, with a reduction in assaults and a drop in suicide. However, the system was also abusive, and in 2004 the High Court found the regime to be unlawful, with certain segregations made illegally and some classification systems breaching the New Zealand Bill of Rights Act. During hearings into the regime it was revealed that some inmates had been locked up 24 hours a day without exercise, had had their lights kept on 24 hours a day, had inadequate heating and ventilation and did not get regular medical checks or bedding changes. They were denied watches and calendars and the supply of items like toilet paper was pointlessly controlled. Aspects of hygiene were of a dangerously low standard. By this time the regime had ceased but, in a move reminiscent of the Mangaroa affair in the 1990s where four inmates were awarded $325,000 in compensation, a court subsequently ordered a total of $130,000 in damages and $358,000 in legal costs to five inmates. Following the success of this action, 175 more former behaviour-management-regime inmates commenced legal proceedings against the Department of Corrections.

The department's problems were not confined to Paremoremo. In 1999 there was more trouble at Paparua where in June, as a part of toughening security measures, a dedicated, full-time Canterbury Emergency Response Unit (CERU) of 11 officers was established to deal with the drug problem and any other crises that might occur. Members of the team – known locally as the 'Goon Squad' – got special instruction in inmate control and riot suppression. It was the first unit of its type ever established in

New Zealand. Nonetheless, the unit lacked adequate training, management and lines of accountability, with the result that it soon became involved in serious breaches of the department's code of conduct. A 2001 internal investigation found, *inter alia*, that members of the squad had misused timesheets and handed in inaccurate timesheets; had inaccurately and improperly used and approved expenditure; had failed to properly document and secure confiscated items such as cannabis and alcohol; and had organised surveillance, armed with prison batons, of guests at a hotel in Dunedin, which it had no mandate for. In November 1999, squad members forced their way into the cell of inmate David Haimona (42), who had become agitated and barricaded himself in. A violent struggle ensued, during which Haimona, who was overweight and suffered from a heart condition, died. Although the staff involved were exonerated in subsequent investigations, squad member Nigel French sued the Department of Corrections for stress and humiliation and was awarded $25,000 from the Employment Court. Finally, as part of a build-up to potential trouble that might arise on New Year's Eve 1999/2000, members of the squad, accompanied (against the regulations) by off-duty police and military personnel, stomped through the prison at night after lockup, dressed in full riot gear. They deliberately provoked inmates who were locked in their cells and unjustifiably subjected them to control and restraint procedures when they reacted. In June 2000, a year after it had been formed, the unit was disbanded.

Two Corrections-initiated reports[61] into the activities of the unit indicated that it had virtually become a law unto itself, and on 17 December 2004 a devastating report ordered by the State Services Commissioner and written by Ailsa Duffy QC, was publicly released. This confirmed that the Canterbury Emergency Response Unit had routinely flouted standard procedure for the treatment of inmates, had probably acted outside the law and that the nature of its activities should have been known to senior prison management. The fact that previous inquiries had failed adequately to address the issue led to a ministerial review of prison complaints procedures.

It will be recalled that Mark Byers' predecessor, David Oughton, had been compromised by the debacle at Mangaroa. Now it was Byers' turn. In Wellington it was known that Byers was devastated when he discovered what had been going on at Paparua, and as chief executive of the Department of Corrections he felt ultimately betrayed by it. His ten-year contract was due to expire in May 2005, but in August 2004, before the Duffy inquiry had concluded, Byers announced his early retirement.

In the meantime there had been political changes as well. Nick Smith was relieved in a Cabinet reshuffle early in 1999. Changes during his watch had been considerable, however, and he left a prison system far more austere and security conscious than the one he had taken over in 1997. By reducing inmate rations and increasing lockup hours he also partly offset the millions he spent upgrading security. However, escapes continued and some took a high profile. In particular, in June 1998, four dangerous men broke out of the medium-security prison at Paremoremo, led by 41-year-old bank robber Arthur William Taylor. The four were on the run for 11 days before being recaptured in a highly publicised hunt. That same month Zane Sutton (17), doing nine-and-a-half years for rape, broke out of Rolleston prison and was not recaptured for some days.[62] Although escapes now were much fewer than they had been in the 1980s and early 1990s, alongside the tightening of security, annual escapes had risen from 54 in 1994 to 84 in 1998. A third of all escapes were from Canterbury. As a result of the administrative and security improvements, however, after 1998 annual escapes nationally fell by more than half, to their lowest point in recent history. The majority of these were minimum security walkaways and parole non-returns.

The other matter of continuing concern was prison stress and suicides. Again some high-profile suicides grabbed press attention, such as the death of Willie Annear, who immolated himself in his cell at Paremoremo maximum in February 1998. At the inquest it was alleged, but not proven, that certain prison staff had taunted him about his intention to set fire to his cell and had supplied him the flammable material to do it with. In a later incident in August, 17-year-old Damien Meyer hanged himself at Manawatu prison. An inquiry into this incident found that Meyer's mental state had not been monitored properly, despite knowledge that he was a suicide risk. A 111 call had not been made until 15 minutes after his body was discovered and staff had had difficulty finding emergency response equipment. Generally, however, by the late 1990s the suicide problem of the late 1980s and early 1990s had stabilised, averaging only 5.8 per year between 1996 and 2000, notwithstanding overcrowding. The ratio of inmates on protection dropped from 20 per cent in 1995 to 17 per cent in 2001, but rose to 19 per cent by 2003.

'Closing the Gaps'

In the November 1999 General Election the National Government lost to a Labour-led coalition with the Alliance party. Campaigning under the banner 'Closing the Gaps', Labour promised to reduce inequalities between Maori and Pakeha New Zealanders. The Minister of Corrections in the new Cabinet was Alliance MP Matt Robson, an idealist with a bachelor's degree in law and an MA in politics who, like Nick Smith, had firm – but completely different – ideas about crime and justice. A man with strong leftist views, Robson believed that the explanation of criminality lay more in the evils of the class system than in any fault of the individual and, reminiscent of Martyn Finlay in the early 1970s, he tended to sympathise with the underdog. He disliked the concept of prisons completely and said publicly he would prefer a system without them. Given that they were a political necessity, however, he believed that by rehabilitating offenders and reducing social inequalities, the new government could staunch crime and cut the need for incarceration.

Robson had had only three years in parliament when he became minister and his lack of political nous soon showed. Sensational publicity about violent offending had hardened public attitudes to the extent that a referendum on crime accompanying the 1999 General Election had found almost 92 per cent support for tougher penalties and greater assistance for victims. Careless of public opinion, and contrary to departmental predictions that musters would increase by 50 per cent in the next ten years, Robson put plans for three new prisons in Northland and Auckland on hold almost as soon as he took office, stating that if priority was given to rehabilitation, he doubted the new facilities would be needed.[63] Although a contract for the private management of the new Auckland Central Remand Prison (ACRP) had just been signed, Robson declared himself opposed to it in principle and said the private contract would not be renewed when it expired in 2005. Later he announced, without consulting Cabinet, that he intended to introduce conjugal visits to prisons, a proposal that the government quickly rejected.[64] Then, to the outrage of victim support groups, in September 2000 Robson proclaimed that the general public had no right to know when convicts were eligible for parole. This added to a furore created three months earlier when Robson, as Minister for Courts, and Minister of Justice Phil Goff, announced the allocation of $4.8 million over three years for the creation of restorative justice projects that might divert offenders from imprisonment. Asked whether criminals might try to use the scheme to avoid going to jail, Robson agreed but stated (without any evidence) that restorative justice was the best way of changing criminal behaviour.[65]

Under rebuke from the Prime Minister and the Minister of Justice, by the end of the year Robson's more extreme pronouncements ceased. However, he retained his ideological precepts for the rest of his three years in office.

The Department of Corrections, with its culturally conscious integrated-offender management system already at an advanced stage, was quick to fall into step with the beat of the Labour–Alliance Government. The department's annual report for 1999–2000, released on 30 June, contained a special section titled 'Closing the Gaps', in which accelerated efforts to 'close the gaps' in Maori and Pacific Islander offending were itemised. A large variety of Maori-based programmes was listed. "All of Corrections' mainstream activities have been, or will be, reviewed in terms of their relevance and effectiveness for Maori and Pacific peoples," the report said.[66] Two years later the department declared having spent $5.86 million on dedicated Maori programmes.[67]

Some of Robson's early plans did bear fruit. By 1995 three pilot restorative justice schemes – at Timaru, Waitakere and Rotorua – had already commenced. By 2001, assisted by the $4.8 million cash injection promised the previous year, 14 restorative justice programmes were being run by the Ministry of Justice.[68] In 2000 a bicultural therapy model for Maori was announced by the minister. Following the lead taken by Mangaroa in 1997, a second Maori focus unit was established at Rimutaka in 1999, followed by another at New Plymouth in 2000 (moved to Wanganui in 2002), and at Waikeria prison (2001) and Tongariro/Rangipo (2002). Additionally, in April 2001, Robson and Goff announced a youth strategy which involved, among other things, allocating $12 million to set up day-care centres to help keep youth out of jail.

But Robson's hopes to reduce imprisonment never came to anything. In fact musters increased from 5,500 to almost 6,000 during his term. To be fair, this was due largely to matters beyond his control. There were fewer releases than anticipated with the removal of parole for violent offenders in 1987, and minimum sentences introduced in 1993 caused long-term violent prisoners to accumulate in jail. Thus, between 1993 and 2002, while the prison population grew by 23 per cent, the number of inmates granted parole fell by 26 per cent. After the murder of Auckland journalist Kylie Jones by the newly released Taffy Hotene in 2000, parole conditions were enforced even more stringently, with breaches increasing by 40 per cent between 2000 and 2001. In addition the new drug-testing rules, which prohibit any inmate testing positive for drugs from appearing before a parole board for three months, caused a large number of inmates to remain in prison for longer than usual; of the 9,042 drug tests carried out in 2002/2003, 26 per cent, or 2,350, were positive. The Bail Act 2000 also affected prison population numbers. This law, which came into force on 1 January 2001, made it harder or impossible for serious repeat offenders to get bail, and the remand muster grew by 25 per cent to over 1,000 within a few months. Tough new sentencing and parole laws drafted by Justice Minister Phil Goff in 2001 increased musters further. Robson had hoped to mothball prison-building projects, but he was soon forced to announce the spending of $56 million on new ones.

Home detention came in a month before Robson became minister – introduced in an attempt to divert short-term prisoners from jail – and expanded hugely during his term (see chapter 12). The courts favoured the new alternative, with home-detention orders increasing from 302 in 2000 to 1,575 three years later. In the meantime, however, there were significant reductions in the number of sentences of community programme, community service and supervision. Periodic detention was the only community-based sentence to hold its numbers in the early years of the new century, and in June 2000 an experimental marae-based programme commenced in Mangere, Auckland, as an alternative to periodic detention for Maori violent offenders. Generally, however, the use of community alternatives declined as public attitudes towards crime hardened.

The Sentencing Act 2002 and the Parole Act 2002

Robson had commenced his term with visionary intentions of reforming prisons, but he was frustrated from the start by reality. The most serious criminal justice issue for some time had been violence. Between 1991 and 2000 convictions for violent crime had increased by 53 per cent. The largest rises were in crimes such as threats to kill (up 135 per cent), serious assault (up 129%) and grievous assault (up 90%).[69] Although homicides had remained stable and violent crimes had begun to decline in the second half of the 1990s the public perception was that violence was accelerating out of control. This notion was enhanced by several incidents of particular savagery, which remained fixed in people's minds and directed criminal justice policy in the late 1990s and early 2000s.

On 12 November 1998 at Whangaparaoa, Auckland, Joanne McCarthy, a 28-year-old kindergarten teacher, was battered to death with a hammer in a random home invasion. Her killer, Travis Burns, who had been awarded $30,000 and granted witness protection by police in the almost identical (and still unsolved) murder of Howick housewife Tania Furlan two years before, was eventually given life with a 15-year minimum. One evening just 18 days after the McCarthy killing, four young men entered the home of Reporoa farmer Henk Bouma and his wife Beverly. Over several hours the couple were terrorised and robbed before Beverly Bouma was shot in the neck and killed. The case received high publicity and within three months an amendment to the Crimes Act, known as the 'Home Invasion Bill', had been drafted. Passed in July 1999, the law increased the maximum penalties available for serious violent and sexual crimes by up to five years, if the offence involved the invasion of an occupied dwelling. Non-parole periods for murder were automatically increased to at least 13 years in home invasion cases.

The home invasion law was a band-aid response to a few particularly horrifying incidents and had many flaws, including the artificial distinction it made between a crime committed inside somebody's house, as opposed, say, to on their doorstep or in their back yard, and the fact that in non-finite cases the add-ons were discretionary. Few were satisfied with it and lobbyists continued to gain support for stronger measures. One effective voice was that of Norm Withers whose mother Nan (71) had been bashed over the head with an iron bar in July 1997 while she was caring for his menswear shop in Christchurch. Nan Withers received cuts requiring 75 stitches in the attack and her assailant, Harry Houkamau (25), who was on parole at the time, got 10 years' imprisonment.

In January 1998 Norm Withers organised a petition seeking the necessary 252,336 signatures (10% of registered voters) for a citizens-initiated referendum on violent crime. The petition, with an estimated 285,000 signatures, was successful and the referendum was carried as a part of the 1999 election. In the weeks before the election, a middle-aged couple in Auckland were savagely beaten with a car jack in a frenzied attack at their home, a 69-year-old man was slashed with a machete and burned in a robbery at his house in Naenae, and two young men were jailed for six and seven years for attacking and robbing a 92-year-old woman in her home in Paekakariki. All incidents received significant publicity. On election day, 27 November, the Withers petition received 91.75 per cent affirmation to the question: "Should there be a reform of our justice system placing greater emphasis on the needs of victims, providing restitution and compensation for them and imposing minimum sentences and hard labour for all violent offences?"

Following this Norm Withers remained an active and outspoken advocate of victims' rights.

Another prominent voice was Mark Middleton. Middleton was stepfather of Carla Cardno (13) who had been kidnapped, sexually tortured and murdered in 1989 by Paul Joseph Dally. In May 1999 it was revealed that Dally had been granted leave from Paremoremo prison several times in preparation for a possible release. Middleton protested vigorously, publicly and repeatedly, vowing to kill Dally if and when he ever got out of jail. In a story on the case, journalist Rosemary McLeod published details of Dally's many previous convictions, together with statistics indicating that nearly half of all murderers released in the decade before 1997 had re-offended in some way.[70] It was Middleton's actions and the media response that cancelled further leaves for Dally and his chances of parole along with it.

A direct product of the Middleton case was an organisation known as the Sensible Sentencing Trust. During August and September 1999 Middleton had continued his threats to kill Dally despite police warnings to desist. In October 1999 Wanganui police charged him with threatening to kill. Convicted and remanded in custody early in February 2001, Middleton was sentenced two weeks later to nine months imprisonment suspended for two years. On 16 February, the day of Middleton's sentencing, large rallies formed outside 64 New Zealand courthouses, chanting slogans and taking signatures. On that day 16,000 people signed a petition demanding life without parole for the most serious cases of murder. From these gatherings the Sensible Sentencing Trust was formed which, led by Garth McVicar, the Hawkes Bay farmer who organised the nationwide rallies, is today one of the most energetic and successful victims' advocacy groups in New Zealand.

To begin with the new government was deaf to such calls. Immediately after the 1999 election Robson met with Withers about the results of the referendum but informed him that in spite of its clear message, longer sentences were not part of the government's agenda.[71] Six months later, however, Kylie Jones (23), an Auckland journalist on her way home from work, was dragged into a reserve, robbed, forced to strip and then stabbed to death. Her killer was Taffy Hotene (30), a career criminal and rapist who had been released from prison just five weeks before. During his short period of liberty, Hotene had breached his parole conditions with impunity and Justice Minister Phil Goff was quick to respond. Soon after the Jones murder he promised to completely redraft the country's parole and sentencing laws. In February 2001, while Mark Middleton was in custody awaiting sentence, Goff said he sympathised with Middleton and promised to change the law so that killers like Dally would stay in prison for longer. The instrument of change was the Sentencing and Parole Reform Bill, which was taken to Parliament that very month. Split into two separate bills in April 2002, the Sentencing Act and the Parole Act came into force on 1 July 2002.

The two new acts repealed large chunks of the Criminal Justice Act 1985 and completely reorganised the way sentences in New Zealand were administered. The legislation was was an attempt, on the one hand, to respond to calls from the 1999 referendum for tougher sentences, while also clearing up weaknesses and anomalies within the old system. Abolishing corrective training and community programmes was a response to these sentences falling out of favour with the courts, whereas creating parole eligibility for violent offenders was in line with the philosophy of IOM, which is based on the presumption that all types of offenders are potentially redeemable. The need for section 102(1), which introduced a proviso to the assumption of life imprisonment for murder, had been highlighted by a small number of cases where a verdict of murder should have been pronounced, but a jury had apparently rejected it because the automatic life sentence would clearly have been unjust. The most influential case at the time was that of Janine Albury-Thompson, who in a premeditated but desperate act had strangled her severely autistic daughter Casey (17) in a Feilding street in 1997 before giving herself up to the police. Acquitted of murder but convicted of manslaughter, Albury-Thompson's sentence of four years' imprisonment was later reduced to 18 months on appeal. Had she been convicted of murder, as she probably should have been, under the old law the court would have had no option but to jail her for life. Given the circumstances most would have considered this unjust.

Corrections after the 2002 Acts

Four months after the new laws came into effect there was another general election. During a two-week period in December 2001, 11 murders had taken place, including the terrible bludgeoning of four RSA workers in Panmure, Auckland, three of whom had died. Hoping to cash in on this, National leader Bill English commenced his campaign in January 2002 on a promise that life would mean life for the worst murderers. But the public now seemed satisfied with the law and the way new sentencing standards were being applied. The courts were responding to public opinion, resulting in a virtual cessation of calls for harsher penalties. The new judicial attitude was quickly demonstrated by the Court of Appeal in August 2002 when Mark Lundy, who had originally been sentenced to life with a 17-year minimum for the axe-slaying of his wife and seven-year-old daughter in August 2000, had his minimum raised to 20 years. At the time it was the longest non-parole term ever given for a murder in this country.

The Sentencing Act 2002: Main Points

- The Crimes (Home Invasion) Amendment Act 1999, which brought add-on prison time for violent offences committed during a home invasion, was repealed.
- Suspended sentences were abolished but replaced by a provision allowing judges to discharge an offender but order him/her to come up for sentence if called upon within a period of up to one year (ss.110, 111).
- Corrective training, which research had shown to be ineffective and losing favour with the courts, was abolished.
- The sentence of community programme, which was also losing favour with the courts, was abolished.
- The sentences of periodic detention and community service were combined into a single sentence called community work (ss.55, 61).
- Habilitation centres were deleted in the law change and thus expired as legal entities. They still exist but have been re-named 'residential community centres'.
- Home detention was re-defined to apply in two situations:
  a. 'Front end' home detention, which refers to persons sentenced to two years or less, for whom there is a presumption that they may apply to the parole board to serve their sentences at home (s.97; cf. Parole Act s.33).
  b. 'Back end' home detention for persons serving finite sentences of more than two years, who may apply to the parole board to serve the latter portion of their sentences on home detention from five months before their parole eligibility date (Parole Act s.33).
- Preventive detention was made available on a first offence for all offenders aged 18 and over who commit a 'qualifying' serious violent or sexual offence (s.87).
- The minimum non-parole period for preventive detention was reduced from ten years to five years, provided a longer non-parole period had not been set by the court (s.89).
- The normal minimum non-parole period for life remains ten years, (c.103, cf. Parole Act s.84). But if at least one serious aggravating factor exists, the automatic minimum is now 17 years. Briefly, the aggravating factors are (s.104):
  a. The murder was committed in order to avoid detection;
  b. The murder involved calculated or lengthy planning or was committed under paid contract;
  c. The murder involved unlawful entry of a dwelling place (ie a home invasion);
  d. The murder was committed in the course of another serious offence (e.g. rape or robbery);
  e. The murder was committed with a high degree of depravity, cruelty or callousness;
  f. The victim was a police officer or prison officer acting in the course of duty;
  g. The victim was particularly vulnerable (e.g. as a result of age or infirmity);
  h. More than one person was murdered, or the killer had previously been convicted of murder;
  i. Any other exceptional circumstances.
- Life imprisonment is presumptive but no longer completely mandatory for murder. If the circumstances of a murder make a life sentence clearly unjust – for example in a mercy killing – a judge may pass any other sentence or discharge an offender without conviction and/or penalty (s.102(1)).
- In the case of determinate sentences, the longest non-parole period a judge can impose is ten years (s.86).
- The general limitation on imprisonment of young offenders convicted of non-purely indictable offences was raised from those under 16 years to those under 17 years.

The Parole Act 2002: Main Points

- The 17 district prisons boards and the national parole board were abolished and replaced by a single authority known as the New Zealand parole board. This is chaired by a High Court Judge or a District Court Judge and has nine separate three-member panels that are presided over by District Court Judges (ss.111–115).

- In the case of sentences of more than two years, automatic remission at two-thirds of sentence was struck out. In its place came parole eligibility at one third of sentence, unless a judge had stipulated a longer minimum. Crimes of serious violence, which had been removed from parole eligibility in 1987, are thus now paroleable (s.84). By this section the indeterminate sentence, which had been virtually abolished in 1954, was fully resurrected.

- The provision by which offenders, once eligible for parole, were entitled to have their cases heard annually was altered. Under s.27, if parole in the short term is unlikely, postponements of up to two years in the case of finite terms, and three years in the case non-finite terms, were created.

- Offenders serving two years or less are not eligible for parole but are automatically released at half sentence (s.86).

- Section 105 of the 1993 Criminal Justice Amendment, by which specified offenders could be ordered to serve their entire sentences, is repealed.

- All released persons are subject to conditions until expiry of full sentence and in any case for at least six months, even if this is longer than the remaining portion of the sentence (ss.18, 29, 32).

- In a controversial provision, the new parole laws apply only to offenders sentenced after the act came into force on 1 July 2002 (s.20). Thus the normal requirement that law changes which benefit offenders should be applied retrospectively, has been disregarded.

- In 2004 the Parole (Extended Supervision) and Sentencing Amendment Act allowed the continued monitoring of high-risk child sex offenders for up to ten years after completion of their prison sentences. The amendment came as a result of publicity surrounding a small number of repeat child sex offenders serving finite terms who, once they had completed their sentences, would have been ineligible for ongoing supervision despite their high chances of reoffending.

The 2002 election was won by another Labour-led coalition, and Matt Robson was replaced as Minister of Corrections by Labour's Mark Goshe. The Lundy sentencing, and the standards implied in the new laws, had introduced a higher premium for the sentencing of violent offenders. In September 2002 Daniel Luff (17) was the first person given a mandatory 17-year minimum for murdering policeman Duncan Taylor the previous July. In November Shane Hoko got life with a 17-year minimum for killing hitch-hiker Jennifer Hargreaves in December 2001. Then in December 2002 a peak was reached when Bruce Howse received a 28-year minimum for killing his two stepdaughters a year before. This was later reduced to 25 years, but it was surpassed in February 2003 when William Bell (26) got a 33-year minimum for the Panmure RSA triple-murder of December 2001. This too was later reduced, to 30 years, but up to the end of 2006 it was the longest non-parole period ever imposed.

These are but a few of a growing list of lengthy minimums that have been given for violent and sexual crimes of exceptional brutality. The standard now operating not only affects recent and future crimes; it will also make it almost impossible for lifers sentenced for crimes that contained aggravating features committed before

July 2002 to win paroles before they have served something like 17 years. In today's climate some may never see freedom again. The harder line on parole taken by the new parole board is evidenced in the reduced numbers of paroles given and the high proportions of sentence served. In the 12 months before the Parole Act, 2,390 inmates were granted parole, a figure that had been stable for the previous five years. But in the 12 months following the law change paroles dropped by 20 per cent, to 1,923. After that they dropped even further. In 2002–2003 51 per cent of parole hearings were unsuccessful. By 2004–2005 the figure had risen to 68 per cent.[72] On average, paroled inmates served 62 per cent of their sentences.[73] Sentence lengths have grown as well. In 1991, 11.5 per cent of inmates serving finite sentences were doing three years or more; by 2001 the figure was 31.5 per cent. At the same time, the ratio of those serving time for a crime of violence grew from 54 per cent to 62 per cent. The number of lifers and preventive detainees grew from 233 to 441.

An inevitable consequence was further increases in prison numbers. Even the 28,000 sentenced to community work in 2003, or the 1,575 inmates granted home detention in 2003 (almost double the intake of 2002), were unable to cushion the impact of the new sentencing and parole regimes. In the 22 months following the November 2001 census the prison population grew an unprecedented 20 per cent to about 7,000, and in 2006 it exceeded 7,500. Another consequence of the longer sentences is an ageing prison population. Where in 1991 14 per cent of the prison population was 40 years or older, by 2003 the figure was 27 per cent.[74] These trends may be expected to continue.

The sharp rises took the Department of Corrections completely by surprise. In December 2002 the Ministry of Justice had told the Department of Corrections to expect a muster of about 6,000 by August 2004. In fact the population was almost 1,000 higher than this. Consequently, prisons at the end of 2005, as so often in the past, were again filled to overflowing, with the excess held in police lockups and court cells. In the meantime, community-based sentences were in decline, dropping 16 per cent between 1997 and 2004. Hardest hit was supervision, which after peaking at 11,613 in 1997, more than halved by 2004. Accommodating the unexpected rises is not easy. It takes approximately 18 months to build a new facility on an existing site, but the need for resource consents and iwi consultation mean that building on new sites takes much longer.[75] In March 2005 a prison for 350 offenders opened at Ngawha in Northland, and a 286-bed prison for women opened at Manukau in June 2006. Prisons at Spring Hill, Meremere (650 beds) and Milton, Otago (330 beds) are due for completion in 2007. The value of the four new facilities was originally estimated at $745 million and would eventually generate annual operating costs of $125 million.

Surprisingly – and very likely because of the better management and security systems installed after 1995 – the 33 per cent increase in musters between 2000 and 2005 has shown no obvious impact on prison tensions. Prison suicides, averaging less than 0.1 per cent since 2000, are at one of their lowest points ever. The number of inmates on protective custody has stabilised at about 19 per cent and, no doubt partly due to improved custodial and classification procedures, escapes hovered at about 30 per year, the majority of them walkaways or parole non-returns. The 2004 escape ratio of 0.3 per cent was only a sixteenth of what was common in the mid-1980s.

Against that, serious violence continued and there were four prison homicides

Spring Hill Corrections Facility under construction.

Artist's impression of a typical new regional prison, such as those at Ngawha and Milton.

in the 2000–2006 period. In May 2001 Justin Kaa (27) was stabbed to death in the low-security unit at Manawatu prison. In March 2003 Christopher Hereora (30) was beaten to death in the showers at Kaitoke, just 24 hours after being transferred from Mangaroa. Interestingly, Hereora had been serving 14 years for his part in the previously mentioned home invasion and beating of a middle-aged Auckland couple with a car jack in 1999. In March 2004 Rex Hopper (51), serving life imprisonment for murdering his fiancée in 1995, was beaten and stabbed in the throat with a gardening fork while in a work party outside the Christian Faith Unit at Rimutaka. Finally, in March 2006, senior Black Power member Sonny Keremete (25) was stabbed to death at Mangaroa and in August Liam Ashley was strangled in a Chubb escort van en route to Mt Eden prison. Ashley's was the tenth New Zealand prison killing and the eighth since 1990.

The Future of Integrated Offender Management

In 2002 the Ministry of Justice published results of a recidivism study based on the pre- and post-conviction histories of 22,340 inmates released from prison between 1995 and 1998. The study showed that 86 per cent had been reconvicted within five years of release and 51 per cent had been re-imprisoned. Most of the inmates (73% of the total sample) had been reconvicted within two years.[76]

The inmates in the study had all been released before IOM commenced, and thus give no indication of how well the new regime is performing. But they do show that IOM's predecessor, He Ara Hou, was ineffective. Since 1998 reoffending has been measured by an instrument known as the Recidivism Index, which indicates reconvictions and re-imprisonment within 12 and 24 months of release. Crimes against the administration of justice are excluded from these figures. The index shows that during the time IOM has been in operation, the reconviction rates of released inmates after two years' liberty dropped a little from 59 per cent of those released in 1999 to 56.4 per cent of those released in 2004 – a decrease of 2.6 per cent. But percentages of discharged inmates who were re-imprisoned during the same periods grew from 37.4 per cent to 39.2 per cent).[77] Reconvictions and re-imprisonment after a one-year follow-up had all risen slightly. It is therefore not possible to deduce from these data that IOM is having any real impact on either reconviction or re-imprisonment rates. Also, IOM programmes are funded to apply to only 18 per cent of eligible offenders. Moreover, the group upon which the greatest energy has been expended, Maori, still re-offends at a significantly and increasingly higher rate than non-Maori and its presence in prison is, if anything, rising. The percentage of sentenced inmates who self-identified as Maori or part-Maori increased from 48.9 per cent in 1997 to 51.1 per cent in 2003.[78]

Alongside this, sentences have been expanding steadily, and in New Zealand longer sentences produce lower recidivist rates than shorter ones. Specifically, Corrections figures show that recidivism among those who have served 1–2 years is more than one-and-a-half times that of those who have served more than five years.[79] Since 1995 the number of inmates serving more than five years has risen slightly, and the small drop in two-year follow-up reoffending between 1999 and 2004 may be due to the fact that a greater proportion of released inmates had served longer sentences. There may be good news, however, from the sex offender programme. A comparison of recidivism at Kia Marama and Te Piriti (where a tikanga Maori programme is incorporated) showed lower recidivism among Maori at Te Piriti than at Kia Marama. Interestingly, though, recidivism for Pakeha was also lower at Te Piriti, so the full implications of these findings are not clear.[80]

One of the great weaknesses of IOM has always been its confusing complexity. Entry of data into the IOMS computer base, translation of those data into criminogenic needs, and identification and application of programmes to meet the needs requires staff who are competent to apply the intricate machinery of IOMS and IOM, and committed enough to its objectives to put in the effort. This was always going to be a problem since prison staff have traditionally been cynical about the possibility of rehabilitating criminals, and many do not even care.[81] A 2003 questionnaire about IOM sent to 1,000 corrections officers found 70 per cent support for the concept but received only a 24 per cent response rate.[82] This suggests there is a significant apathy or cynicism about IOM in the Prisons Service. Moreover, high staff turnover is eroding the pool of experienced personnel.

In a personal letter to Corrections chief executive Mark Byers on 23 May 2000, the author observed that the practical problems Byers would face in the execution and implementation of IOM would likely result in far lower success rates than the 25 per cent overall improvement he anticipated. This prediction appears to have been realised. An evaluation of IOM carried out in 2003 found application of the programme to be haphazard and incomplete. In particular, the study found that:

- Assessment information about offenders was mostly unavailable or missing.
- Staff performed less than half the required assessment tasks necessary to apply the offender management model.
- Some staff had technical problems with the IOM assessment process and data entry to IOMS.
- Approximately one-third of assessment levels based on risk of reconviction/risk of imprisonment (RoC/RoI) scores were subsequently overridden by staff or by judicial request because the staff or the judiciary felt they were inappropriate. This resulted in inmates being directed into response categories inconsistent with their actual risk scores.

An internal memorandum on the report said, "The primary finding about offender management is that the resulting information needed for the proper functioning of IOM is in most cases missing, inaccessible, or incomplete".[83] Although IOM cannot be applied to all inmates IOMS, which is the data system that accompanies it, is supposed to. But the study found that only 84 per cent of inmates had any record on IOMS; only 22 per cent had a sentence plan recorded on IOMS, and only 13 per cent showed any link between IOMS and programme attendance.

Where assessment data were available the study found that, when offender needs were identified, the resources seldom existed to address those needs. Instead, in the majority of cases, inmates were given programmes that were irrelevant to their identified needs, or did not get programmes at all. Where the Community Probation Service was concerned, only 14 per cent of recipients were allocated criminogenic programmes linked to their identified needs. In prisons the situation was slightly better, with 26 per cent of those who attended programmes getting treatment appropriate to their needs. However, the majority of inmates either did not have a sentence plan or did not receive any programmes.

Although not all the study findings were negative, it appeared that deep-seated problems existed in the way that IOM was operating, both in prisons and within the Community Probation Service. The evaluation report concluded "The possibility must be faced that IOMS may in fact not be capable of providing the flexible, user-friendly case management database that the Corrections management model requires. Arguably the sentence management model is not able to function adequately until a satisfactory data management system is available".[84]

Where this leaves IOM has yet to be determined. In a letter to the author on 12 January 2006, national prisons boss Phil McCarthy assured that the findings of the 2003 review related to teething problems and that most of the issues identified in the report had been remedied. Whether this is actually the case will no doubt be revealed in the next review, which is due in 2008. What is clear is that in spite of over $18 million being spent over a six-year period establishing the database and adapting it to the 2002 law changes, a year after full implementation it was not operating as expected and there was doubt about its ability to do so. The effectiveness of IOM, on which more millions have been spent, is dependent on the data carried in IOMS. If IOMS cannot be made to work properly, if a large proportion of staff continue to display apathy toward it, and if programmes that match the identified needs of inmates cannot be found, then the whole IOM concept is nonsensical. This is confirmed by the very literature that the IOM concept was based on. As noted earlier, in order for a programme to have any chance of success, staff need to be trained and highly committed; programmes need to be properly resourced and tailored to the specific needs of individual offenders. If these requirements are not met, the literature says, the effects will be zero or negative.[85]

The 2003 IOM evaluation results must have been extremely frustrating for Byers who had worked so hard for, and was so committed to, its success. His disappointment was aggravated by news of the abuses reported at Paparua and within the behaviour management regime at Paremoremo. As noted, Byers announced his intention to take early retirement in August 2004 and stood down in February 2005. His replacement was Barry Matthews, former Deputy New Zealand Police Commissioner, who came directly from an appointment as Police Commissioner to Western Australia.

Matthews is an experienced administrator and a hard-nosed pragmatist, but he inherited a department facing serious challenges. In June 2005 the Corrections Act 2004 was brought fully into force, accompanied by the Corrections Regulations 2005. Although they largely codified existing process, the two documents also placed greater pressure on management accountability and compliance. There were also some fairly deep-rooted problems within the department itself. In December 2004, in the wake of the scandals involving the BMR at Paremoremo and the 'Goon Squad' fiasco at Paparua in the late 1990s, the Ombudsmen, using powers conferred by the Ombudsmen Act 1975, took the rare step of conducting an 'own motion' to investigate the department's current practices and procedures in relation to the detention and treatment of prisoners. Their intention was to focus primarily, but not completely, on Paremoremo and Paparua. They released their 77-page report early in December 2005.

Although the investigation failed to find any systemic ill-treatment of prisoners of the type seen in the behaviour management regime and the Canterbury emergency response unit, nor any culture of abuse among staff, the report was critical of the department on a number of fronts. Of greatest importance among the identified faults were that:

- Between 1994 and 2003, the average amount of time spent by those remanded in custody rose by 37 per cent, to 64 days, in spite of the fact that only half of all remandees eventually received custodial sentences (p. 10). (This is a matter for statute and the judiciary rather than the Department of Corrections).

- In some prisons, blanket punishments as a result of the actions of a few are carried out (p. 31).

- Prisoners sometimes have incident reports filed against them without their knowledge and without the chance to challenge their contents (pp. 31–32).

- For a significant proportion of New Zealand prisoners, there is no meaningful work or industry (p. 8), and budget constraints have caused a number of industries to close down. Only 26 per cent of prisoners are on official employment programmes and 36 per cent are employed (primarily in part-time domestic duties) in their units. Over a third are completely unemployed (pp. 43–47). The employment problem is particularly bad for young offenders (p. 40).

- Most maximum-security prisoners at Paremoremo are locked in their cells or on their cell landings, with almost no work or recreation, for 24 hours a day (p. 7).

- In relation to high risk of reoffending (HRX) prisoners, there is misunderstanding among inmates and staff as to how the HRX system works and how the label is attributed, and that a blanket ban on HRX prisoners (many of whom are low escape risks and easily managed) from outside working parties is discriminatory and unreasonable (pp 47–49).

- In most cases, prison library, recreational and sporting facilities are inadequate (pp. 22–24).

- In spite of the fact that 89 per cent of inmates have identified drug or alcohol problems and 60 per cent have at least one major personality disorder, in 2005 only 145 prisoners (out of over 7,000) underwent residential treatment. The only dedicated drug and alcohol unit for men is at Waikeria, and this is fully booked until 2008. In addition, in 2005 there were just 103 dedicated '100-hour' programmes (pp. 40–42).

- One of the most serious criticisms the Ombudsmen recorded concerned the '66 per cent rule'. This relates to a department policy that inmates should not be subject to criminogenic

Barry Matthews, Chief Executive, Department of Corrections 2005–.

programmes until they have served at least two-thirds of their sentences. Since parole is available at one-third, most inmates appear before the parole board and many are released before they can access any programmes. Moreover, due to population pressure, many inmates are unable to take programmes even when they do become eligible (pp. 50–52).

- There are sometimes unacceptable delays in the preparation of inmate sentence management plans and that the procedure for preparation of plans is complicated and time consuming. Many staff struggle to understand the procedure and inmates become disinterested. Planned objectives such as "spend the majority of time in the company of less criminally-oriented companions", and "gain/improve employment skills" seem ridiculous in the prison context. Many 'intervention services' required by the plans are unavailable in any particular prison (pp. 59–61).
- Due to high turnover many staff are inexperienced. In 2005 only half of all staff had more than five years' experience and 20 per cent had less than six months. Many middle-ranking supervisory personnel are 'acting' in more senior positions (p. 72).
- Some of the information supplied to the Ombudsmen by the Department of Corrections was wrong (p. 16), or conflicted with what the Ombudsmen observed (pp. 45–46).
- In spite of the efforts of IOM, the proportion of inmates reconvicted and re-imprisoned after 12 months between 2002 and 2005 had increased (p. 11).

On receipt of the report the department announced it was remedying the problems, but even for inmates who had access to programmes the news was bad. Since 2002 controlled studies had been conducted in New Zealand on the effectiveness of individual programmes in reducing recidivism. The results, released in 2005, were devastating. Few of the programmes showed any significant impact on reoffending rates over a one- or two-year follow-up period. In fact in most cases recidivism was higher in the treatment groups than in the controls. The much-vaunted 'straight thinking' programmes fared particularly poorly: those who did the 70-hour course were significantly more likely to re-offend than those who did not. The only programmes that showed any truly positive results were those related to special focus units dealing with drugs and alcohol, and units for sex offenders.[86]

The 2006 *Effective Interventions* Initiative

In 1999 the prison population had been predicted to reach 6,800 in 2008. By August 2006, with the muster already in the region of 7,600, a revised figure of 8,600 for 2008 was forecast (*Corrections News*, August 2006: 9). Apart from factors such as the Bail Act 2000, a major driver behind the blowout was the Parole Act 2002. With parole available at one third of sentence under the Act, judges seemed to have been calculating how long an inmate would actually serve and increasing sentences accordingly. This had led to a 'creeping up' of prison sentences overall. On the other hand, the parole board had been more conservative than expected, with the average inmate, as noted earlier, serving an average of 62 per cent of his/her sentence before being paroled.

In February 2006 the government asked the New Zealand Law Commission to report on the current operation of the sentencing and parole system, and to consider possible improvements. Headed, ironically, by Sir Geoffrey Palmer, the Justice minister who had vastly liberalised parole in the Criminal Justice Act 1985, the Commission's report, released in August, criticised the excessive use of parole and argued for a return to a form of 'truth in sentencing'.

The main problems with extensive use of parole, which are well known, are these:

1. It tends to lead to a 'creeping up' of sentence lengths.

2. Parole is based on an assumed ability to predict post-release reoffending chances, which in reality is extremely difficult to do accurately on a case-by-case basis.

3. If parole was used as intended – that is for those judged to have 'reformed' and to be unlikely to reoffend – it would rarely be given, since 86 per cent of all prison releases reoffend within in five years.

4. Extensive use of parole undermines public confidence in the criminal justice system because sentence length may bear little relation to actual time served.

5. Liberal parole regimes make it difficult for inmates to plan their sentences, as they have little idea for how long they will be in prison and when they will be released.

6. Each time inmates apply for parole they have to present a release plan which normally indicates where they intend to live and work. Parole systems are unfair on members of the public who may hold jobs and/or accommodation open for parole candidates, only to be told that parole has been denied. This task of finding work and lodgings must be repeated every time an inmate appears for parole (normally once or twice a year).

7. Liberal parole systems make it hard to predict prison populations on a year-by-year basis, leading to blowouts of the type currently being experienced.

Recognising these factors the solution proposed by the Commission (2006b: 9–16) contained two main points:

1. There should be 'truth in sentencing', with inmates serving at least two-thirds of their terms before becoming eligible for parole. For sentences of 12 months or less, the entire term should be served.

2. It was predicted that under such a system inmates would serve an average of 80 per cent of their terms. In order to account for greater proportions of sentences being served, average sentence lengths would have to reduce by 25 per cent. To achieve this and to remove current regional and individual judicial differences in sentencing patterns, a 10-person Sentencing Council was proposed, with the job of providing guidelines about sentencing and the use of parole. Judges and the parole board would be bound by these guidelines.

The government's response to the report was positive. Under its new *Effective Interventions* initiative, released straight after the Commission's report, the government announced its intention to reform the parole system and to establish a Sentencing Council in the form suggested by the Commission. Truth in sentencing, dismissed as 'simplistic' and rightist by former Minister of Justice Phil Goff in 2002, now became central to the government's correctional philosophy. In addition to the above and as part of the *Effective Interventions* initiative, the government announced that there would be:

- increased emphasis on rehabilitation efforts and an expansion of special focus units
- greater use of restorative justice
- an expansion of community sentencing alternatives (these had been reduced in the 2002 legislation)
- as part of the above expansion home detention would be created as a sentencing option in its own right for low-risk offenders. Front-end home detention would be abolished.

Enabling legislation in the form of the Criminal Justice Reform Bill was introduced in November 2006, with implementation expected in 2007.

Thus, just four years after introducing major changes to the sentencing and parole structure of New Zealand, 2006 saw the country contemplating yet more alterations, many of which reversed the policies that had been created in 2002.

With nearly $46 million spent on programmes that year the department came under stinging fire from NZ First MP Ron Mark.[87] Its response was to extend the length of some programmes and to create a new position of General Manager Integration, late in 2005, to oversee and co-ordinate the department's reintegrative services. In February 2006, Phil McCarthy, formerly General Manager Public Prisons, took on this role.

In the meantime, the ballooning costs of running prisons and the building of new ones combined with construction budget blowouts in excess of $490 million (more than double the original estimate due mainly to faulty construction calculations) forced the department to economise on accommodation and cut back further on programmes and services. In November 2005 it was revealed that inmates in Auckland had been held temporarily in vans parked on public streets, and in January 2006 the government made a deal with prison staff to allow inmates to be routinely housed two to a cell. Closures of prison horticulture, nurseries and other employment programmes in 2005 put more inmates out of work, albeit saving the department $4.8 million. At the time of the Ombudsmen's report 26 per cent of inmates were on work programmes; this figure had fallen to 20 per cent by April 2006.[88] There were cutbacks in education courses and substance-abuse programmes. With the growth in prison numbers expected to continue beyond the department's capacity to provide new cells, in early 2006 the government began considering further changes to parole law and the law of home detention.[89] Enabling legislation, in the form of an amendment to the Criminal Justice Act, was tabled in parliament in November 2006. In December 2006, as this book was going to press, convicted murderer and life parolee Graeme William Burton (35) breached his parole conditions after only five months of liberty. Arrested in January 2007 and charged with 23 offences, including another murder, the case created immense publicity and is highly likely to affect the content of the amendment as it develops into law.

Notes

1 AJHR E.61, 2003: 17.

2 Pers. comm. 12 February 2006.

3 Powers and Witmer, 1970.

4 Allen, 1959:226–230; Bailey, 1966; Cressey, 1958; Wooton, 1959.

5 Bailey, 1966.

6 Adams, 1970; Hawkins, 1976: 45-55; Hood, 1967; Little, 1963; Morris and Hawkins, 1970: 118; N. Walker, 1968: 255; Walker, 1969:93–44; Wilkins, 1969.

7 Martinson, 1974: 25.

8 Andrews *et al.*, 1990.

9 Martinson and Wilks, 1977; Martinson, 1979.

10 Greenberg, 1977: 141.

11 Lundman, McFarlane and Scarpatti, 1977; Romig, 1978; Wright and Dixon, 1977.

12 Palmer, 1975.

13 Glass, 1976.

14 Cook *et al..*, 1992: ch 1.

15 Andrews *et al.*, 1990; Gendreau, Little and Goggin, 1996; Gendreau and Ross, 1986; 1987; Latessa, Cullen and Gendreau, 2002; Lipsey, 1992; Palmer, 1986; S. Walker, 1989; Wilson, 1986.

16 Gendreau and Ross, 1987: 395.

17 Whitehead and Lab, 1989.

18 Lipsey, 1992: 125–6.

19 Glass, McGaw and Smith, 1981: ch 7.

20 Lipsey, 1992: 87.

21 Lipsey, 1992: 125.

22 Lipsey, 1992: 126.

23 Lipsey, 1992: 87; Gendreau, Goggin and Smith, 2000: 59.

24 Lipsey, 1992: 122.

25 Israel and Chui, 2006; Walker, 1989: 228–231.

26 Latessa, Cullen and Gendreau, 2002.

27 Andrews *et al.*, 1990: 372.

28 Andrews *et al.*, 1990: 386.

29 Ward, 2006.

30 Penal Policy Review Committee, 1981: 62.

31 Penal Policy Review Committee, 1981: 62.

32 Umbreit, 1994; Van Ness, 1990; Zehr, 1994.

33 Morris and Maxwell, 1993.

34 Maxwell *et al.*, 2004.

35 *Corrections Quarterly* 1992, issue 1: 3–5; *Corrections News* December 2001: 7; *NZ Herald*, 22 September 2004.

36 *Criminal Justice Quarterly* 1994, issue 7: 10–11.

37 Gendreau and Andrews, 1990; Gendreau and Ross 1980; 1983; 1984; 1987.

38 McLaren, 1994; 1995.

39 *Corrections News*, June 2001: 5.

40 Department of Corrections, 2001c: 42.

41 McLaren had been working on the concept since late 1994. Her therapeutic model was published in the Criminal Justice Development Group's in-house journal *Criminal Justice Quarterly* in December 1994 and March 1995, and was presented in updated form to the annual conference of the Australian and New Zealand Society of Criminology in 1996.

42 *Corrections News*, September/October 1996:2.

43 *Justice Matters*, no.2, November 1996.

44 The four phases were: planning and phased introduction; piloting of induction programmes; piloting of offender management programmes; and establishment of re-integrative services.

45 At p. 377.

46 McFarlane-Nathan, 1999.

47 Department of Corrections, 2001a; 2001b; 2003.

48 *Justice Matters*, 1998, issue 5: 15.

49 *Corrections News*, November 2001: 2.

50 Corrections News, November 2001: 3.

51 *The Press*, 20 October 1998.

52 *Corrections News*, September 2004: 5.

53 AJHR E.61, 2003: 45, 91, 103.

54 *Corrections News*, February 2000: 5.

55 Byers, pers. comm., 20 March 2002.

56 Department of Corrections, 2001c: 6, 10.

57 AJHR E.61, 2003: 21.

58 AJHR E.61, 1998: 9.

59 *The Press*, 6 July 1996.

60 See Newbold, 1982.

61 See Duffy, 2004; Love, Kinney and Dyer, 2001a; 2001b.

62 Zane Sutton is brother/co-offender of Joel Sutton who had escaped with Barry Johansen in 1996.

63 *NZ Herald*, 18 January 2000.

64 *The Press*, 26 May, 2000.

65 *The Press*, 12 June 2000.

66 AJHR E.61, 2000: 21.

67 AJHR E.61, 2002: 19.

68 *Justice Matters*, June 2001.

69 Spier, 2001: 14.

70 *Sunday Star-Times*, 5 September 1999.

71 *The Press*, 17 December 1999.

72 *The Press*, 10 August 2006.

73 NZ Law Commission, 2006: 52.

74 Harpham, 2004: 56.

75 Letter from Phil McCarthy, GM, PPS; *Police News,* 37(9): 189.

76 Spier, 2002.

77 AJHR E.61, 2003: 34–35; 2006; 51.

78 Harpham, 2004: 19.

79 AJHR E.61, 2004: 40.

80 Nathan, Wilson and Hillman, 2003.

81 Goffman, 1971: 73–88; Hawkins, 1976: ch. 7; McLeery, 1960:69–71; Morris and Morris, 1963:95–98; Thomas, 1972: 199–208.

82 Mullen, 2003: 8.

83 Mullen, 2003: 3.

84 Policy Development, 2003b: 19.

85 Ward, 2006.

86 AJHR E.61, 2005: 40–42.

87 *NZ Herald*, 16 February 2006.

88 *The Dominion Post*, 17 April 2006.

89 *The Press*, 8 March 2006.

References

Adams, Stuart (1970) 'The PICO Project'. In Norman Johnston, Leonard Savitz, and Marvin Wolfgang (eds), *The Sociology of Punishment and Correction*. New York: Wiley.

Allen, Francis (1959) *Journal of Criminal Law, Criminology and Police Science* v.50(3): 226–230.

Andrews, D.; Zinger, I.; Hoge, R.; Bonta, J.; Gendreau, P.; and Cullen, F. (1990) 'Does Correctional Treatment Work? A Clinically Relevant and Psychologically Informed Meta-Analysis'. *Criminology*, v.28(3): 369–404.

Bailey, Walter C. (1966) 'Correctional Treatment: An Evaluation of 100 Studies of Correctional Outcome'. *Journal of Criminal Law, Criminology, and Police Science* v.57(2): 153–160.

Cook, T.; Cooper, H.; Cordray, D.; Hartmann, H.; Hedges, H.; Light, R., Louis, T. and Mosteller, F. (eds) (1992) *Meta-Analysis for Explanation: A Casebook*. New York: Sage.

Cressey, Donald (1958) 'The Nature and Effectiveness of Correctional Techniques'. *Law and Contemporary Problems* v.23: 754–771.

Department of Corrections (1988) *Prisons in Change: The Submission of the Department of Justice to the Ministerial Committee of Inquiry into the Prisons System*. Wellington: Department of Justice.

Department of Corrections (2001a) *Let Maori Take the Journey*. Wellington: Department of Corrections.

Department of Corrections (2001b) *Treaty of Waitangi Strategic Plan 2001–2003*. Wellington: Department of Corrections.

Department of Corrections (2001c) *About Time: Turning People Away from a Life of Crime and Reducing Reoffending*. Wellington: Department of Corrections.

Department of Corrections (2003) *Maori Strategic Plan: 1 July 2003–30 June 2008*. Wellington: Department of Corrections.

Duffy, Ailsa (2004) *Report for the State Services Commissioner into the Department of Corrections Canterbury Emergency Response Unit (CERU)*. Wellington: State Services Commission.

Gendreau, Paul and Andrews, D. (1990) 'Tertiary Prevention: What the Meta-analyses of Offender Treatment Literature Tell Us About "What Works"'. *Canadian Journal of Criminology* v.32(1): 173–184.

Gendreau, Paul; Little, T. and Goggin, C. (1996) 'A Meta-Analysis of the Predictors of Adult Recidivism: What Works!'. *Criminology*, v.34(4): 575–607.

Gendreau, Paul and Ross, Robert (1979) 'Effective Correctional Treatment: Bibliotherapy for the Cynics'. *Crime and Delinquency* v.25: 463–489.

Gendreau, Paul and Ross, Robert (1980) *Effective Correctional Treatment*. Toronto: Butterworths.

Gendreau, Paul and Ross, Robert (1983) 'Success in Corrections: Programs and Principles'. In R. Corrado, M. Le Blanc and Jean Trepanier (eds), *Current Issues in Juvenile Justice*. Toronto: Butterworths.

Gendreau, Paul and Ross, Robert (1984) 'Correctional Treatment: Some Recommendations for Successful Intervention'. *Juvenile and Family Court Journal* v.34: 31–40.

Gendreau, Paul and Ross, Robert (1986) 'Correctional Treatment: Some Recommendations for Effective Intervention'. In Kenneth Haas and Geoffrey Alpert (eds), *The Dilemmas of Punishment: Readings in Contemporary Corrections*. Prospect Heights, IL: Waveland.

Gendreau, Paul and Ross, Robert (1987) 'Revivification of Rehabilitation: Evidence from the 1980s'. *Justice Quarterly*, v.4(3): 349–399.

Glass, G.V. (1976) 'Primary, Secondary and Meta-Analysis of Research'. *Educational Researcher*, v.5: 3–8.

Glass, G.V.; McGaw, B. and Smith, M. (1981) *Meta-Analysis in Social Research*. Beverly Hills, CA: Sage.

Goffman, Erving (1971) *Asylums: Essays on the Social Situation of Mental Patients and Other Inmates*. Middlesex: Pelican.

Greenberg, D.F. (1977) 'The Correctional Effects of Corrections: A Survey of Evaluations'. In D.F. Greenberg (ed), *Corrections and Punishment*. Newbury Park, CA: Sage.

Harpham, David (2004) *Census of Prison Inmates and Home Detainees 2003*. Wellington: Department of Corrections.

Hawkins, Gordon (1976) *The Prison: Policy and Practice*. Chicago: University of Chicago Press.

Hood, Roger (1967) Council of Europe, European Committee on Crime Problem. *Collected Studies in Criminological Research* v.73:79–83.

Israel, Mark and Chui, Wing Hong (2006) 'If "Something Works" is the Answer, What is the Question? Supporting Pluralist Evaluation in Community Corrections in the United Kingdom'. *European Journal of Criminology*, v.3(2): 181–200.

Lipsey, M. (1992) 'Juvenile Delinquency Treatment: A Meta-Analytic Inquiry into the Variability of Effects'. In Cook, T.; Cooper, H.; Cordray, D.; Hartmann; H.; Hedges, L.; Light, R.; Louis, T.; and Mosteller, F. (eds), *Meta-Analysis for Explanation*. New York: Sage.

Little, Alan (1963) 'Penal Theory, Penal Reform and Borstal Practice'. *British Journal of Criminology*, v.3: 257–275.

Love, Maureen, Kinney, John and Dyer, Tony (2001a) *Report on the Investigation of Tony Bird, Doug Smith and Mike Kelly*. Unpublished.

Love, Maureen, Kinney, John and Dyer, Tony (2001b) *Management Issues Report: Identified as a Consequence of the Investigation of Staff Associated with the Emergency Response Unit in Canterbury Prisons*. Unpublished.

Lundman, R.J, McFarlane, P.T and Scarpatti, F.R. (1976) 'Delinquency Prevention: AQ Description and Assessment of Projects'. *Crime and Delinquency*, v.22: 297–308.

Nathan, Lavinia, Wilson, Nick and Hillman, David (2003) *Te Whakakotahitanga: An Evaluation of the Te Piriti Special Treatment Programme for Child Sex Offenders in New Zealand*. Wellington: Department of Corrections.

Martinson, Robert (1974) 'What Works? – Questions and Answers about Prison Reform'. *The Public Interest* v.35: 22–54.

Martinson, Robert (1979) 'New Findings, New Views: A Note of Caution Regarding Sentencing Reform'. *Hofstra Law Review* v.7(2): 243 248.

Martinson, Robert and Wilks, Judith (1977) 'Save Parole Supervision'. *Federal Probation*. v.41: 63–76.

Maxwell, Gabrielle; Robertson, Jeremy; Kingi, Venezia; Morris, Allison and Cunningham, Chris (2004) *Achieving Effective Outcomes in Youth Justice: An Overview of Findings*. Wellington: Ministry of Social Development.

McFarlane-Nathan, Garry (1999) *FReMO: Framework for Reducing Maori Offending*. Wellington: Department of Corrections.

McLaren, Kaye (1992) *Reducing Reoffending: What Works Now?* Wellington: Department of Justice.

McLaren, Kaye (1994) 'What do Offenders Need to Stop Reoffending and Who Needs it Most?' *Criminal Justice Quartlerly*, issue 9: 6–9.

McLaren, Kaye (1995) 'Assessing What Offenders Need'. *Criminal Justice Quarterly*, issue 10: 8–11.

McLaren, Kaye (1996) 'Dazed and Confused: New Evidence on What Works in Reducing Offending'. Unpublished paper presented to the annual conference of the *Australian and New Zealand Society of Criminology*, Victoria University of Wellington, 1996.

McLeery, Richard (1960) 'Communication Patterns as Bases of Systems on Authority and Police'. In R.Coward, D. Cassey, R. McLeery, L.Ohlin, G. Sykes and S. Messinger (eds), *Theoretical Studies in Social Organisation of the Prison*. NY: Social Science Research Council.

Morris, Allison and Maxwell, Gabrielle (1993) 'Juvenile Justice in New Zealand: A New Paradigm'. *Australian and New Zealand Journal of Criminology* v.26(1): 72–90.

Morris, Norval and Hawkins, Gordon (1970) *The Honest Politician's Guide to Crime Control*. Chicago: University of Chicago Press.

Morris, Terence and Morris, Pauline (1963) *Pentonville: A Sociological Study of an English Prison*. London: Routledge and Kegan Paul.

Mullen, Jared (2003) *Internal Memorandum to ISC on Draft IOM Evaluation Report, 26 June 2003*. Unpublished.

Nathan, L; Wilson, N.J and Hillman, D (2003) *Te Whakakotahitanga: An Evaluation of the Te Piriti Special Treatment Programme for Child Sex Offenders in New Zealand*. Wellington: Department of Corrections.

New Zealand Law Commission (2006) *Reforms to the Sentencing and Parole Structure: Consultation Draft*. Unpublished.

Newbold, Greg (1982) *The Big Huey*. Auckland: Collins.

Ombudsmen (2005) *Ombudsmen's Investigation of the Department of Corrections in Relation to the Detention and Treatment of Prisoners*. Wellington: Government Printer.

Palmer, Ted (1975) 'Martinson Revisited'. *Journal of Research in Crime and Delinquency*, v.12: 133–152.

Palmer, Ted (1986) 'The "Effectiveness" Issue Today'. In Kenneth Haas and Geoffrey Alpert (eds), *The Dilemmas of Punishment: Readings in Contemporary Corrections*. Prospect Heights, IL: Waveland.

Policy Development (2003a) *Census of Prison Inmates and Home Detainees*. Wellington: Department of Corrections.

Policy Development (2003b) *Draft Report: Sentence Management in the Department of Corrections – A Process Evaluation*. Unpublished report.

Powers, Edwin and Witmer, Helen (1970) 'The Cambridge-Somerville Study'. In Norman Johnston, Leonard Savitz and Marvin Wolfgang (eds), *The Sociology of Punishment and Correction*. New York: Wiley.

Report of the Ministerial Committee of Inquiry into the Prisons System (1989). 'Prison Review: Te Ara Hou: The New Way'. (1989) Chair: Justice Sir Clinton Roper. Wellington: Government Printer.

Report of the Penal Policy Review Committee 1981. (1981) Chair: Mr Justice Casey. Wellington: Government Printer.

Romig, D. (1978) *Justice for our Children*. Lexington, MA: Lexington Books.

Spier, Philip (2001) *Conviction and Sentencing of Offenders in New Zealand: 1991–2000*. Wellington: Ministry of Justice.

Spier, Philip (2002) *Reconviction and Reimprisonment Rates for Released Prisoners*. Wellington: Ministry of Justice.

Thomas, J.E. (1972) *The English Prison Officer Since 1850*. London: Routledge and Kegan Paul.

Umbreit, M. (1994) *Victim Meets Offender: The Impact of Restorative Justice and Mediation*. Monsey, NY: Criminal Justice Press.

Van Ness, D. (1990) 'Restorative Justice'. In B. Galaway and J. Hudson (eds), *Criminal Justice: Restitution and Reconciliation*. Monsey, NY: Criminal Justice Press.

Walker, Nigel (1968) *Crime and Punishment in Britain: The Penal System in Theory, Law and Practice*. Edinburgh: Edinburgh University Press.

Walker, Nigel (1969) *Sentencing in a Rational Society*. New York: Allen & Lane.

Walker, Samuel (1989) *Sense and Nonsense about Crime: A Policy Guide*. Pacific Grove, CA: Brooks/Cole.

Ward, Tony (2006) 'What Works?' Unpublished paper presented to the Prison Fellowship of New Zealand National Conference, Silverstream, Wellington, 12–14 May 2006.

Wilkins, Leslie (1969) *Evaluation of Penal Measures*. New York: Random House.

Wilson, James Q. (1985) '"What Works" Revisited: New Findings on Criminal Rehabilitation'. In Kenneth Haas and Geoffrey Alpert (eds), *The Dilemmas of Punishment: Readings in Contemporary Corrections*. Prospect Heights, IL: Waveland.

Whitehead, J.T. and Lab, S.P. (1989) 'A Meta-Analysis of Juvenile Correctional Treatment'. *Journal of Research in Crime and Delinquency*, v.26(3): 276–295.

Wooton, Barbara (1959) *Social Science and Social Pathology*. London: Allen and Unwin.

Wright, W.E and Dixon, M.C. (1977) 'Community Prevention and Treatment of Juvenile Delinquency: A Review of Evaluation Studies'. *Journal of Research in Crime and Delinquency*, v.14: 35–67.

Zehr, Howard (1994) 'Justice that Heals: The Vision and the Practice'. *Stimulus* 2(3): 5–11.

PART II

*Aspects of
New Zealand
Corrections*

CHAPTER 7
THE NEW ZEALAND PRISON SYSTEM TODAY

As seen in Part I, after annexation to the British Crown in 1840, the New Zealand prison system developed along lines similar to those of England, particularly after consolidation under Arthur Hume in 1880. Although Hume assisted in the development of the world's first national probation system, his was a highly conservative administration and prisons did not evolve in any significant way until after his retirement in 1909. But from that point a number of changes that would last occurred. The most notable of these were the parole system and the agrarian and youth reformatory programmes of the 1910s and early 1920s, the abolition of corporal punishment in 1941, the experiments in ad hoc reformism of the 1950s, the legislative measures of the Hanan–Robson era which implemented detention centres and periodic detention, and finally the experiments of He Ara Hou and Integrated Offender Management from 1990. The prison system of today is a legacy of many of these initiatives and their vestiges, in one form or another, remain within the modern correctional context. Since the complete abolition of capital punishment in 1989, imprisonment has continued as the most severe sanction available to the courts. This chapter reviews the primary features of the New Zealand prison system as it exists in 2006.

The Purposes of Imprisonment

Although some decry imprisonment as inhumane and would like to see it abolished, prisons are nonetheless an essential component of a modern criminal justice system. Incarceration may be a rather blunt implement, but there is at this point no better way of dealing with those who seriously threaten the property or safety of others, or the wellbeing of society at large. Like them or not, prisons perform a number of essential functions, some of which are obvious, while others are less so. The principal purposes of prisons are these:

Custody

A clear function of imprisonment is the safe custody of offenders who present a risk to society or who have failed to respond to non-custodial measures. Some criminals are dangerous and have high likelihoods of reoffending, and the state has a duty to keep such people secure during their period in custody. In extreme cases this may mean forever. Preventive detention is an example of a sentence that is specifically designed for the dangerous criminal, allowing violent and sexual offenders to be locked up indefinitely when they are considered an ongoing threat. In a similar way, life sentences and long finite terms are often used to keep dangerous criminals in safe custody. Moreover, in law, section 28(2) of the Parole Act 2002 states that no offender shall receive parole unless the board is satisfied that he/she will not pose an "undue risk" to the safety of the community.

Rehabilitation

Since 1910, a manifest purpose of imprisonment has been 'rehabilitation', that is, turning offenders' lives away from criminal pursuits and toward law-abiding alternatives. Not all offenders can be rehabilitated and not all want to be. Many criminals like the way they are and prefer the way they live. However, others desire a lifestyle that does not involve the risk of further imprisonment, and one of the functions of prison programmes is to assist those who wish to live crime-free lives when they are released. Thus prisons provide, to varying degrees, programmes aimed at developing skills such as employment, life management, cognitive thinking, parenting, basic numeracy and literacy, spirituality, cultural awareness, control of alcohol and drug abuse, and so on. Even if an inmate goes on to reoffend, exposure to prison programmes has the potential to create a more thoughtful, compassionate human being than one who receives no treatment at all. Thus, provision of programmes and humane treatment in prison is likely to pay a dividend even if full 'rehabilitation' is not achieved.

Punishment

Another obvious aspect of incarceration is punishment. The essence of imprisonment is the deprivation of liberty, including loss of conjugal rights and other freedoms. It is often said that people are sent to prison *as* punishment, not *for* punishment, in other words the loss of freedom is punishment in itself. The extent to which the experience of incarceration deters people from further offending is moot – high recidivist rates suggest its effect may be small. Nonetheless, the vast majority of inmates detest being in prison, are impatient to get out, and while inside at least, most swear that their current 'lag' will be their last. Without doubt, as the small number of prisoners in the 50-plus age bracket (only 9.3% of all inmates) suggests, most criminals give up offending at some stage in their lives[1] and a loathing of lockup is one explanation.

Deterrence

Sometimes known as 'general deterrence', this refers to the impact of the threat of imprisonment on people's decisions about whether or not to engage in criminal activity in the first place. Some offences, such as crimes of passion, involve little rational forethought and people who commit them seldom consider consequences before acting. In these situations prison is a minor deterrent. Many crimes, however, particularly white-collar crimes, involve considerable planning and assessment of consequences, in addition to weighing the chances of success or failure. Suit-wearing businessmen and entrepreneurs, most of whom are middle or upper class, are generally fearful of prison and thus prison must act as a significant deterrent to criminal activity for them. A good example of the 'advertisement' function of incarceration is seen in the old Victorian prisons, with their forbidding, fortress-like appearance. These institutions (Mt Eden being a good example) were deliberately designed to inspire awe and dread in onlookers, thus to remind them of the awful consequences of law-breaking.

Retribution

Sometimes known as 'just deserts', '*jus talionis*', 'an eye for an eye', or 'making the punishment fit the crime', the retributive function of imprisonment is something that many people have difficulty accepting. Yet retribution it is fundamental to any criminal justice system. Terrible crimes produce strong emotional reactions, which demand the retributive delivery of misery upon an offender. This is why the maximum penalty for manslaughter – the killing of a person without murderous intent – is life imprisonment, whereas attempted murder – where no life is lost in spite of the homicidal motive of the offender – carries only 14 years. Although the *mens rea*, or guilty intent, of someone who tries to kill another is greater than that of an unintentional killer, the penalty for manslaughter is larger because the consequences are worse. In our law, causing a fatality accidentally requires heavier retribution than attempting to kill but failing to do so.

Where retribution is concerned, the offender's likelihood of reoffending is of little importance. If Mark Lundy, who axed his wife and child to death in 2000, was released tomorrow he would probably never kill again. But the callous brutality of the murder produced such revulsion nationwide that few would argue that his punishment of life, with a 20-year minimum, was unjust. One of the greatest causes of public protest where sentencing for serious crimes is concerned is that the punishment inadequately reflects the gravity of the offence. A government which denied the public its 'pound of flesh' in sentencing policy would not govern for long.

Affirming the Power of the State

The final, and somewhat more nebulous, function of punishment is that it reaffirms the power and legitimacy of the state. From a legal point of view, when a person breaks a law the offence is technically against the state, not against an individual, and normally it is the state which prosecutes, not an injured party. This is why criminal proceedings are normally titled *The Queen* v. [*Accused*]. It is also why prosecutions do not always require a complainant. For example, in an assault, the Crown may decide to proceed with charges even though a victim refuses to lay a complaint. In *R* v. *Pauga*[2] an accused was convicted of rape on his own admission, even though no victim was ever identified. If the law is broken, the state is offended and therefore the state prosecutes.

So, one of the functions of criminal justice is to affirm the power of the state by ensuring that law-breakers are held to account. In order to retain public faith in the law, the state must successfully defend itself against those who challenge it. Justice must be 'seen to be done'. In New Zealand, imprisonment is the most powerful statement the state can make about its power over the wrongdoer. Bert Dallard, Controller-General of Prisons 1925–1949, was one who appreciated the symbolism of this aspect of law enforcement. In 1931 he issued the following instructions on executions procedure:

> As the Union Jack is emblematic of British Justice, such a flag will be hoisted to the main flagstaff on the morning of an execution. At the time the execution takes place a black flag will be hoisted to a lower flagstaff, the Union Jack in the ascendant, silently proclaiming the suzerainty of the law.[3]

The Prisons of New Zealand

At the end of 2006 New Zealand had 19 public prisons in operation, all but five of them in the North Island. Three prisons – two in the North Island – were dedicated female institutions and there was a temporary 60-bed unit for women at Waikeria. This chapter deals with the public prisons of New Zealand. The recently-closed private prison will be considered in chapter 10.

All prisons in New Zealand are overseen by a senior management team located at head office of the Department of Corrections in Wellington, but administration is divided into five regions, each with a regional manager. Beneath this, individual prisons are controlled by site managers, and units within these institutions are run by unit managers. Thus there is a trickling-down of authority and responsibilities from top to bottom, with unit managers, who are normally in charge of about 60 inmates, having fairly close acquaintance with the men and women under their control. With a ratio of approximately two inmates per staff member (including non-uniformed personnel), staffing in New Zealand is low relative to countries such as Canada, Australia, England/Wales and Scotland, which have ratios in the region of 1:1 or 1:1.5. Approximately 80 per cent of the cost of running prisons is taken up in wages, and the average running cost of New Zealand prisons, at roughly $69,000 per inmate per year, is similar to the above nations, save Scotland.[4]

The public prisons operating in New Zealand in 2006 and their respective regional affiliations are as follows:

Northern Region: Northland Region Corrections Facility (Ngawha), Auckland prison (Paremoremo), Mt Eden prison, Mt Eden Women's prison (closed 2006), Auckland Central Remand prison (ACRP), Auckland Region Women's Corrections Facility (ARWCF).

Waikato/Central Region: Waikeria prison, Tongariro/Rangipo prison.

Midland Region: New Plymouth prison, Hawkes Bay Regional prison (Mangaroa), Wanganui prison (Kaitoke), Manawatu prison (Linton).

Wellington Region: Rimutaka prison, Arohata Women's prison, Wellington prison (Mt Crawford).

Southern Region: Christchurch prison (Paparua), Christchurch Women's prison (Paparua Women's), Rolleston prison, Dunedin prison, Invercargill prison.

Within these establishments there are four major security classifications: maximum, high medium, low medium, and minimum, with some institutions catering for just one security level, others for several. The old prisons at Mt Eden and Mt Crawford, for example, mainly accommodate high medium security risks, and Rolleston and Tongariro are primarily for minimums. But some prisons, for example Paparua and Waikeria, have significant proportions of high–mediums, low–mediums and minimums located in different areas. High–medium-security prisoners are usually contained in the older buildings on a site (for example, at Paparua) and are transferred to the more modern and pleasant 60- or 80-bed units if they achieve low medium or minimum security status.

Conditions in different prisons vary greatly, depending largely on when the institution was built. The oldest prisons in New Zealand are Dunedin, New Plymouth and Mt Eden, all designed in the 19th century, and none have the capacity to provide

Entrance to Mt Eden prison.

Wing interior, Mt Eden prison.

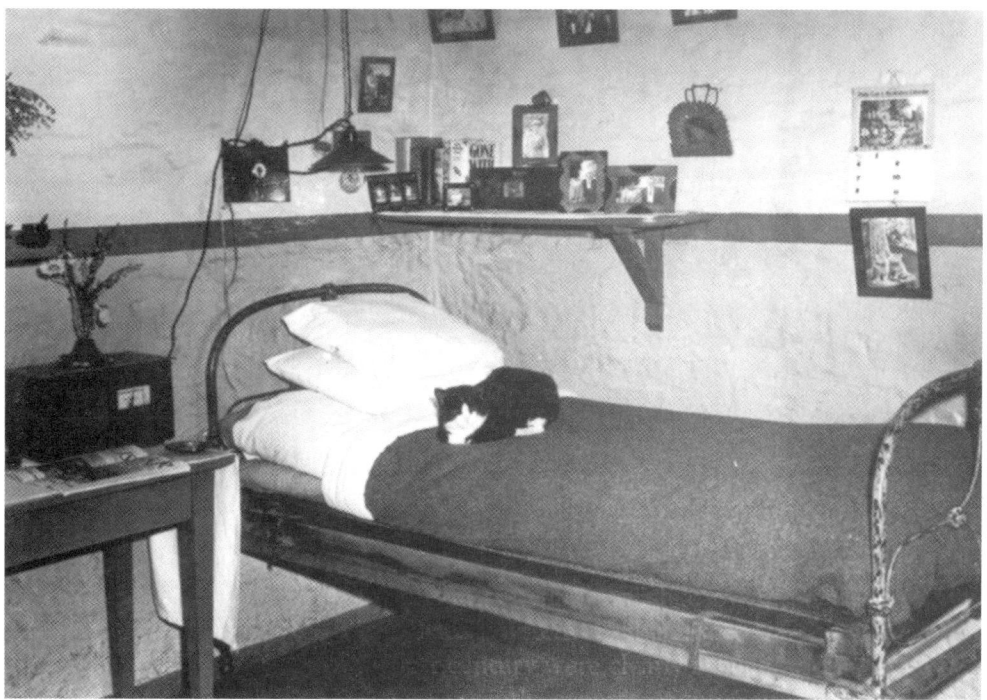

Decorated long-termer's cell at Mt Eden in the 1950s.

the quality of programmes that are desirable today. Mt Eden, the largest of the three with about 380 inmates, has an interior reminiscent of a medieval castle, with echoing stone and concrete floors and walls, rattling grilles, and cell doors of 2cm-thick steel plate. Until 2000 there was no plumbing in the cells. Now used primarily for short termers and transfers, Mt Eden has limited capacity for programmes and recreation.

Even on a single site, conditions can vary markedly. Paparua and Waikeria, for example, are large complexes with old buildings that were constructed in the early 20th century. Here conditions are as poor as at Mt Eden, with a shortage of meaningful employment and only limited programmes and recreation. Inmates in these institutions are often doubled-up in their cells. Alongside these old jails, however, are a number of more modern units – where conditions are far better and which cater for low medium-security prisoners and minimums. The modern units normally consist of 60 or 80 cells set in a rectangle around a central area, with a tennis court and/or basketball court. The units are surrounded by high double-mesh fences topped with razor wire. Inmates all have their own cells, have access to a weight room, and many work outside the wire. Conditions here are far better than in the cellblocks of the old jails. In addition to the units, there are also several more modern medium security institutions – such as Mangaroa, Paremoremo medium and Ngawha – where conditions are relatively good and opportunities exist for job training, programmes and sport.

Minimum-security prisons, often known as camps, are usually located in rural areas, such as Rolleston and Tongariro. Here inmates have their own cells and are

Modern housing units, Rimutaka prison.

often employed in farming, gardening or forestry work. Camps afford freedoms unavailable in other prisons, such as unsupervised work and sporting excursions with outside teams. Many minimum security inmates qualify for 72 hours home leave, as well as travel, every two months to allow them time with their families.

There are three women's institutions in New Zealand, located at Manurewa (ARWCF), Arohata and Paparua, which in the past have catered for 200–300 inmates, although by August 2004 the female muster had increased to almost 400. There is also a temporary 60-bed women's unit within the Waikeria complex. The three prisons hold mainly minimum and medium-security inmates, but ARWCF and Paparua also

Modern unit interior, Rimutaka prison.

have capacity for secure accommodation. With the majority of women coming from the Auckland region, it was a legacy of poor planning that until recently the two largest women's prisons in the country were located in Wellington and Christchurch, with the Mt Eden building accommodating just 54. The opening of ARWCF for 286 women at Manukau, South Auckland, in June 2006 was a remedy that was long overdue. The imprisonment of women is covered more fully in chapter 9.

New Zealand has only one maximum-security prison, Paremoremo's East Division, which was built in 1969. Catering for around 200 inmates at a time, the management philosophy of Paremoremo maxi has undergone significant changes in the 36 years of its existence. Currently the regime at Paremoremo is more restrictive than at any other time in its history. This institution is dealt with in detail in chapter 8.

Special Focus Units

Although the abolition of borstal training in 1981 and corrective training in 2002 saw the end of specialist institutions, New Zealand has a number of special-focus units that are dedicated to specific kinds of inmates. The principal specialist units operating in New Zealand are as follows:

Sex Offender Units

The idea of providing specialised units for sex offenders has been around since the early 1980s, but an actual project was not approved until 1987. Two years later the first dedicated sex-offenders' unit, for 60 men, administered by the Psychological Services Division of the Department of Justice, opened at Rolleston prison. It was named 'Kia Marama' (Behold the Light). Early perceived success of Kia Marama soon led to plans for a second 60-bed unit at Paremoremo, which became known as 'Te Piriti' (The Bridge). This opened in 1994. Both units now offer volunteer programmes for child-sex offenders, and many of the staff have psychological training. Inmates accepted for treatment are transferred from their resident institutions to the sex offenders' unit toward the end of their sentences, where they work in teams of 8–10 on a course that lasts 33 weeks in the case of Kia Marama, and 40 weeks at Te Piriti. After the programme has been completed, these inmates often remain in the unit until their release dates.[5]

New Zealand's sex offender programmes are among the few treatment regimes to have produced significant and sustained reductions in recidivism. Figures compiled by the Department of Corrections indicate that untreated child sex offenders have a recidivist rate of approximately 22 per cent within seven years of release. Those who complete the programmes at Kia Marama and Te Piriti reoffend at approximately half the rate of the untreated, and Maori who complete the Te Piriti program, with its tikanga focus, have a reoffending rate of 4.41 per cent, against 13.58 per cent for Maori at Kia Marama.[6] Interestingly, as noted, Pakeha inmates who complete the Maori programme are also slightly less likely to reoffend than those who do not. The reasons for the difference are unclear.

Maori Focus Units

There are five units in New Zealand specifically devoted to a Maori 'bicultural therapy' model. Bicultural therapy essentially involves instilling ethnic pride in Maori offenders by introducing them to Maori language, culture and 'values', in an attempt to divert them from further offending. The first of these units was a 60-bed facility opened at Mangaroa in December 1997. Reviewed and deemed a success, a second unit was established at Rimutaka in 1999, followed by New Plymouth later that year. In 2002 the New Plymouth unit was shifted to Wanganui and that same year two more units opened, at Waikeria and Tongariro. These five units are able to cater for approximately 270 inmates at any one time.

Youth Offender Units

Following the recommendations of an internal discussion document in 1998, the first of a number of youth offender units opened at Mangaroa in October 1999. The Mangaroa unit initially contained only 17 high medium security beds (later expanded to 28) and was designed for young males under the age of 20. A second unit, with 35 beds, was opened at Waikeria in June 2000, followed by 40-bed units at Rimutaka and Paparua in 2001. There is a unit at the new Northland prison at Ngawha and one is planned for the prison being built at Spring Hill, Meremere. Youth units provide structured programmes involving basic education, trade training, life skills and offender awareness programmes for young men aged 14–19 who have frequently come from disturbed, deprived and dysfunctional backgrounds. Each unit is supposed to have access to a half-time psychologist, but this has not materialised and Stone[7] argues that the units actually perform far below capacity.

Violence Treatment Unit (VTU)

Operating along similar lines to those which have proven successful at Kia Marama and Te Piriti, in March 1998 a special treatment unit for violent offenders was established at Rimutaka. Originally known as the Violence Prevention Unit, this 30-bed facility, run jointly between the Psychological Service and the Public Prisons Service, provides 36 weeks of intensive treatment for inmates nearing the end of their sentences who have committed serious violent offences. A Department of Corrections survey in 2004 found that inmates who complete the VTU programme are only half as likely to reoffend as similar offenders who are untreated.[8] It must be remembered, however, that violent offenders who volunteer for this programme and proceed to complete it, may not be fully comparable with those who do not.

Drug and Alcohol Treatment Units

The Department of Corrections runs three specialised units for inmates with substance abuse problems which, can cater for about 120 inmates at any time. Located at Rolleston and Arohata women's prison, these units are run in partnership with the National Society on Alcohol and Drug Dependence (Care NZ). Prisoners with drug/alcohol problems are identified at the commencement of sentence, and admission to one of the specialist units is normally timed to occur toward the end of a term. The programme is psychology-based and is designed to help inmates recognise addictive relapse indicators, develop skills to deal with potential relapse, and to recognise the link between addiction and offending.

Faith Unit, Rimutaka prison.

Faith Unit

In October 2003 a pilot 60-bed Faith Unit, known as He Korowai Whakapono, opened at Rimutaka prison. The unit provides a programme developed by the Prison Fellowship of New Zealand (headed by former Assistant Secretary for Justice, Kim Workman) that is based on Christian principles, regular prayer, visits by church groups and regular spiritual retreats. Transfer to the unit is voluntary and is designed for longer-term inmates nearing the end of their sentences. The unit works in concert with a faith-based reintegration programme operating out of Wellington, known as Operation Jericho. Although the unit appears now to be operating well with good results, it got off to an unfortunate start when in March 2004, just a few months after opening, inmate Rex Hopper (54) was murdered by fellow inmate Emani Seu (46) during a dispute over a screwdriver in an outside gardening party.

Self Care Units

Self care units are designed for offenders in the final months of their sentences, to assist with the transition from prison into the free community. Normally situated outside of prison compounds but with their own fences and security, self care units consist of a number of four-bedroom flats, each with its own cooking and laundry facilities. Inmates in self care units are trusted prisoners who usually work on prison property during the day, but otherwise look after themselves within the confines of their units. Each unit has a weekly budget, and every week one member is taken shopping with a correctional officer to purchase food and other items. Thus, essential living skills are learned in preparation for release. The first self care unit was established at Paparua women's prison in May 1998, and was followed by units at Paparua men's prison, at Mangaroa, at and at Wanganui. In 2002, a fifth self care unit opened at Arohata women's prison and there is also one at the new Northland facility. In mid 2006 there were nine self care units in operation, catering for approximately 100 inmates. Five of them were located in women's facilities.

Figure 7.1: Prison Musters

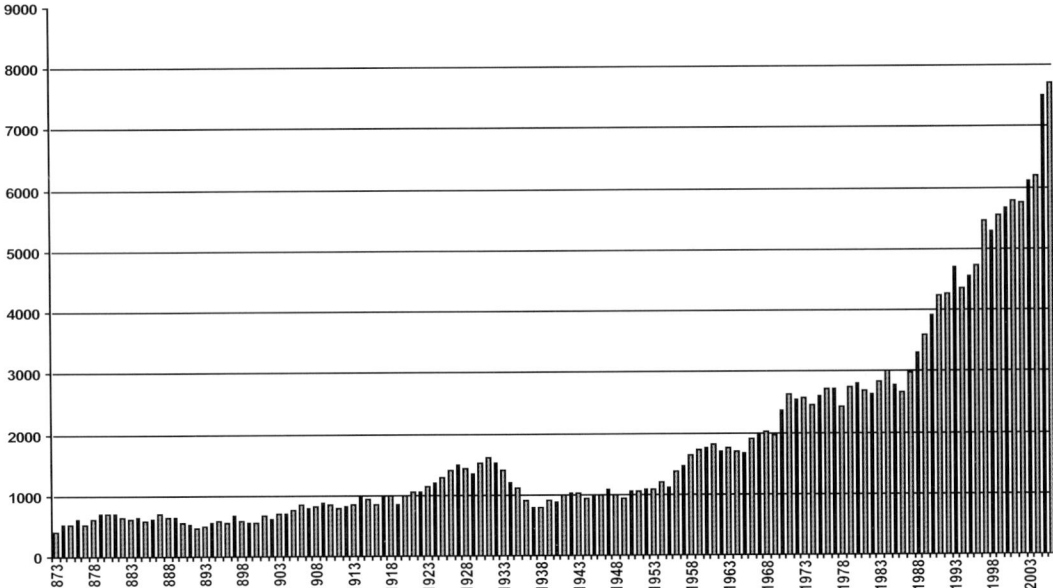

Figure 7.2: Prison Musters per 100,000 Mean Population

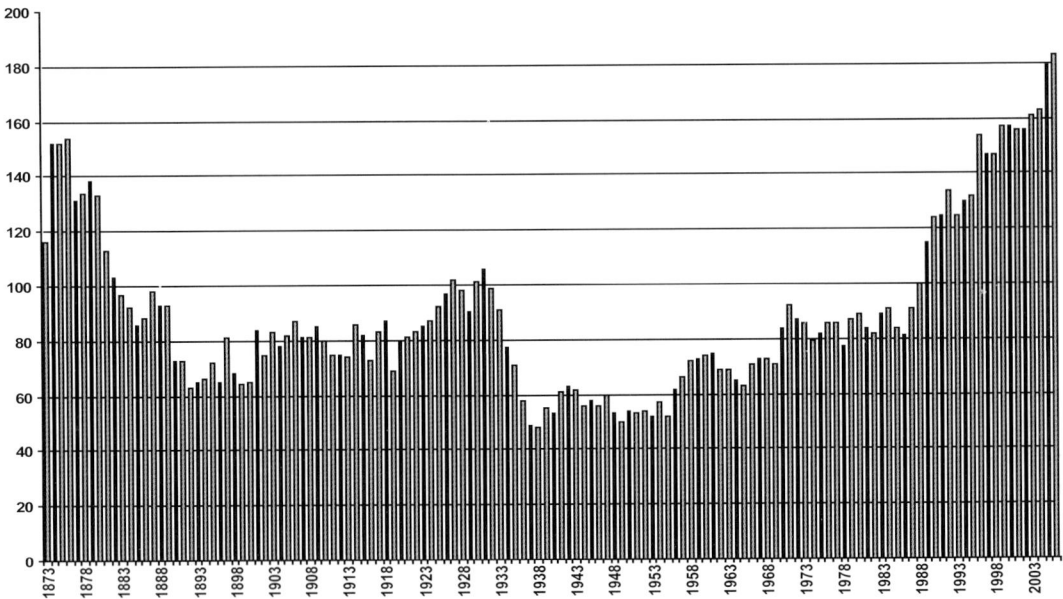

The Prison Population

As can be seen from the graph below, the prison population of New Zealand grew quickly during the 19th century, rising from about 70 in 1854 to over 1,000 in 1870 probably as a result of the gold rushes. The prison muster in the 1870s was high relative to total population. From here numbers dropped and remained quite stable at around 1,000, from about the time of the First World War until 1955. But in 1956 a series of leaps occurred, so that by 2000 the muster was five times what it had been 45 years before.

After 2000 there were unprecedented increases in prison populations in New Zealand, partly as a result of the Sentencing Act and the Parole Act which became effective in July 2002. The first of these acts toughened penalties for some types of offences, while the second removed automatic release on remission for all prisoners serving over two years. From this point on, all such releases were at the discretion of the parole board. In addition, the Bail Act 2000 made it harder for accused persons to get bail. Thus, if the rising proportion of remand inmates is included in the equation, the total prison population of New Zealand grew from 5,780 in 2001 (156/100,000) to over 7,700 in 2006 (188/100,000) – a numerical increase of 33 per cent. Apart from the growth in custodial remands (which more than doubled between 1991 and 2006, to 20 per cent of the total muster), the primary reason for the jump is longer overall sentences, combined with conservatism of the new parole board in the granting of parole.[9]

Children and Young Offenders

In New Zealand, offenders aged between 10 and 13 are referred to as 'children', whilst those aged 14 to 16 are, 'young persons'. In the Children and Young Persons Act 1974, the minimum age at which a person could be prosecuted for an offence was set at 14, but was dropped to 10 in 1977. In both cases, children aged 10–13 can only be prosecuted for murder or manslaughter; others are normally dealt with through the Department of Child, Youth and Family (CYF). Young persons are seldom prosecuted either. Eighty per cent of apprehended young persons aged 14–16 are dealt with by the Police Youth Aid Section and given a warning or diversion. Diversion is a process whereby a young first offender can avoid conviction by completing a programme (normally involving an apology and repair of any damage) overseen by the police. The majority of the remaining 20 per cent are referred to CYF for a family group conference (FGC), which is a restorative justice initiative introduced in 1989 aimed at attempting reconciliation between a young offender and his or her victim/s.[10] If the circumstances of an offender or his/her offence make an FGC inappropriate, a young offender may be prosecuted in the youth court.

There is a general restriction in the Sentencing Act 2002 which limits the imprisonment of offenders under 17 to offences that are purely indictable (such as murder, manslaughter, sexual violation and dealing in Class A or B drugs). Thus, although approximately 30,000 young offenders aged 14–16 are apprehended every year, and in spite of the fact that apprehensions for violent offences within this group increased by 21 per cent between 1994 and 2001, very few children and young people enter the prison system,[11] and their percentages relative to other inmates are declining. Young offenders sent to prison for serious crimes are normally detained in youth facilities administered by CYF until they reach the age of 15, when they are transferred, usually to youth units run by the Department of Corrections. This, for example, was the case with New Zealand's youngest convicted killer, Bailey Kurariki. Kurariki was only 12 when, along with five other teenagers, he killed pizza delivery man Michael Choy in 2001. Sentenced to seven years imprisonment for manslaughter, he was held initially in the care of CYF before being transferred to a Corrections youth unit.

Corrections census figures show that the percentage of prison inmates aged 15–19 declined from eleven per cent in 1991 to 6.7 per cent in 2003. The percentage of young adults aged 20–24 also dropped in the same period, from 28.9 per cent to 18.6 per cent. The prison population is in fact ageing considerably, with the percentage of inmates aged 35 and over growing from 22.5 per cent in 1991 to 40.2 per cent in 2003.[12]

Maori

As seen in chapter 3, the number of Maori prisoners received was insignificant in the 1900s but rose after the First World War. By 1940, 15 per cent of prisoners were Maori, and during the 1950s, as Maori moved in increasing numbers into the towns, the percentage of Maori prisoners grew steadily, reaching 50 per cent by 1980. The percentage of Maori received into prisons has remained at about that level since. In the 2003 prison census, 51.1 per cent of sentenced inmates were Maori or part-Maori.[15] Relative to their presence in the general population, Maori are imprisoned about three times as often as non-Maori.

Women

Where women are concerned the above is reversed. The number of women in New Zealand prisons are low by comparison with men and were lower in the 19th century than today. In 1875, 18 per cent of all prisoners were female, but by 1892 this had dropped to 11 per cent, and it mostly remained at between nine and 11 per cent until after the First World War. From 1922 until the end of the Second World War, the percentage of women in prison generally fluctuated at between four and seven per cent of the prison population, but after the war it dropped again, and has tended to hover between four and five per cent since then. Recently, as happens from time to time, there has been a jump in female incarcerations, and in August 2004 the women's muster stood at 393, or 5.7 per cent of the total inmate population. This represented a 68 per cent increase over the muster in November 2001. Women's imprisonment is dealt with more fully in chapter 9.

Remands

Unlike the United States, where those awaiting trial or sentence are normally held in designated jails, most custodial remands in New Zealand are contained in segregated sections of existing prisons. The only dedicated remand facility in New Zealand is Auckland Central Remand prison (ACRP), which until July 2005 was a private institution run by Australasian Correctional Management (see chapter 10). ACRP contains about 230 remanded inmates out of the national total of 860 custodial remands, in a state-owned building that is modern and was well-managed by its private contractor. Conditions at ACRP were exceptional, however, and in state-run institutions conditions are poor. Because they have not yet been convicted or sentenced by the courts and may only be in a prison for days or weeks, remands are not classified and are held with a minimum of privileges. They usually have no access to programmes or facilities and if denied bail they are usually contained in spartan segregated conditions until trial and sentencing are over. This may involve over a year of 'dead time'.

Publicity over some bail remands reoffending before trial led to a study in 1990 which found that 13.6 per cent of bailed offenders re-offended while bonded.[16]

Major Changes to Sentencing and Parole Law Since 1987

1987

- The presumption of imprisonment threshold for violent offences was reduced from offences punishable by at least five years imprisonment to offences punishable by at least two years imprisonment.
- The non-parole period for lifers and preventive detainees was increased from seven years to ten years.
- Most violent offenders sentenced to more than two years imprisonment became ineligible for parole and had to serve at least two thirds of sentence, before being released on remission.
- Parole boards gained the power to order that certain offenders serve their entire terms.

1993

- Courts were empowered to impose minimum terms that exceed normal non-parole periods.
- Release conditions were made more rigorous and recall procedures were simplified.
- Preventive detention was broadened to become available to sex offenders on a first offence and violent offenders on a second offence.
- The maximum penalty for rape was increased from 14 years to 20 years.

1999

- The home invasion law increased the maximum term available for violent offences committed during the course of a home invasion by up to five years, depending on the charge.

2002

- The Parole Act and the Sentencing Act removed automatic release on remission for all sentences over two years and made all such sentences paroleable. Under a new parole board, parole was awarded less liberally than before. As noted, inmates today serve an average of 62 per cent of their full sentences.[14]
- 17 year minimums were mandated for murders committed under certain aggravating circumstances.
- The applicability of preventive detention was broadened and made available to both serious violent and sex offenders, on a first offence.

During the 1990s, offending on bail increased to over 20 per cent.[17] This, along with publicity over some high-profile bail crimes, resulted in the Bail Act 2000 which, when brought into force in January 2001, toughened bail conditions by placing the onus on defendants to prove that bail is safe, and introduced a presumption against bail in some cases. A consequence of the act has been a larger proportion of offenders remanded in custody. Between 1991 and 2006, the number of remands as a ratio of all inmates grew from 9.7 to 20 per cent.

Contemporary Issues

Sentence Length

Apart from restrictions on youth imprisonment, a major factor in the ageing of the prison population is sentence length. Between 1992 and 2001, the number of sentences given which exceeded two years increased from 1,490 to 2,414.[13] In 1991, 35.9 per cent of sentenced inmates were doing more than two years. By 2003 this had increased to 50.8 per cent. The number of inmates doing life or preventive detention grew from 230 in 1991 to more than 500 in 2005. Average sentence lengths increased as well, particularly for violent offences. The average custodial sentence for violence almost doubled between 1985 and 2002. In addition, since 1987 various law changes have added both to sentence length and the proportion of sentence served.

Such changes have significantly lengthened the amount of time that sentenced offenders spend in prison, hence the ageing population. This has particularly been the case with violent and sexual offenders. In addition to age changes, between 1987 and 2003 violent and sexual offender numbers in prison grew from about 50 to 58 per cent.

Protective Segregation

A feature of the post-1980s period has been an increase in the proportion of inmates requiring protective custody. Prior to the 1980s, protective segregation was rare. Even in the maximum-security prison at Paremoremo there was no need for a protection unit, because demand was insignificant. In the 1970s, the few inmates who came under threat from others were either placed in another block, or the source of the threat was removed to administrative segregation. But during the 1980s, as sentences got longer and prisons were populated by more violent offenders, protective segregation became a permanent feature of the prison environment. In 1972, for example, only 87 out of a total of 1,645 sentenced prisoners (5.2%) were serving sentences of over seven years.[18] By 2003, the number of inmates doing more than seven years had risen to 1,290, or 25 per cent.[19] Likewise, prison censuses indicate that the percentage of inmates doing time for violence as their major offence grew from about 20 per cent in 1972, to 42 per cent in 1987, then to 68 per cent in 2001. So there has been a significant shift in the constitution of the inmate population, which is one reason why nine of New Zealand's 10 prison homicides have occurred since 1984.

Figure 7.3: Inmates in Protective Custody

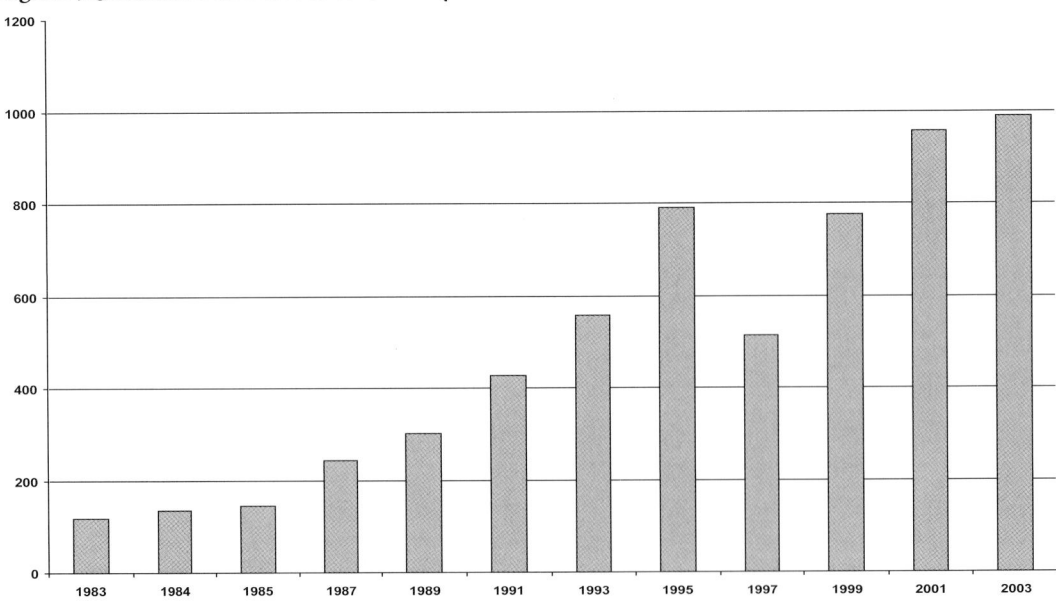

Figure 7.4: Inmates in Protective Custody as % of Muster

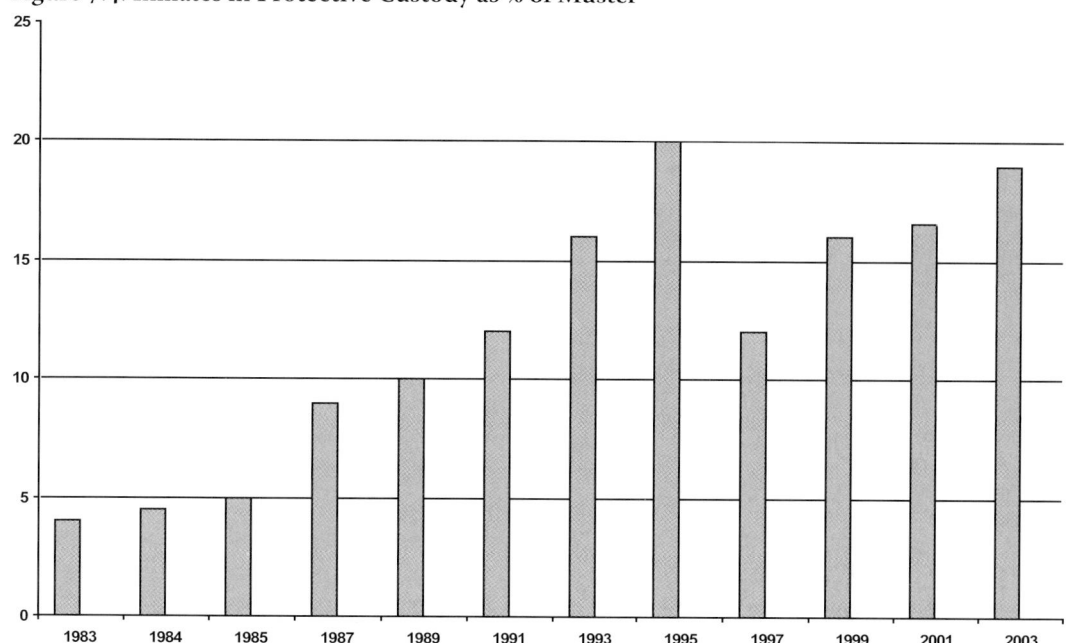

Another factor in the growing demand for segregation was that, after a Committee of Inquiry into Auckland's Oakley forensic psychiatric hospital reported in 1983, the standing practice of transferring psychiatric inmates to hospital for treatment, ceased. After this they had to be treated in prisons, which were ill-equipped for the purpose. A corollary result, as discussed in chapter 8, was the spate of suicides at Paremoremo maximum in the 1980s.

These factors have all contributed to the sudden growth of protective custody after the 1970s. Nearly all inmates in protective custody are male. The earliest figures available are for 1983, when 117 inmates (4% of the total) were reported to be held under protective segregation. This increased to 136 (4.5%) the next year, to 146 in 1985 (5%), and to 244 in 1987 (9%).[20] Since then, between 16 and 20 per cent of inmates have been segregated in protective custody.

The increases in protective custody are thus a direct consequence of the rising levels of tension that have been a growing feature of New Zealand prisons since the beginning of the 1980s.

Employment and Programmes

The last chapter dealt at some length with the development and philosophy of Integrated Offender Management (IOM), which is the Department of Corrections' primary vehicle for addressing the problem of recidivism. This programme involves, in part, the teaching of work habits and skills and the provision of various other services to offenders.

i. Employment

With more than half of the New Zealand prison population never having had regular employment, the development of regular work habits and employment skills is seen as an essential component of the reform process and in 2004, approximately 20 per cent of all sentenced inmates had commenced training towards a recognised job qualification, with a completion rate of 80 per cent. Prison censuses from the early 1990s indicate that at that time approximately two-thirds of inmates were listed as 'employed'. Work was unavailable for about 20 per cent.[21] Today, more detailed information on employment is contained in annual reports and biennial censuses. According to the department's report for 2003–2004,[22] its goal was to provide each inmate eligible for work with 1,410 hours employment per year (an average of 27 hours per week). It achieved 90 per cent of this objective.

The 5.7 million hours actually worked indicates that employment was available for 4,042 (64%) of the approximately 6,300 inmates in custody at that time. This is confirmed by the 2003 census, which shows that 38 per cent of the prison population was unemployed on census day.[23] The majority of inmates who were unemployed were remands, short-termers, maximum-security prisoners, and those in protective segregation. As the accommodation crisis intensified in 2005 and running costs increased, a large number of work programs, which normally run at a deficit, closed down. These included horticulture, joinery and light engineering enterprises. Between 2004 and 2005 there was almost a one-third drop in the number of hours worked by inmates per week and a 23 per cent decline in inmate work-scheme placements. There were cutbacks in education, drug, alcohol, and other programmes as well.

Employment, when it is available, takes various forms, from routine duties such as cooking, cleaning, laundry, and vehicle maintenance, to production in workshops, and farm and forestry work in minimum-security institutions. It should be noted that figures indicating an inmate is 'employed' are artificially inflated by many forms of prison labour, such as 'cleaner', 'librarian', and 'kit-locker attendant' which, although listed as full-time duty, in fact only involve a few hours a day. Moreover, with a maximum 'incentive allowance' of just $1.00 per hour, the reward for employed inmates who work hard is low. Finding real work for inmates can be difficult, and the cost of equipment, training and supervision is what makes it uneconomic. Even industrial workshops are hard-pressed to make a profit, and in any case cannot compete fairly with private industry which has to pay employees a proper wage and thus must remain 'competitively neutral'.[24] So product sales tend to be restricted to the public sector. Thus, in reality, many 'employed' inmates are able to work far less than what is reported by the department.

One of the greatest aids to an inmate's chances of successful post-release adjustment is work parole, now known as Release to Work (RtW). Work parole commenced in New Zealand in 1961 and has grown significantly since. Minimum-security inmates may apply for work parole during the latter months of their sentences. Those serving two years or less can be granted up to three months work parole; others can be released to work by the parole board after they have reached their parole-eligibility date. Work parolees live in prison but are released every day to attend an approved paid occupation within the community. A proportion of a parolee's earnings are deducted to pay for his/her cost of living, and other deductions may be made for fines, reparation or family support. Since the introduction of home detention as a parole condition in 1999, work parole has become somewhat redundant. Whereas in 1985, 681 inmates commenced work parole while in custody,[25] in November 2003 only 13 out of a total of nearly 5,000 sentenced inmates were involved in a RtW programme.[26]

ii. Programmes

The other component of preparing inmates for release is rehabilitative programmes. A variety of programmes is available to inmates and at any time, approximately 16 per cent of inmates live in the special focus units discussed earlier.

Outside of this, inmates in standard accommodation are also involved in programmes, but as discussed in the last chapter, in spite of the high expectations of IOM, actual participation levels are low. As noted, by 2005 budget constraints had caused a reduction in the number of programmes offered, although the November 2003 census[27] gives a snapshot of programme participation among sentenced inmates on census night:

Straight Thinking	123	2.4% of sentenced inmates
Tikanga Maori	89	1.7%
100-hour 'cirminogenic' programmes	57	1.1%
Living skills course	7	0.1%
National Certificate in Employment Skills	658	10.29%

These are all short-term courses, which only occupy an inmate for a small proportion of his/her sentence, which is why participation levels are low at any particular time. The completion rate of those who start programmes is generally between 70 per cent and 80 per cent. The annual cost of supplying rehabilitative programmes and reintegrative services within prisons and probation, which in addition to the above includes whanau liaison services, reintegration services, specialised treatment for Maori, specialised treatment in sex and violent offender units, community residential centres, psychological services, youth offending programmes and chaplaincy services, is about $45 million. The bulk is spent in prisons, and yet we have seen that approximately 86 per cent of inmates reoffend within five years of release. The reasons for this will be explored in chapter 14.

Home Leave

Although not a programme in itself, an important privilege, designed to reduce the deleterious effects of incarceration, is home leave. Under the Criminal Justice Act 1954 provision was made for temporary release for special purposes, which became utilised from 1965 in the form of home leave. The purpose of home leave is to allow certain low-security prisoners time with their families and/or friends in order to maintain linkages with the community. In the case of married persons (to which the scheme was originally restricted), home leave also helps to preserve family bonds. Since 1975 home leave has been generally available to minimum-security prisoners for 72 hours plus travelling time, every two months and thus it remains today. Apart from its usefulness in assisting reintegration, the availability of home leave and the fact that it can be forfeited for misconduct, is a powerful incentive for good behaviour.

Disturbances

Departmental rhetoric notwithstanding, the primary function of a prison management team is not, and never has been, the rehabilitation of inmates. Rehabilitation programmes cannot operate effectively unless the institutional environment is right. So the first obligation of prison government is maintaining order among a difficult population of men and women who are confined against their will, and who generally see their interests to be in opposition to the governors. More than anything else, the job of a prison management team involves ensuring that the safety and wellbeing of prisoners and staff are not compromised, that inmates do not escape, and that good order and discipline are maintained. In a well-run prison the incidence of escapes, suicides, assaults and other disturbances is low. Conversely, badly managed and/or badly designed prisons are generally marked by high levels of violence, disorder, escapes and suicides.

Suicides

Inmate suicides have been a problem for the department over a number of years, particularly at Paremoremo maxi in the 1980s. A look at national prison suicide rates since 1980 fails to reveal any consistent pattern, except that they appear to have escalated from 1984 onward, peaking in 1985. The fact that they have been low and stable since 1996 may be taken as a mark of good management.

Internationally, New Zealand's suicide rate is lower than Australia and Scotland, and is similar to England and Wales, and Canada.[28] Prisons generally contain a disproportionately high number of psychologically disturbed inmates who are prone to psychiatric episodes, self-mutilation and suicide. The 1987 prison census, which looked at inmates' socio-biographical profiles, found that 15 per cent of males and 25 per cent of females had been admitted for psychiatric treatment at some point in their lives.[29] A decade later, a representative study of psychiatric morbidity in prisons found the incidence of mental disorder – such as schizophrenia, bipolar disorder, major depression, obsessive-compulsive disorder and post-traumatic stress disorder – was significantly higher than in the rest of the community. Moreover, at least 60 per cent of inmates surveyed had at least one major personality disorder.[30] Suicidal tendencies can be aggravated or mitigated by the institutional environment as well as by detection and treatment strategies.[31] Management of the suicidal is thus a critical component of reducing suicide risks.

Escapes

In New Zealand there is a long series of data relating to prison escapes, extending back as far as 1946. Unlike suicides there are a number of trends discernible in escapes, although explaining the trends is difficult. As can be seen from the graph on page 94, escape rates were high during the early 1950s, fell during the late 1950s and 1960s, rose again during the 1970s, reaching a high point in 1972, but began to fall once more from the mid-1980s to a nadir in 1994. They then rose slightly, but since 2000, escapes have occurred at a very low rate – another mark of good management.

Comparing escape rates internationally makes little sense, because the majority of New Zealand escapes are 'walkaways' and 'non-returns' which typically involve inmates absconding from open work parties or sports teams, or failing to return from temporary parole. In New Zealand, approximately 45 per cent of all inmates are held in minimum security, where they may have access to home leave, unsupervised recreation and labour, and sport with outside teams. Thus they have ample opportunity to abscond. Part of escape-risk minimisation in these circumstances involves accurate security classification procedures, and the effective detection and handling of inmates during personal crisis periods when escape risk is heightened. Breakout escapes do provide opportunity for meaningful international comparison, however, and since new security measures such as razor wire were installed in prisons the late 1990s, New Zealand's breakout rate has been small relative to Canada, comparable with Australia, but still slightly higher than England and Wales, and Scotland.[32]

Perhaps surprisingly, the majority of escapes in New Zealand do not occur because an inmate wishes to avoid a prison sentence. As an island nation New Zealand is without contiguous international borders and few inmates possess the knowledge, resources, ability, or even the will, to leave these shores forever and never return. A study of prison escapes conducted in the mid-1990s found that the great majority of escapees expect to get caught and know they will receive extra time for their trouble. Yet still they choose to abscond. Most escapees interviewed in the survey cited either internal prison pressures (such as bullying) or external pressures (such as family problems) as their main reasons for escaping. A small number escaped simply because it seemed like a good idea at the time.[33] Apart from classification and security, therefore, a major element of escape risk reduction is individualised inmate management, that is: identifying prisoners who may attempt to escape and dealing with their problems in a way that reduces the impulse to do so.

Inmate telephone facilities may reduce tensions associated with suicides and escapes.

Assaults

By their very nature prisons are prone to violence, which can take a number of manifestations. Violence by inmates upon others is relatively common, but, of course, due to the inmate code of silence,[34] inmate–inmate assaults are seldom reported. We may guess, however, from the spate of prison homicides and from the dramatic increases in the population undergoing protective segregation since the 1980s, that serious prison violence has probably increased significantly in the last 25 years. According to Corrections data, however, the rate of reported serious inmate–inmate assaults has dropped sharply since 2000, from an average of 1.7 serious assaults (requiring hospitalisation or ongoing medical treatment) per hundred in 1998 and

1999, to an average of .34 since 2000. The exact reasons for the sudden drop are unclear, but, like escapes and suicides, probably have to do with better management practices introduced as a part of IOMS.

Due to definitional differences international comparisons are difficult, but New Zealand's serious assault rate appears to be low compared to Australia, and on a par with Canada.[35] Interestingly, however, and in contrast to the United States where prison rape is a serious problem,[36] rape is little known in New Zealand prisons. During five years of incarceration in the 1970s this author heard of only two instances of rape and a study published by Winfree, Newbold and Tubb in 2002 confirmed that this is still the case. The reasons for the trans-Atlantic difference have never been systematically analysed but may have to do with shorter sentences, smaller prisons, a less oppressive penal environment, high numbers in minimum security with access to home leave, and a general ethic of egalitarianism that prevails in New Zealand generally, as well as in its penal establishments.

Assaults on staff are more frequently reported than those on inmates. Like inmate assaults, serious assaults on staff, where hospitalisation or ongoing medical treatment is required, fell sharply after 2000.[37] Once more, the reasons for the sudden drop are unknown, although there have been significant crack-downs on prison security since 1998. Again due to inconsistencies with definition international comparisons are difficult, but before 2001 New Zealand had a very high serious-assault rate on staff relative to Canada and Scotland and after 2000 its assault rate was lower than Scotland's but still higher than Canada's. Assaults on staff are treated extremely seriously by prison authorities and injurious assaults almost invariably result in police action and the laying of criminal charges in an outside court.

Mutinies

The ultimate signal of administrative failure in prison is the mutiny. Mutinies can take the form of passive strikes, but of greater concern is the riot, sometimes accompanied by the taking of hostages. There is a wide literature on the causes of mutinies and riots and a brief review only is provided here. Prison riots have existed for almost as long as prisons,[38] but the first real attempt to analyse their causes occurred after the epidemic of disturbances that spread across the United States between 1951 and 1953. In 1953, the American Prison Association's Committee on Riots issued a pamphlet that identified the basic causes of riots as:

1. Lack of financial support and official and public indifference

2. Substandard personnel

3. Enforced idleness

4. Lack of professional leadership and professional programmes

5. Excessive size of prison populations and overcrowding

6. Political domination of management

7. Unwise sentencing and parole practices.[39]

A mass of literature has been published since which reinforces the above findings, but adds other factors such as low budgets, unqualified personnel in positions of authority, poor segregation practices, changes in administrative procedure, a worsening of prison conditions, inconsistency and favouritism in the treatment of inmates, destruction of the inmate elite privilege system, a breakdown in administrative control and routine, and lapses in security procedures.[40]

New Zealand has been relatively free of riots, but there have been some notable exceptions in the past 40 years which display many of the characteristics identified in the American literature. The Mt Eden prison riot of 1965, discussed in chapter 3, was the most destructive prison disturbance in New Zealand's history and resulted in the temporary decommissioning of that institution. Here, lax security procedures, archaic design, low staff morale, overcrowding, a breakdown in the prisoner elite privilege system, and oppressive management practices, all contributed to the explosive violence that erupted. Some of these same factors – low staff morale and oppressive management – were also present at Paremoremo prison between 1969 and 1972, when riots, strikes, assaults, floods and fires were almost daily occurrences. Trouble at Paremoremo did not cease until after the original superintendent was replaced in 1972 and a new, firm but liberal, management philosophy was installed.

Since that time there has been a major riot at Addington prison in 1988, sparked over the searching of female visitors for drugs; however, substandard accommodation and generally poor living conditions created the tensions that underlay the outburst. At Paparua prison in October 1997, four lifers took six officers hostage for 26 hours in protest at the murder conviction of their leader, Rex Haig. Here it was intransigence of judicial authorities over a perceived injustice, rather than prison administration itself which appear to have been at fault, although questions were later raised about security procedures at the institution resulting in a major security upgrade in 1998 and 1999. The formation in 1999 of the fated Emergency Response Unit at the prison may have been a partial reaction to the hostage crisis, and would almost certainly have caused a riot itself had its aggressive activities been allowed to continue.

Conclusion

New Zealand has had a liberal tradition in its prison system and for an inmate the experience of imprisonment is somewhat more benign than in, for example, the United States and Australia. Prisons in New Zealand tend to be small or, if not, are divided into small administrative units, sentences are relatively short (but increasing), multiple cell accommodation is minimal, and there are no dormitories. Nearly half of all inmates live in open, minimum-security conditions and are thus eligible to apply for 72 hours home leave every two months. A variety of programmes and employment options are offered. Suicide rates have fallen, and in recent years so has the rate of escape and serious assaults on staff and other inmates. Riots are infrequent, homosexual rape is rare and prisons seldom have a stable and recognised inmate hierarchy.

Nonetheless, New Zealand still faces many of the problems that beset penal settings in other parts of the Western world. Due to financial constraints, the actual provision of programmes is less than optimal and the potential for training in meaningful occupation areas is slim. A third of inmates are unemployed and a large proportion of those listed as employed are under-employed. These difficulties have been aggravated in recent years by budgetary constraints, burgeoning prison numbers and by a renewed emphasis on security since the late 1980s. Increases in inmates requesting protective segregation and a number of prison murders since the 1980s suggest that for many, life in prison can be difficult and dangerous. Finally, in spite of what is done in prisons to provide for the rehabilitation of prisoners, recidivist rates are high and have shown no trending downwards in recent years.

Notes

1 Harpham, 2004: 19.
2 *R v Pauga* (1992) 3 NZLR 241.
3 Cited in Newbold, 1986: 49.
4 AJHR E.61, 2006: 39.
5 Department of Corrections, 1995; Nathan, Wilson and Hillman, 2003.
6 *Corrections News*, June 2002: 9; Nathan, Wilson and Hillman, 2003: 9.
7 Stone, 2005.
8 *Corrections News*, August 2004: 6–7.
9 NZ Law Commission, 2006: 53–54.
10 Ministry of Justice, 1995.
11 Spier, 2002: 107–109.
12 Harpham, 2004: 56.
13 Spier, 2002: 76.
14 NZ Law Commission, 2006: 52.
15 Harpham, 2004: 19.
16 Lash and Luketina, 1990: 21.
17 Howard League, 2000.
18 Department of Justice, 1975: 39.
19 Harpham 2004: 23.
20 Department of Justice, 1988: 98.
21 Southey, Spier and Edgar, 1995: 53.
22 AJHR E.61, 2004.
23 Harpham, 2004: 34.
24 Department of Corrections, 2001: 5.
25 Department of Justice, 1988: 339.
26 Harpham, 2004: 34.
27 Harpham, 2004: 35.
28 AJHR E.61, 2004: 48.
29 Braybrook and O'Neill, 1988: 158.
30 Simpson *et al.*, 1999: 31–51.
31 Committee of Inquiry into Procedures Used in Certain Psychiatric Hospitals, 1988.
32 AJHR E.61, 2004: 49.
33 McLellan, Saville-Smith and Newbold, 1996.
34 See Newbold, 1989; Sykes and Messinger, 1960.
35 AJHR E.61, 2004: 45.
36 Hogshire, 1999: 70; Ross and Richards, 2002: 85–86.
37 AJHR E.61, 2004: 46.
38 Fox, 1956: ch 1.
39 MacCormick, 1954: 23–24.
40 See, e.g., Colvin, 1982; DiIulio 1987; Fox, 1956, Hartung and Floch, 1956–57; Irwin, 1980; MacCormick, 1954; Martin, 1954; Schrag, 1960; Sykes, 1956; Useem, 1985; Useem and Kimball, 1991.

References

Braybrook, Beverley and O'Neill, Rose (1988). *A Census of Prison Inmates*. Wellington: Department of Justice.

Colvin, Mark (1982) 'The 1980 New Mexico Prison Riot'. *Social Problems*, v.29(5): 449–463.

Committee of Inquiry into Procedures at Oakley Hospital and Related Matters (1983) *Report*. Wellington: Government Printer.

Committee of Inquiry into Procedures Used in Certain Psychiatric Hospitals in relation to Admission, Discharge or Release on Leave of Certain Classes of Patients (1988) *Psychiatric Report*. Wellington: Government Printer.

Department of Corrections (1995) *Kia Marama: A Description of the Treatment Programme*. Wellington: Department of Corrections.

Department of Corrections (2001) *Inmate Employment Policy*. Wellington: Department of Corrections.

Department of Justice (1975) *Justice Department Penal Census 1972*. Wellington: Department of Justice.

Department of Justice (1988) *Prisons in Change: The Submission of the Department of Justice to the Ministerial Committee of Inquiry into the Prisons System*. Wellington: Department of Justice.

DiIulio, John (1987) *Governing Prisons: A Comparative Study of Correctional Management*. New York: Free Press.

Fox, Vernon (1956) *Violence Behind Bars*. New York: Vantage.

Harpham, David (2004) *Census of Prison Inmates and Home Detainees*. Wellington: Department of Corrections.

Hartung, Frank and Floch, Maurice (1956–57) 'A Social–Psychological Analysis of Prison Riots: An Hypothesis'. *Journal of Criminal Law, Criminology and Police Science*, v.47: 51–57.

Hogshire, Jim (1999) *You Are Going to Prison*. Port Townsend, WA: Breakout Productions.

Howard League for Penal Reform (2000) 'Remand on Bail and Remand in Custody'. *Fact Sheet 14*, November 2000.

Irwin, John (1980) *Prisons in Turmoil*. Boston: Little, Brown.

Lash, Barbara and Luketina, Francis (1990) *Offending While on Bail*. Wellington: Department of Justice.

Martin, John Bartlow (1954) *Break Down the Walls: American Prisons: Present, Past and Future*. New York: Ballantine.

MacCormick, Austin (1954) 'Behind the Prison Riots'. *Annals of the American Academy of Political and Social Science*, v.293: 17–27.

McLellan, Velma; Saville-Smith, Kay and Newbold, Greg (1996) *Escape Pressures: Inside Views of the Reasons for Prison Escapes*. Wellington: Ministry of Justice.

Ministry of Justice (1995) *Restorative Justice: A Discussion Paper*. Wellington: Ministry of Justice.

Nathan, Lavinia; Wilson, Nick and Hillman, David (2003) *Te Whakakotahitanga: An Evaluation of the Te Piriti Special Treatment Programme for Child Sex Offenders in New Zealand*. Wellington: Department of Corrections.

New Zealand Law Commission (2006) *Reforms to the Sentencing and Parole Stucture: Consultation Draft* (unpublished).

Newbold, Greg (1986) *The Maximum Security Prison in New Zealand*. Unpublished PhD thesis, Sociology Department, Auckland University.

Newbold, Greg (1989) 'Criminal Subcultures in New Zealand'. In D.Novitz and B.Willmott (eds), *Culture and Identity in New Zealand*. Wellington: GP Books.

Report of the Committee of Inquiry into Procedures used in Certain Psychiatric Hospitals in relation to Admission, Discharge or Release on Leave of Certain Classes of Patients (1988) Chair: Kenneth Morgan DCJ. Wellington: Government Printer.

Ross, Jeffrey and Richards, Stephen (2002) *Behind Bars: Surviving Prison*. Indianapolis, IN: Alpha Books.

Schrag, Clarence (1960) 'The Sociology of Prison Riots'. *Proceedings of the American Correctional Association*, v.90: 136–145.

Simpson, A., Brinded, P., Laidlaw, T., Fairley, N., and Malcolm, F. (1999) *The National Study of Psychiatric Morbidity in New Zealand Prisons*. Wellington: Department of Corrections.

Southey, Pamela; Spier, Philip and Edgar, Nicolette (1995) *Census of Prison Inmates 1993*. Wellington: Department of Justice.

Spier, Philip (2002) *Conviction and Sentencing of Offenders in New Zealand 1992–2001*. Wellington: Ministry of Justice.

Stone, Geoff (2005) *New Media Evaluation: Improving Practice and Organisational Culture in the Department of Corrections*. MA (Applied) thesis in Social Science Research, Victoria University of Wellington.

Sykes, Gresham (1956) *The Society of Captives: A Study of a Maximum Security Prison*. New York: Atheneum.

Sykes, Gresham and Messinger, Sheldon (1960) 'The Inmate Social System'. In Richard Cloward *et al., Theoretical Studies in Social Organization of the Prison*. New York: Social Science Research Council.

Useem, Bert (1985) 'Disorganization and the New Mexico Prison Riot of 1980'. *American Sociological Review* v.50 (Oct): 677–688.

Useem, Bert and Kimball, Peter (1991) *States of Siege: US Prison Riots 1971–1986*. New York: Oxford University Press.

Winfree, Tom; Newbold, Greg and Tubb, Houston (2002) 'Prisoner Perspectives on Inmate Culture in New Mexico and New Zealand: A Descriptive Case Study'. *The Prison Journal*, v.82(1): 213–233.

CHAPTER 8
THE MAXIMUM-SECURITY PRISON

For most of the 19th century, when prisons were designed primarily for punitive purposes, there was little differentiation between them. In America this began to change with the introduction of the reformatory system in 1876. In New Zealand prison administration was haphazard and largely provincial until Hume took over in 1880.

Developing a Prison Classification System

Under the Prisons Act 1882 the penal system was centralised, and one of Hume's early moves was to call for the classification of prisoners to allow for differential forms of treatment. Hume thought it essential to separate penal servitude and long-term hard labour inmates from the others, and in 1883 he had prisons divided into two classes: first-class prisons (at Auckland, Wellington, Lyttelton and Dunedin), which were for penal servitude and hard labour inmates serving more than a year, and second-class prisons (at New Plymouth, Napier, Wanganui, Nelson, Addington, Timaru, Hokitika, Invercargill and Westport), for less serious offenders.[1]

Overcrowding prevented Hume's method ever being put fully into operation, and the work camps he established from 1901 effectively created a third class of prison. These work camps were designed for the employment of low-risk prisoners who could be trusted with extra freedoms, and were thus distinguished from the rank and file. Initially the camps were designed for first-time offenders, but due to the demand for labour, they were later extended to other categories of low-risk prisoner. In 1909 he retired and the Minister of Justice, John Findlay, became the main voice in penal reform. His primary objective was to refine the classification of prisoners. Findlay proposed five categories of inmate: corrigible, incorrigible, criminally insane, sexual, and alcoholic, and he designated New Plymouth for sexual criminals and Invercargill for young offenders. With the introduction of reformative detention in 1910, further distinction was necessary and Waikeria was decided upon as the nation's first reformatory, although this did not last long either.

Findlay's problem was that most of the inmates (about 700), apart from the tree-planting camps which held about 70 low-risk prisoners, were contained in relatively undifferentiated central prisons in Auckland, Dunedin, Hokitika, Invercargill, Lyttelton, Napier, New Plymouth, Wanganui and Wellington.[2] When Findlay lost his seat in 1911, his role was taken over by Inspector of Prisons Charles Matthews. Matthews continued as Findlay had started, and in 1917 classified prisons as:[3]

- Auckland: long-term and dangerous prisoners
- New Plymouth: sex 'perverts'

- Rotoaira: military defaulters
- Kaingaroa: military defaulters, first offenders and reformables
- Waikeria: reformative detainees and reformables
- Wellington: short-termers and receptions
- Napier: short-termers
- Paparua: South Island inmates
- Dunedin: short-termers
- Invercargill: borstal (youth reformatory).

So, from 1917, the year its construction was completed, Mt Eden became New Zealand's chief, safest and strongest penal institution. Although the term 'maximum security' was not routinely used until the 1950s, Mt Eden was effectively a maximum-security prison from 1917. Other institutions had maximum-security facilities, and Wellington continued to carry out executions until 1935. After capital punishment was reintroduced in 1950, all hangings took place at Mt Eden.

The country's first maximum-security prison was built according to a radial model popularised at Eastern Penitentiary, Philadelphia, and copied in England with Pentonville prison which opened in 1842. When the decision was made to build a

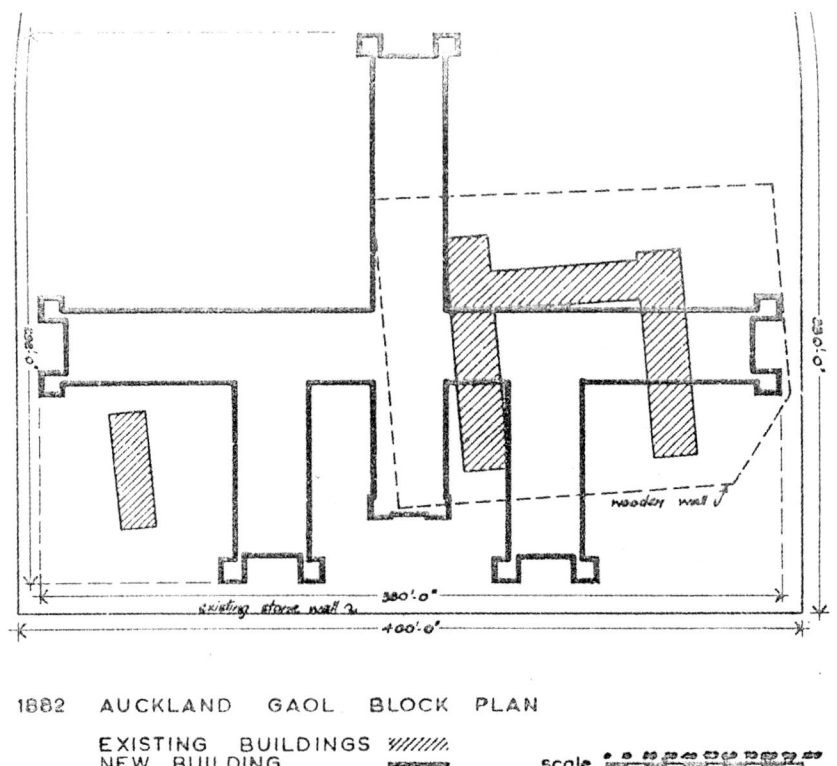

Original site plan for Mt Eden prison, designed by Pierre Finch Martineau Burrows in 1882. The existing 'Stockade' buildings are shaded.

new prison for New Zealand in 1882, the plans came from England and the prison – known originally as Auckland prison but commonly referred to as Mt Eden – served as the country's only maximum-custody institution until it was wrecked in a riot in 1965.

The history of the maximum-security prison before 1965 is covered in my book *Punishment and Politics*[4] and will not be repeated here. This chapter briefly traverses the history of Mt Eden's replacement, Paremoremo, and shows how and why administrative philosophies at this institution have changed so dramatically and uniquely during the 36 years of its existence.

Paremoremo prison was built to an American model, most particularly the highly secure United States Penitentiary (USP) at Marion, Illinois. Although once a showpiece of liberal experimentation, Paremoremo has recently followed certain United States trends and reduced its offerings to little more than secure custody. Before considering Paremoremo therefore, it is useful to look briefly at its sister institution, USP Marion.

USP Marion

In 1963, the year the federal penitentiary on the island of Alcatraz in San Francisco Bay closed, a Federal prison camp was established a few miles out of Marion, a small rural town in southern Illinois. In January the following year a penitentiary was opened on an adjacent site. A maximum-security institution, USP Marion was built originally to contain just 350 men and is currently the smallest penitentiary in the US federal system. Erected during a reformative era in American corrections,[5] Marion was an experimental facility that attempted to modify behaviour by offering three levels of security, with the lower grades offering greater privileges. The 1973 Marion rulebook itemises a range of facilities, programmes and activities for residents, indicating a high level of concern for their rehabilitation and welfare.

In its early years Marion catered mainly for young prisoners, but by the beginning of the 1970s a number of older convicts, some of them former Alcatraz men, had begun to accumulate in the prison. Many were violent, intractable convicts, and in 1973 the Federal Bureau of Prisons (FBP) decided to open a special control unit at Marion to contain the worst of them. Violence, race and gang wars, and assaults on staff became increasing problems throughout American prisons in the 1970s, however,[6] and in 1979 the FBP created a new security level above the five already in place, to cater for the very worst criminals in the federal system. Marion was chosen to be the nation's only Level 6 penitentiary, and its population and programme began to change dramatically.

Concentrating the most dangerous and unmanageable criminals in one institution caused numerous difficulties. Inmates still had work and association privileges within their units, but violence and serious misconduct became a chronic problem. Between February 1980 and June 1983 there were 14 escape attempts, 28 serious assaults on staff, 54 serious prisoner-on-prisoner assaults and eight prisoners killed at Marion. In September another convict was killed and on 22 October 1983 two officers were stabbed to death in separate incidents. On 27 October a tenth prisoner was killed. The following day a state of emergency was declared and the institution was locked down.[7]

This lockdown regime has been maintained since October 1983. Men are kept in their cells for up to 23 hours a day and have virtually no privileges or programmes. When this author visited the institution in November 2002, six of the eight housing units operated under this routine. The exceptions were C ('Intermediate') and B ('Pre-Transfer') units, to which prisoners are sent before being relocated in less secure facilities.[8]

A New Maximum-Security Prison for New Zealand

Paremoremo prison began taking prisoners five years after Marion, on 13 March 1969, after almost a decade of planning. As early as 1960 the incoming Secretary for Justice, Dr John Robson, had been aware of the shortcomings of the 70-year-old institution at Mt Eden. Its plate-steel cell doors could be opened with simple home-made keys; the mild steel bars in the cell windows could be cut with serrated knives; and the high stone walls were easily scaled with a rope or ladder. As noted in chapter 3, there had been an embarrassing series of escapes in the late 1950s, and within a few months of Robson's appointment as Secretary for Justice in 1960, the department's building policy was reviewed and the erection of a new maximum-security prison became a top priority.

Planning and Delays

By June 1961 the prioritising of the new prison was official and a site at Paremoremo, 30km north of Auckland, was purchased in 1963. In the meantime research had started on the prison's design. A number of overseas institutions were looked at, including the maximum-security facilities under construction at Blundeston in Suffolk, England and at Marion, Illinois. Both opened in 1963 and that year they, as well as another that was nearing completion at Kumla, Sweden, were visited by the government architect. The plans for all three were studied, but not until March 1964 were sketches for a five-block, 244-cell New Zealand institution complete.

The drawings for Paremoremo incorporated some of the features of the English and Swedish prisons. But the structure that had easily the greatest influence was USP Marion. The design of the sentry towers, the centralised control area, the cellblock layout and the 'telegraph pole' plan of the overall structure were unmistakeably from Marion. The gymnasium, too, was modelled on Marion's. From the air, in fact, Paremoremo looks like a miniature version of Marion.

Physical security was North American in origin. The remote door-locking mechanisms were made in Joliet, Illinois, and the tool-proof manganese steel grilles were freighted from Canada. The major departure from American policy related to firearms. The perimeter of Marion is secured by armed personnel; however the New Zealand Justice department insisted that sentries should not be armed. At Paremoremo inmates would be kept inside most of the time, and playing fields were excluded from its design. The only time prisoners would be outside would be in the small, high-walled, concrete exercise yards adjacent to each of the cellblocks. This would markedly reduce the risk of escape. Robson and his minister Ralph Hanan, both passionate opponents of capital punishment, believed that escapees should not be shot at unless they were posing a direct threat to human life.

The original estimated cost of the project was £1 million ($2 million) and this proved a sticking point. Within government and Treasury, opposition to what was seen by some as an extravagant use of funds held up progress and at times, although it was never officially admitted, the project was almost cancelled.

Mt Eden in Crisis

However, ongoing crisis at Mt Eden kept the project alive. In 1960, with over 400 men at Mt Eden, there were more prisoners in maximum security than at any other point in New Zealand's history. This created enormous pressure on the old jail, which had been designed for no more than 320. Related to this pressure, in the early 1960s, there were some embarrassing escapes as well as several disturbances where convicts and staff viciously assaulted one another.

As a result of ongoing troubles the superintendent Horace (Horry) Haywood, who had run the jail since 1951, was transferred in 1963. His replacement was Eddie Buckley, a hard, old-school authoritarian, who governed Mt Eden on a regime of strict discipline. Highly unpopular with both prisoners and staff, Buckley proved unable to prevent further disturbances. Assaults, arsons and strikes continued. Early in 1965 three inmates armed with a sawn-off shotgun took an officer hostage and escaped. Although they were soon found and apprehended, the hostage incident, which occurred in the most secure section of what was supposed to be the tightest prison in the land, intensified pressure to get a replacement as soon as possible.

By this time Paremoremo prison, which Hanan had hoped would be finished by the end of 1966, was far behind schedule. Earthworks had still not commenced and working drawings were incomplete. Even at this point, in spite of all that had happened at Mt Eden, there were moves afoot in parliament to have Paremoremo postponed indefinitely.

In the winter of 1965 these deferment moves came to a sudden halt with the Mt Eden riot. Inmates took over the institution and set it alight. It was three days before the rioters surrendered and Mt Eden prison, now a blackened shell, was temporarily uninhabitable.[9]

Waikeria

The Mt Eden riot of 1965 was the most serious prison insurrection in New Zealand's history, and from that point the jail ceased to function as a maximum-security facility. Building Paremoremo became an immediate priority. Mt Eden's residents were

East Wing, Waikeria Borstal.

shipped to other prisons and the most dangerous 89 were transferred to a hastily adapted secure unit in the East Wing of Waikeria borstal, 130km to the south.

For the next three-and-a-half years, the high-security men remained at Waikeria while the new prison was constructed. Knowing what happened in the East Wing is critical to understanding the culture the men took with them to Paremoremo in 1969. To begin with, no work was available, the cells had no radios and there was almost no recreation. Conditions were especially bad for the riot leaders, who were kept in an area known as the 'top twelve'. Cells here had no furniture. Inmates slept on mattresses on the floor and read sitting on the toilet. Most of the time they were locked up alone and when, after several weeks, they were allowed an hour's exercise, it was in wire cages that admitted little sunlight. Elsewhere in the wing prisoners had furniture and were eventually allowed radios, but by any standards conditions were extremely austere. After the riot, relationships with staff were tense and disobedience was dealt with harshly and often summarily. Of the environment when the first receptions arrived, officer Ross Hannah said:

> Naturally, they didn't get any exercise. I remember when we put them in there we said, "That's it!" and they shut up, mate. I think even the guys that had done a while were a bit frightened. They were a bit upset. They didn't know what was coming next. Because there was no compassion shown to them in any shape or form. If they stepped out of line, they were in for it. And that's how it worked.[10]

As an example, when one convict tried to escape he was batoned to the ground by staff and then sat upon while a doctor stitched a cut to his head. No anaesthetic was used.[11]

By the time Paremoremo began taking prisoners in March 1969 there were only 50 men left at Waikeria, and they had endured such conditions for nearly four years. They had become a small compact group united by their shared misery and intensifying hatred of 'screws'. Whereas at Mt Eden staff and prisoners had interacted in an often casual and friendly way, now a sharp line divided the keepers from the kept. A powerful ethic of anti-authoritarian solidarity had grown, and alongside it developed an almost ritualistic commitment to the prisoners' social code. A convict brotherhood kept internecine conflict to a minimum. The officers felt the new attitude too. Of working conditions in the East Wing, an old Irish screw called Ted Molloy said:

> Oh Jesus, tough down there, boy. That was really crucial, that one was. That was about as tough a situation as I've ever handled anywhere. The tension. The tension between inmates and staff. You know, there were chaps down there that I knew, that I used to talk freely to and that, and it was as if I didn't know them. I couldn't break them. Couldn't break them. … Well you never knew what was going to bloody happen there from one minute to another, you don't know. Never knew what the bloody hell was going on.[12]

When the escorts to Paremoremo began, the prisoners took this culture up north with them.[13]

Paremoremo's Early Years

Like Marion, Paremoremo was constructed during a decade of progressiveness in corrections, which had begun in New Zealand in 1960. Secretary for Justice John

Robson and his minister Ralph Hanan were both avid reformists, dedicated to the provision of humane, salutary care to prisoners irrespective of their security level. They hoped to apply these principles at Paremoremo, but the man chosen as superintendent was Eddie Buckley, the unpopular officer from Mt Eden, who resolved to run the new prison with the same authoritarian method he had used at Mt Eden. Prisoners were to have few privileges unless they had been earned, and security and discipline would be tight. Hanan and Robson were both concerned about this, and Buckley was given clear written instructions to relax discipline and introduce reformative programmes. But Buckley was a man of narrow vision and low self-confidence, who felt more comfortable in the coat of the autocrat. The nature of the prisoners and the thought of losing another prison scared him, and he proved largely unable to adjust to his bosses' requirements.

The first escort to arrive contained 20 'intractables' from Waikeria who were moved straight into segregation in D Block. Here they got no privileges and, as at Waikeria, were locked in single cells for most of the day. However, like Marion, Paremoremo's cells had barred frontages, allowing convicts to communicate and weakening the ability to segregate. D Block men were thus able to transmit their gripes to one another, and it was here that the first trouble started.

The D Block men had arrived expecting to be mixed with the general population. Their designation as 'intractable' had been made arbitrarily, anonymously and without explanation. In fact, initially they were not even told of their special status, and when they found out, their sense of injustice was acute. Such a policy was a recipe for trouble and it began in D Block almost immediately. There were violent demonstrations, which staff attempted to suppress with tight discipline. Prisoners, unified by the contempt for authority that had been seeded at Waikeria, reacted violently. Assaults, strikes, fires and cell flood-outs became commonplace. Convicts began baiting duty staff, who retaliated with charge-sheets and solitary confinement. The first serious incident occurred in November 1969 when Dempsey Roberts and a powerful Samoan called Atenai Saifiti were ordered not to speak to other prisoners while sweeping a corridor. When the pair ignored the order the officer called reinforcements. As soon as the reinforcements stepped out of the sally port Roberts and Saifiti attacked, injuring two of them. The staff retreated and the rebels barricaded themselves behind a grille. They smashed two security cameras and fought off further reinforcements with a fire hose before finally being subdued. Although the pair received three-year extensions of their sentences for this incident, from that point on, staff in D Block were assaulted with increasing regularity.

In the 'open' blocks (A, B, and C), conditions were better than in D Block, but not by much. The prison was in fact not completely finished, the workshops were inoperative and prisoners were inactive for most of the day. There was no education officer and nobody to organise the programmes that head office had ordered. Trouble began almost as soon as the prison opened, and by the beginning of 1970, the situation was becoming critical. In its first six months, with the 244-bed prison still more than half empty, there were 10 serious assaults on staff. In the 10 months following, 15 more serious incidents were recorded. There were minor attacks as well – in fact Buckley's former deputy later reported it was not uncommon for two or three staff to be assaulted in a day.[14] Attacks might occur on provocations as minor as being told

Eddie Buckley, Superintendent Mt Eden prison 1963–1968; Paremoremo prison 1968–1972.

to tuck their shirts in or delays in the delivery of mail. Institutional equipment, such as telephones, windows, clocks, lights and cameras, was smashed regularly and fires were common.

Staff responded with counter-assaults and charges resulting in solitary confinement or loss of remission. They also needled prisoners, serving meals cold, putting pubic hairs in their food or supplying broken plastic cutlery to eat with. They withheld mail and read out sensitive sections from incoming letters over the p.a. system. Grievance procedures were ineffective. Requests to see the superintendent went unanswered; letters to the Secretary for Justice were often never posted. Communication between prisoners and staff virtually ceased and Buckley was losing control. Lifer Stan Rangi commented:

Things were getting worse by this stage. They were getting fucking worse with the screws. There was no communication whatsoever by them. You could not communicate with fucking screws and they would not communicate with you, other than to tell you what to do.[15]

Convicts gave up using official complaints channels and resorted to their own devices. One evening after lockup in July 1970, for example, Dempsey Roberts asked an officer called Smith to pass a package of bread down to his friend Stan Rangi. Smith threw the bread into the rubbish and Roberts screamed that next time he saw him he would "Punch [Smith's] fucking lights out". Two weeks later, when Smith was standing by the D Block sally port, Roberts bashed him to the ground and kicked him until he was unconscious. An officer called Downs tried to intervene, but was knocked over by another inmate called Tamarua. Roberts, Tamarua and later Atenai Saifiti were charged in an outside court. Smith had been hospitalised, and Roberts received an extra eight months' imprisonment after a guilty plea. Tamarua and Saifiti, who pleaded not guilty, got two years each.

Saifiti was, in fact, innocent and following his conviction on 11 October, prisoners decided to retaliate. Five staff were attacked, one of whom was badly injured. The other four were taken hostage. They were tied up and beaten, and threatened with death unless Saifiti got a new trial. After a six-hour siege the prisoners were promised an inquiry and no repercussions, provided they released their captives. The rioters finally agreed and returned to their cells. However, the leaders were charged and sentenced to extra time.

Cell landing, D Block.

Exercise Yard, A Block, Paremoremo prison.

Following the hostage incident, with the threat of a staff strike, security in D Block tightened considerably. Extra grilles were installed. Convicts were escorted three-on-one when leaving their cells and were exercised irregularly and infrequently. Hobbies and other privileges were curtailed. All this simply hardened resolve and intensified the hatred that was boiling between them and the staff. "The minute you walk through the D Block sally port you feel it because there's no outlets for your tensions and frustrations, they build up until they finally explode", Wickliffe said. "We take it out on those nearest to us, ourselves or the screws."[16] Under these conditions nobody was safe. In 1971 Saifiti badly injured a popular officer called Savage, for nothing more than being late unlocking Saifiti to exchange his books. Of this, Stan Rangi said:

> Savage was a good guy, boy. He's a *fucking* good screw. But even though you know a screw's a good fucking screw, you couldn't sorta favour him, because he represented the screws and *that* was *it*, man. After they started putting in these double doors and all that, you know, you had to suppress your own thing and look at it from the guys' point of view and fuck your own. So even though some of us thought Sai was a bit out of hand breaking his jaw, you still had to back him up.[17]

Men developed a fatalism that made them careless of penalties. Roberts, for example, who had entered prison with 18 months, finished up with nearly nine years. Saifiti's original 21-month sentence increased to almost seven years as a result of accumulated assault charges. The attitude of prisoners was that in a sacrifice for the greater good their personal welfare was irrelevant.

This made them unpredictable and dangerous, and created deep tensions for

Central Control in Paremoremo prison, the jail's electronic 'nerve centre'.

Landing entrance in Paremoremo's D Block, showing remote door-locking mechanism.

front-line staff. Because Buckley offered little support, morale eroded further and large numbers resigned. Those who stayed often took their tensions home to their families, causing marriages to suffer. One career officer who lasted there until 1975 said that he would not work at Paremoremo again "for $2,000 a week".[18]

Inmates in the 1970s were of a different feather to those of previous decades. As noted in chapter 4, this was the era of radical protest and 'liberation consciousness', when young people were more politically active than ever before. A small number of self-styled 'revolutionary' activists were imprisoned in the early 1970s and these men encouraged prisoners to identify with a number of high-profile American prison counterparts. Thus did

Riot damage in D Block, Paremoremo, August 1971.

the prisoners easily adopt the mantle of oppressed martyrdom. Dean Wickliffe, an intelligent and articulate lifer sentenced to life for robbery-murder, became a political leader in this vein. "This was the era of Che Guevara and George Jackson and The Weathermen", he later wrote. "All over the world street riots and bloody revolts like that at Attica were occurring. And we in D Block were having our own little war with our jailers."[19]

From 1971, support from the reformist group, Project Paremoremo, enhanced the prisoners' sense of self-awareness. By visiting prisoners, these educated liberals apprised themselves of the situation at the new jail and campaigned the government for an investigation. Hanan had died just four months after the prison opened and Robson had retired at the beginning of 1970. The new minister, Dan Riddiford, had little interest in prison reform, but his secretary, Eric Missen, was, like Robson, an educated career public servant with a good feel for administration. Neither could ignore the pressure that was being brought and late in 1971, following a representation from Project Paremoremo to the Ombudsman and a work-to-rule by staff, Riddiford ordered the Ombudsman to conduct an inquiry into the prison.

Jack Hobson, Superintendent Mt Eden prison 1968–1972; Paremoremo prison 1972–1984.

The period during which the inquiry took place was punctuated by assaults, floods, strikes and fires, and although investigators found many of the prisoners' complaints groundless, a number of recommendations for improvement were made. Moreover, the committee believed that there was reason to doubt the soundness of Saifiti's conviction for the 1970 assault on officer Smith and in June 1972 Saifiti received a judicial pardon.

Conspicuously absent from the Ombudsman's report was any reference to the prison superintendent. This may have been politic, because by the time it was received on 21 January Buckley had gone. Head office was already well aware of Buckley's shortcomings and Missen said it was clear that Buckley had "lost his nerve"[20] and that many of the situations at Paremoremo could have been avoided by more effective action. Thus, on 7 February 1972, Jack Hobson took over as superintendent of New Zealand's toughest jail.[21]

Hobson Takes Over

Jack Hobson was a former WWII Royal Navy gunner who had migrated to New Zealand after the war. On arrival he joined the prison service and quickly rose through the ranks. Intelligent, strong-willed, compassionate and with a good understanding of men, his leadership potential was soon recognised. Hobson had taken over Mt Eden prison when it was recommissioned after the 1965 riot, and when Buckley was sidelined from Paremoremo he was the obvious successor.

Hobson brought a management style almost the opposite of Buckley's. Where Buckley had been aloof, nervous and unapproachable, locating his office outside the institution proper, Hobson was a confident, hands-on administrator. He moved his office to the centre of the prison and walked around frequently, talking to men informally and taking notes. He promised and gave direct, prompt access for interviews and requests. Moreover, instead of holding interviews once a week and requiring prisoners to stand to attention in a line in front of his desk, with two prison officers in attendance (as was protocol in other institutions), he often invited men to sit down and discuss a problem without anyone else present. He responded to requests promptly and gave clear reasons for any denial. Whereas Buckley's policy had been to give nothing unless it had been earned, Hobson believed in full privileges for all unless something warranted denial.

This included D Block, and within a few weeks all but three of D Block's prisoners had been transferred to the standard blocks. Some subsequently, returned but many never went back.

Hobson's Reforms

Hobson introduced a multitude of reforms. All cellblocks were given permanent managers, known as Divisional Officers (DOs), who

Paremoremo's boot shop.

were allowed a degree of freedom in running their units. Dressed in civilian clothing, they were often on first-name terms with their charges. Correspondence restrictions were lifted and prisoners were allowed to write and receive as many letters as they wished. Visiting hours were extended and some jewellery was permitted. Restrictions on reading material were stopped. Virtually any literature available on the outside was now allowed. Hobbies were encouraged and two full-time activities officers were appointed. In the cellblocks, special rooms were set aside for pastimes like basket weaving and wood carving. The

Paremoremo's A team winning the Auckand Debating Association Athenaeum Cup final in 1977. The author is seated far right.

workshops became fully commissioned and many prisoners were employed making furniture, clothing or mailbags. A Maori culture club was formed, weightlifting began in the gymnasium, and inmates from all standard blocks were allowed to socialise in the gym outside working hours. During recreation time movement was also allowed between cellblocks.

There was a deliberate policy of encouraging community participation. A debating club went on to compete successfully at an elite level in Auckland's annual competitions. Outside sports teams came regularly to play badminton or volleyball. Concert parties were invited in and voluntary education courses started. In the blocks inmates were allowed musical instruments, and to paint and decorate their cells as they wished. Goldfish, canaries and pot plants began to adorn prisoners' cells. In essence, there was a complete metamorphosis in administrative philosophy and living conditions at Paremoremo after Hobson arrived in February 1972.[22]

The Honeymoon Ends

Hobson's general plan was to give prisoners a stake in conformity by allowing them privileges that could be removed for misbehaviour. The idea eventually worked, but the effect was not immediate. To begin with, they tested the new superintendent's mettle. Some grew complacent about their privileges and pushed for more than even Hobson was prepared to give.

Many staff were resentful of what they saw as a mollycoddling of criminals. Some began quietly to sabotage Hobson by ignoring rule infractions and deliberately misapplying his directives. Discipline slipped. Convicts started refusing strip searches before visits, and alcohol and drugs began to appear. Conditions soon reached crisis point, and only five months after taking over Hobson faced his first test. For not only had he relaxed conditions in the standard blocks; D Block had been eased as well. The few men in this unit were permitted limited contact with the standard blocks – mixing in the visiting room and occasionally attending concerts. Thus they sometimes got

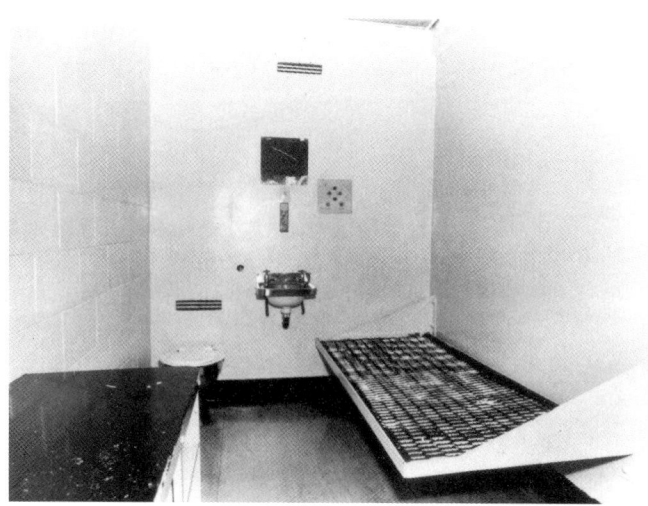

Stripped cell, Paremoremo prison.

access to alcohol illicitly brewed in the standard wings.

One Sunday in June 1972, following a confrontation between men from B and D blocks and the discovery of alcohol, Hobson cancelled permission for D Block to attend a concert in the gymnasium scheduled for later that day. Angered by the decision, six men armed with broom handles and chair legs refused to be locked up at lunchtime. They had been drinking, and Hobson decided to confront them head on. He waited for the strikers to sober up and asked them to surrender. They refused. At 6pm he sent the riot squad in, armed with shields and batons. The strikers resisted and were beaten badly and dragged, some unconscious, into their cells. They were then taken to the punishment cells, where – without Hobson's knowledge – some were beaten again. Hobson then ordered a two-day general lockup, during the course of which each man was searched and all cells stripped of non-standard equipment. Strike leaders were removed to D Block.

The 1972 baton charge marked a turning point in Hobson's administration. Realising his liberalisations had gone too far, he returned D Block to its previous status as an isolation unit for long-term disciplinary segregation.

For the rest of 1972, in spite of Hobson's decisive action in June, prisoners continued to challenge the boundaries. In the tailor shop they made non-regulation clothing, and one prisoner even crafted a pin-striped suit. When the sartorial attire was confiscated, the men retaliated by destroying standard prison uniforms. Finally, in November, Merv Rich, an intelligent desperado doing seven years for possessing explosives, escape, and kidnapping a Crown witness, was discovered attempting an audacious escape. Hobson immediately ordered another lockdown, and over three days the prison was systematically searched and the cells stripped. Several prisoners were beaten up, and 26 were removed to D Block. New rules were established, banning long hair and jewellery and limiting the contents of cells. Movement between cellblocks ended. From then on, standard block residents could mix only in the gym, visiting room, chapel and workshops.

Project Paremoremo was outraged by the November 1972 lockup and petitioned government for another inquiry. Paremoremo had seldom been out of the media since it opened, and there was growing support for the prisoners among Auckland's liberal and left-wing intellectuals. The convicts had never known such popularity, and being constantly in the limelight boosted their aspirations. Hobson knew this and commented, "Some of these chaps just play up to publicity such as this. They think they have an ally on the outside and away they go".[23]

In an attempt to stop what he saw was unwarranted interference, Hobson banned Project Paremoremo from the prison, doing his best to deny the inmates the attention they coveted. Thus, when three men barricaded themselves in the D Block recreation area in November 1973, Hobson just locked the grille and left them there without food or bedding. After 14 days, in the absence of publicity or fuss, they gave in.[24]

Tranquillity Returns

In the general election of November 1972 the National Government, which had been in power since 1960, was replaced in a Labour landslide. The new Minister of Justice, Dr Martyn Finlay, was a likeable, liberal-minded idealist with a PhD in law from the London School of Economics. Finlay had friends in the protest movement and as an avid reformist, was sympathetic to Project Paremoremo. Petitioned by the group as soon as he came to office, one of the first things he did was to order a second inquiry by the Ombudsman into the maximum-security prison.

Five times larger than its predecessor, the second Ombudsman's inquiry into Paremoremo supported the activities of groups such as Project Paremoremo. Disloyal officers earned a sharp rebuke and the regime of Superintendent Hobson received the committee's full support. Now, with Project Paremoremo still banned, unco-operative officers chastised, and rebellious prisoners moved to D Block, the jail at last became quiet.

The bulk of the men, having challenged Hobson twice and suffered as a result, now seemed content with what they had. As the threat to his regime subsided, Hobson once more relaxed controls and allowed more freedoms. The prison disappeared from newspaper headlines and Project Paremoremo dissolved. In the cells, extra furniture began to appear, fancy bedspreads returned and curtains were allowed across cell frontages. There was calm about the place, born of a *détente* between officers and inmates. Like old revolutionaries, veteran convicts taught new arrivals about the 'dark days' of Buckley; of how the struggles and sacrifices of the past had helped make the prison what it now was, and of the advantages of keeping the peace. Seasoned inmate agitators now actively discouraged and refused to become involved in further riotous activity. In this environment, prison programmes flourished and the quality of life improved.

There were isolated incidents. In July 1974 guards in the prison workshops were attacked by A Block residents in retaliation for the beatings of two drunk prisoners who had seriously assaulted staff the night before. But for the most part, problems now were of a different type. Before 1973 the targets of aggression had principally been staff; now increasingly convicts turned their violence on each other. In 1973 and 1974, for the first time, there were incidents of prisoners being hospitalised after assaults by

Decorated cell, Paremoremo prison.

others. In December 1975 the first serious racial conflict occurred when a Pakeha was almost stabbed to death by a Maori prisoner during a fight in the gymnasium. Staff were now seldom attacked. In 1971 a population of about 160 prisoners recorded 18 serious assaults on staff, compared with seven in 1976, even though the prison muster had risen to 200. Numbers stabilised at between five and 10 assaults a year through to 1984.[25] In 1985 Superintendent Syd Ward observed, "[Aggression] is not directed at staff, not in this prison anyway".[26]

Life at Paremoremo 1975–1978

For several years, apart from sporadic confrontations, trouble at the prison was rare. The most dramatic incident was in 1976 when Dean Wickliffe escaped from a D Block exercise yard. Recaptured after just 20 minutes, Wickliffe was the prison's first successful escapee.

Between 1975 and 1978 the jail was probably as peaceful as it has ever been. Programmes and freedoms were at their zenith. Among prisoners the old ethic of solidarity was strong and there was rigid adherence to the convict social code. Because of the divisive nature of gangs, a consensual rule prohibited the wearing of gang insignia or colours anywhere in the jail. "You're an inmate first, a gang member second," members were told. For the same reason, racism was seldom visible although pockets existed below the surface.

Prisoners were committed to the principle of egalitarianism, and there was resistance to the idea that any inmate should be privileged over any other. For this reason there was no observable hierarchy and although fights occurred, the bullying of the weak by the strong was rare. 'Tea leafing' (theft) from cells was actively condemned. In the standard cell blocks, officers and men got to know one another well. Here the approved protocol on both sides was formal politeness, without overt intimacy.

As long as things were running smoothly, block staff took a rather hands-off approach to governance. Apart from routine searches, they seldom interfered in convict business. In the mid-1970s a sort of *Gemeinschaft*[27] existed, and it was generally agreed that 'Parry' was 'a good jail to do a lag in'.

A New Breed

This situation was a direct legacy of past conflict in a prevailing atmosphere of tolerance and peace. As the old leaders were released or transferred, however, so early traditions expired. Like the United States, the idealism that had bonded prisoners in the early 1970s gave way to individualism, racial and gang factionalism and a corresponding rise in violence.[28] Although not obvious at the time, the gymnasium stabbing in December 1975 had been a sign of things to come.

In New Zealand in the early and mid-1970s there were sharp increases in reported crimes of serious violence such as homicide, robbery, serious assault and rape. These rises continued until the early 1990s, amid constant calls from the public for harsher penalties. Disproportionately represented in these rises were Maori and Pacific Islanders. Comprising about 15 per cent of the national population in 1985, Maori and Pacific Islanders accounted for 53 per cent of convictions for violent offences – four percentage points up on 1979.[29] Paremoremo, which received the most serious violent offenders, had this imbalance reflected in its population. Where in the 1970s the prison's Maori/Pacific Island: Pakeha ratio had been about 1:1; by May 1985 Maori and Pacific Islanders outnumbered Pakeha almost 2:1.[30] Moreover, a revival in Maori ethnic awareness that began during the protest era of the 1970s increased racial tensions. In prison, this was largely expressed through gang membership.

The two largest gangs in New Zealand are the Mongrel Mob and Black Power; both overwhelmingly Maori. In fact, about 80 per cent of all gang members in New Zealand in the 1980s were Maori.[31] Gang membership and gang violence increased dramatically after 1975,[32] and many members ended up in maximum security. After sentencing, gang members were 43 per cent more likely to be sent to Paremoremo than non-gang members, in consequence of which, by 1985, nearly a third of its inmates belonged to gangs. Most were Maori and most had been sentenced for crimes of violence. In May 1985, 82 per cent of the high-security men were doing time for violence, including 25 per cent who had committed homicides.[33]

At Paremoremo these demographic changes brought two important outcomes. First, while the profile of gangs had previously been low, by 1985 gangs were the dominating feature of the prison's infrastructure. Until the late 1970s allegiance to the inmate code was seen as paramount, but by 1985 gang allegiance had, in many cases, usurped it. This tendency toward factional solidarity radically affected power relations. In 1985 one inmate, in Paremoremo for bank robbery, said:

> If you did attack a gang member you would be taking your life into your hands because – let's say this – they know not to say "fuck" with me too much. But if I ever had cause to attack one of them, well it's quite possible that the others would be in. And I'm always aware of this. In prison 10 years ago you knew that if you had a fight with someone the worst that was going to happen was *maybe* a kicking. But today you've got to size up each situation. "Do I go on with this, or what?" Because it might be worth a killing. My own.[34]

In 1979 New Zealand had its first prison homicide, when child-sex killer Keith Hall had his throat cut in A Block. As noted, Cedric James was charged but acquitted of his murder. A second homicide occurred in January 1985 when former Paremoremo man Ross Appelgren beat Darcy Te Hira to death at Mt Eden. Appelgren was returned to Paremoremo to begin a life sentence. In March 1993 there was a third killing, when a double-murderer called Steve Matchitt was stabbed in A Block. His assailant was dismissed on the grounds of self-defence. As in the USA, this tendency toward extreme violence was a nationwide problem. Of the 10 prison murders in New Zealand prisons since 1979, two have been at Paremoremo.

The prison's record of growing convict-on-convict violence began to attract media attention in 1979. Between 1978 and 1984, although the incidence of violence between staff and prisoners remained low, internecine fighting increased almost threefold. Reciprocally, the number of prisoners segregated for protection more than doubled. At the end of 1980, after a serious attack on a sex offender, a complete landing of the Classification Block had to be set aside for protective custody. Soon after that the entire block was taken over for protective segregation, and classification services were transferred to Mt Eden.

Paremoremo's gymnasium.

As a result of the influx of gang members, by the end of the 1970s the prison had split into factions, dictated by gang designation. A Block contained the Head Hunters and those acceptable to them; B Block held the Mongrel Mob, Black Power and admissible others and C Block had weaker groups and the unaffiliated. The blocks were still integrated at work and recreation, but the deepening entrenchment of gang allegiance caused continual friction. Tensions rose steadily in the early 1980s, and at the end of 1984 they exploded. On Christmas Eve, as prisoners gathered in the gymnasium for a movie, a brawl erupted between the Mongrel Mob and the Head Hunters. In the fracas two Mongrel members were stabbed and a third suffered severe head injuries. Seven Head Hunters were eventually shifted to D Block. Two weeks later another man was stabbed in the Classification Block.[35]

Security Tightens

To prisoners the Christmas Eve incident came as no particular surprise, but it marked another turning point for the prison administration. Mob retaliation was likely and a bloody gang war seemed imminent. Averting the ubiquitous threat of gang upheaval required radical steps, so from January 1985 total cellblock segregation was put into effect. The blocks became discrete sub-units as they had been under Buckley. Communion between cellblocks at work, recreation and in the visiting room was stopped. Blocks were given access to the gym at different times, they had visits on separate days and the workshops were closed down. Inter-block sporting competitions ceased, as did visits from outside teams. Maori culture and discussion groups were severely curtailed and the debating programme, once the flagship of the prison's intellectual achievement, ended altogether.

The impact of gangs thus severely eroded the quality of life at Paremoremo. Routine became one of chronic inactivity and boredom. Certainly related to this was an increase in self-mutilation and suicide, which had coincided with the rising gang presence. Up to 1980 the prison had had only one self-killing – in 1972 when a fetishist accidentally hanged himself in the psychiatric unit during the course of sexual stimulation. In 1980 this suddenly changed. In April two brothers committed suicide at Paremoremo, beginning a trend that swept prisons nationwide. Of the 29 New Zealand prison suicides recorded between 1971 and 1985, more than half were in 1984–85. Between 1980 and 1987 Paremoremo had 15 suicides, 13 of them between 1984 and 1987.[36]

Administrators searched frantically for a solution. At Paremoremo, three suicides in 1985 and a hunger strike led to an increase in D Block's hours of unlock from three to seven a day, and permission for televisions in D Block cells. In July 1985 the psychiatric unit was upgraded and a landing of the Classification Block set aside for psychiatric purposes. At first, the new measures had little effect, but an upgrading of services in the psychiatric unit in March 1987 solved the problem. After 1988, suicides in maximum security occurred occasionally, but not often enough to cause concern.

At the start of this trouble, in 1984, Jack Hobson retired. He was followed by a succession of superintendents of varying ability. The gang situation continued to deteriorate. Much of the trouble was in B Block, dominated by the Mongrel Mob. Serious attacks on officers doubled, and there was a 50 per cent increase in men needing protective segregation. By mid-year, 81 of the prison's population of 200 were in segregation, and a landing in D Block was taken over to accommodate them. More than half of B Block's cells were now empty because prisoners refused to go there for fear of violence.

Les Hine, Superintendent of Paremoremo prison 1985–1987.

Attempts to control the block by restricting privileges and increasing hours of lockup caused Mob resistance to harden. In 1987 there were 37 assaults on officers, nearly double the 1985 figure. Most were in B Block. Staff wanted to introduce emergency measures and gave the superintendent, Les Hine, one week to solve the problem. Four days later it was announced that Hine would take early retirement.

Hine's replacement was Max Hindmarsh, a 51-year-old former police sergeant who had been one of the hostages threatened with death in the D Block hostage crisis of October 1970. A humane, courageous and straightforward man, Hindmarsh had similar qualities to Hobson and was liked and respected for the same reason. With the Mongrel Mob still causing trouble, he immediately cleared them from B Block. From then on the policy of allowing gang members to live in separate blocks ceased. Gang members were dispersed throughout the prison, and those unable to leave their rivalries at the gate were sent to D Block. The prison stabilised under

Max Hindmarsh, Superintendent of Paremoremo prison 1987–1991; threatened with death during the 1970 hostage crisis.

this regime, and there was a dramatic reduction in assaults on staff (down 64%), assaults on inmates (down 62%), and self-mutilations (down 81%) in 1988. That year there were no suicides.

For the next eight years, Paremoremo virtually disappeared from the public eye. The prison was quiet and the routine was punctuated by only a few newsworthy incidents, including two escapes. In 1991 Dean Wickliffe, serving seven-and-a-half years and a recall for an armed robbery committed while on life parole, escaped for a second time from a D Block exercise yard. This time it was a month before he was recaptured. Two years later came the escape of Michael Bullock and Brian Curtis. After the Curtis-Bullock escape, razor wire was piled between the two perimeter fences, making penetration almost impossible.

The Government Gets Tough

As noted in chapter 5, the early 1990s was a period of change, with the commencement of He Ara Hou on the one hand, and concern about drugs and escapes on the other. At Paremoremo maximum, apart from the escapes of Wickliffe in 1991 and Curtis/Bullock in 1993, and the murder of Steve Matchitt that same year, the prison remained largely invisible. In May 1993 a Paremoremo officer was convicted of possessing cannabis for the purpose of supplying it to a prisoner, but the event attracted little attention. Although the blocks remained segregated as a result of the 1984 gang brawl and formal activities were still limited, procedures and discipline within the units were again relaxed. A research project visit in 1995 showed the cellblocks looking rundown and unkempt.[37] Prisoners marvelled at how easy drugs were to procure, and at the lively trade in items such as coffee, alcohol and non-standard food issue from the kitchen. Staff seemed happy to ignore such things as long as the place ran smoothly.

After 1996, however, things started to unravel again. That year an officer was stabbed in the lung and spleen. Early the following year a fight between men in B Unit who had been drinking resulted in prisoners refusing to be locked up and using weightlifting bars to smash through a concrete wall to the kitchen, where knives were taken. Although they eventually surrendered, a lockdown revealed a large amount of contraband including alcohol, drugs and an array of weapons. In September 1997 a young lifer was beaten and stabbed in the lungs, and three weeks later an officer was stabbed in the stomach and legs. In April 1997 a man in D Unit almost died after setting himself alight, and ten months later lifer William Annear (32) was asphyxiated in D Unit while burning out his cell.

Before long, plans were developing for a radical change in prison organisation. The 1996 General Election brought a National-led coalition into government with the conservative Nick Smith as Justice minister. Almost as soon as he took office Smith set about tightening prison discipline and security nationwide. In a press release at the end of January 1988, Smith promised, *inter alia*, to get all prisoners into work and to adopt a zero-tolerance policy towards drugs and prison gangs. Some of the promises were impracticable but, when a law allowing random drug testing came into effect on 1 February 1998, testing commenced immediately. Stiff penalties were imposed for those failing mandatory tests. In an attempt to make cell searches easier, national cell standards were set, rigidly circumscribing what inmates could have in their cells.

Smith believed that conditions in Paremoremo were softer than at lower-security prisons. The quality of meals was higher and staff had attempted to appease inmates, he said, with a less rigorous regime than elsewhere in order to keep them settled. Ignoring the fact that privileges and freedoms in maximum security were already far lower than in other jails, he promised to reduce the quality of life at Paremoremo to a level that he thought was consistent with other New Zealand institutions.[38]

Plans for a Marion-style Regime

At Paremoremo there was concern about the stabbings and burnings of 1996 and 1997. In 1997 a new management team at the prison attributed the recent problems to a climate of fear that had developed among staff. They believed that staff had adopted a 'peace at any price' approach. In an effort to control the situation some privileges and programmes were curtailed. This created unrest throughout the institution; in fact it was in protest at the changes that, on 13 February 1998, Willie Annear had set fire to his cell and accidentally caused his own death.

Not satisfied that the measures were effective, the new team had started planning a radical restructuring even before Smith took office in December 1997. According to documents released under the Official Information Act, the Auckland Prison Business Plan for 1997–98 had identified an intention to divide the maximum-security division into a progressive-privilege regime.

The objective was to deter disruptive behaviour in the standard blocks by introducing a new system of 'Precautionary Segregation' to D Unit.[39] An American influence in the proposal was clear. American terminology such as 'Supermax' and 'visitation' was used in the planning documents, and early discussion papers made specific reference to the system at USP Marion. A similar type of behavioural modification regime to was envisaged for Paremoremo.

By November 1997 planning for the new regime was well underway and by January 1998 a project brief had been developed. That month, men targeted for the regime (all existing D Unit residents) were identified and by 5 March a skeleton programme had been worked out. To be known after introduction as the 'Unit for Reducing Disruptive Behavior' (RDB Unit), the D Unit 'Development Program' would consist of four phases of highly restricted privileges through which dangerous or unruly men would pass before eventual relocation in one of the standard blocks. By March 24 the new regime was in place.

In the meantime the prison was preparing to introduce the new national cell standards that were already effective in other institutions. In addition, due to budget overruns, daily lockup was to be increased by four-and-a-half hours, meaning the men would now spend 15 hours a day in their cells and lose their evening recreation period. Hours of visiting would be cut as well.

The 1998 Riot and its Aftermath

When prisoners heard about the proposals they were furious, and speculation was rife about what else may be in store. On 26 March 1988, the day before the restrictions were due to take effect, an organised protest took place. At 3pm convicts jammed the A Unit sally port gate shut, isolating the unit from the rest of the prison. Trapped, four duty staff fled to their office, which they locked before being rescued through a hatch in the roof. In the block, rioters began burning and trashing equipment, including bedding and most of the cell toilets, joined soon afterward by their neighbours in B Unit. As armed police surrounded the perimeter wire, A Unit men smashed holes through their cell walls, accessing the service tunnels behind them.

From outside, electricity and water were cut off, and crisis squads moved in to regain control. A negotiation team was sent to A Unit and at 7.45pm the men returned to their cells. Several cells were now uninhabitable, however, and 12 rioters had to be shifted to Mt Eden.

The riot of March 1998 was the first serious prison disturbance since 1972 and the most destructive in the institution's history. Paremoremo now came under total lockdown and an inquiry commenced. In the meantime, the Justice minister promised even tighter controls and a reduction in rations. He pledged to provide $4.2 million to improve security at Paremoremo and Mt Eden. Eleven inmates were sent to D Unit. Here, they were initially deprived of access to showers and staff were prohibited from speaking to them or referring to them by name. Fearing further protests, a strategy of rigorous repression was now adopted.

The existing D Unit residents had not taken part in the riot; in fact, block representative Dean Wickliffe brokered a deal with the administration for D Unit inmates to retain their limited privileges – such as the five-hour-a-day unlock – in return for full co-operation with staff. But the riot of 26 March changed everything. In a letter to the author soon after the event, Wickliffe explained what happened:

> We in D Unit did not participate in the riot. As far as we were concerned we had a deal and we didn't want to jeopardise what little we did have. I personally made a point of speaking to every inmate in upper D Unit and got a commitment from all of them to 'stay cool', the day after the riot. We assured our own staff that we would cause no problems and for the first two days we were unlocked without incident.
>
> But then on Saturday night, 30 or 40 officers in full riot gear and armed with batons marched into D Unit up and down all landings and lined up in the corridor shoulder to shoulder facing the cells. I occupied the first cell and when I asked, "What the fuck's this all about?" I was ordered, "Inmate, get to the back of your cell and place your hands against the wall!" When I asked why I was struck in the face with a torch with enough force to send me reeling back into the centre of my cell. The officer who struck me said, "Inmate, you had your chance. C & R [Control and Restraint] team, remove this inmate!"
>
> They opened the door and crashed me to the floor with their shields. I had been sitting on my bed, putting on my shoes. I was not given any option to go quietly as the rules require. I was handcuffed with my hands behind my back and C & R'd to the lower landing of the Classification Block.[40]

According to the Department of Corrections, C & R teams are allowed to inflict enough pain to stop a man from struggling or endangering staff. Dean Wickliffe, aged 49, weighing less than 65kg and already handcuffed, was apparently deemed in need of such restraint. He continued:

> Pain was achieved by bending my thumbs and wrists back almost to breaking point. Three or four times on the way we stopped for a 'torture session' to try and make me scream. When they couldn't it seemed to infuriate them even more. I was punched and kicked and had my head banged on the floor repeatedly while being held by the hair. My thumbs took weeks to get the feeling back in them and my left wrist, which suffered a chipped and fractured bone, is now in a cast. But they never got me to scream for them.
>
> After I had been removed, four other D Block prisoners were C & R'd. Each has a similar story to tell. In the two weeks following, over a hundred more men throughout the prison were subjected to C & R. Not one of them was given the option of going quietly. Most of them were C & R'd from their cells to the end of the corridor and back, solely to intimidate them. Many suffered thumb and wrist injuries, abrasions, sprains, and swollen joints.

The New Regime in Place

The psychological purpose of the C & R exercises was to soften prisoners up for the changes that were about to be imposed. Backed by the conservative new minister, the riot had provided management with a mandate to tighten security even more than had been in place under Eddie Buckley. On 11 May a new regime, known as the sentence management system (SMS), was introduced. The system consisted of six graduated phases, three of them in D Unit and one in each of C, B, and A units. In phase 1, which was set for 14 days, there would be lockup 23 hours a day, one hour exercise in isolation, and no smoking. In phases 2 and 3, association with one or two other prisoners and small privileges (such as having toiletries in one's cell) were allowed. In general, however, D Unit's three phases were completely spartan. The minimum time an inmate would be held in D Unit was six months.

The biggest changes, however, took place in the old standard blocks. Previously all standard block inmates had full privileges within the block confines; now they too became part of a punishment system. Inmates in B and A units (phases 5 and 6) were allowed dining-room privileges, but the dining rooms were partitioned so that only a small number could congregate at any one time. Where all standard-block men had been allowed contact visits, now all visits were non-contact and phases 1–4 had visits in a security booth. Convicts would be locked up for most of the day, with B Unit allowed three hours unlock and A Unit four hours. Hobbies and activities were limited, no work was offered other than routine cleaning duties and education was highly restricted. Along with the workshops, the gymnasium and the library were also virtually unused.

One rationale for SMS was to control misconduct and make life unpleasant, so as to encourage prisoners to seek transfer to less secure institutions. Before this, particularly when Jack Hobson was superintendent, Paremoremo was considered one of the better places to do time, and some men preferred to stay there rather than move to one of the old and decrepit medium-security prisons such as Mt Eden, Mt Crawford or Paparua.

Under SMS, this was no longer the case. Men wanted to get out. The problem now was that there were not, and never had been, enough classified maximum-security men in New Zealand to fill Paremoremo's 244 beds. In order to keep the place relatively full, the prison had always allowed men of lower security rankings to remain if they really wanted to. After March 1998 the situation was different. Lower-security men wanted to get out, but because other prisons were full they had to stay in the new punitive regime, even though they did not qualify for it. There was no bed space elsewhere. In fact, in March 2002 only two-thirds of the prisoners at Paremoremo max had been classified maximum security. The rest were high- or low–medium security.

Moreover, within the prison itself, SMS was flawed by this same factor. The logic of SMS was that when a man exhibited the appropriate conduct he would be rewarded by moving to a higher phase in the programme. But with only 48 beds in each phase – and all full – men were stuck in their existing phases, irrespective of conduct, until accommodation became available elsewhere.

From the outset the sentence management system was defective and it is not surprising it did not last. Within 12 months it was replaced by another system known as the behaviour management regime (BMR). Unlike SMS, BMR operated only in

D Unit and had four phases involving a graduated system of privileges. BMR inmates had a maximum of two hours unlock per day and limited association with other prisoners. Smoking was not allowed anywhere.

The regime was designed to eliminate disruptive behaviour in men who had been identified as a significant risk to safety and discipline. They could be sent to BMR from any prison in the country, subject to the approval of the General Manager Public Prisons in Wellington. The minimum term for BMR placement was six months.

By 2003, the old standard units (A, B, and C), conditions had become fairly uniform. The exception was the upper landing of A Unit where 24 men had slightly more privileges. But even here conditions were far more restricted than they were before the March 1988 riot. Prisoners were unlocked for about two-and-a-half hours in the morning and again in the afternoon. Only Upper A had dining-room privileges; the rest were fed in their cells. Apart from Upper A, men could only associate with the 12 convicts on their own landings, and the yards had been divided up to facilitate this. During unlock they had access to the yards or to a weight machine downstairs but most preferred to hang about in the cellblock corridor. Only A Unit had access to the gymnasium. No hobbies were permitted, there was limited education only and no work. There were no contact visits. On 12 March 2003, Arthur Taylor, doing 15 years at Paremoremo for armed robbery and escape, wrote:

> The place is now basically a concrete warehouse … in the whole of Maxi life is just an existence, mate. One day is the same as the next, it's everything, and worse, that I would expect a third world prison to be.[41]

From an administrative point of view, BMR was a partial success. It was a strong deterrent to misconduct, and when this author visited in March 2002 only eight men were undergoing it – not all from Paremoremo. This left 40 cells in D Unit potentially unoccupied, so this area was being used for men in transit or for overflows in protection. Site Manager Bryan Christy said the new regime had resulted in a reduction of assaults, both on staff and on other inmates, and a cessation of suicides.[42] This may be so, but the whole of C Unit and part of D Unit – that is, more than a quarter of the entire prison – are now housed in protection.

In the end, redress was found in the civil courts. In July 2002 nine men who had been subjected to BMR sued the prison, the Department of Corrections and the Attorney General for psychological torture and gratuitous punishment. Although BMR had by then been disestablished due to underuse, in 2004 the High Court found the regime to be unlawful and in some cases in breach of the Bill of Rights and awarded four of the applicants a total of $325,000 in compensation (see also chapter 6).

Discussion and Conclusion

Since receiving its first residents in 1969, New Zealand's maximum-security prison has undergone significant changes. Many have been driven by administrative initiatives, but in all cases a complex political interplay between prisoners and staff has been evident.

Clearly throughout there has been an American influence. The institution was modelled on Marion and opened during a time of progressiveness in corrections.

Both Marion and Paremoremo initially offered an impressive range of programmes and facilities and made serious efforts to rehabilitate prisoners. But in both cases, administrative efforts were thwarted by problems with gang rivalry and rising levels of violence. At Marion, restrictions began in 1973 with the opening of the Control Unit and continued with its designation as a Level 6 penitentiary in 1979. At Paremoremo, the gang brawl on Christmas Eve 1984 was the defining moment. After that all association between cellblocks ended, which meant closure of the workshops and an end to inter-block sporting competitions and most externally run programmes such as the Maori culture group and the debating club.

At neither institution did interim control measures solve the problem of violence. At Marion, the killing of 10 inmates and two staff between 1980 and 1983 led to the implementation of the lockdown regime in October 1983. At Paremoremo there have been just two murders, but violence and gang conflict resulted in suicides and increasing numbers of men requesting protective segregation in the 1980s. The situation at Paremoremo has never been as critical as at Marion, but when, under the governance of a conservative minister, management decided to lock the prison down, it took its lead directly from Marion. Thus, the two institutions, already related in their physical appearance and architecture, operate on very similar lines as well. Both prisons were once state-of-the-art in terms of activities and facilities and both are now long-term, punitive holding pens.

The critical difference between Marion and Paremoremo is their draft populations. Marion caters for men who, for the most part, have been sent for punitive segregation after serious misconduct – such as rape, murder or escape – at other federal facilities. They have earned their placement and are deemed in need of behavioural modification. Paremoremo, on the other hand, simply takes all men who, due to various factors such as length of sentence or previous history, have been computer-classified as maximum security. Many have arrived straight from the courts. Moreover, as noted, only two-thirds of Paremoremo prisoners are classified maximum security. Most of the others are high-mediums, detained there to fill the numbers until lower-security housing can be found elsewhere. These men are subjected to the same conditions as the maximum-security prisoners.

What the future holds for Paremoremo is difficult to predict. Since 1999 New Zealand has been run by a Labour-led coalition that has championed issues such as environmentalism and the rights of workers, women and Maori. Prisons have not been forgotten. The rehabilitation scheme called integrated offender management (IOM) has been introduced nationwide, and in 2002 the government restored parole eligibility – removed in 1987 – to all violent offenders. This change in climate is unlikely to have much effect at Paremoremo and, because of the absence of programmes, IOM exists there in name only. Currently, with the prison running smoothly, management is satisfied with things as they are. Supported by a public that has little interest in the welfare of violent criminals, it appears that in the short term at least, the course of the prison is set.

Notes

1 Mayhew, 1959: 57–58.
2 Matthews, 1923: 12.
3 Ritchie, 1984: 98.
4 Newbold, 1989.
5 See Schmalleger, 2001: 453–456.
6 Irwin, 1980: 89–92.
7 See Consultants' Report, 1985.
8 See also Richards, 2005.
9 See Newbold, 1989: ch. 12, for a fuller treatment of the Mt Eden riot.
10 Personal comment to author, 8 April 1983.
11 Ibid.
12 Personal comment to author, 16 July 1983.
13 See Newbold, 1989: ch. 12, for fuller treatment of the Waikeria period.
14 *NZ Herald*, 14 September 1985.
15 Personal comment to author, 6 March 1983.
16 Interviewed in *Red* no.2, December 1970.
17 Personal comment to author, 6 March 1983
18 Personal comment to author, 1 May 1983.
19 Cited in Bungay and Edwards, 1983: 127. See also, Irwin, 1980.
20 Personal comment to author, 13 September 1983.
21 For a fuller treatment of the Buckley era see Newbold, 1989: ch. 10.
22 For a fuller treatment of Hobson's arrival see Newbold, 1989: 235–241.
23 *NZ Herald*, 22 November 1972.
24 For a fuller treatment of the Hobson era see Newbold, 1989: ch. 17–20.
25 AJHR E.5, 1984: 13.
26 *NZ Herald*, 14 Sept, 1985.
27 Tonnies, 1963.
28 Colvin, 1982; Austin and Irwin, 2001: 121–129; Irwin, 1980: 196–206.
29 Department of Justice, 1986: 79.
30 Meek, 1986: 54.
31 Meek, 1986: 97.
32 See Dennehy and Newbold, 2001: 167–191.
33 Meek, 1986: 41–44, 57.
34 Personal comment to author, 14 November 1983.
35 For a fuller treatment of events during the 1980s see Newbold, 1989.
36 Meek, 1986: 84; *The Dominion*, 24 March, 1985; *Sunday News*, 29 March, 1987.
37 Personal visit by author, 24 August 1995.
38 *The Dominion*, 30 March 1998.
39 The term 'Unit' replaced the term 'block' at Paremoremo in the early 1990s.
40 Letter from Dean Wickcliffe to author, 26 June 1998
41 Letter from Arthur Taylor to author, 12 March 2003
42 Personal comment to author, 24 August 1995.

References

Austin, James and Irwin, John (2001) *It's About Time: America's Imprisonment Binge*. Belmont, CA: Wadsworth.

British Journal of Criminology (1961) v.1 (4): 305–375. (Special edition on prison architecture).

Bungay, Mike and Edwards, Brian (1983) *Bungay on Murder*. Christchurch: Whitcoulls.

Cleaver, Eldridge (1968) *Soul on Ice*. New York: McGraw-Hill.

Colvin, Mark (1982) 'The 1980 New Mexico Prison Riot'. *Social Problems*, v.29(5): 449–463).

Consultants' Report Submitted to the Committee of the Judiciary, US House of Representatives (1985) *The United States Penitentiary, Marion, Illinois*. Washington: US Government Printing Office.

Committee of Inquiry (1983) *Report of the Committee of Inquiry into Procedures at Oakley Hospital and Related Matters*. Wellington: Government Printer.

Dennehy, Glennis and Newbold, Greg (2001) *The Girls in the Gang*. Auckland: Reed.

Department of Justice (1986) *Submission to the Committee of Inquiry Into Violence*. Wellington: Department of Justice.

Hogshire, Jim (1999) *You Are Going to Prison*. Port Townsend, WA: Breakout Productions.

Irwin, John (1980) *Prisons in Turmoil*. Boston: Little, Brown.

Jackson, George L. (1972) *Blood in My Eye*. London: Cape.

Matthews, Charles (1923) *Evolution of the New Zealand Prison System*. Wellington: Government Printer.

Mayhew, P.K. (1959) *The Penal System of New Zealand: 1840–1924*. Wellington: Department of Justice.

Meek, John (1986) *Paremoremo: New Zealand's Maximum Security Prison*. Wellington: Department of Justice.

Newbold, Greg (1978) *The Social Organization of Prisons*. Unpublished MA thesis in anthropology, University of Auckland.

Newbold, Greg (1986) *The Maximum Security Prison in New Zealand*. Unpublished PhD dissertation in sociology, University of Auckland.

Newbold, Greg (1989) *Punishment and Politics: The Maximum Security Prison in New Zealand*. Auckland: Oxford University Press.

Richards, Stephen (1985) 'Marion, US Penitentiary'. In Mary Bosworth (ed), *Encyclopedia of Prisons*. Thousand Oaks, CA: Sage.

Ritchie, Brian (1984) *Prison Industries in New Zealand*. Unpublished: Department of Justice.

Ross, Jeffery I. and Richards, Stephen C. (2002) *Behind Bars: Surviving Prison*. Indianapolis, IN: Alpha.

Schmalleger, Frank (2001) *Criminal Justice Today: An Introductory Text for the 21st Century*. Upper Saddle River, NJ: Prentice-Hall.

Tonnies, Ferdinand (1963) *Community and Society (Gemeinschaft und Gesellschaft)*, Tr. Charles P. Loomis. New York: Harper and Row.

CHAPTER 9
WOMEN IN PRISONS

Although the amount of material available about women's prisons overseas is growing, there is still a dearth of data about such institutions in New Zealand. Apart from several university theses,[1] no extensive inquiry into this area has been published. The matter of women prison officers has likewise been ignored. In 1993, a thesis was presented to the School of Government at Victoria University Wellington on the subject of women prison officers at Paremoremo prison;[2] however an article by this author[3] is the only published research on women working in men's prisons. Of women prison officers generally, there is no literature.

A Brief History of Women's Prisons

One of the earliest known prisons specifically for women was the Dutch Spinhuis, opened in 1645 in Amsterdam.[4] The Spinhuis was a house of correction, where deviant women were employed in industries such as fabric production and in community services such as cooking, cleaning and laundry. Most houses of correction and jails in Europe at the time, however, provided no such services, and men and women were often herded together in conditions that were crowded and unsanitary and where women were subjected to sexual exploitation by staff and other inmates. Pregnancies were a persistent problem, and many prison babies, denied proper medical care, died in infancy. In the 18th and 19th centuries hundreds of thousands of criminals were also locked up in old ship hulks or sent to convict colonies. In Australia, a 'factory' for female transportees was set up at Parramatta in 1821, but this was soon used as a brothel and marriage recruiting centre for male convicts and settlers.

To combat the problem of sexual exploitation, by the 1820s almost all French jails had segregated accommodation for women, and in England a separate section had been set aside for females at Wakefield. In England in 1823 Sir Robert Peel's Gaol Act required women to be confined separately from men and forbade any male to visit the female part of a prison unless he was accompanied by a matron. In the 1820s separate female institutions were established in Cambridge and London, but for the most part women remained segregated in sections of men's prisons.[5]

When the penitentiary system was established in the United States in the 1820s, female prisoners were located in sections of male institutions. Pennsylvania's Eastern Penitentiary admitted women almost from its first day in 1929,[6] and six years after opening in 1819 women were committed to New York's first penitentiary, Auburn State prison. At Auburn women inmates were largely excluded from the system of silence and regimentation that applied to men. With no cells of their own they lived in an attic and worked during the day in the prison kitchen, frequently unsupervised. This neglect typified the lot of women prisoners generally – isolated from the mainstream and often denied access to work, exercise and programmes. Sexual abuse of female inmates by male staff continued to be common in many institutions.

As numbers of women prisoners grew, matrons were appointed to the sections reserved for females, but still women tended to be deprived of the attention invested in men.[7] In 1839 a separate facility for women was created at Mount Pleasant Female prison, which was administratively annexed to Ossining (Sing Sing) prison in New York. This was the first prison explicitly created for women by legislation.[8] Run from 1844 by matron Eliza Farnham, Mount Pleasant offered education, music, flowers and frequent visitors – to the annoyance of administrators in the men's facility where the rule of silence and hard labour were in force – which led to Farnham's removal after just three years. For more than two decades thereafter most women in American prisons, often written off as irredeemable, received little attention or were treated similarly to men.

England, which had begun transporting convicts to Australia in 1787, lost this means of dealing with women criminals in 1852 when Van Diemen's Land refused to accept any more. This caused a crisis which demanded accommodation for 1,000 prisoners. That year Holloway prison was opened for 683 male and female inmates.[9] And, in addition to female accommodation in the prisons of Millbank and Fulham in London, Brixton in Surrey was opened in 1853 with housing for up to 800.[10] Where the United States was giving women little specialised attention, England was developing a strong emphasis on trying to reform women morally and encourage femininity, responsibility and self-respect. The punitive rule of silence in men's prisons was waived for women, who were rewarded for reformative compliance with greater privileges and freedoms. The Gaol Act 1823, which had barred men from women's institutions, virtually stopped sexual exploitation by male staff, but did not prevent a proliferation of lesbian relationships between inmates, or between inmates and matrons, or other forms of corrupt practice.[11]

By and large, British patterns continued into the 20th century and eventually spread to the United States. In the Detroit House of Correction, penal innovator Zebulon Brockway hired Emma Hall as matron in 1869, who introduced religious, domestic and academic training to install 'womanly virtues' in her charges.[12] This was followed by female reformatories at Indiana in 1873, Massachusetts in 1877, and New York in 1887, where women came to be seen not as profligate and irredeemable but as wayward children in need of benevolent instruction.[13] Increasingly, as the reformatory movement took hold, America followed the English example in replacing male managers with women and installing regimes less severe than those for men.

The first federal women's facility was constructed at Alderson, West Virginia, in 1923 and is still in operation. By 1940 separate women's facilities existed in 23 states; this number had increased to 34 by 1975 and to 92 by 1978.[14] A feature of British women's prisons in the first half of the 20th century, as the courts grew less inclined to lock up petty offenders, was a dramatic decline in female musters. A large number of female institutions closed.[15] Where, for example, 33,000 women had been imprisoned in 1913, only 11,000 were imprisoned in 1921 and by the 1960s the annual figure was less than 2,000. In the United States there was no decline but populations remained quite level between 1925 and 1970. In New Zealand the female prison population, as a proportion of the male population, also fell dramatically in the first two decades of the 20th century before becoming relative stable.

New Zealand Women's Imprisonment in the 19th Century

Because of its small size and because organised colonisation did not start until after 1840, New Zealand had no dedicated male or female prisons for almost the whole of the 19th century. Prisons were haphazardly administered and maintained and, until Arthur Hume arrived from England in 1880, they lacked effective central administration and control. Transport and communication throughout the country were difficult, and all prisons catered for both male and female convicts. Most settlements had a lockup, and women serving short sentences were kept in separate sections of these jails as much as possible. By the 1860s New Zealand's more than 500 inmates were held in 11 major prisons and a number of smaller jails, with Auckland, averaging 175 inmates, easily the largest, followed by Dunedin with 112 and Lyttelton, Hokitika and Wellington all containing more than 50.[16]

In 1861 the judges of the Supreme Court wrote to the governor, complaining about prison conditions throughout the colony. Auckland's City gaol was typically primitive, with all classes of prisoner, male and female, held in the same institution. The women were contained in three cells in the debtors' yard, two of which were "dank dens" below the Supreme Court, which usually held a number of women and their babies as well. The other cell was a "ricketty (*sic*) lean-to" ventilated by a steel grille and beside a stinking ditch containing lavatory effluent.[17] At this time the total number of women in prison would have been less than 50.

Prison conditions in the 19th century were generally poor for all classes of inmate, but because of their small numbers and short sentences, in New Zealand, as in America and Britain, there was little special provision for women. Segregation of female prisoners did not become standard until the 1860s and often, due to the lack of separate facilities, women were put in solitary confinement for the duration of their terms. Sometimes they were not properly kept apart and frequently there was no matron or female attendant to guard them. At Auckland, there was no separate accommodation for its five women prisoners until 1850 and a female attendant was not appointed until 1851. At Wellington, clothing for women was not issued until 1868.[18] During a Commission of Inquiry into Dunedin prison in 1883 it was alleged (but not proven) that the gaoler, James Caldwell, had placed female prisoners in with the men and had made immoral suggestions to prisoners' relatives. One female inmate alleged that Caldwell and one of his friends had forced her to have sex with them. Consequently, a recommendation was made that a matron or assistant matron should always be on duty at the prison. Similar problems occurred at Auckland where male staff were reported to have regularly harassed female prisoners. Even the appointment of a matron there in 1863 failed to end the practice of male staff searching female inmates.[19]

Work for female prisoners was minimal and, if provided at all, consisted mainly of domestic chores and picking oakum – which involved tearing old rope apart for re-use and sale. As early as 1844 Governor FitzRoy had ordered oakum to be supplied to women at Auckland and to other prisoners without work. Women were also engaged in making prison clothes, doing the laundry of male prisoners and carrying out general cleaning duties. At times, however, scant labour was available to women and there was little attempt to reform them. Even after 1880, when Inspector of Prisons Arthur Hume began transforming the New Zealand penal system and developing rudimentary reform programmes, women remained largely forgotten.[20]

Women in the 20th Century

In 1890 the first single-sex prison was created – the all-male road-building camp at Humeville in Milford Sound. This experiment was a failure, but it was followed by a number of tree-planting camps, starting with Waiotapu in 1901. These camps catered for men only. Arthur Hume, who was in charge of prisons until 1909, believed many male prisoners to be capable of reform, but had little confidence in the redemption of women. In his second report of 1882 he wrote:

> The majority of male criminals in New Zealand Prisons is, I am glad to find, not of the habitual and hardened class … and many of them may therefore be deemed not wholly dishonest or irreclaimable.

Of women, however, he observed:

> The female criminal population of the colony, I regret to report, is, with few exceptions, of the most degraded class, and long past all possible chance of reformation …[21]

Although Hume believed that some male and young female offenders could be reformed through rigorous discipline, he thought that attempting to treat adult females was largely pointless.

When Hume retired in 1909 his ideas were already considered out of date and the reformatory movement, which had started in New York in 1877, was now influencing correctional policy around the world. The reformatory was based on the assumption that offenders, particularly the young and criminally naïve, could be diverted from future offending by exposure to the right kinds of influences, such as training, education and religion. The movement had been responsible for the creation of male and female borstals in England in 1908, and by 1910 the reformatory system had come to the notice of certain New Zealand politicians, in particular the Liberal Government's Minister of Justice, Dr John Findlay. On Hume's retirement, Findlay attempted to modernise the New Zealand prison system by creating a regime where the previous emphasis on discipline was replaced by an accent on correctional care. On this basis the sentence of reformative detention was created in 1910 and Invercargill prison was gazetted as a borstal in 1917.

Findlay lost his seat in a snap election in 1911, but William Massey's Reform Party which now became the government, was no less enthusiastic. Supported by Inspector of Prisons Charles Matthews, the Reform Party established (all-male) prison farms at Invercargill, Paparua, Waikeria, Wi Tako, Hautu and Rangipo, as well as the road making/sawmilling camp which later became known as Waikune. Serious efforts were made to rehabilitate prisoners by providing healthy work in agriculture and land development. In addition, apart from creating the sentences of reformative and borstal detention, Massey's administration abolished release on fixed remission in favour of universal parole.

Special Prisons for Women

When it opened in 1871 Addington prison in Christchurch was designated primarily for women, but after 1872 it was largely taken over by men. In 1909 the 60-odd women

Interior of Addington prison in Christchurch.

inmates were distributed through eight separate men's prisons, with only Auckland, Wellington and Lyttelton holding more than 10 women each. A primary correctional objective of the Reform Government was to end the dispersal of female prisoners into special sections of men's prisons and establish a special facility for them. By 1924 the policy of dispersal had ceased.

Addington became the country's primary institution for females in 1913. Originally intended for the reformable, it soon catered for the mature and 'irredeemable', and continued in this role until June 1950 when it was closed and passed over to the army. The second institution for women was Pt Halswell in Wellington, built as a reformatory for adult women in 1920. A girls' borstal was opened on the site in 1924. These facilities continued operating until 1944. The third women's facility was the female division at Mt Eden in Auckland.[22] At first women at Mt Eden were held within the North Wing Extension of the main buildings, but in 1924 a separate wooden unit, consisting of 11 double cells, was constructed beside the North Wing, and this housed female prisoners for the next 40 years. Although most prisons still had facilities for receiving women, until 1944 no other institutions held them on a long-term basis.

The type of work offered to women depended on where they were located. At the Pt Halswell reformatory inmates were employed in duties such as domestic science and housekeeping, as well as receiving instruction in health, nursing, first aid, child care and some academic subjects. At Mt Eden and Addington, which were for older and more hardened types, the emphasis was more industrial and prisoners here performed primarily domestic chores as well as sewing and laundry.[23] The programme for women, whether deemed reformative or not, was geared to the expectations of the time that women would spend the majority of their lives as mothers and homemakers.

Dalley[24] points out that after 1920 neither Addington nor Pt Halswell operated smoothly. Ideals were subordinated to practicality and little real effort was put into providing programmes. Inmates got whatever was available. She writes:

> In practice and indeed in principle, reformatories did not represent a progression over any other forms of detention … The department maintained a veneer of reformation, but punishment remained the guiding principle as the majority of imprisoned women continued to be viewed as irredeemable and beyond any influence.

After the death of prisons chief Charles Matthews in 1924, and his succession by Bert Dallard the following year, New Zealand entered a non-progressive era in corrections which lasted until about 1950. Described in chapter 2, the reasons for this long 'fallow period' were economic instability in the 1920s followed by the Depression in the early 1930s, international political uncertainty in the later 1930s and the start of the Second World War in 1939. The conservative, parsimonious character of Dallard also contributed. For women prisoners, the only major development during this time was the closure of Pt Halswell due to its proximity to an ammunition dump, and the opening of Arohata Girls' Borstal, north of Wellington, in 1944. Arohata was the first purpose-built female penal institution in over a century of justice administration in New Zealand.

Conditions of Confinement

Little is known about conditions in women's prisons during this time, but Molly Molloy, who worked as assistant matron, matron and later deputy prison superintendent between 1931 and 1966, sheds some light. In 1983, in a two-hour interview about her years in New Zealand women's prisons, Molloy described the generally poor conditions that women were subjected to.[25] In the 1930s, women prisoners wore coarse, unbleached calico underwear with a denim skirt and blouse. At work they wore an apron of sacking, and a white apron at meal times and on Sundays. If they chose to go to Sunday chapel, they also had to wear a starched collar and white Victorian bonnet. The uniform for female staff in the 1930s was a grey nurse's uniform with a cap and apron, and a veil for the matron. About 1940, uniforms for women staff were abolished and during the war female staff wore civilian clothing. In the 1950s, navy serge uniforms were introduced.

In the women's division at Mt Eden the 11 rooms were each equipped with two wire-wove beds, a kapok mattress, woollen blankets and flax sheets. There was a table and two chairs for meals, a wardrobe for storing extra kit and eating utensils and chamber pots for a toilet. Lockup was from 5pm until 6.30am, and as there was no messroom, meals were eaten under lockup. Mt Eden catered for all classes of prisoner, and separating adults from the younger and more vulnerable females was impossible. Most women were employed in the laundry, where clothing was hand-scrubbed with soap before being boiled in huge wood-fired coppers then rinsed and put through hand-wringers. In the afternoons, the laundry was cleaned out and the coppers were polished with vinegar and sand soap. Women not employed in the laundry were usually put to work repairing prison clothing and darning socks, and on Fridays the whole institution was spring-cleaned with kerosene and soap and the wooden floors scrubbed and polished.

Meals were cooked in the men's division and were the same as the men's. Breakfast at 6.30am was a dixie of porridge and one of hash, with bread and dripping. Prisoners 'slopped out' the contents of their chamber pots and were then locked up again until work parties were called at 8am. The main meal, of hash or stew and suet pudding, was served at 11.30am and the women were then locked up until 1pm. Dinner was at 4.45pm. At this time a small ration of semolina or porridge was served – sometimes with a rissole – and bread, dripping and jam. Tea or cocoa came with each meal. Staff got the same rations as inmates, except they were allowed to cook their own and to provide their own butter. At 5pm the prison was locked down for the night.

In the 1930s, conditions for women prison workers were also inferior to those of the men. The women's division had just one matron and an assistant, and either the matron and/or the assistant matron was on duty at all times during hours of unlock. At Mt Eden the two women staff worked staggered shifts – on duty 6.30am to 5pm one day, and 8am to 9.45pm the next. Unlike the male prison staff, who won a 40-hour week in 1946, Molloy claims there was no overtime allowance for women officers and until 1965 the basic hourly rate paid to women was less than that for male prison officers. Once employed, female staff could be transferred at any time to any of the three institutions that were then available for women. About 1945 a third woman was employed at Mt Eden and in 1951, as pressure on female facilities grew, more were hired.

Changes in the 1950s

After the Second World War the use of Addington as a women's prison began to decline and in 1950, with the reintroduction of military conscription the previous year, part of the site was taken over by the army. In 1951 the remains of the women's division (built in 1870), were demolished.[26] The women at Addington were transferred to a small, specially constructed unit at Paparua, and also Mt Eden's North Wing Extension, which had the prison laundry in its basement, was also reopened for women prisoners. The North Extension now held all maximum-security females and the old wooden division took the overflow. The only other long-term female institution still in operation was Arohata.

In 1949 Dallard retired as prisons boss, and his replacement Sam Barnett proved to be far more liberal than his predecessor. Prison conditions nationwide lifted considerably under Barnett, and as they did, so did the lot of women. Rations and facilities improved. At the behest of Molloy, coarse calico underwear was replaced by cotton. Canteens were introduced, where women prisoners could buy luxuries such as makeup and toilet soap. Lockup hours were reduced (with inmates' doors unlocked over lunchtime), facilities for education were created and evening hobbies, such as dressmaking classes (commenced 1953) and embroidery began. Extra staff were employed to assist with the added duties prison officers now faced.[27]

By 1958, in spite of the many improvements made by the Barnett administration, the prison system fell into crisis. Between 1951 and 1958 the total number of inmates in New Zealand, which had hovered around 1,000 since 1936, increased to 1,600. The women's population exploded from about 40 to 75 in the same period and exceeded 100 in 1959. Barnett considered the rise in the women's population administratively insignificant however,[28] and, as had always been the case, pressure in the men's prisons directed policy for women.

In June 1958 it was discovered that a group of men in the overcrowded maximum-security prison at Mt Eden had created removable bars in their communal 'association' cell which had allowed them to escape after lockup, commit crimes in the city overnight, and return to their beds before morning. As described in chapter 3, this caused a national scandal that almost cost Barnett his job. The existence of association cells was blamed on population pressure and the immediate reaction of the Department of Justice was to make more space for men by temporarily transferring the 40 or so women from the North Wing Extension to the women's borstal and reformatory at Arohata. The wooden 11-cell female division remained. Early the following year, 44 cells for women were opened in part of the old Dunedin prison, which had been reclaimed from the army. The police continued to occupy some of the ground floor. Although, according to Barnett, Dunedin had "nothing to commend it and much to condemn it" and was intended only as a stopgap,[29] the prison remained the primary facility for criminally mature women and security risks for the next 15 years.[30]

Within a few months of arriving at Dunedin the women rioted over conditions, hanging out their windows and shouting at passers-by. But troubles in the men's prisons were worse, as musters continued to rocket and escapes and disturbances became commonplace. By the 1960s the female inmate population had settled at about 100, while the male population continued to grow, exceeding 2,000 in 1969.

A New Prison for Women

Barnett's replacement, Dr John Robson, inherited a prison system bursting at the seams. In his first report of 1961, Robson announced an extensive building programme, including two new prisons for women, one of which would be in the South Island.[31]

But of more urgent priority was the need for a new maximum-security jail for men. Following a series of escapes and disturbances at Mt Eden in the early 1960s, the 1963 annual report recommended closing the wooden women's division to make room for a small high-custody unit for men. At the same time, Robson announced an intention to replace Dunedin with a new female facility at Paparua, in Christchurch. A riot at Dunedin the following year made these plans a priority, but once more nothing was done. Again, events in male prisons forced the government's hand. In 1965 three dangerous prisoners at Mt Eden smuggled a sawn-off shotgun into the security division, took an officer hostage, and escaped in a prison truck. Although they were quickly recaptured, the incident was yet another embarrassment for the beleaguered institution and the justice department now took action. The 40-year-old women's division was closed almost immediately and demolished and the women moved outside the prison walls to the old superintendent's quarters. A small concrete security block for men was built on the site. A few months later a major riot temporarily decommissioned the entire Mt Eden prison, and the building of a new male maximum-security prison at Paremoremo, north of Auckland, occupied departmental attention for the rest of the decade. Not until June 1974 was a new purpose-built, four-wing facility for 44 women finally opened in Christchurch. Dunedin was then converted for short-term males and remands.

Why the department chose to build its major female prison in the southern city of Christchurch when the vast majority of women inmates came from the North Island has never been explained. Even the Minister of Justice at the time Paparua Women's opened was not able to offer an explanation when he was asked about it in 1983. As far as he was aware, the decision had been made years before (by Robson) and did not seem to have been questioned since.[32] Perhaps it was based on economic and practical expediency, with free land available on the Paparua farm site. Whatever the

Christchurch women's prison.

reason, once again the needs of women prisoners, many of whom had children, was completely overlooked. Reflecting on justice department policy for women prisons generally after 35 years working in them, Molly Molloy said:

> I've often said, "Head office doesn't solve its problems, it shifts them". And that's what they've done with women right back as far as I can remember. They haven't really tackled the building [problem] – until Christchurch, which is in the wrong location. It was always makeshift for women. Women have just been forgotten, they really have.[33]

Female Inmate Numbers

One of the reasons women in New Zealand prisons have been marginalised for so long is that, as in America and Britain, they have always constituted a small proportion of the total inmate complement, their numbers have been distributed thinly among different institutions and they have often only been imprisoned for minor offences and short periods of time. As noted, women have seldom constituted more than 10 per cent of the national muster, and numerically did not exceed 100 until 1959.

During the late 1870s and early 1880s, when numbers of women held in New Zealand prisons approached 100, they represented up to 18 per cent of the total inmate population. The large numbers of women at this time reflect the attempts of the judiciary to control prostitution and other 'immorality' by imprisoning women for brief periods under the Vagrant Act 1866, the Contagious Diseases Act 1869, or for drunkenness.[34] From the early 1890s, however, the number of incarcerated women dropped to between 50 and 90 – less than 10 per cent of the total muster.

In the early 1920s, primarily as a result of rising male numbers, the percentage of women in prison fell and remained at between four and five per cent until the Second World War. During the war there was a sudden surge in female prosecutions and imprisonment as women took advantage, through prostitution, of the influx of relatively well-paid American servicemen. The female inmate figure of nine per cent of the inmate population reached in 1943 – the year after the Americans entered

Figure 9.1: Female Prison Musters

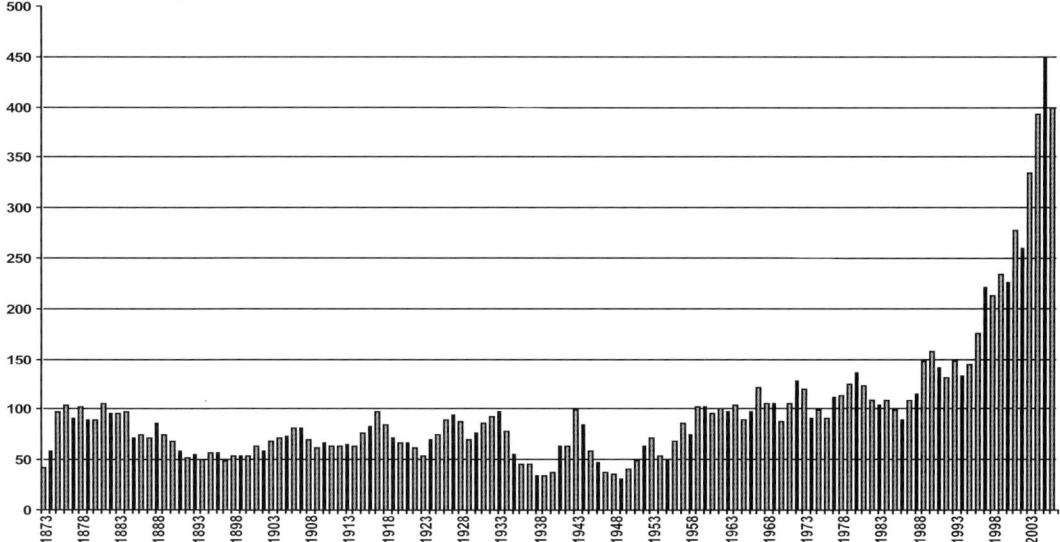

Figure 9.2: Female Prison Musters as % of Total Muster

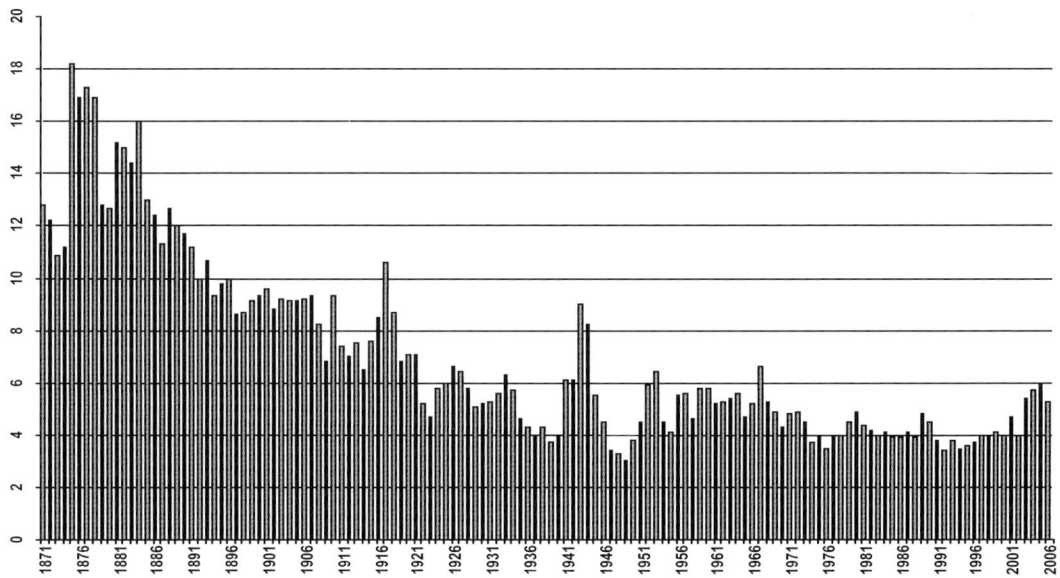

the war – was a 20th-century high. This was followed by a 20th-century low of three per cent six years later, as American troops withdrew and New Zealand soldiers returned, found girlfriends, got married and had families. Thus the demand for illegal commercial sex declined.

Not until the 1960s did women's figures rise regularly above 100, but as male musters boomed also, the proportion of female prisoners remained relatively stable, mostly between four and five per cent. From the 1980s, as a result of mandatory sentencing laws and lower levels of tolerance toward female offending, the numbers of women incarcerated worldwide jumped. In the United States, for example, the 'war on drugs' of the 1980s saw large numbers of people imprisoned for extensive periods[35] – between 1980 and 2002 the prison population of women increased by 700 per cent.[36] In Australia the percentage of women prisoners relative to men rose from 2.6 per cent in 1977 to 5.7 per cent in 1997.[37] In England and Wales the increase started in 1993 and by March 2005 the population of women prisoners had grown by 178 per cent.[38] This increase has been attributed to the rising tendency in England and Wales to put petty offenders in prison.[39]

In New Zealand the large increases started in 1988. That year there was a sudden hike in musters, both male and female, as a result of longer sentences being given and greater proportions of sentences being served following the Criminal Justice Act 1985 and its amendments.[40] At first the rise in female musters paralleled that of men, but after 2001, possibly due to the Sentencing and Parole Acts in 2002 which toughened aspects of sentencing, parole and recall, the number of women in prison began to grow faster than that of men. The August 2004 figure of 393 female prisoners more than trebled that of 1987, with women constituting 5.8 per cent of the total inmate complement in 2004, compared with 4.1 per cent in 1987. This was the highest proportion of women held in prison since 1960. After that, however, numbers stabilised – on 12 June 2006, for example, there were 411 women in prison, 5.4 per cent of the total prison muster.

Women's Prisons Today

Before the Auckland Region Women's Corrections Facility (ARWCF) in Manukau started operating in 2006, the primary institutions for women were Arohata and Paparua. When Paparua women's prison opened in 1974 it was one of three facilities that routinely received female sentenced inmates. In the later 1970s, apart from the approximately 40 maximum-, medium- and minimum-security inmates at Paparua, the Arohata reformatory and borstal held about 50 low-security prisoners and the new women's division at Mt Eden contained a dozen or so short-termers and remands. In the late 1980s and early 1990s, with rising pressure in Auckland, the Mt Eden women's division was expanded to accommodate up to 54 prisoners, and from 1994 it started taking more long-term prisoners as well as short-termers and remands, although it lacked proper provision for education, training and employment. The Mt Eden unit closed in 2006.

Because of the small numbers of female inmates and the short sentences most are serving, work programmes in women's prisons are limited. Apart from routine maintenance duties such as wing cleaning, gardening, laundry and kitchen, a small number of women are employed sewing. Most women inmates in New Zealand are unemployed or under-employed.

Compared with men, and for similar reasons, rehabilitation programmes for women are limited too, and those that exist are largely cut-and-paste versions of systems designed for men. In 2004 a Tikanga (Maori customs) syllabus and a criminogenic needs programme were piloted at Arohata. Apart from these, women have some access to standard offerings such as numeracy, literacy, parenting skills, budgeting,

Interior of Auckland Region Women's Corrections Facility.

straight thinking, life skills and kapa haka. In addition Arohata has a special drug treatment unit to which up to 20 women can be assigned for a set six-month period. In practice, however, facilities for women have always been somewhat unkempt and the programmes, compared with those for men, have been haphazard.

This situation may be improving. In 2000 a commissioned review of the management of women inmates by Celia Lashlie and Kathleen Pivac identified a number of issues requiring attention. As a consequence the position of Assistant General Manager – Women's and Specialist Services (reporting to the GM Public Prisons) was created at national office to deal specifically with female issues. There was recognition that criminogenic needs assessments and security classifications for women had been improperly, and sometimes inappropriately, based on programmes designed for men. It was in this light, for example, that the maximum-security classification of women has been abolished. Facilities for women have been improved and an attempt made to provide special programmes and procedures specifically suited to the needs and social realities of female prisoners. Accordingly, visiting and searching regulations for women have been altered, male-based risk scores and targeting rules have been changed so that women are not excluded unnecessarily from programmes, and the programmes themselves have been modified. Of particular importance in the 2000 review was a call for a comprehensive policy on women with babies, allowing mothers of very young children to have their infants with them in prison in a safe and nurturing environment. This policy is discussed below.

At Arohata and Paparua a large number of physical upgrades have occurred, with new health, at-risk management, and self-care units built or under construction. Better visiting and feeding and bonding areas have been provided and work areas improved. There have also been changes in health centres, control rooms, reception offices, property stores and segregation areas. The department also hopes that ARWCF, with its 286 beds, will relieve much of the pressure that has prevented the efficient working of female facilities.

Such improvements may look well on paper; however, it is possible the changes are more rhetorical than real. Inmates spoken to by this author suggest that little of significance has really altered, and Celia Lashlie, out of corrections since 1999 and now working as an independent consultant, is highly sceptical about the claims. In

Figure 9.3: Female/Male Inmate Age Profile 2003 (%)

Figure 9.4: Female/Male Inmate Sentence Length 2003 (%)

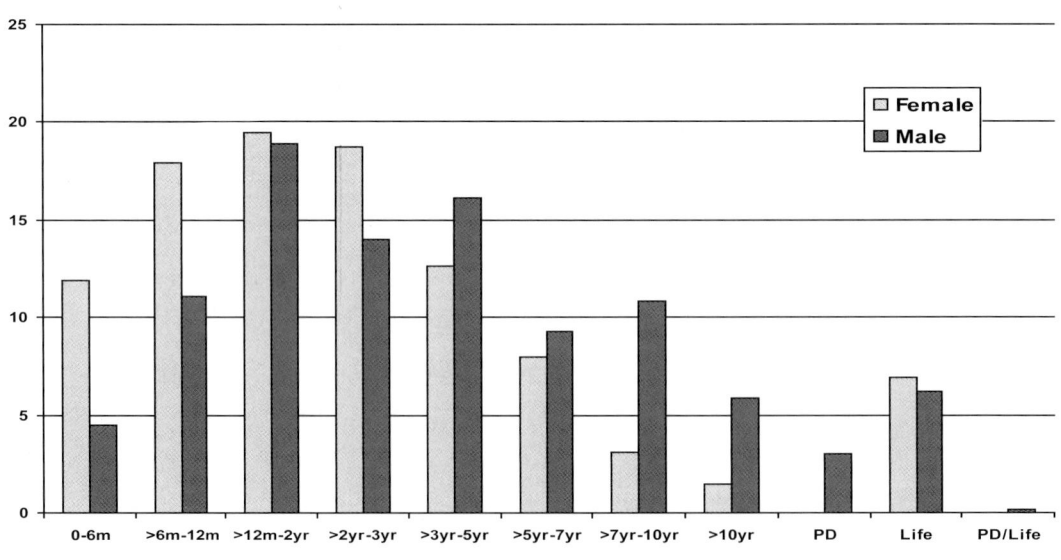

her view, the position of AGM – Women's and Specialist Services is largely a toothless palliative and improvements have been primarily superficial. In June 2005 she wrote:

> I have no doubt that some positive things are happening ... About damn time ... [but] if the information I am receiving from a variety of sources is only half-true [significant change] is definitely not the case. On the surface the right steps are being taken, but I have yet to be convinced that it is anything but lip-service. There has been no change in the basic philosophy that has existed for years that women should be grateful for whatever they get and that they are not important because their numbers are so low. There is almost no understanding of the deeper issues surrounding women in prison and no interest in exploring deeper than the top half an inch.[41]

The 2004 Muster Increase

A feature of the women prison population is its numerical volatility. Predicting female musters is difficult; because of small numbers they are prone to sudden short-term fluctuations. In the late 1980s the average female prison muster jumped from about 100 to about 150, and stayed there until 1996 before climbing steadily to 335 in 2003. An unexpected upswing caused numbers suddenly to leap to 420 in late 2004. This 180 per cent hike in eight years – the last 25 per cent of which occurred in 2004 – put intense pressure upon female facilities; an overflow of about 56 inmates was transferred to a converted 80-bed unit at Waikeria prison (Nikau Unit) in the Waikato in 2003, and temporarily to a standby 40-bed modular unit at Mt Eden men's prison. By 2005 Arohata had been expanded to 154 beds and Paparua Women's to 98 beds, with further accommodation under construction. By March 2005 musters had fallen again to about 370 and the standby unit at Mt Eden was emptied. In the first half of 2006 numbers rose again to over 400, but the proportionate increase was less than that of the male population.

Reasons for the 2004 rise are unclear, but the explanation offered by Corrections Department analysts Bridgman and Mullen[42] for the longer term are: a seven per cent increase in women sent to prison; longer sentences mandated or permitted under the Sentencing Act 2002; larger proportions of sentences being served under the Parole Act 2002 and more inmates remanded in custody.

The Profile of Women Prisoners

The 2003 prison census[43] indicated that approximately 40 per cent of all female inmates were at Arohata, with 28 per cent at Paparua, 17 per cent at Waikeria and 16 per cent at Mt Eden. When ARWCF became fully operational at the end of 2006, more than half of the female inmate complement of New Zealand was located at this modern facility.

Ethnicity

As is the case internationally, minorities are over-represented in New Zealand prisons. In England and Wales 31 per cent of women in custody are from minority groups,[44] and in the US more than half of all female inmates are African-American or

Hispanic.[45] In New Zealand about 57 per cent of female prisoners are Maori or part-Maori is (compared with about 50 per cent for males), but sentenced Maori women are far more likely than Pakeha to be held in the low-security facility at Arohata. In 2003, 54 per cent of sentenced Maori women were at Arohata, compared with just 28 per cent of Pakeha. Similarly, nearly half of all Pakeha women prisoners were held at Paparua compared with only 22 per cent of Maori. This may be because Maori women inmates tend to be younger (and presumably less criminally experienced) than Pakeha. With the majority of Maori offenders coming from the North Island, the distribution also reflects the desire of the Department of Corrections to keep prisoners as close to their homes as possible.

Age

In the United States about two-thirds of all female inmates are under the age of 34.[46] New Zealand female (and male) age profiles are similar, with 60 per cent of inmates under the age of 35. But among Maori women inmates, 35 per cent are under 25, compared with only 16 per cent of Pakeha. Pakeha are about twice as likely as Maori to be aged 40 or over. A comparable pattern can be found among Maori and Pakeha men.

Sentences

The 2003 census provides no ethnic breakdown on sentence length, but female inmates tend to serve shorter sentences than their male counterparts. Thirty per cent of women are serving 12 months or less, compared with 16 per cent of men, and 12 per cent of women are serving more than seven years (including life and preventive detention), compared with 26 per cent of men. This differential is partially because women offend less seriously and are 50 per cent more likely than men to be first offenders. But it also reflects the fact that even where relevant sentencing factors are held constant, New Zealand judges tend to treat men more harshly than women.[47]

Crimes

Reflecting the legal presumption of imprisonment for violent offenders, men and women are equally likely to be doing time for non-sexual violence (about 36% are in for such offences), but women are about a third more likely to be inside for property crime (31.7%). They are more than twice as likely to be in prison for drugs (17.6%). Conversely, 22 per cent of men are imprisoned for sexual crimes, which is far greater than for women.[48] In the United States, by comparison, women are about half as likely as men to be in prison for violence (14.9%), and slightly more likely to be in for property crimes (31.7%) or drugs (27.4%).[49]

Security

New Zealand male inmates are three times as likely as females to have a reoffending risk score of 70 per cent or more, and are more likely to be classified at least high-medium security (16% compared to 9%). No women are classified as maximum security in New Zealand because, as noted, the category no longer exists for women. Conversely, 71 per cent of females are classified minimum security compared to 45 per cent of males.[50] The tendency for women to have a low-security classification is replicated in the United States, where about half of women inmates are classified minimum security and only 7.6 per cent maximum (compared with about 13% and 20% in the case of men).[51] The reason for this is mainly that women seldom escape from prison. An exception in New Zealand is lifer Melissa (Missy) Wepa (32), leader of a prison gang called the Deadly Fucking Bitches. Imprisoned in 1997 for stabbing another woman to death and with an ongoing reputation for extreme violence, Wepa has escaped twice from women's prisons in this country.

Figure 9.5: Female/Male Inmate Major Offence 2003 (%)

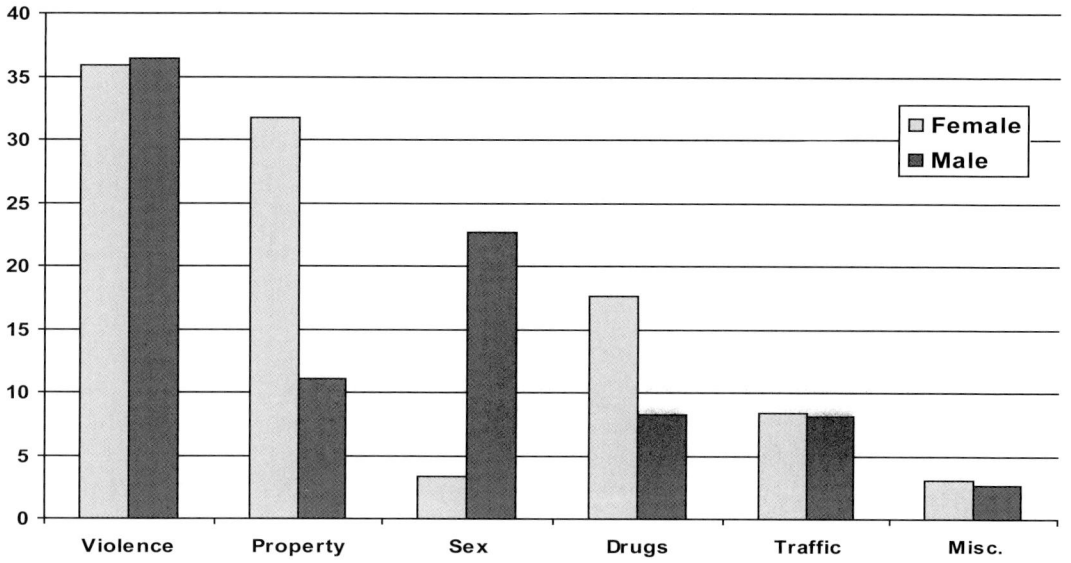

Figure 9.6: Female/Male Security Classification 2003 (%)

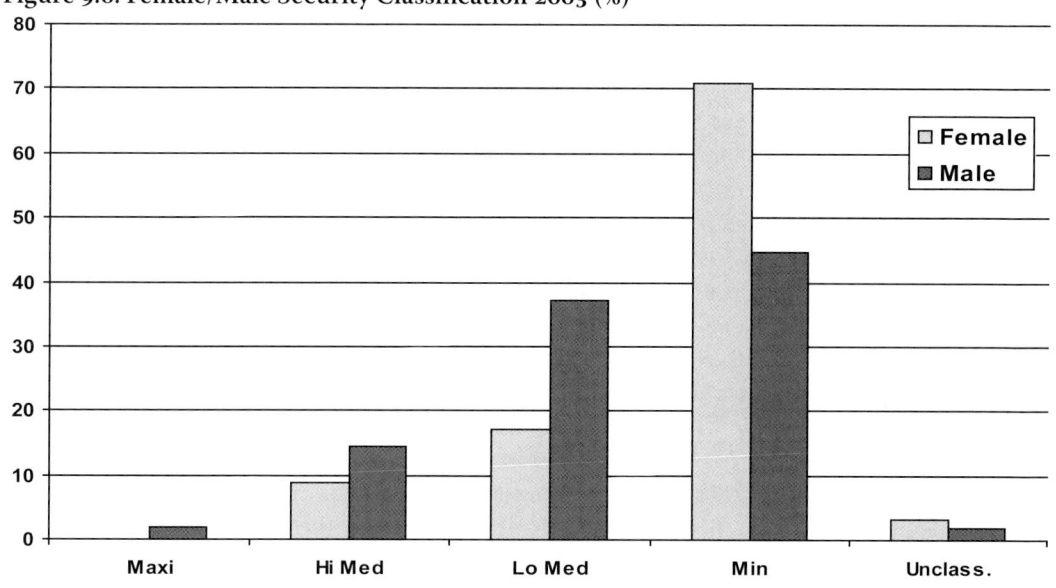

Children and Pregnancy

One of the major issues relating to the incarceration of women is that they are often primary caregivers of children. In the United States, two-thirds of all women prisoners have at least one dependent child under the age of 18.[52] In England and Wales more than half have a child under 16, and over a third have a child under five.[53] In New Zealand the figures are similar, with 47 per cent of women caring for dependent children at the time of their imprisonment. By comparison only 26 per cent of men have dependent children. Women are three times as likely as men to have at least two dependent children,[54] probably because, although male inmates are generally older than women, they are less likely to assume parental responsibilities.

A specific problem for managers of women's prisons is pregnancy. Some women arrive in prison pregnant or with new babies, and sometimes they get pregnant while serving their sentences. This issue has faced administrators since the inception of prisons and has been tackled in a number of ways. At Mt Pleasant prison in New York in the 19th century, and in some other institutions such as Brixton in the UK, nurseries existed where women could take their children, often until their sentences had expired. However, under legislation enacted in England in the second half of the 19th century, the children of women inmates were removed to industrial schools.[55] In modern British prisons women are permitted to have their children with them to the age of two, although they are discouraged from doing so.[56] In the United States an estimated four to nine per cent of women entering prisons and jails are pregnant.[57] To appreciate the size of the problem, in 1998 for example, 1,900 women entered prison pregnant and 1,400 gave birth in prison. In the United States the treatment of women prisoners who have babies varies between jurisdictions. Often the best options are abortion or some form of foster care. Some institutions allow furloughs and overnight visits or provide nurseries for extended mother–child visits.[58] Only a small number of states allow women to keep their children with them, and then only for short periods of time. In most cases a baby is removed from her mother soon after birth.[59]

In New Zealand, when it is considered to be in the best interests of the baby and prison security is not threatened, a woman who comes to prison with a child under the age of six months, or who has a baby in prison, may be allowed keep the child until it reaches six months. In such cases mother and child are transferred to one of the self-care units inside the wire where they cook and care for themselves and their infants. The women's self-care units each contain units with four bedrooms each. Units are clean, modern and well-appointed, and can provide a baby with a relatively normal life within a safe and secure environment. Of the seven self-care units in operation in New Zealand at the beginning of 2005, five were in women's facilities: one at Arohata and four at Paparua.

If a woman decides not to keep her baby full-time or fails to meet the eligibility criteria for transfer to a self-care unit, she may have the child brought in to her daily for up to 12 hours for feeding and bonding. Today, all permanent women's prisons (ARWCF, Arohata and Paparua) have feeding and bonding facilities. Almost half of women inmates serve two years or less, and as such are eligible for statutory release after serving half their sentences. Women who are to be released before an infant is nine months old are allowed to keep their child beyond the normal six-month period. There is a good chance, therefore, that a woman who has a baby in prison will be able to spend all of the child's early life with it, in conditions likely to be better than those on the outside. Allowing mothers to bond properly with their children in prison is intended to reduce the women's chances of reoffending and to deflect problems that may develop with the children in later life.

Health

Another area where specific attention is needed in women's prisons is health. Compared to men, women prisoners suffer more often from health problems, both physical and mental. In the United States and Britain the large numbers of women in prison with drug addictions create specific problems with HIV, TB and hepatitis. Women are also afflicted with a variety of genital complaints and are more likely than men to suffer from anxiety neurosis, depression and other mental illnesses.[60] Women prisoners are typically characterised as suffering from low self-esteem[61] and more women than men report histories of physical and sexual abuse.[62] It is estimated that between 25 and 60 per cent of women inmates require mental health services.[63]

The situation is similar in New Zealand. Women are more likely to have been abused and are more often identified with mental and psychological conditions than men. Women inmates are more than twice as likely to be doing time for drugs (21%) and three times as likely to be in drug and alcohol treatment units. Thirty-nine per cent of women inmates receive prescribed non-psychiatric medication, compared with 15 per cent of men. The difference in diagnosed psychiatric conditions is even more pronounced. Among women inmates, 15.4 per cent receive prescribed psychiatric medication, compared with only 6.7 per cent of men.[64] The personality defects of female inmates and their higher likelihood of inflicting harm upon themselves create special problems for prison administrators.

The Society of Women Prisoners

There is very little formal research on the society of women inmates in New Zealand.[65] But the area has been well investigated in Britain and the United States, and much of the information from these countries accords with (at least anecdotal)[66] information on the situation in New Zealand prisons. As noted, New Zealand women prisoners tend to be predominantly Maori, aged less than 35 and considered relatively low reoffending and security risks. They are mostly serving short sentences for drug or property crimes and, compared with men, are more likely to have dependent children.

Discipline

Security in women's prisons is less stringent, female inmates seldom escape and in New Zealand, as in England,[67] they do not wear uniforms. The conflict that often characterises staff–inmate relationships in men's prisons is less pronounced in women's prisons;[68] in fact there is evidence that women form relationships with staff and factionalise vertically rather than horizontally.[69] Serious violence is less evident, but female prisons are nonetheless volatile and petty squabbles and rule infraction are common. Internationally, women in prison are charged with disciplinary offences more than twice as often as men,[70] and are more willing to argue a point with an officer than men are.[71] Apparently New Zealand women are no different. Of the women's prison at Paparua, former manager Celia Lashlie writes:

> The things I learned in my first few months are as follows. Everybody does everybody's sentence. No new rule will be obeyed until the reasons behind the rule have been explained ... to everyone. If the rule isn't based on sound reasoning, or even if it is, the muttering about the rule will continue long after the women have been told the rule is here to stay. The women affected by the rule may return three or four times to challenge the reasoning behind it ... Unfortunately for those who have to manage them, in the minds of the majority of female inmates, a good day in prison is a day in which a new rule was modified, or perhaps even abandoned, as a result of their challenges.[72]

Discussions with prison officers and administrators also suggest that when denied a request women inmates are more likely to take personal offence than men, they tend to react more emotionally than males, and consequently are less predictable on a day-to-day basis.[73] This can make the running of a women's prison considerably more complex than running a prison for men.

On the other hand, researchers report that women are subject to a great deal of petty and senseless rule enforcement from staff, are treated like children and are put on report for behaviour – such as bad language – that would be overlooked in a men's institution.[74] In their research at Cornton Vale in Scotland, for example, Dobash, Dobash and Gutteridge,[75] and Carlen[76] report that women are restricted as to whom they may associate with and where they may do it, their conversations are electronically monitored and they are forbidden to share any of their possessions or even to light one another's cigarettes. Some staff see themselves as 'mothers' of the inmates and constantly scrutinise their deportment and cleanliness. Cornton Vale is perhaps an extreme example of female infantilisation, but the situation is not atypical.

Social Organisation

One of the reasons women inmates are vulnerable to such trivial controls is that they tend to lack solidarity and seldom engage in collective violence in the way that men do.[77] At Cornton Vale, for example, strong relationships seldom form between inmates, there is little sense of group solidarity and prisoners tend to think primarily in terms of their own interests.[78] Although in the United States an inmate social code has been identified among women that is similar to men's,[79] the code is frequently violated and 'snitching' or 'grassing' on fellow inmates is commonplace.[80] Ward and Kassebaum, for example, write:

> Our interviews suggested that any prohibition against *ratting* at Fonterra was almost universally violated and that the role of the *snitch* had been articulated to a point where differentiations were made, not between those who kept quiet and those who ratted, but in terms of the kind of stool pigeon one was.[81]

Explaining this phenomenon, Giallombardo observed:

> It is clear that the cultural definition of the female role and the popular culture on the woman-to-woman level preclude any expectations of strength or moral

toughness on the part of the female inmate. Traits such as 'courage', 'nerve', and 'toughness' are not meaningful concepts to the female and thus arouse no anxiety on her part. In the words of the inmates: "The hardest part of living in a prison is to live with other *women*".

... It is not the constant fear of violence or exploitation which creates a hardship for the Alderson prison inmates ... but rather it is the adjustment that living in close proximity with other women in general engenders, the strain involved in being in the forced company of others who are believed to be untrustworthy and capable of predatory tactics. There is a widely held belief that women stand ready to take advantage of one another, and one must remain alert to the possibility and must take the necessary precautions.[82]

In New Zealand there is no reliable information, but the situation is probably the same. At Arohata, distrust among fellow inmates is common,[83] an observation that has frequently been repeated by former and serving prisoners at Paparua women's.[84] Treachery among inmates is a powerfully divisive factor that makes united action among female inmates difficult. Thus they become exposed to nitpicking and capricious rule enforcement from staff, which in a united men's prison would not be tolerated. In men's prisons, rules and the way they are enforced are mediated by the endemic possibility of collective retaliation from prisoners.[85]

Pseudo-families

Given the centrality of families to the lives of most women, it is perhaps not surprising that family-type structures are replicated in female prisons. This is a unique and apparently universal phenomenon unknown in the male world. At Cornton Vale the creation of a family structure is part of official policy,[86] but there is also evidence of the spontaneous formation of pseudo-families in prisons for women.[87] In her study of Central California Women's Correctional Facility, Owen[88] describes a culture in which older, prison-wise convicts take on the role of 'Mom' with younger or naïve inmates responding as daughters. 'Moms' provide a degree of protection for the younger inmates and give advice and guidance throughout their sentences.

Sexuality

Often the protective mother–daughter situation becomes emotional and sexual, and the dominant partner may adopt a masculine role. Unlike male prisons, where sexual relationships tend to be purely physical and where taking a submissive sexual role results in social demotion,[89] there is little negative stigma attached to feminine role-playing in a women's prison. In these situations 'butch' females often take a male identity, perhaps wearing men's shorts and boots and cutting their hair short, and may see themselves as fathers, sons or brothers of other inmates. In a sexual role they act as husbands to their inmate 'wives', 'femmes' or 'mommies' and create 'play families' within the cellblock context in a mimicry of the normal domestic relationship.[90]

According to Owen, lesbian associations are a predominating feature of women's prisons and a significant number of women become involved in them. Because of the emotional vulnerability of many female inmates, because they are easily drawn into pseudo-families, and because homosexual activity carries little stigma, same-sex love affairs are far more common in women's prisons than in men's. Ward and Kassebaum[91] found a large majority of inmates estimated that at least 30 per cent of female inmates become involved in homosexual affairs.

Conversations by this author with women inmates and prison workers in New Zealand suggest that lesbian behaviour among inmates here is also high, with estimates of 30–50 per cent engaging in such activity while in prison. Dalley[92] reports that lesbianism is common at Arohata. Compared with the United States, where sentences are long, the relatively brief amounts of time that New Zealand's women inmates spend in prison might reduce the pressure to engage in homosexual behaviour.

A related issue in all prisons where inmates are guarded by members of the opposite sex, is sexual misconduct between inmates and staff. According to Silverman,[93] female inmates in the jurisdictions of Texas, California and the Federal Bureau of Prisons made 506 allegations of staff-on-inmate sexual misconduct between 1995 and 1998.

In New Zealand, men have always worked in women's prisons, and since 1985 women have worked in a frontline capacity in men's institutions. By the end of 2003, of the 2,869 staff working in the nation's 18 prisons, 500 were female. Approximately 350 women were assigned to men's prisons, while 33 men worked in women's prisons. Here, as in the United States, although co-sexual staffing policies benefit prisons by normalising the institutional environment, an unfortunate by-product is the inevitable risk of corrupt sexual relationships occurring between the keepers and the kept.

In New Zealand women's prisons there is a policy of having at least three female staff on duty for every male (and likewise, three male staff per female in men's prisons). Nonetheless, between December 1999 and March 2005 six male officers were investigated for having affairs with female inmates. When a male officer has a sexual affair with a female inmate, due to the inherent inequality in the relationship it is often assumed that the affair is abusive or exploitive in nature. However, that is not always so. In New Zealand it appears that for the most part sexual relationships are consensual and may result in special favours for the women involved. For this reason sometimes other inmates volunteer to act as lookouts while sexual activity takes place. There is a similar problem in men's prisons. Between December 1999 and March 2000 18 female officers were investigated for having affairs with male inmates, and at least two officers became pregnant.[94] Often allegations cannot be proven or an officer resigns before any formal allegation is made. On a number of occasions also, male and female staff who have had affairs with inmates have continued their relationships after the prisoner has been released. Although the Department of Corrections is aware of the problem and has robust procedures in place to prevent corrupt associations occurring,[95] the realistic objective is minimisation, not eradication, of these types of affair.

Conclusion

From the time the first comprehensive penal systems were set up in America and Europe in the early 19th century, the treatment of women was largely an afterthought, and if any programmes existed at all they tended to follow on the heels of programmes for men. This changed in Britain and the United States toward the end of the century as female inmate numbers increased and philanthropic administrators began attending to women's specific needs.

In New Zealand, where the female muster did not begin regularly to exceed 100 until the 1960s, women prisoners have continued to be largely ignored. Women have always comprised only a small proportion of prisoners overall, so events in men's prisons that have driven government decisions about accommodation for women inmates; the women have tended to be shunted here and there as demand required. When a modern women's facility was finally opened at Paparua in 1976, as before, economy and expediency rather than practical utility determined its location. Today, the limited number of programmes and employment available to women prisoners is a reflection of their continued low numbers relative to men.

The nature of the New Zealand women's prison population and the structure of its society bear strong similarities to what is reported from women's institutions internationally. Reflecting their status and profile in the wider community, women inmates everywhere tend to be incarcerated for less serious offences than men and to serve shorter sentences. They are more likely to be first offenders and their security classification is generally lower.

The society of women inmates, likewise, reflects their role in society and their innate propensities as women. The environment of female prisons tends to be more volatile than males' prison environment, and women inmates are inclined to form social and sexual attachments that reflect, loosely at least, the structures of families that provide the focus of much female activity in the outside world. The need for emotional bonding and security, combined with the lack of stigma attached to femininity, impel women to form long-term homosexual relationships with other inmates, and occasionally with staff, far more frequently than is the case with men.

In New Zealand, rising inmate numbers, the recent opening of the new female facility in Manukau and procedural changes in the treatment of women prisoners, provide rays of hope for the future. Recognition that in the past women have been subjected to procedures and programmes designed for men, and an understanding that the needs of women demand separate consideration, hold the promise that dedicated female-specific programmes are becoming a fixed feature of the New Zealand correctional environment. However, as noted, there is informed opinion that the department is claiming substantially more than it is in fact achieving. The truth of the matter awaits future judgement.

Notes

1 Ph.D. thesis by Dalley, 1991; McKenzie, 2004, and master's level theses by Dalley, 1987; O'Neill, 1989; and Taylor, 1996.

2 Hansen, 1993.

3 Newbold, 2005.

4 Zedner, 1995: 329.

5 Zedner, 1995: 332.

6 Mays and Winfree, 2002: 135.

7 Rasche, 2003; Ryder, 2003; Silverman, 2001: 195.

8 Ryder, 2003.

9 The prison was converted to a women-only facility in 1903. Hall Williams 1970: 243; Rock, 2003.

10 Zedner, 1995: 336.

11 Zedner, 1995: 332, 344.

12 Rasche, 2003: 302.

13 Mays and Winfree, 2002: 135; Rasche, 2003.

14 Mays and Winfree 2002; Zedner, 1995.

15 Zedner, 1995: 356.

16 Royal Commission, 1868.

17 Judges of the Supreme Court, 1861.

18 Burnett, 1955: 71–75.

19 Dalley, 1993; Royal Commission, 1883.

20 Auckland Gaol Commissioners, 1877; Burnett, 1995; Mayhew, 1959.

21 AJHR H.6, 1882: 1–2.

22 Dalley, 1993; Mayhew, 1959: 101.

23 Dalley, 1993:45.

24 Dalley, 1993: 59–60.

25 Molloy interview with author, 15 June 1983.

26 Andrews and van Zoggel, 2001: 109.

27 Molloy interview with author, 15 June 1983.

28 AJHR H.20, 1959.

29 AJHR H.20, 1959.

30 See Martin, 1998: 163–164.

31 AJHR H.20: 1961.

32 Finlay interview with author, 21 June 1983.

33 Molloy interview with author, 15 June 1983.

34 Pratt, 1992: 104–108.

35 Allen and Simonsen, 2001: 196–197; Bloom, 2005; Chesney-Lind, 1997: 149–151.

36 Bloom, 2005.

37 Baldry, 2003.

38 Howard League, 2005.

39 Cavadino and Dignan, 2002: 328–329.

40 See Kettles, 1988.

41 Lashlie, 2005: personal letter to author, 18 June 2005.

42 Bridgman and Mullen, 2004.

43 Harpham, 2004: 13.

44 Howard League, 2005.

45 Chesney-Lind, 2003.

46 Zaitzow, 2003:22.

47 Jeffries, Fletcher and Newbold, 2003.

48 Harpham, 2004: 24.

49 Allen and Simonsen, 2001:420.

50 Harpham, 2004: 26.

51 Allen and Simonsen, 2001: 247; 425.

52 Chesney-Lind, 2003.

53 Howard League, 2005.

54 Harpham, 2004: 66.

55 Zedner, 1955: 343–344.

56 Dobash, Dobash and Gutteridge, 1986: 198.

57 Owen, 2002: 240.

58 Allen and Simonsen, 2001: 427–428; Silverman, 2001: 204–205.

59 Zaitzow, 2003: 31.

60 Bloom, 2005; Mays and Winfree, 2002: 140–141; Morris, 1987: 124; Silverman, 2001: 216;

Zaitzow, 2003: 32–33.

61 Carlen, 2005: 119.

62 Chesney-Lind, 1997: 153–154; 2003; Lashlie, 2002: 100–101.

63 Owen, 2002: 240.

64 Department of Corrections, 2005; Harpham, 2004: 37.

65 O'Neill, 1989. Interviews with eight women prisoners conducted by O'Neill for her M.Soc.Sci. project,

66 Discussions with inmates, prisoners and officers by the author (various).

67 Carlen, 1998: 96; Morris, 1987: 116.

68 Morash, 2003.

69 Dobash, Dobash and Gutteridge, 1986: 191; Harper, 1951.

70 Morris, 1987: 121.

71 Carlen, 1998: 86–88; Zaitzow, 2003: 29.

72 Lashlie, 2002: 96.

73 Informal discussions with author (various).

74 Allen and Simonsen, 2001: 430–431; Carlen, 1983: ch5; 1998; Dobash, Dobash and Gutteridge, 1986; Lashlie, 2002: 92; Morris, 1987: 123; Zaitzow, 2003: 28.

75 Dobash, Dobash and Gutteridge, 1986: 186.

76 Carlen, 1983: 89–115.

77 Carlen, 1983: 113.

78 Dobash, Dobash and Gutteridge, 1986: 186.

79 Owen, 2002: 243; Silverman, 2001: 201; Smith and Natalier, 2005; Sykes and Messinger, 1960.

80 Giallombardo, 1966: 99–100; Ward and Kassebaum, 1966; 1970.

81 Ward and Kassebaum, 1966: 32.

82 Giallombardo, 1966: 99–100.

83 Dalley, 1987: 56.

84 Informal discussions with former prisoners, Newbold (various).

85 See, e.g. Newbold, 1978: 298–307; 1982.

86 Dobash, Dobash and Gutteridge, 1986: 184–185; Carlen, 1983: 94.

87 Giallombardo, 1966; Ward and Kassebaum, 1966; Zaitzow, 2003.

88 Owen, 1998.

89 Hogshire, 1999; Sykes, 1958: 95–99.

90 Giallombardo, 1966; Owen, 1998; Ward and Kassebaum, 1966; 1970.

91 Ward and Kassebaum, 1970: 469.

92 Dalley, 1987: 56.

93 Silverman, 2001: 207.

94 Newbold, 2005: 112–113.

95 See Newbold, 2005.

References

Andrews, Mike and van Zoggel, Peter (2001) *Addington: The Prison*. Whitecliffs: Purple Barn Conspiracy.

Allen, Harry and Simonsen, Clifford (2001) *Corrections in America: An Introduction*. Upper Saddle River, NJ: Prentice Hall.

Auckland Gaol Commissioners (1877) *Report*. H.20, 1877.

Baldry, Eileen (2003) 'Women in Prison, Australia'. In Nicole Hahn-Raft (ed), *Encyclopedia of Women and Crime*. NY: Checkmark Books.

Bloom, Barbara (2005) 'Women Prisoners'. In Mary Bosworth (ed), *Encyclopedia of Prisons and Correctional Facilities*. Thousand Oaks, CA: Sage.

Bridgman, Andrew and Mullen, Jarrod (2004) *Further Explanation of Trends in Inmate Numbers.* Unpublished briefing paper to the Minister of Justice and the Minister of Corrections (min 3/1), 3 August 2004.

Burnett, R.I.M. (1995) *"Hard Labour, Hard Fare and a Hard Bed": New Zealand's Search for its Own Penal Philosophy.* Wellington: National Archives NZ.

Carlen, Pat (1983) *Women's Imprisonment: A Study in Social Control.* London: Routledge and Kegan Paul.

Carlen, Pat (1998) *Sledgehammer: Women's Imprisonment at the Millennium.* London: Macmillan.

Carlen, Pat (2005) 'Risk and Responsibilities in Women's Prisons'. In O'Toole, Sean and Eyland, Simon (eds), *Corrections Criminology.* Sydney: Hawkins.

Cavadino, Michael and Dignan, James (2002) *The Penal System: An Introduction.* London: Sage.

Chesney-Lind, Meda (1997) *The Female Offender: Girls, Women and Crime.* Thousand Oaks, CA: Sage.

Chesney-Lind, Meda (2003) 'Women in Prison, USA'. In Nicole Hahn Rafter (ed), *Encyclopedia of Women and Crime.* New York: Checkmark.

Dalley, Bronwyn (1987) *From Demi-Mondes to Slaveys: A Study of the Te Oranga Reformatory for Delinquent Women, 1900–1918.* Unpublished MA thesis, History Department, Massey University.

Dalley, Bronwyn (1991) *Women's Imprisonment in New Zealand 1880–1920.* Unpublished PhD thesis, History Department, Otago University.

Dalley, Bronwyn (1993) 'Prisons Without Men: The Development of a Separate Women's Prison in New Zealand'. *New Zealand Journal of History* v.27(1): 37–60.

Department of Corrections (2005) *United Nations Quaker Office: General Information.* Wellington: Department of Corrections (unpublished).

Dobash, Russel; Dobash, Emerson and Gutteridge, Sue (1986) *The Imprisonment of Women.* Oxford: Basil Blackwell.

Giallombardo, Rose (1966) *Society of Women: A Study of a Women's Prison.* New York: Wiley.

Hall Williams, J.E. (1970) *The English Penal System in Transition.* London: Butterworths.

Hansen, Pleasance (1993) *A Theoretical Analysis of the Phenomenon of Resistance as an Aspect of Organisational Change.* An unpublished M.Pub.Policy thesis, Department of Government, Victoria University of Wellington.

Harper, Ida (1952) 'The Role of the "Fringer" in a State Prison for Women'. *Social Forces,* v.31: 53–60.

Harpham, David (2004) *Census of Prison Inmates and Home Detainees.* Wellington: Department of Corrections.

Hogshire, Jim (1999) *You Are Going to Prison.* Port Townsend, WA: Breakout.

Howard League for Penal Reform (UK) (2005) *Women in Prison in England and Wales.* Unpublished.

Jeffries, Samantha; Fletcher, Garth and Newbold, Greg (2003) 'Pathways to Sex-Based Differentiation in Criminal Court Sentencing'. *Criminology,* v.41(2): 701–722.

Judges of the Supreme Court of New Zealand (1861) *Reports and Memoranda.* AJHR D.2A, 1861.

Kettles, Sue (1988) *The Recent Increase in the Female Prison Muster.* Wellington: Department of Justice.

Lashlie, Celia (2002) *The Journey to Prison: Who Goes and Why.* Auckland: Harper Collins.

Lashlie, Celia and Pivac, Kathleen (2000) *He Kete Pokai: Suitcase of Hope.* A working document on the management of women in prison in New Zealand. Wellington: Department of Corrections (unpublished).

McKenzie, Anna (2004) *'Trying to Stem their Downward Course': The Development of Penal Governance for Women in New Zealand, 1840 to 1974.* Unpublished PhD thesis, Institute of Criminology, Victoria University of Wellington.

Martin, Bill (1998) *Dunedin Gaol: A Community Prison Since 1851.* Dunedin: Bill Martin.

Mayhew, P.K. (1959) *The Penal System of New Zealand 1840–1924.* Wellington: Department of Justice.

Mays, Larry and Winfree, Tom (2002) *Contemporary Corrections*. Belmont, CA: Wadsworth.

Morash, Merry (2003) 'Women's Prison Administration, Contemporary'. In Nicole Hahn Rafter (ed), *Encyclopedia of Women and Crime*. New York: Checkmark.

Morris, Allison (1987) *Women, Crime and Criminal Justice*. Oxford, Basil Blackwell.

Newbold, Greg (1978) *The Social Organization of Prisons*. Unpublished MA thesis in Anthropology, Auckland University.

Newbold, Greg (1982) *The Big Huey*. Auckland: Collins.

Newbold, Greg (2005) 'Women Officers Working in Men's Prisons'. *Social Policy Journal of New Zealand* issue 25: 105–117.

O'Neill, Rose (1989) *The Experience of Imprisonment for Women: A New Zealand Study*. Unpublished M.Soc.Sci. thesis, Department of Sociology, Waikato University.

Owen, Barbara (1998) *In the Mix: Struggle and Survival in a Women's Prison*. New York: SUNY Press.

Owen, Barbara (2002) 'Understanding Women in Prison'. In Jeffrey Ross and Stephen Richards (eds), *Convict Criminology*. Belmont, CA: Wadsworth.

Pratt, John (1992) *Punishment in a Perfect Society*. Wellington: Victoria University Press.

Rasche, Christine (2003) 'Women's Prison Administration, Historical'. In Nicole Hahn Rafter (ed), *Encyclopedia of Women and Crime*. New York: Checkmark.

Rock, Paul (2003) 'Holloway Prison'. In Nicole Hahn Rafter (ed), *Encyclopedia of Women and Crime*. New York: Checkmark.

Royal Commission (1868) *Reports*. AJHR A.12, 1868.

Royal Commission (1883) *Report on the Management of Dunedin Gaol*. AJHR H.31, 1883.

Ryder, Judith (2003) 'Women's Prisons, History of'. In Nicole Hahn Rafter (ed), *Encyclopedia of Women and Crime*. New York: Checkmark.

Silverman, Ira (2001) *Corrections: A Comprehensive Review*. Belmont, CA: Wadsworth.

Sykes, Gresham (1958) *Society of Captives*. Princeton: Princeton University Press.

Sykes, Gresham and Messinger, Sheldon (1960) 'The Inmate Social System'. In Richard Cloward, Donald Cressey, George Grosser, Richard McCleery, Lloyd Ohlin, Greasham Sykes and Sheldon Messinger (eds), *Theoretical Studies in Social Organization of the Prison*. New York: Social Science Research Council.

Smith, Philip and Natalier, Kristin (2005) *Understanding Criminal Justice: Sociological Perspectives*. London: Sage.

Taylor, Annabel (1996) *The Imprisonment of Women in New Zealand 1840 to the Present Day: A Social and Historical Perspective*. Unpublished M.Soc.Wk. thesis, Department of Social Work, Massey University.

Ward, David and Kassebaum, Gene (1966) *Women's Prison: Sex and Social Structure*. London: Weidenfeld and Nicolson.

Ward, David and Kassebaum, Gene (1970) 'Homosexuality in a Women's Prison'. In Norman Johnston, Leonard Savitz and Marvin Wolfgang (eds), *The Sociology of Punishment and Correction*. New York: Wiley.

Zaitzow, Barbara (2003) '"Doing Gender" in a Women's Prison'. In Barbara Zaitzow and Jim Thomas (eds), *Women in Prison: Gender and Social Control*. London: Lynne Reiner.

Zedner, Lucia, (1995) 'Wayward Sisters: The Prison for Women'. In Norval Morris and David Rothman (eds), *The Oxford History of the Prison*. New York: Oxford University Press.

CHAPTER 10
THE PRIVATISATION OF CORRECTIONS

Internationally, the privatisation of correctional services has had a long and often chequered history. The contracting of punishment was known in England as early as medieval times[1] and was supported by prison reformer Jeremy Bentham in the 18th century.[2] Privatisation fell out of favour after England adopted the penitentiary system in 1839, and in 1877 the prisons of England and Wales were taken over entirely by the state.[3]

In America, a degree of privatisation existed from the start. The first convict transports to Virginia in 1607 were by contract to the British Government and in the early 19th century several of the earliest prisons were privately managed, including New York's prisons at Auburn and Sing Sing. Privatisation declined during the next 100 years as a result of ongoing scandal, political pressure and changing market forces, however, and by the end of the 1920s all US prisons were under state control.[4]

In the 1980s, as rising incarceration costs forced some jurisdictions to search for cheaper alternatives, a second era in private contacting began. In 1975 the first modern facility to be tendered out wholly to private management was opened for juveniles at Weaversville, Pennsylvania.[5] A second privately managed juvenile facility, the Okeechobee School for Boys, commenced operation in Florida in 1982.[6] In 1983 the Corrections Corporation of America (CCA) was formed in Nashville Tennessee, followed by the Wackenhut Corrections Corporation (WCC) (known as the GEO Group Inc since January 2004) in 1984. Today, although 14 separate companies now offer private correctional services, these two multinational giants dominate the private prisons industry worldwide, controlling 74 per cent of the American contract corrections market and more than half of the international capacity.[7]

CCA's first contract was for the Hamilton County Jail in Chattanooga, Tennessee, in 1984, and in 1985 CCA commissioned, in Kentucky, the first privately owned and operated state facility for adult males. Federal interest in proprietary detention centres for aliens started in 1979 and general involvement in privatisation began in the early 1980s. The first federal contract of any size involving a detention centre for the Immigration and Naturalization Service, went to CCA in 1984, and the first private contract with the Federal Bureau of Prisons was signed with Wackenhut in 1987, for running the Taft Correctional Institution in California.[8]

During the 1990s, as US state and federal prison populations continued to boom – growing nearly threefold between 1980 and 1999[9] – private contracting, which promised cost savings of between 10 and 20 per cent, proceeded apace. In 1990 a total of 38 jails and prisons in 11 different states were being managed by the private sector.[10] Ten years later 32 states had contracted a total of 162 private facilities.

Accordingly, the rated capacity of US private secure adult facilities grew from 15,300 in 1990 to 138,243 in 1999.[11]

Eighty per cent of private correctional contracts are in the United States,[12] but in 1990 Australia became the first country to follow America's example, opening a private prison at Borallon in Queensland.[13] Run by the Corrections Corporation of Australia (a CCA subsidiary), Borallon was followed by the Arthur Gorrie Correctional Centre, operated by Australasian Correctional Management (ACM) (a Wackenhut subsidiary) in Queensland in 1992, then Junee in NSW, run by ACM, in 1993. England opened a private prison at The Wolds, Humberside, in 1992 (Group 4 Prison Services), followed by Blakenhurst (CCA) the next year. By 1998 four companies were competing for the non-American market share, with Wackenhut taking 52 per cent, followed by the British company Group 4 (29%), CCA (14%) and Securicor (5%). In 1998 four countries had contracted correctional services with these corporations. Australia was the largest, with 12 private facilities, followed by England with 10, and Scotland and South Africa with two each.[14] New Zealand opened its first and only private prison in 2000. Globally, the amount of revenue collected by private correctional companies is estimated today at US$1 billion a year.[15]

New Zealand's First Private Prison

As was the case in England,[16] New Zealand's move toward privatisation was influenced by overseas developments was driven by overcrowding, and was consonant with the move toward state corporatisation and the *laissez-faire* economics that had commenced in New Zealand in the 1980s.[17] Discussion about the prospect of prison privatisation had started by 1988, with the Department of Justice and its minister both initially indisposed to the idea.[18] But in 1989 a Ministerial Committee of Inquiry into prisons commented on the need for a new remand facility and suggested the option of private management. Then at the end of 1990, when the sitting Labour Government was replaced by National, the incoming Minister of Justice, Doug Graham, began musing publicly about the possibility of private-sector involvement.[19] His interest in some form of contracting continued, and in November the following year approval in principle for private prisons was endorsed by Cabinet. In October 1992 the Cabinet Strategy Committee gave substantive approval to private-sector contracting. The empowering bill – the Penal Institutions Amendment (No.3) Bill – was introduced into parliament in May 1993 before being referred to the Justice and Law Reform Select Committee.

The prospect of a new opening for investment caused a flurry of excitement in the business community, with a number of overseas and local firms showing interest in tendering for a contract.[20] Cabinet had approved private-sector involvement in a 250-bed remand centre in central Auckland in November 1992. Late that month calls for expressions of interest were made and a total of 53 replies received. By July 1993 the field was reduced to six applicants, who would be invited to tender for contracts to design, build, finance and manage two prisons. The successful candidates were: Australian Correctional Services; Corrections Corporation of New Zealand Consortium; Civil and Civic; Fletcher Construction/Group 4 International; McConnell Dowell/Corrections Services Group; and Serco Corrections.

At this stage the process hit a political snag. The National Government was re-elected in November 1993 with an effective voting majority of only two and was under pressure to avoid controversy. This put the matter of contract corrections on hold. A year later, however, Labour MP Peter Dunne backed the Penal Institutions Amendment Bill, which would open the door to private contracting. This allowed the bill to be revived, and in November 1994 it was passed by 41 votes to 36. In March 1995 an Order in Council brought the act into law.

By this time it had been decided to contract initially for a single prison, a 275-bed remand facility adjacent to Mt Eden prison in Auckland City. In August 1995 an evaluation committee of four was established to assess the tender proposals to finance, build and manage the new prison. Of the five parties invited to tender only two responded: Fletcher Challenge/Group 4 and Gibson O'Connor/ACM (Wackenhut). After several months of deliberation the committee found that while one tender had a clearly superior architectural design, the other's operational proposal was better. In May 1996 it was decided that neither applicant fulfilled the specifications laid down in the invitation to tender and so no contract would be awarded. The committee recommended that, in order to avoid the construction/management dilemma of the previous round, the government invite separate tenders – one to build, the other to manage the new prison.[21]

Another political snag appeared at this point. After the 1996 General Election – the first under the new MMP system – neither Labour nor National held a clear majority and New Zealand First had the balance of power. After some uncertainty a coalition government between NZ First and National was formed, with Winston Peters, NZ First's leader, as Deputy Prime Minister and Treasurer. Peters was opposed to private prisons, and without his support the process could go no further. However, in August 1998 the coalition agreement was terminated and from then until the general election of 1999, National governed alone.

The weakening of the alliance between National and NZ First, followed by the removal of NZ First from government, allowed National to resurrect its plans for privatisation. In June 1998 Minister of Corrections Nick Smith announced that three new prisons built by the state would be tendered to private management. The first would be the $40 million, 275-bed, state-owned remand prison being built at Mt Eden. Tenders for running this institution were called in August and a five-year contract was awarded in mid-1999. The successful bidder was Australasian Correctional Management – the Wackenhut subsidiary that had the contract for Australia's second private prison, the Arthur Gorrie Centre, which is also a remand facility. The Mt Eden remand centre, known as Auckland Central Remand prison (ACRP), opened in July 2000. In 2003, apart from accommodating 32 sentenced inmates in a service capacity, the role of ACRP was to house all remand prisoners from the Auckland region. Catering initially for 299 in total, including 22 with special needs, the prison employed 81 male and 68 female staff, with an ethnic staff mix of 60 per cent Maori/Pacific Islands.

No sooner had the ACRP contract been awarded than there was another change of government, and once more politics entered the fray. In the election of November 1999 the National Government had been defeated by a Labour/Alliance coalition. Almost as soon as he took office the new Minister of Corrections, Matt Robson of the Alliance Party, had begun talking about closing prisons down and terminating the ACM contract, using a $1 million exit clause written into the deal. In the end the government opted to let the contract run, but plans for further privatisation were cancelled and opposition to the idea continued. In 2004 the Penal Institutions Act was repealed by the Corrections Act which, among other things, prohibited extensions on private management contracts. Accordingly, on 13 July 2005 when the ACM (known from 16 January 2004 as GEO Group Australia) contract expired, the prison reverted to state control.

The decision to lapse the ACM contract was ideologically driven and had nothing to do with performance: Robson had made it clear before the prison even opened that he opposed private management in principle and wished to terminate the contract. His position remained unchanged in spite of the acknowledged fact that the company was fulfilling its terms well. In 2004, for example, filled to maximum capacity with 360 inmates, the prison had one suicide and only three serious assaults – a low level of serious incidents for an institution of this type and size. Only 5.5 per cent of inmates returned positive drug tests, compared with over 20 per cent in the public sector. ACM had, in 1999, won the right to run the prison by submitting a bid that was eight per cent lower than its competitor, the New Zealand Department of Corrections. The prison's first manager was Terry Easthope, a former probation officer, who had been an innovative manager at the minimum-security public prison of Rolleston in Canterbury. He was fully familiar with New Zealand Government requirements and practices and he recruited some top-performing staff from the public sector to his senior management team.

ACRP had a low public profile during its time of operation, and few people remembered it was privately managed. Monitored constantly by the government, its degree of contract compliance was high, which allowed it to collect regular bonus payments for exceptional service delivery. The only incident of note (and its first and only escape), occurred in December 2000 when an inmate managed to walk out the front gate with visitors. In accordance with the contract, this error cost ACM a $50,000 financial penalty and was never repeated. By the time the institution closed, still operating well below the state budget, it had won a variety of awards and accreditations. The most eminent was in December 2001, when ACRP became the first prison in New Zealand to be granted the prestigious AS/NZS ISO 9001:2000 Quality Management System Accreditation. At the time of its handover to the state, ACRP was the only prison in the country with NZQA programmes in alcohol, drug and anger management, and to have achieved Quality Health New Zealand accreditation. In the EEO Trust Work and Life Awards of 2003, ACM was identified as one of New Zealand's preferred employers.

The author spent two half-days touring ACRP and talking to management – once soon after it opened and again shortly before it closed – and on both occasions was struck by the professionalism, dedication and enthusiasm of its employees. ACRP was far more sophisticated than, and in a completely different league to, similar government-run institutions. For example, where remand inmates in the New Zealand state system are normally locked up for 20 hours a day and get almost nothing in the way of facilities or programmes, 75 per cent of the 360 inmates at ACRP under private management had access to a gymnasium and a wide variety of vocational, educational and cultural training activities. Its reversal to state ownership signalled the end of the correctional careers of a large number of staff, and ended one of the most innovative and successful experiments in prison management this country has known.

Private Contracting to Public Prisons

Although the state's experiment with private prison management has ended (for the time being anyway), aspects of privatisation have always existed within New Zealand's public prisons, and no doubt always will. The construction of prisons, for example, has been tendered out to contractors for over a century, and limited contracting for prison produce on the open market has been going on since the 19th century as well.[22] Inmates nearing completion of their sentences have taken up employment in the private sector since 1961, and for many years privately contracted personnel have operated within the prisons. Prisoners' Aid volunteers have been around since 1877, and the Prisoners' Aid and Rehabilitation Society currently operates under contract to the Department of Corrections. Schoolteachers were seconded to the Department of Justice from about 1912 and some still work on a contracted basis. The Country Library Service started supplying books to prisons in 1945, and in the 1950s the prison activities of educationalists, welfare workers, doctors, psychologists and chaplains all grew dramatically and have continued to do so.

Today, services from psychiatrists, psychologists, counsellors, cultural workers, educationalists, doctors and dentists are all contracted to the Department of Corrections. Drug test analysis, which commenced in 1998, is also tendered out, as is the post-release support and monitoring of certain offenders. In particular, the Parole (Extended Supervision) Amendment Act 2004 allows a sentencing court, on application from the Chief Executive of Corrections, to impose extended supervision orders on high-risk child-sex offenders. These can require such offenders to serve 12-months' home detention and/or 24-hour personal monitoring after the termination of their sentences, and to subscribe to other special conditions for up to 10 years. Some of these extra-departmental providers are drawn from government agencies, while others involve private operators. In 2004 the Department of Corrections contracted rehabilitative, motivational, educational and re-integrative services from at least 15 private providers and spent $3.8 million on purchasing services, both public and private, to assist its operations.[23]

Since the mid-1990s there has been a growing tendency for private contracting in newly created correctional alternatives or to replace services previously handled by the state. In 1995, the year private prison management became legal, a pilot home detention scheme was started in Auckland, with Justice for One Ltd supplying the equipment and monitoring. When the scheme was expanded into its current form in August 1999, the security firm Chubb New Zealand Ltd won a $6.5 million contract to provide this service. As can be seen in chapter 12, home detention has expanded significantly in the past six years. In 2004, 1,950 offenders commenced a home detention order. Chubb has been the preferred tender in other government contracts. In October 1998 they won the contract for a five-year pilot prison escort and courtroom custody service in Auckland, which was renewed for a further five years in 2004. That year Chubb carried out over 31,000 prisoner escorts and over 7,000 court custody tasks in Auckland and Northland.[24]

Privately Contracted Community Corrections Services

Private contracting has also entered corrections in the area of community programmes. Internationally, privately run community programmes have a long history, with the United States providing a number of well researched examples. The Chicago Area Projects and the Cambridge-Somerville Youth study from the 1930s are two early instances, followed by well-known experiments at Highfields, New Jersey, in 1950; the Provo Experiment in Utah in 1959; and the California Community Treatment Project of 1961.[25]

A popular version of the community programme is the 'halfway house', which normally provides residential treatment for offenders after they have completed prison sentences, or after having been sent directly from the courts. The concept of the halfway house originated in England, Ireland and the United States in the early 1800s, but did not flourish until the 1950s and 1960s following rising cynicism about the effectiveness of imprisonment. The biggest growth occurred after the mid-1960s. In the United States, for example, the number of functioning halfway houses grew from 40 in 1966 to at least 1,800 in 1982.[26] Two of the most famous American examples are Synanon, established in Santa Monica, California, in 1958 to deal with released drug offenders, and the Delancey St Foundation, an offshoot of Synanon, which was formed in San Francisco in 1971.

The movement of the New Zealand Government into this area did not really begin until the early 1980s. In 1981 a state-sponsored inquiry into penal policy supported the involvement of community organisations in corrections.[27] The inquiry endorsed the new sentence of community service, which had been introduced the previous year. Community service was a sentence that allowed a court to substitute a sentence of imprisonment with a set term of free service (initially between eight and 200 hours) in, with or for some community agency. The agency had primary responsibility for overseeing the offender, although it was unpaid work and ultimately the offender reported to the probation service.

The next development came in 1985, when the Criminal Justice Act 1954 was repealed and replaced. Changes to the Criminal Justice Act 1985 had a significant impact on community organisations. The act attempted to divert property offenders away from prison by mandating that they should not be incarcerated except in special circumstances. To assist this objective it created a new sentence called community care (re-named community programmes in 1993). Community care allowed a court to sentence an offender to up to 12 months' care with a community agency (such as a halfway house or a marae), up to six months of which could be residential. Furthermore, broadened parole provisions in the primary act and subsequent amendments gave greater powers to parole authorities to commit some offenders to community programmes as a condition of release.

In the case of community care, payment to the contracting sponsor could be made, and since inmates thus discharged were deemed still to be serving their sentences and could be recalled to prison, community care providers were, in effect, privately run correctional agencies. Community care thus represented the first example of a contracted correctional service in New Zealand. These private schemes, which were (and still are) used for sentencing and parole purposes, did not usually operate for profit. Typically they were set up under the Charitable Trusts Act and governed by volunteer boards of trustees that hired professional staff to run them. Partial funding came from the Department of Justice; this was supplemented by alternative sources such as other government departments and charitable organisations.

Programmes took a variety of forms, but normally catered for fewer than 20 inmates each. In 1991, with almost 600 offenders serving community care sentences at any given time – plus an unknown number of inmates directed to community organisations as a condition of parole – approximately 100 private, partially government-funded community care schemes were in operation. Twelve houses owned by the Department of Justice were leased to such organisations through its Community Programme Fund.

It was some of these agencies that landed the Department of Corrections' first private community corrections contracts, under the 'habilitation centre' scheme. Habilitation centres were conceived in the 1989 Ministerial Committee of Inquiry into prisons, and the establishment of these centres was a central recommendation of the committee. As initially conceived, habilitation centres would operate as a series of small, semi-custodial halfway houses that would provide specialist services to rehabilitate offenders and would virtually replace the prison system as we know it. The government knew that, if implemented, the scheme would be inordinately expensive and would very likely be ineffective,[28] and in the end the recommendation was ignored.

But the idea of habilitation centres remained alive within the Department of Justice and a Habilitation Centre Development Group was set up in 1990.[29] This group refined the Committee of Inquiry recommendations into a practicable form, which eventually appeared in section 102 of an amendment to the Criminal Justice Act in 1993. Section 102 allowed the parole board or the district prisons board to direct that an offender be released to a habilitation centre. Habilitation centres, as such, still did not exist in 1993, but charitable organisations – such as Montgomery House in Hamilton, Beck House in Napier, Te Moana Marae in Wellington, the Salisbury St Foundation in Christchurch and the Downie Stewart Foundation in Dunedin – had been operating for some time as de facto halfway houses for persons sentenced by the courts under community care or sent as a condition of parole. The Criminal Justice Amendment Act 1993 provided the legal machinery to alter the status of such centres by paving the way for full-time funding contracts to centres that could satisfy a rigorous set of 'habilitation centre' requirements.

In 1994, soon after the legislation was passed, the Department of Corrections began to prepare the way for five pilot habilitation centres, which it would contract and fully fund. In December 1994 contract guidelines, specifications and a draft tender agreement were circulated to more than 275 potentially interested groups and individuals. Of the 22 organisations which responded and were subsequently assessed, five were invited to proceed with a full proposal – Higher Ground Drug Rehabilitation Trust in central Auckland, for five male or female residents; Te Whanau o Waipareira Trust in West Auckland, a kaupapa Maori programme for 12; Te Ihi Tu Trust in New Plymouth, a kaupapa Maori programme for 10 males; Aspell House in Plimmerton, for 10 females with alcohol or drug-related problems; and the Salisbury St Foundation in Christchurch, a non-specific programme for 10 male residents.

After a lengthy and drawn-out assessment process, in April 1996 the Salisbury

St Foundation was awarded $320,605 to operate as the country's first government-contracted pilot habilitation centre. This agreement was followed by three more, with Higher Ground the only programme to be denied a contract.

Subjected to rigorous departmental requirements and quarterly reviews, several of the centres soon began to falter. In November 1996 faults within the Aspell House programme caused it to be suspended, but it began operating again under a new programme in April 1997. By December 1997 problems were identified in the financial statements of the Waipareira Trust as well as a large number of serious incidents involving absconding, drug use and other criminal offending. All of the four pilot centres reported relatively high absconding and non-completion rates, and low occupancy was a problem in all centres except the Salisbury St Foundation, which had an average occupancy rate of 91 per cent.[30]

By the end of 1998, when an overall assessment was carried out, Aspell House, Te Ihi Tu and Waipareira were all in trouble, with occupancy at times dropping to between zero and three residents each, and high operating costs. Moreover, on occasion residents at Waipareira had been left alone and without supervision. Salisbury St was the best performing programme in value for money, occupancy levels and reoffending, and the only centre that consistently operated within the requirements of its contract. Approximately half of those who attended this programme for more than three months had not re-offended during its 32-month operational period.[31]

Late in 1998 Aspell House, which was temporarily closed in 1996 and 1997 and which continually struggled with organisational problems and zero residency, closed down permanently, and in 1999–2000 a fifth habilitation centre, Challenge Trust in South Auckland, was denied resource consent and was thus unable to open. In March 2000 Waipareira Trust was closed as a result of mismanagement and continuing high levels of criminal offending among its residents. Due to re-open in May 2000 under the name of Te Wairua Rangi Marie, in mid-2001, after repeatedly failing to comply with financial auditing requirements, the trust had its contract terminated. Thus, of the five habilitation centres granted contracts in or after 1996, only two, Te Ihi Tu and Salisbury St, were still operating by the end of 2001.

In 2002 the Sentencing Act repealed the sentences of community service and community programme, and habilitation centres were abolished as a legal entity. At this time they became known as 'residential community centres' and continued to receive funding as before. A third community residential centre was Montgomery House in Hamilton, established in 1987, which had operated independently as a fully funded programme for the treatment of violent offenders during the habilitation-centre period.[32]

The Salisbury St Foundation

Of the five habilitation centres established under the 1993 Criminal Justice Amendment, the Salisbury St Foundation (SSF) has been consistently the most successful and trouble-free. Two MA theses have been completed on this organisation,[33] and the author has served on its board of trustees since 1989. Before concluding this chapter on privatisation, therefore, it will be useful to briefly review the history and current operation of the SSF programme, and comment on the reasons for its success.

Early in 1979 David Hall, an inmate at Paparua prison, influenced by a book he had read about California's Delancey St Foundation,[34] decided that a similar concept might work in New Zealand. He approached Dave Robinson, a Canadian-born psychologist, probation officer and prison counsellor, and together they made plans for a halfway house in Christchurch. In October 1979, after Hall's release, the Salisbury St Foundation was established as a charitable trust in central Christchurch.[35]

Like Delancey St and Synanon, the Salisbury St Foundation was initially conceived as an inmate-run programme. The regime was haphazard and unstructured, however, and soon the operation, located in a four-bedroomed house leased from the Methodist Mission and overseen by Hall, fell apart. In 1980 the programme closed down, but due to the efforts of Robinson, was relocated and re-opened in 1981. Its new placement was a 12-bedroomed house owned by the Department of Justice in the upper-class suburb of Merivale.

Funded by a small grant from the Department of Justice and by money from other government departments and charitable handouts, SSF initially applied a psycho-therapeutic model. This was later supplanted by one based on encounter recreation, before reverting to a mixture of encounter recreation and therapy. Overall governance came from a publicly elected, unpaid board of trustees, which hired management and other staff, as required and according to what it could afford. Board-member turnover was high. Maintaining stability was difficult in this uncertain financial and governance environment; between 1981 and 1994 the organisation had no fewer than 10 different directors. Poor organisation, recurring crises and meddling from board members eroded morale and led to high levels of drug use, criminal offending and absconding among residents – along with expensive recreational equipment repeatedly being broken or stolen.

The Foundation's salvation was the awarding of the habilitation centre contract in 1996. By this time an experienced board of trustees was in place; they adopted a hands-off approach to governance and left day-to-day administration to professional staff. Full government funding removed the burden of having constantly to apply for charitable grants to stay afloat, and regular Department of Corrections supervision and performance evaluation ensured the programme met the terms of its contract.

In 2000, in order to prevent the possibility of a hostile takeover – always a potential problem with publicly-elected boards – the board of trustees rewrote the constitution and public election of board members ceased. Instead the board co-opted its own members as required. It now became a highly stable and effective body, with a lawyer as chair and a District Court judge as treasurer, and supported by a committee comprising a medical doctor, an investment businessman, a prison-unit manager, an operations manager for Child, Youth and Family, and a criminologist (the author). Most board members, all unpaid volunteers, have served for more than 10 years. The board meets monthly and hires full- and part-time professional staff to design, manage and carry out the programme. The director is a trained social worker.

The organisation has now run smoothly, efficiently and with a minimum of disruption for over a decade. There have been only three directors since 1994 and by 1998 SSF was secure enough to raise a mortgage and buy the Merivale premises it has rented since 1981. In 1984 a nearby block of four, two-bedroom flats was purchased to ease the transition of residents advanced in the programme back into the community.

The flats have raised the potential residential complement of the programme to 19, and with the appreciation in land value, the cashed-up equity of the organisation is now well over a million dollars.

Today Salisbury St offers what is normally a six- or 12-month structured residential programme with 24-hour supervision that is not limited to, but is particularly suited to, long-term violent recidivists. A few enter directly from the courts as a condition of probation, but most are prison parolees. The highly organised programme consists of: discussion groups; training in life skills, anger management and problem-solving; individual counselling; drug abuse counselling; sporting activities and outdoor recreation. Toward the end of their terms, residents are assisted with finding a job and a place to live, or they may move into the flats. The programme costs about $450,000 a year to run.

Prospective residents initially attend the house on day-parole from prison. If they are assessed as motivated and suitable, a recommendation to release them to SSF is forwarded to the parole board. Once on the programme new residents are normally on tight curfew; however conditions are progressively relaxed, eventually allowing residents to leave the premises – at first accompanied and ultimately without escort. Toward the end of their time, successful residents are allowed weekend leaves with their families or sponsors. 'Graduating' residents are awarded a certificate at a low-key graduation ceremony attended by the board of trustees. They may then live in the flats and are encouraged to maintain contact with the house. Most do so, particularly in the early adjustment phase.

All residents are subjected to random drug testing. If they are found to have taken illegal substances they are initially warned and have their freedoms restricted. If drug use continues or other aspects of the programme are not engaged with, residents can ultimately be expelled – which often means being returned to prison by the parole board.

In spite of rigorous pre-admission screening and a professionally administered programme, levels of failure are relatively high. Forty per cent of inductees re-offend, abscond or are recalled to prison while in the programme, and 34 per cent are discharged for non-compliance. Among the 26 per cent who graduate, however, recidivism is unlikely, with only 20 per cent reoffending within four years. Most SSF graduates get jobs or careers and live relatively stable lives after discharge. A number of the best graduates have also been successfully employed by the organisation in counselling and management capacities.

The Salisbury St Foundation is necessarily small and caters for only a limited number of prison releases, but it has proved highly successful in placing some serious long-term recidivists on the path to successful life. It establishes a model for private halfway house management which could well be emulated elsewhere, but its levels of failure are also a stark reminder of the difficulties faced in criminal rehabilitation.

Conclusion

Although the private provision of correctional services has existed in New Zealand since formal criminal justice began here, its reception has been ambivalent. For well over a century, prisons have been constructed by private companies operating for profit, and a wide variety of services – from routine maintenance to supply of food, essential materials and treatment facilities – have been and are still privately contracted. Recently custodial activity in the form of prison and courtroom escorts, the monitoring of home detainees, and management of pre-release custody and care, have been contracted out to private organisations operating either for profit or voluntarily. These developments have all taken place without significant controversy. The area of greatest contention, however, has been contracted prison management. The issue of private prisons was hotly debated at the outset, and then, oddly, the first one came into being without ongoing comment. The acknowledged success of the move notwithstanding, political idealism has since caused the private prison experiment to come to an end, leaving the management of prisons as one of the few correctional provinces in New Zealand where the state still retains an operational monopoly.

Notes

1 Borna, 1986: 327.
2 Roper, 1986:77.
3 Ryan, 1993:319.
4 DiIulio, 1993: 158–160; Durham, 1989; Kunkel and Capps, 2005.
5 Young, 1987: 6.
6 Austin and Irwin, 2001: 70.
7 Westerberg, 2005 a, b.
8 Kunkel and Capps, 2005; Westerberg, 2005.
9 Schmalleger, 2001: 458–459.
10 Kinkade and Leone, 1992: 58–59.
11 Allen and Simonsen, 2001: 323–327.
12 O'Toole, 2005: 63.
13 Moyle, 1992; 1993: 234.
14 Austin and Irwin, 2001: 66.
15 Austin and Irwin, 2001: 65–66.
16 Lilly and Knepper, 1992: 180–181; Rutherford, 1990.
17 See Deeks and Perry, 1992; Duncan and Bollard, 1992; Roper and Rudd, 1993; Russell, 1996.
18 Department of Justice, 1988: 63; *Northern News Review*, July 1989; *NZ Herald*, 17 Jan 1989.
19 *The Dominion*, 12 Dec 1990.
20 *National Business Review*, 13 Nov 1992.
21 Yuill *et al.*, 1996.
22 Lingard, 1936: 14.
23 AJHR E.61, 2003: 137; 2004: 128.
24 AJHR E.61, 2004: 129, 161.
25 Champion, 1996; Empey, 1977; McCord and McCord, 1959; McCorkle, Elias and Bixby, 1958; Miller and Montilla, 1977; Weeks, 1958.
26 Champion, 1996: 363.
27 Penal Policy review Committee, 1981: 36.
28 Directly after its submission, the Minister of Justice commissioned the author to critique the report, which he did, pointing out the numerous flaws of the proposal. See Newbold, 1989.
29 Hough, 2003: 159.
30 Department of Corrections, 1997; Yeboah, 1999.
31 Yeboah, 1999.

32 See Berry, 1998.

33 Jamieson, 1991; Hough, 2003.

34 See Hampden-Turner, 1976.

35 See Hough, 2003: 79–83.

References

Allen, Harry and Simonsen, Clifford (2001) *Corrections in America: An Introduction*. Upper Saddle River, NJ: Prentice Hall.

Austin, James and Irwin, John (2001) *It's About Time: America's Imprisonment Binge*. Belmont, CA: Wadsworth.

Berry, Steve (1998) *An Evaluation of the Montgomery House Violence Prevention Programme*. Wellington: Department of Corrections. Unpublished.

Borna, S. (1986) 'Free Enterprise Goes to Prison'. *British Journal of Criminology*, v.26: 321–334.

Champion, D.J. (1996) *Probation, Parole and Community Corrections*. Upper saddle River, NJ: Prentice Hall.

Deeks, J. and Perry, N. (eds) (1992) *Controlling Interests: Business, the State and Society in New Zealand*. Auckland: Auckland University Press.

Department of Corrections (1997) *Habilitation Centres: Contract Compliance to 31 December 1997*. Unpublished report.

Department of Justice (1988) *Prisons in Change: The Submission of the Department of Justice to the Ministerial Committee of Inquiry into the Prisons System*. Wellington: NZ Department of Justice.

DiIulio, John (1993) *Governing Prisons*. New York: Free Press.

Duncan, I. and Bollard, A. (1992) *Corporatization and Privatization: Lessons from New Zealand*. Auckland: Oxford University Press.

Durham, A.M. (1989) 'Managing the Costs of Modern Corrections: Implications of Nineteenth-Century Privatized Prison-Labor Programs'. *Journal of Criminal Justice*, 17: 441–455.

Empey, Lamar T. (1977) 'The Provo Experiment'. In E.E. Miller and M.R. Montilla (eds), *Corrections in the Community*. Reston, VA: Reston Publishing.

Hampden-Turner, Charles (1976) *Sane Asylum: Inside the Delancey St Foundation*. San Francisco: San Francisco Book Company.

Hough, Donna (2003) *A History and Analysis of the Salisbury Street Foundation in Christchurch*. Unpublished MA thesis in sociology, University of Canterbury, Christchurch.

Jamieson, Kath (1991) *The Social Organisation of Grosvenor Foundation*. Unpublished MA thesis in sociology, University of Canterbury, Christchurch.

Kincaid, P.T. and Leone, M.C. (1992) 'The Privatization of Prisons: The Wardens' Views'. *Federal Probation*, 4: 58–65.

Kunkel, Karl and Capps, Jason (2005) 'Privatization'. In Mary Bosworth (ed), *Encyclopedia of Prisons and Correctional Facilities*. Thousand Oaks, CA: Sage.

Lilly J.R. and Knepper P. (1992) 'An International Perspective on the Privatisation of Corrections'. *The Howard Journal* v.31: 174–191.

Lingard, F. (1936) *Prison Labour in New Zealand*. Wellington: NZ Government Printer.

McCord, W. and McCord, J. (1959) *Origins of Crime: A New Evaluation of the Cambridge-Somerville Youth Study*. New York: Columbia University Press.

McCorkle, L.W., Elias, A., and Bixby, F.L. (eds), *The Highfields Story: An Experimental Treatment Project for Youthful Offenders*. New York: Henry Holt.

Miller, E.E. and Montilla, M.R. (1977) 'Halfway Houses: An Overview'. In E.E. Miller and M.R. Montilla (eds), *Corrections in the Community: Success Models in Correctional Reform*. Reston, VA: Reston Publishing.

Ministerial Committee of Inquiry into the Prisons System (1989) *Prison Review Te Ara Hou: The New Way*. Chair: Sir Clinton Roper. Wellington: NZ Government Printer.

Moyle, Paul (1992) 'Privatising Prisons: The Underlying Issues'. *Alternative Law Journal*, v.17: 114–119.

Moyle, Paul (1993) "Privatisations of Prisons in New South Wales and Queensland: A Review of some Key Developments in Australia". *The Howard Journal* v.32(3): 231–250.

Newbold, Greg (1989) *Observations on the Report of the Ministerial Committee of Inquiry into the Prisons System 1989*. Unpublished report commissioned from the Department of Justice.

O'Toole, Sean (2005) 'Privatisation in the Corrections Industry'. In Sean O'Toole and Simon Eyland (eds), *Corrections Criminology*. Annandale, NSW: Hawkins.

Penal Policy Review Committee (1981) *Report*. Wellington: NZ Government Printer.

Roper, B. (1986) 'Market Forces, Privatization and Prisons: A Polar Case for Government Policy'. *International Journal of Social Economics*, v.13: 77–92.

Roper, B. and Rudd, C. (eds) (1993) *State and Economy in New Zealand*. Auckland: Oxford University Press.

Russell, Marcia (1996) *Revolution: New Zealand from Fortress to Free Market*. Auckland: Hodder Moa Beckett.

Rutherford, A. (1990) 'British Penal Policy and the Idea of Privatization'. In D.C. McDonald (ed), *Private Prisons and the Public Interest*, New Brunswick, NJ: Rutgers University Press.

Ryan, M. (1993) 'Evaluating and Responding to Private Prisons in the United Kingdom'. *International Journal of the Sociology of Law*, v.21: 319–333.

Schaffer, L. (1995) 'Synanon's History and Influence in Therapeutic Communities and Emotional Growth Schools: A Three-Part Series'. *Woodbury Reports Archives – Options and Essays*, Issue 2, available online: http:wwwstrugglingteens.com/archives/1995/2/oe05.html

Schmalleger, Frank (2001) *Criminal Justice Today*. Upper Saddle River, NJ: Prentice Hall.

Weeks, H.A. (ed) (1958) *Youthful Offenders at Highfields: An Evaluation of the Effects of Short-Term Treatment of Delinquent Boys*. Ann Arbor MI: University of Michigan Press.

Westerberg, Charles (2005a) 'Corrections Corporation of America'. In Mary Bosworth (ed), *Encyclopedia of Prisons and Correctional Facilities*. Thousand Oaks, CA: Sage.

Westerberg, Charles (2005b) 'Wackenhut Corrections Corporation'. In Mary Bosworth (ed), *Encyclopedia of Prisons and Correctional Facilities*. Thousand Oaks, CA: Sage.

Yeboah, David (1999) *National Evaluation Report on the Habilitation Centres Programme*. Unpublished report. Wellington: Department of Corrections.

Young, P. *The Prison Cell*. London: Adam Smith Institute.

Yuill, John; Smith, Mel; Newbold, Greg; and Tumahai, Danny (1996) *Private Sector Contract Prison: Evaluation of Proposals for Mt Eden Remand Facility*. Unpublished report prepared for the Department of Corrections.

CHAPTER 11
CAPITAL PUNISHMENT

C apital punishment is one of the earliest criminal sanctions known to civilisation. From the books of the Old Testament it is evident that around 900BC, penalties such as death by stoning, burning, decapitation and strangulation existed in the ancient cities of Israel. In the Twelve Tables written in 451BC, the first laws of Rome prescribed death by burning, falling, clubbing, hanging, drowning, decapitation and being buried alive, for certain offences. And in 400BC Athenian law provided for stoning, being thrown off a cliff, being bound to a stake to die slowly in public (an early form of crucifixion) and compulsory suicide.[1]

England

In medieval Europe a variety of methods of execution was used, including hanging, beheading, burning, drowning, pressing, garrotting, being buried alive, mutilation and being broken on the wheel;[2] however, the commencement of the Enlightenment in the 17th century, with its emphasis on human rights, saw a general reduction in the more brutal forms of execution. In England, death by hanging had been introduced by the 12th-century Norman king Henry I and soon became the nation's primary method. Most other European countries eventually followed. Initially death in hanging, favoured for its publicity value, was caused by strangulation but in the later 18th century a quest for greater efficiency began. The search was largely a hit-and-miss affair. At Tyburn in 1760 experiment began with the long drop method, designed to cause instantaneous death by breaking the neck. Due to inconsistent application and a lack of expertise the method was only partially successful, with many botch-ups. A more sophisticated drop was built at Newgate in 1783, and in 1880 Downing St issued specific, handwritten instructions for hanging with the long drop. In 1888 a table of calculated drops and rope lengths was issued,[3] and in 1891 fresh instructions were given, altering the placement of the noose on the neck in order to improve effectiveness.

In England, from which New Zealand derived its criminal justice traditions, hanging became increasingly popular from the beginning of the Tudor era in 1485. Other forms of execution were used as well. Executions reached a peak between 1530 and 1630 when an estimated 75,000 people were put to death in England.[4] Judicial killings declined after this, with the commencement of transportation to the Americas. Up until the mid-17th century no more than 50 offences carried the death penalty, but the number of listed capital crimes increased again after the Restoration in 1688, largely as a result of the growth of urban capitalism and the desire of the bourgeoisie to protect their property. As late as 1830, under what was known as the 'Bloody Code', more than 220 crimes were punishable by death, for offences as minor as forgery, pick-pocketing, and robbing a rabbit warren.[5] Accordingly, in the second half of the 18th century there was a precipitous jump in executions; between 1750 and 1800 about 1,400 executions took place in London alone, nearly five times as many as in the first half of the century.[6]

Between 1800 and 1830 more than 2,000 people were executed in England and Wales, but after 1832, with the continuing growth of liberal humanitarianism, the death penalty declined once again. In 1837 it was confined to 12 offences and with the Offences Against the Person Act 1861 was cut to four: high treason, murder, piracy with violence and the destruction of public arsenals and dockyards. As a result of these changes, just 347 people were hanged between 1837 and 1868. With the exception of traitors or cowards in war, there were no executions in England and Wales from 1838 for any crime except murder.[7]

Most of the 19th-century hangings in Britain were conducted in public, but in 1856 a Select Committee of the House of Lords recommended that public executions cease, and in 1868, after a similar recommendation by a Royal Commission on Capital Punishment (1864–1866), an amendment to the Capital Punishment Act decreed that henceforth all executions should take place in a prison.[8]

Between 1900 and 1949, 621 death sentences were carried out in England and Wales and the rate of executions remained quite steady.[9] But opposition was gathering. A select committee of the House of Commons on capital punishment reported on the issue in 1930, and between 1949 and 1953 another royal commission on capital punishment examined the matter, under the chairmanship of Sir Ernest Gowers.[10] Both investigations failed to effect any significant changes, but in 1952, while the Gowers commission was sitting, the murder case of two teenagers caused widespread outrage throughout England. Christopher Craig (16), abetted by Derek Bentley (19), had killed a policeman with a pistol shot. The minimum age for hanging was 18, and because of his age Craig was given life imprisonment. Bentley, however, mentally immature and mere accomplice to the crime, was hanged.[11]

The Craig and Bentley matter highlighted concerns about the fairness of the death penalty and fed growing pressure for reform. Hanging also fell out of favour with the judiciary and the executive. In the first half of the 20th century a relatively stable average of 62 executions a year took place; this dropped to an average of 3.6 by the late 1950s and into the 1960s.[12] The abolitionist movement in Britain in the 1960s never achieved a majority, but pressure from organisations such as Amnesty International and a strong trend toward abolition among other European countries finally persuaded the government to strike it out.[13] Capital punishment for murder was suspended by law in 1965 and abolished in 1969. Today it exists in England only for the crimes of treason and piracy and for certain offences committed by military personnel in wartime.

The United States

Today nearly all European nations have abolished capital punishment for murder; the United States is the only English-speaking democracy that still has the penalty on its books.[14] A former British colony, North America initially followed English tradition and in its early years used death by hanging as its principal mode of civil execution.

The first execution took place in 1630 when John Billington, one of the original *Mayflower* signatories, was hanged in Massachusetts for murder.

After the United States gained independence in 1783 and developed as a leading industrial power, it experimented with more 'modern' forms of execution. In 1888 New York approved use of the electric chair, Utah introduced the firing squad in 1903 and in 1924 in Nevada the gas chamber was tried out for the first time.[15] Finally, in 1982, Texas executed the first felon with a lethal injection.

Historically, executions in the United States have been ordered by a variety of jurisdictions – federal, state, county and so on – and before 1890, executions at state level were uncommon. Between 1850 and 1889 there were only 56 state executions from a total of over 5,000 carried out between 1850 and 1967.[16] Data[17] which include all executions under civil authority in the US, reveal a larger picture, however, with 5,381 executions between 1880 and 1899 and another 7,555 between 1900 and 1967. State executions peaked at 1,520 in the 1930s, with the largest single year being 1935 when 199 people were put to death. Thereafter capital punishment declined steadily with each decade – 1,174 executions in the 1940s, 682 in the 1950s and only 191 in the 1960s. In 1965 there were seven executions, in 1966 there was just one, and there were two in 1967.[18] In mid-1967, executions temporarily ended.

Detailed material relating to the nature and frequency of execution in the United States has been kept by the federal government since 1930 and, largely as a result of the burgeoning civil rights movement, it became accepted from the early 1960s that in its application, capital punishment was heavily discriminatory towards blacks and other minorities. In 1967 the President's Commission on Law Enforcement and the Administration of Justice conceded as much[19] and in June 1967, as a result of a number of pending legal challenges to the constitutionality of execution, a moratorium on death sentences commenced. Further challenges soon materialised, driven by civil rights activists, but the issue was not decided until the case of *Furman v. Georgia* in 1972. One of three cases of its type on the US Supreme Court agenda at the time, *Furman* affirmed the petitioner's view that capital punishment was, because of its arbitrary and discriminatory application, a 'cruel and unusual' punishment and was in violation of the United States Constitution. This decision declared capital punishment illegal throughout the United States, and the lives of 620 death-row inmates were spared.[20]

The decision was soon challenged. In 1976, just four years after the Furman case, *Gregg v. Georgia* declared the death penalty to be constitutional provided that a bifurcated proceeding – one part for the determination of guilt; the other for argument over penalty – was in place. *Gregg* also determined that states could remove jury discretion in punishment by making death mandatory for some crimes.[21]

In the wake of the *Gregg* decision, some states wasted no time resurrecting death-penalty statutes. In 1977 the first execution in 10 years was carried out when Gary Gilmore, convicted of two robbery-murders, was shot by firing squad in Utah. Thereafter the penalty was used with increasing frequency. There were only two more executions in the 1970s, but in the 1980s there were 117, and the 1990s saw 478 executions. Executions declined after reaching a peak of 98 in 1999 – with only 85 in 2000, 66 (2001), 71 (2002), 65 (2003) and 59 in 2004.[22] In December 2005, North Carolina double murderer Kenneth Lee Boyd became the one-thousandth person executed in the United States since 1976. By 2002, 38 of the 50 states, the federal government and the military had reinstated the death penalty. In 1999, 31 states had carried out the sentence. Gassing, electrocution, hanging and the firing squad were still on the books in many jurisdictions, but most used the lethal injection as an alternative or as the sole method. Only four executing states – Alabama, California, North Carolina and Nebraska – did not have the lethal injection and used the electric chair.[23]

In 2003 there were about 3,500 inmates on death row in the United States, but with fewer than 100 executions a year it was clear that the majority would never be executed. Most would have their sentences overturned or commuted, and a small number would die before their execution date; due to the complex appeals process the average time between sentencing and execution is about 12 years.[24]

A number of factors affect a person's chances of being executed. Blacks are more likely than whites to commit murder and to have a sentence of death carried out. Thirty-five per cent of those executed are black – that is, they are three times more likely to be executed than other Americans on the basis of population. People who kill whites are also more likely to be executed than those who kill black people. Men are far more likely to be executed than women. Of the 820 executions between 1977 and the end of 2002, only 10 were women.[25] Some states are more likely to execute criminals than others. California, for example, with more death-row inmates than any other, executed only seven people between 1977 and 1999. Texas, on the other hand, executed 185 – far more than any other state. About a third of all US executions since 1977 have taken place in Texas, and over three-quarters have been carried out in southern jurisdictions.[26]

From the above figures, it would appear that many of the factors that led to the *Furman* decision in 1972 remain in the United States. But debate based on the arbitrary and discriminatory nature of the death penalty is unlikely to succeed in today's climate. Seventy-seven per cent of Americans generally approve of capital punishment.[27] Some arguments for and against the penalty will be discussed later in the chapter, but an effective opposition strategy currently popular in the United States is to emphasise the fallibility of the criminal justice system, and the certainty that innocent people have been executed. Three American criminologists have identified 416 cases in the 20th century where men or women in North America were wrongfully convicted of crimes punishable by death. About a third received death sentences and 23 were executed. In each case the state had admitted that an error had occurred and had taken steps to correct it.[28]

Due partly to the growing sophistication of DNA testing, cases of wrongful convictions in capital crimes have continued to accumulate. Between 1977 and 2000 in the state of Illinois, for example, when 12 men were executed, 13 death row inmates were freed as a result of new evidence that pointed toward their innocence. As a result, in 2000 Governor George Ryan, a former death-penalty advocate, declared a moratorium on the penalty in Illinois. In the next two years another seven alleged killers were cleared in that state. Describing capital punishment as being "haunted by the demon of error", Ryan then commuted the sentences of all 167 of the state's death-row inmates.

The problem was not restricted to Illinois. Nationwide, in the 26 years after 1977, 99 death-row inmates were cleared of the crimes for which they had been sentenced to death.[29] In the light of this, some other states may follow Ryan's example, but it is unlikely that the murder rate will be affected either way. Whether or to what extent the penalty may be an effective deterrent to murder is unknown.[30] Whatever the case, in America strong support for capital punishment remains.

Capital Punishment in New Zealand Before 1935

The roots of New Zealand's criminal codes and its approach toward capital punishment lie in Victorian England. When the territory was annexed to the British Crown by the Treaty of Waitangi in 1840 it inherited much of England's law and the Westminster system of government. Britain had once relied heavily on the sanction of execution, but by the time New Zealand became a British possession capital punishment was in rapid decline. So in New Zealand use of the penalty was always restricted. New Zealand followed English common law until 1893 and thus, in 1861, the death sentence was limited to four crimes: high treason, murder, piracy with violence and the destruction of public arsenals and dockyards. In 1893 New Zealand passed its own Criminal Code Act which defined culpable homicide and made it, along with high treason and piracy, punishable by death. In fact, beyond murder, the death penalty has been used only once in New Zealand. Hamiora Peri, a follower of Ringatu Church leader Te Kooti, was hanged in 1869 for high treason in bringing war against the Queen. Although the penalty for treason also required Peri to be beheaded and quartered after death, this refinement was dispensed with.[31]

After the Treaty of Waitangi, the first person hanged in New Zealand was Wiremu Maketu, the teenage son of a Nga Puhi chief, who killed two Pakeha adults and three children at the Bay of Islands in 1841.[32] Wiremu's execution in 1842 was followed by that of labourer Joseph Burns in 1848. Burns had killed a family of three during a robbery in Auckland and was hanged publicly in Devonport on the site where the murders were committed.[33] A commemorative plaque now marks the location.

Until the Execution of Criminals Act 1858 abolished public executions, all hangings in New Zealand – a total of eight – were public. After that they took place inside prisons. About half of the 85 executions in New Zealand between 1840 and the date of final repeal in 1961 were conducted at Mt Eden prison in Auckland. Only one involved a woman. Minnie Dean, the so-called 'Winton baby farmer', convicted of taking unwanted babies for adoption and then killing them, was executed at Invercargill in 1895.

In the 19th century there were 57 executions, which were generally carried out at the prison closest to the place of trial. Scaffolds and miscellaneous equipment were held in at least two jails and were transported about as required, but occasionally scaffolds were built on the spot.[34] In 1880 the Home Office in London issued a handwritten 'Memorandum upon the Execution of Prisoners by Hanging with a Long Drop', together with hand-drawn diagrams, which was forwarded to New Zealand. In this, the knot on the rope was set so that it slipped to the back of the neck after the drop, the objective being to cause death by "dislocation of the neck or nervous shock". New instructions relating to hangings were codified into the Criminals Executions Act 1883 and a revised set of instructions (this time typed) was issued in December 1891. In this later document the positioning of the knot was changed so that it moved

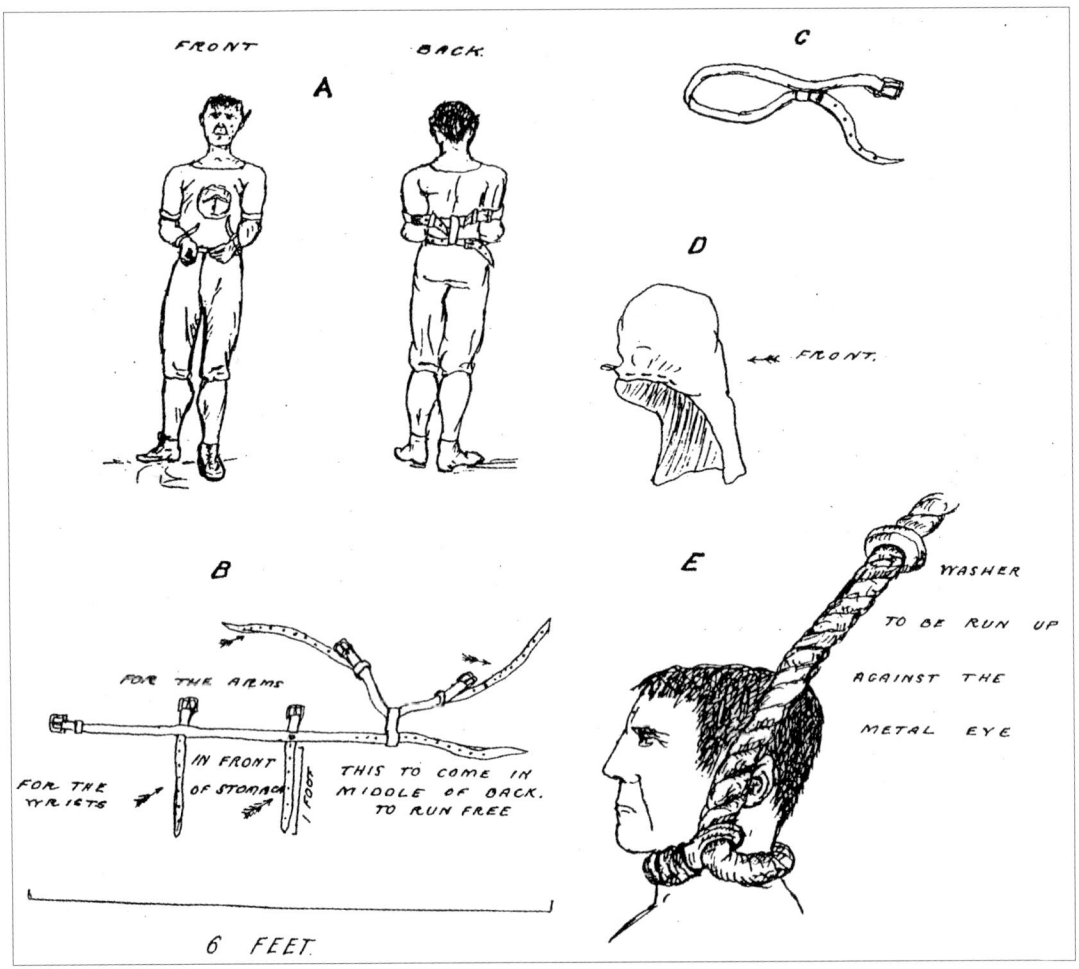

Hanging instructions sent to New Zealand from Downing St, London, in 1880. Note the incorrect setting of the noose, which was rectified in a revised set of instructions drafted in 1891.

under the chin instead of to the nape. In New Zealand the 1891 instructions were carried in a confidential circular dated 24 March 1905, but it is unclear whether they were in operation before this.

Capital punishment became less common in New Zealand as the 20th century progressed. Although the dominion's population expanded from 800,000 to 1.5 million between 1900 and 1935, the number of executions reduced to 20, or 0.57 per year, compared with 0.95 per year in the previous 60 years. In the first 35 years of the new century 56 people were convicted of murder, almost two-thirds of whom had their sentences commuted to life imprisonment. Before 1917, lifers could be discharged from prison only on exercise of the royal prerogative, but in 1917 they became eligible for release on probation after serving a minimum of eight years. This was reduced to five years in 1920 and increased to 10 years in 1962.[35]

The Move to Abolition

Until the 1920s the issue of capital punishment was seldom questioned and it remained uncontroversial. But after the First World War and the growth of left-wing politics that it generated, a trickle of anti-death penalty petitions began appearing on Department of Justice files. During and after the Depression of the 1930s, with increasing sympathy for the plight of the underdog, flourishing leftist sympathies resulted in the election of New Zealand's first Labour Government in 1935. Labour had the abolition of capital (and corporal) punishment written into its manifesto, and when it took office it automatically commuted all death sentences to life imprisonment.[36] The last hanging to take place before Labour came in was that of William Price, executed at Mt Crawford prison five months before the November election.

The suspension of capital punishment in New Zealand, in the same year the United States executed more murderers than ever in its history, was an extension of Labour's liberal/humanitarian philosophy. Being committed to a heavy social reform programme, however, Labour was initially too busy to deal with something as contentious as capital punishment. So abolition remained *de facto* and was not passed into law for some years. Had it not been for an unusual train of events, in fact, executions would probably have recommenced during the Second World War. For although the Labour caucus remained opposed to capital punishment, Prime Minister Peter Fraser was uneasy with abolition and favoured execution in extreme cases. In fact, in 1940 Fraser vigorously but unsuccessfully opposed the clemency application of a double murderer-rapist called Douglas Cartman. Fraser's leadership was a significant obstacle to legislative change.

The strange circumstances that led to the abolition of capital punishment began in 1940 when a reprieved murderer (RRD Smith) and three accomplices escaped from Mt Eden prison, permanently disabling a warder in the process. Quickly recaptured, the trio was sentenced in February 1941 to 12 years' hard labour each and 20 strokes of the cat-o'-nine tails. When these penalties were confirmed by the Court of Appeal, the government was placed in an extremely embarrassing situation. Having for years promised to abolish flogging it was now required to carry out a practice it abhorred.

The only way out was to exercise executive clemency, which it attempted to do. But clemency could not be extended without royal assent, and Governor General Sir Cyril Newall, an avid abolitionist, refused to sign the Cabinet's remittal order while flogging was still on the statute books. Fortunately Prime Minister Fraser was out of the country on war business at this time, and the deputy prime minister seized the opportunity to have abolition of both corporal and capital punishment brought through the House, without his leader's opposition.[37]

So it was that through a string of circumstances unrelated to the issue of hanging itself, New Zealand became an abolitionist state. In spite of the somewhat irregular manner

Rex Mason, Minister of Justice 1935–1949; 1957–1960, and an avid opponent of the death penalty.

of its passing, and notwithstanding the continued huge public support for executions, the law went through without great fuss. Hitler's domination in Europe, the invasion of Russia and the increasing belligerence of Japan were of far weightier concern to New Zealanders in 1941 than the treatment of murderers. There had been only six capital convictions since 1935, none particularly dramatic. However, without the mass of public opinion behind aboliton, it was probably inevitable that opposition would grow. As hostilities in Europe neared an end in 1945, dissatisfaction about abolition increased in pitch.

Capital Punishment Restored

New Zealand had six reported murders in 1941 and five in 1942. The following year, however, murders doubled, and in 1944 they doubled again. There were another 20 in 1945. Not all reported murders ended in convictions, but in the six years before abolition (1935–1940) there had been an average of one murder conviction a year. In the next six years (1941–1946) there were 20 convictions: an average of 3.3 per year.[38] These jumps were unprecedented in 20th-century New Zealand and seemed clear evidence that abolition was failing.

After the war annual reported murders fell again, but stayed high relative to pre-1942 figures, with a steady average of 11.8 reported murders per year between 1946 and 1950. But cold facts are not the stuff of successful campaigns and homicide figures were really only a rationalised baseline to an emotional upsurge that had been brewing since the early 1940s. The real energy for retentionism came from sensation. After 1941 every brutal murder in the dominion was blamed by death-penalty lobbyists on the absence of an effective deterrent. The outcry began in August 1942 with the slaying of two elderly sisters, and was repeated in 1946, 1947 and 1948 with four

Figure 11.1: Murders Reported to the Police

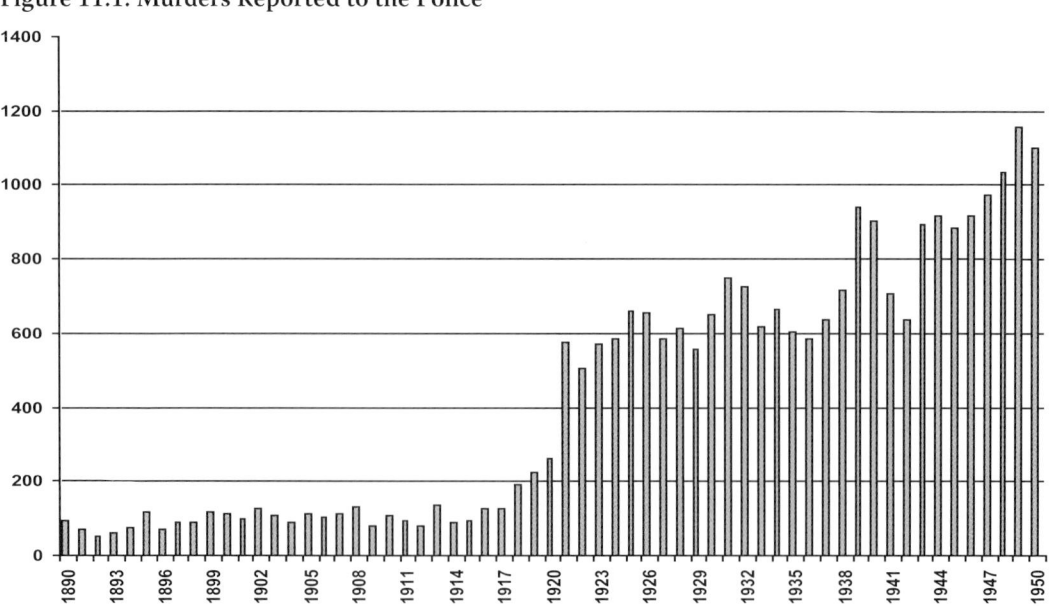

murders that remain unsolved to this day. From the end of the war, reported murders began to receive richer and richer press coverage. This attention was complemented by a crescendo of calls from grand juries for a return to capital punishment.

In August 1948 in Wellington, Edward Horton, a young sex offender on parole from borstal, sexually maimed and murdered a middle-aged English woman out for a Sunday walk, inflicting injuries so ghastly that they were described as "beyond the experience" of the Crown pathologist.[39] The so-called 'Kitty Cranston murder' sent shockwaves through the nation and caused an Imprest Supply Bill in parliament to be interrupted by a spontaneous debate on hanging. In opposition, the National Party pledged that if elected in 1949 it would "not flinch to give the people the protection they are entitled to".[40] No sooner had this furore died down than a man called John Tume battered his son, his mistress and her mother to death in a psychopathic frenzy. At trial the following year the offender displayed no remorse and evidence was given that he had been openly contemplating the slaying for some months. His words before the incident, "Even if you do murder these days you only get eight years, that's because of the good government we've got", drew wide notice, as did the convicting jury's rider calling for the restoration of the death penalty.

The murders and murder trials of 1948 and 1949 ensured that the issue of hanging had no chance to cool in the vital months preceding the November polls. Though not a major election matter, the National Party in 1949 had restoration written into its manifesto, and when the country went to the hustings that year feeling about it was simmering. The positions of the two major parties were clear: a vote for Labour meant a vote for continued abolition; a vote for National would be one for the gallows. The result was a resounding victory for National. With a margin of 12 in an 80-seat House, it wasted no time in fulfilling its promise.

The Hangings of the 1950s

As soon as he was sworn in as the new Justice minister, Clif Webb began preparing the ground for the return of capital punishment. Parliament resumed in June 1950 and the death penalty was high on the agenda. Debate over the Capital Punishment Bill ended in November, and despite the concession of a free vote, only one National member, Ralph Hanan, crossed the floor to vote with a united opposition. The Bill was passed with a majority of nine, and from 1 December 1950 New Zealand returned to retentionism.

In February 1951, only 11 weeks after hanging had been restored, a man called Malcolm McSherry was condemned for killing a bank clerk during a robbery. He was speedily reprieved but the ensuing outcry was warning that pusillanimity would not be tolerated. There had been eight convictions for murder in 1950, the highest figure on record. If that trend continued, the death sentence would soon be confirmed.

Clif Webb, Minister of Justice 1949–1954, who sponsored the Capital Punishment Act 1950.

Between 1951 and 1957 the sentence of death was passed 22 times for murder in New Zealand, and it was put into effect on eight separate occasions. All hangings took place at Mt Eden prison.

In the 1950s the decision of whether or not a death sentence would proceed was normally made by Cabinet, sitting in its capacity as the Executive Council. The Minister of Justice made the case for consideration, and legal issues were explained to sitting members by the Attorney General. When the Executive Council had made its decision over a person's fate its duty was to advise the Governor General and recommend that the penalty either stand or be commuted to life imprisonment.[41] At the time, and somewhat anomalously, the minimum non-parole period for life was only five years.

The first person hanged in New Zealand after the restoration of capital punishment was Urewera millhand William Fiori (30), convicted in February 1952 of shooting his employer and his employer's wife, for money. Described officially as "borderline feeble-minded",[42] Fiori had lodged no appeal against conviction; however, a recommendation for clemency had been made by the trial jury. Having received this prisoner following his sentencing, therefore, the authorities anxiously awaited the decision of the Executive Council.

Since the verdict, Horace Haywood, superintendent of Mt Eden prison, had had close contact with Fiori. The trial had been conducted 120 kilometres away in Hamilton, and Haywood had been a member of the escort which had transferred Fiori to Auckland. The prisoner was condemned on 14 February and it was almost three weeks before Cabinet decided there were no grounds to interfere with the sentence of the court. Law required that execution take place within 14 days of confirmation by the Governor General.

Prisoners, of course, knew Fiori was due to hang and trouble had already threatened at the jail over an attempt to get them to help erect the scaffold. The gallows mechanism and the rope, with a sandbag attached to it, had to be tested and the prisoner weighed every 24 hours from the time sentence was confirmed so that no one would know when the execution was scheduled. During this period a resounding crash echoed through the prison every time the steel trap was opened. Moreover, the condemned man was held in the West Wing, whereas the scaffold was located in the basement of the East Wing, known as the East Block, at the opposite end of the prison. This meant a long walk down hollow, stone corridors for the hanging party. The imminence of a hanging and the instant of the drop would thus be communicated to most inmates at the institution.

Prison authorities were unsure about how prisoners would react to an execution and the actual date, once fixed, was kept a close secret. Although no hanging had taken place in New Zealand for some 17 years, older prisoners recalled that they usually happened in the morning. They were unaware that the schedule had changed and that executions would now be carried out at night.

On Thursday 13 March 1952, a notice on the walls inside the prison advertised that Kerridge Odeon was to sponsor a movie showing in the prison that evening. Most prisoners attended this rare event, but Fiori, isolated in the capitals division, stayed in his cell. He probably suspected nothing, but shortly after he was showered the hanging party arrived. Fiori was spoken to briefly and escorted to a cell in the

Entrance to the East Block. The stairs lead down to the basement isolation cells where condemned men were prepared for execution.

East Wing basement. There, after he had stripped off his prison clothes and donned a white canvas smock, his arms and thighs were pinioned and, wearing the slippers he was given, he shuffled up the 17 steps to the gallows floor. Standing on the trap his ankles were bound, the noose secured, the white hood fitted, and he was asked if he had anything to say. At 8.03pm the signal was given. The lever was pulled, the trap swung open, the rope snapped taut, and the life of Fiori was extinguished. While prisoners were enjoying their evening's entertainment the condemned man had taken his final walk.

It was not until the following day that prisoners heard the radio news that the hangman's work had been done, and a feeling of revulsion swept through the institution. Although it was now too late to act, inmates resolved never again to be gulled. The movie ploy could work but once and the administration knew that in future it would have to be different. It was 18 months before the next execution took place, and by this time there had been some refinement.

It was now decided that executions would be scheduled an hour earlier – at 7pm – and that all inmates would be locked up, with their peepholes closed, before the event. A long seagrass mat would be rolled out between the west and east wings to soften the footsteps of the hanging entourage. The hangman – reputedly a retired policeman who wore a buttoned-up raincoat with a felt hat pulled over his eyes to

Isolation cells in the East Wing basement. The door at the end leads to the hanging yard.

avoid recognition – always arrived an hour earlier and waited by the scaffold for his victim. Although the trapdoors were now padded to muffle the sound of their opening, there was still no foolproof way of preventing inmates from knowing whenever an execution was imminent.

The next man hanged was Eruera Te Rongopatahi (23), who in a mood of drunken depression after being jilted by his girlfriend, gratuitously shot an Ashburton taxi driver. Te Rongopatahi died in 1953, and just over three months later, two weeks before Christmas, Harry 'Darkie' Whiteland (56), an Indian-born railway worker and an epileptic, was hanged for shooting a teenage female co-worker in Reefton after a minor argument.

For the next 18 months there were no further hangings, but in the five months between July and December 1955 there were four. On 7 July English immigrant Frederick Foster (26) was hanged for shooting his teenage ex-girlfriend in a central Auckland milk bar. Edward Te Whiu (20) was hanged on 18 August. Te Whiu, whose family had produced a number of prominent Auckland criminals, strangled an old woman in Whangarei after she discovered him burgling her house. On 13 October Harvey Allwood (34) was executed for shooting a friend at Te Anau during a drunken argument, and on 5 December Albert 'Paddy' Black (20) was hanged. Black, an Irish immigrant, had stabbed a romantic rival in the back of the neck with a knife in a central Auckland café.

After his conviction Foster feigned insanity, and on the scaffold refused to raised his chin for the noose. Only Allwood showed any bitterness. He was uncommunicative with staff, and after sentencing his guard was doubled because of a threat he had made to "take a screw with him" before he died. But at his appointed time, like the others, Allwood went quietly and duty staff were spared what they feared – a man demonstrating violently against his fate. In order to assist proceedings the condemned were offered a sedative cocktail of morphine and phenobarbitone four hours before their final walk.[43] As a precautionary measure, however, their thighs and arms were pinioned before climbing the scaffold.

The eighth and last execution of the 1950s was James Bolton, 15 months after Black. Bolton differed markedly from the nondescripts who had gone before him. He was 68 years old, a successful Wanganui farmer, convicted of poisoning his wife with arsenic. Bolton, who had been having an affair with his wife's younger sister, vigorously protested his innocence. On 18 February 1957, the day he was scheduled to die (though he was unaware of it at the time), Bolton requested an interview with the superintendent and the prison psychologist. He made an impassioned plea for his life.[44] But the hour of execution had been set and several hours later Bolton was brought to the gallows so distraught and heavily sedated that he could hardly stand up. Scenes like this were extremely upsetting for others involved.

The Impact of Hangings on Inmates

The effect of these ghoulish proceedings on inmates is difficult to assess. Certainly the majority were against capital punishment, but they were remarkably acquiescent about it. A collective sense of political, social and even moral commitment to one-another was only weakly developed among maximum-security prisoners in the 1950s.[45] There had been resistance to assisting with the scaffold and to attending films when hangings were scheduled. On such evenings an expectant hush fell over the whole institution as the hour of seven approached, and there was some banging on doors afterwards. But there was no effective, organised action, and as far as inmates were concerned, routine was very quickly restored.

Some prisoners were more troubled by executions than others, but feelings remained fairly personal. In 1977 Cecil Te Whiu spoke about the execution of his brother Eddie, saying that his sadness and bitterness would remain with him for the rest of his life.[46] In general, however, prisoners were rather blasé. An inmate called 'Maori Mac', who was one of the prominent figures at Mt Eden at the time, described the atmosphere at the time of a hanging:

> Oh, on the day of a hanging, everybody talked about it, eh. And the next day the screws would say, "Oh, he went like this", or "he didn't have nothing to say", or, "he just hung his head". That's all it was, just general conversation around the place. That's all. Nobody felt ill-at-ease. Nobody I knew felt ill-at-ease. I suppose some of them might have, but kept it to themselves.[47]

A senior officer called Dan Cavanagh confirmed[48] that apart from the prison being a bit quieter during executions, they did not seem to affect the prisoners. Some even took a macabre interest. Although everyone was supposed to be locked up at the time of a hanging, a lax administration made it easy for some to remain out of their cells, especially those who worked in the kitchen. By climbing on top of the elevator that brought meals up from the kitchen and lifting a flap at the base of the door, the arrival of the hangman, the escorting of the prisoner and the removal of his body on a stretcher could be watched. Actions, identity, dress and demeanour of the hanging party were accurately described by inmates who had watched through the gap in the door. One described Bolton "crying, dragging his feet, blabbering and frothing at the mouth" as he was shepherded to his appointment in the East Wing basement.[49]

Two of those who watched these proceedings were lifers. One was Les Shortcliffe, convicted of callously killing his young son in 1950, immediately before the passing of the Capital Punishment Act. Shortcliffe, described by prison psychologist Don MacKenzie[50] as "violent, unpredictable, and insensitive", always said he had hopes of recognising the hangman so he could kill him after he was released.

The Impact on Non-Institutional Personnel

In spite of their supposed deterrent function, judicial executions in this country were veiled in secrecy and the justice department was at pains to allow as little publicity about them as possible. But inevitably they were fairly public affairs. Apart from prison personnel, the hangman, the sheriff and the doctor – all of whom played active parts – a limited number of spectators was allowed. Any Justice of the Peace could attend, as could representatives of the Police. News delegates, too, were invited to witness proceedings, provided they exercised 'restraint' in their published accounts. Condemned men were allowed to receive religious instruction from a minister of a denomination of their choice, and to request that this person attend their hanging.

As with the inmates, the effects of executions on witnesses were various. One Justice of the Peace is reported to have attended every one. He was studying their "psychological effects," he said.[51] Most spectators were less intrigued. A *Truth* newspaper representative who witnessed Black's hanging was clearly repelled by proceedings, as reflected in his subsequent detailed and somewhat ghoulish written account.[52] Father AH Hyde, parish priest at St Benedict's Catholic Church, said that there was reluctance among the clergy to attend the condemned, because of the terrific emotional stress it imposed upon them. Some had to be pressured into 'doing their share' of what they clearly considered an unpleasant duty.[53]

Father Leo Downey, Director of Catholic Social Services and a man of great strength and compassion, counselled all four men who requested Catholic instruction before their deaths. Most priests were less resilient, and due to the strain on them, Downey insisted that no padre should ever go to a hanging alone. Father Hyde saw two – Te Rongopatahi and Black – with Downey, and he described the first as the most unnerving experience of his life. The morning after, Hyde was so distressed that he was unable to stand up straight when he got out of bed. It took him a week or two to get over the impact.[54]

Among the worst affected were the sheriffs, the official masters of ceremony whose job was to command the superintendent to "surrender the body of the prisoner" and later to signal the hangman to pull the trap lever, by raising their right hand with the warrant of execution held in it.[55] MacKenzie reports[56] that during the 1951–1957 period, three different sheriffs officiated and each was seriously affected. One suffered a physical collapse at an execution and had to be supported by two prison officers while he performed his sombre duty. Another, prison officer Percy Anstiss reported, so dreaded executions that he began turning up to them drunk. Each of these men went sick – for periods of up to four months – after an execution, suffering symptoms like shock, anxiety, nervous exhaustion and duodenal haemorrhaging.[57]

The Impact on Prison Officers

Officers reckoned that opinion among prison staff was divided about 50/50 on capital punishment, but tended toward abolition as the number of executions rose.[58] Only the most stoic, reliable and accordant personnel were considered for hanging duty, and those chosen were replaced if they showed any signs of nervousness. The job was not for the faint of heart. When Foster refused to raise his chin for the noose, one of the party later boasted of having stuck his fingers into the terrified man's eyes to force his head back.[59] Officer DD Price, who volunteered for hanging duty, openly defended the penalty and made fun of it. It was he who, before Fiori's hanging, had tried to trick an inmate into assisting with work on the gallows. He also went to lengths to try to cajole an obviously distressed Father Hyde into witnessing a practice drop. Where executions were concerned, MacKenzie said that Price was a "tough, unfeeling, bastard".

In 1950, the *Justice Department Memorandum to the Joint Committee on the Capital Punishment Bill* stated that executions in the past had been "an unpleasant duty which [warders] faced without flinching". So they tended to be in the 1950s. Officer Dan Cavanagh, who attended all eight of the Auckland executions, was totally unmoved by them. As far as he was concerned, there was no emotional involvement because staff did not feel individually responsible. "There was nothing *personal* in it", Cavanagh said, "we were only carrying out the sentence of the court."[60]

Cavanagh explained that the older officers who took this duty had been through the Depression and the war and some had seen internment in POW camps. These experiences had inured them to suffering in the same way that a doctor or a nurse could become desensitised to the sight of traumatic injury. He did concede, however, that an air of despondency would descend on the prison whenever an execution was scheduled.

The detachment of Cavanagh and others in the hanging party was not shared by all, for condemned prisoners had to be monitored day and night until they were reprieved or executed. Unlike the hanging party, which had no contact with the prisoner before his final escort, those assigned to 'special duty' (death watch), had intimate involvement with him for weeks on end. Sitting with him while he ate, slept, prayed and wept, they got to know him well. Two of the death-watch volunteers interviewed by the author expressed considerable empathy with the condemned men. But officer Anstiss said that he didn't think anybody had any particular concerns about it. "It was just another job that was there to do, and you did it", he said. "Didn't worry me".

The death watch never walked with the hanging party, but those who counselled the condemned to the grave found a dispassionate stance impossible. Hyde got to know Te Rongopatahi well before he accompanied him on his final walk, a mistake he was not to repeat with Black. MacKenzie commented, too, that he got so acquainted with Foster that when his time arrived he grieved for him as he would a close friend. When asked to witness the execution of Allwood, he made a point of remaining aloof.[61]

The Impact on the Superintendent

The person the executions affected most was Haywood. while they awaited the decision of the Executive Council. His job was the most stressful of all, for it was on

Horace Haywood, Superintendent of Mt Eden prison 1951–1963, who officiated over the eight hangings of the 1950s. The experience undoubtedly contributed toward his eventual breakdown.

him that the entire burden of the ritual fell. The superintendent was in close contact with a capital man and his family from the time he was sentenced to the time his corpse was taken from the institution the day after his death. He thus had no escape from their anguish, their pleading and their suffering. When a reprieve was granted Haywood relayed the news to the death cell. When mercy was denied it was Haywood's job to inform the prisoner that his sentence had been confirmed and he would face the gallows within 14 days. On the evening of the execution it was his miserable duty to have the prisoner prepared for death. The transfer of the condemned to the cell in the basement, the pinioning of the limbs, the positioning of the noose, and the fitting of the hood – all were the superintendent's concern. On 22 occasions Haywood had to receive and care for persons condemned to death by the courts, without knowing whether the sentence would be carried out. Eight times over that seven-year period he had to take them on their final journey.

The effect of this ritual was marked. Each execution took its toll, although some were worse than others. Prisoners like Black and Allwood, who faced their destinies bravely, made the job easier. Those who crumbled made it difficult to bear. Foster, who feigned madness and tried to resist the rope, and Bolton, who denied guilt and collapsed in his last hours, taxed the stoicism of all but the most implacable. But it was Eddie Te Whiu, a youth of just 20 years, who was the most distressing. The Te Whiu family was well known to Haywood; several members had been in his custody, and Eddie's case had evoked much sympathy from the public. To make things worse, the boy's parents waited for him outside the prison after clemency was denied and it was well known that Haywood, at least, was seriously affected. A number of people interviewed by the author commented upon it. Officer Percy Anstiss, for example, said:

> That was a very emotive situation, it was a terrible drain on Haywood. The whole family crying and shouting in the courtyard ... I can particularly remember Te Whiu's father with his big hat on. And his mother and all the carry-on, crying.

Although it seems that the institution as a whole gradually got used to the executions, for Haywood the burden became heavier as time went on. A government publication reproduces a statement by MacKenzie on the matter:

> Each execution was attended by tension which mounted throughout the institution as the day and hour approached. But it was noticeable to me that the tension was less each time. There seemed to be a growing acceptance amongst the inmate population. The tension and anxiety among those who had to carry it out grew no less, however, and the effect on the Superintendent was cumulative ...[62]
>
> The Superintendent always adopted a show of bravado, but the effect on him was all too apparent. He became, and looked, a lonely, ageing man, carrying a burden that grew heavier as days passed. It usually took him several weeks to become his old robust self.[63]

Sam Barnett, who was Secretary for Justice between 1949 and 1960, was in the superintendent's office when the Executive Council's decision to hang a young Maori (probably Te Whiu) came through. The superintendent is reported to have burst into tears.[64] Haywood made no secret that he hated executions and an official, reporting on the matter to head office, wrote, "… adverse effects have been noticed in this superintendent, so that he is minimising the effect executions have on himself".[65] Exactly what these words mean is open to speculation, but the implication is that Haywood was drinking.

For the purposes of executions only, alcohol was permitted for the use of the hanging party. After proceedings were over, the party retired to the superintendent's office where they were given a much-needed drink. It was upon release through this means that Haywood became increasingly dependent during his later administration,[66] and even prisoners knew that Haywood's preference was whiskey. One convict is reported to have personally accused Haywood of drowning his emotions in alcohol whenever a hanging was due and, a former inmate told me, was later put on charge for telling an officer, "Yeah, Haywood would still be sucking on his whiskey bottle after telling the bloke to pull the lever". Another former prisoner said he had heard that Haywood hated hangings so much "he used to get steamed up on a bottle of whiskey before he would even attend". A lifer who knew Haywood well, said:

> Haywood was a good fellow until he started going funny. He went to a hanging in Fiji and when he came back he was off for three weeks. The screw told us he was lying in bed blind drunk, throwing whiskey bottles at the wall.

The evidence that Haywood had a drink problem is thus fairly conclusive. That his abhorrence of hanging exacerbated his problem in quite a significant way is highly probable.

Final Repeal

In 1957 the National Government was ousted and Labour was sworn back in. A single-vote majority in parliament made the new administration hesitant to legislate, so once again it commuted all death sentences to life imprisonment. Seven capital cases were despatched in this way before Labour was relegated to opposition in 1960.

Rejection of the death penalty had increased in the National Party when it returned to power in 1960, but the majority of the caucus still favoured it. Labour remained uniformly opposed. There was a powerful feeling in parliament that, whatever the outcome, a matter as serious as capital punishment should not be subject to the oscillations of party politics. One way or another, a permanent solution should be reached.[67] What direction such a settlement might take was uncertain, but a key to it was the new Minister of Justice and Attorney General, Ralph Hanan.

Hanan was one of the few National Party politicians who opposed the death penalty. He had been a vocal critic of it for most of his political life, and he alone had crossed the floor in the vote of 1950. Now a highly regarded and influential member of Cabinet, Hanan was more committed than ever. An important item on his agenda was the drafting of a new Crimes Act, section 172 of which would deal with the penalty for murder.

Arguments over this section of the bill were hotly contested in the debating chamber, and it is interesting that the name of John Tume, used effectively in 1950 to support hanging, was now raised in opposition. While at Mt Eden, Tume had become the victim of a murder attempt by a deranged prisoner called Brooks. Brooks had decided he wanted to die on the gallows and the abolitionists argued that the existence of the scaffold could become an incentive to murder for people with suicidal tendencies.

Overall, the issue was far more complex than this, of course, and the Brooks-Tume incident was of no great significance. Support for the penalty ebbed as the hangings progressed and sympathy for the condemned increased, but in 1961 perhaps two-thirds of voters still supported it.[68] Tempers frayed in the debate over section 172, and in the final division 10 National members voted with the opposition and succeeded in abolishing capital punishment for murder.

Hanging remained for treason and treachery, but this never became an issue. There was no sudden leap in murders after 1961 and people soon lost interest. In November 1989 the Abolition of the Death Penalty Bill, striking the death penalty out entirely, sailed through the House of Representatives with a 52–14 majority and almost without public comment. Today, although from time to time particularly brutal murders result in passionate calls for the return of the death penalty, such campaigns normally run out of steam fairly quickly. It is thus unlikely that the idea of reinstatement would get any sustained support.

Discussion and Conclusion

In 1764 Cesare Beccaria, the world's first recognised criminologist, wrote an essay in which he outlined his reasons for opposing capital punishment. Many of these same arguments recur today as the issue is passionately and repetitively debated without resolution. In modernising nations, however, the penalty has tended to abrogate or disappear so that, apart from the peculiar exception of the United States, in the Western democracies the execution of criminals has virtually died out. New Zealand provides a good case study of some of the issues relating to the death penalty and the difficulties that surround it.

How effective capital punishment is in reducing murder rates is unknown, and it is difficult to demonstrate a relationship between murder rates and executions.[69] In the United States, although homicides increased during the 10-year moratorium that started in 1967, they continued to rise after executions recommenced, reaching peaks of over 25,000 in 1991 and 1993. They then dropped again to their current level of about 16,000 per year.

What is clear is that policy decisions about capital punishment are influenced more by emotionalism and political expediency than by practical efficacy. Such an observation highlights one of the debate's principal concerns, because history shows just how sensitive opinions are to emotional ebbs and flows. For this reason, calls for referenda on the matter have always been denied by New Zealand governments. But the problem of inconsistency does not end with the general public. Even when decisions are left to the executive, chance and circumstance are prominent players. New Zealand's abolition statute of 1941 for example, came about simply because the Governor General refused to sign a remittal order for a flogging when the Prime

Minister happened to be overseas. In the Crimes Act of 1961, the charisma of a single man – Ralph Hanan – was critical to the final outcome of section 172.

Commutations are another area where fate has played a powerful hand. New Zealand's first and second Labour governments reprieved all condemned men, almost as a matter of course. And in 1951 the main reason that Malcolm McSherry was spared was simply an absence of government resolve. The dynamics of this fatal process were shifting. Bert Dallard, Controller General of Prisons 1925–1949, was an open advocate of capital punishment. He was always consulted in capital cases and reports that before 1935 his personal recommendation was almost invariably followed by government.[70] In the Executive Council the Prime Minister held particular sway, although in Cartman's case we know he was overruled.

In spite of all its legal safeguards, the judicial process is not infallible and in capital cases leaves itself open to irreversible error. Seldom, if ever, are all the facts of a case available to a jury. Verdicts are delivered on the basis of truths, half-truths, suppositions, inferences, deductions, rhetoric, exaggerations, minimisations and often pure falsehoods, which defence and prosecution throw at a jury in order to persuade it toward a particular view. There is clear evidence of false murder convictions in the United States, and obvious injustice in the English case of Derek Bentley. England has a procession of wrongful murder convictions as well.[71] In New Zealand there is the disturbing case of Arthur Allan Thomas, convicted largely on the basis of a police fabrication over a double murder in 1971.[72] He was pardoned in 1979. Another is Dean Wickliffe, convicted of murder in 1972 but whose conviction was reduced to manslaughter in 1986. In 1997 he was again convicted of a murder, but acquitted on a retrial in 1999.[73] There have been a number of other murder cases in New Zealand in which questionable facts and processes have led to controversial convictions. It is the fallibility of the trial process and the possibility of a faulty verdict that presents probably the strongest argument against capital punishment.

The issue of capital punishment will always be contentious, but it is difficult to sustain a pragmatic argument in its favour. For the most part the issues are emotional more than practical.[74] In the United States the principal justification of executions seems to be appeasement of a vengeful public. Everywhere the penalty is dogged by problems of consistency, equity and justice. It does not appear to affect the crime rate and it is not always conducted without partiality. But most important is the certain fact that people have at times been executed for crimes they did not commit, adding more innocent lives to the list of those who have fallen as victims of murder.

Notes

1 Johnson, 1990: 3–17; Newbold, 1999.

2 Peters, 1995: 37; Spierenburg, 1995: 51–58.

3 Gatrell, 1994: 51–54; Young, 1998: 8.

4 Gatrell, 1994: 6–7.

5 Cooper, 1974; Hay, 1982: 103–108.

6 Gatrell, 1994: 7; Koestler, 1956.

7 Gatrell, 1994: 616–619; Royal Commission, 1953: 5.

8 Calvert, 1973: 4; Gowers, 1956: 9–27.

9 Royal Commission, 1953: 9, 308–309.

10 Gowers, 1956.

11 Koestler and Rolph, 1961: 121.

12 Zimring and Hawkins, 1973: 290.

13 Zimring and Hawkins, 1989: 12, 20.

14 See Hood, 1996: App.1.

15 Bowers, 1984: 12–13.

16 Inciardi, 1999: 388.

17 Espy and Smylka, 1994.

18 Zimring and Hawkins, 1989: 27–35.

19 Inciardi, 1999: 388–389.

20 Bowers, 1984: 15–24; Zimring and Hawkins, 1969: 34–37.

21 Inciardi, 1999: 392–393.

22 *USA Today*, 14 November 2005.

23 Mays and Winfree, 2002: 72.

24 Mays and Winfree, 2002: 70.

25 Silverman, 2001: 40–44; http://www.ojp.usdoj.gov/bjs/glance.htm

26 Allen and Simonsen, 2001: 581.

27 Allen and Simonsen, 2001: 589.

28 Radelet, Bedau and Putnam, 1992.

29 *The Dominion Post*, 13 Jan 2003; *USA Today*, 29 March 2002.

30 Mays and Winfree, 2002: 368.

31 Young, 1998: 50–57.

32 Oliver, 1990.

33 Page, 1982.

34 Young, 1998: 7–11.

35 Webb, 1982: 143, 151.

36 Engel, 1977: 10–11.

37 Newbold, 1989: 21, 26; 1990.

38 Engel, 1977: 35.

39 Lynch, 1970: ch.8.

40 NZPD 1948, v.238: 3270.

41 Marshall, 1984: 221.

42 Newbold, 1990: 160.

43 MacKenzie, 1980: 72–83.

44 Interviewed by author, 9 September 1982.

45 Newbold, 1989: 71–83.

46 Prison conversation with author, 1977.

47 Interviewed by author, 7 November 1983.

48 Interviewed by author, 11 June 1983.

49 Interviewed by author, 22 July 1983

50 MacKenzie, 1980: 72.

51 MacKenzie, 1980: 80.

52 *Truth*, 14 December 1955.

53 Interviewed by author, 6 May 1983.

54 Interviewed by author, 6 May 1983.

55 Engel, 1976: 65.

56 MacKenzie, 1980: 76.

57 MacKenzie, 1980: 76–77.

58 Personal comments to author: 1982–1983.

59 MacKenzie, 1980: 83.

60 Interviewed by author, 11 June 1983.
61 MacKenzie, 1980: 80–81.
62 Department of Justice, 1974: 71.
63 Department of Justice, 1974: 70.
64 Engel, 1977: 66.
65 Cited in MacKenzie, 1980: 77.
66 MacKenzie, 1980: 77.
67 Marshall, 1983: 223.
68 Robson, 1987: 169–170.
69 See Bowers, 1984: 25–28; Newbold, 1990: 170–71.
70 Dallard, 1980: 121; 1976.
71 See Newbold, 2000: 233–234.
72 See Yallop, 1978.
73 See Newbold, 2000: 148.
74 For a contrary view, see Garrett, 1999.

References

Allen, Harry E. and Simonsen, E. Clifford (2001) *Corrections in America: An Introduction* (9th ed). Upper Saddle River, NJ: Prentice Hall.

Beccaria, Cesare (1963/1764) *On Crimes and Punishments*. New York: Macmillan.

Bowers, William J. (1984) *Legal Homicide: Death as Deterrent in America, 1864–1982*. Boston: Northeastern University Press.

Calvert, E. Roy (1973) *Capital Punishment in the Twentieth Century and the Death Penalty Enquiry*. Mountclair, NJ: Patterson Smith.

Cooper, David D. (1974) *The Lesson of the Scaffold: The Public Execution Controversy in Victorian England*. Athens, OH: Ohio University Press.

Dallard, Berkeley L.S. (1980) *Fettered Freedom: A Symbiotic Society or Anarchy?* Wellington: Department of Justice.

Dallard, Berkeley (1976) Interview with Margaret Long. Unpublished tape recording. Wellington: Department of Justice.

Department of Justice (1974) *Crime in New Zealand*. Wellington: Government Printer.

Engel, Pauline F. (1977) *The Abolition of Capital Punishment in New Zealand 1935–1961*. Wellington: Department of Justice.

Espy, Watt and Smylka, John (1994) *Executions in the US 1608–1987: The Espy File*. Death Penalty Information Centre.

http://users.bestweb.net/~rg/execution/STATE%20EXECUTION%20TOTALS.htm

http://www.deathpenaltyinfo.org/article.php?scid=8&did=269

Garrett, David (1999) *A Life for a Life: A Case for Capital Punishment*. Christchurch: Hazard Press.

Gatrell, V.A.C. (1994) *The Hanging Tree: Execution and the English People 1770–1868*. Oxford: Oxford University Press.

Gowers, Sir Ernest (1956) *A Life for a Life? The Problem of Capital Punishment*. London: Chatto and Windus.

Hay, Douglas (1982) 'Property, Authority and the Criminal Law'. In Piers Beirne and Richard Quinney (eds), *Marxism and Law*. New York: Wiley.

Hood, Roger (1996) *The Death Penalty: A Worldwide Perspective*. Oxford: Clarendon Press.

Inciardi, James A. (1999) *Criminal Justice* (6th ed). Fort Worth, TX: Harcourt Brace.

Koestler, Arthur (1956) *Reflections on Hanging*. London: Victor Gollancz.

Koestler, Arthur and Rolph, C.H. (1961) *Hanged by the Neck*. Middlesex: Penguin.

Lynch, P.P. (1970) *No Remedy for Death: The Memoirs of a Pathologist*. London: John Long.

MacKenzie, Donald F. (1980) *While We Have Prisons*. Auckland: Methuen.

Marshall, Sir John (1984) *Memoirs, Volume One: 1912–1960*. Auckland: Collins.

Mays, G. Larry and Winfree, L. Thomas (2002) *Contemporary Corrections*. Belmont, CA: Wadsworth Thomson.

Newbold, Greg (1989) *Punishment and Politics: The Maximum Security Prison in New Zealand*. Auckland: Oxford University Press.

Newbold, Greg (1990) 'Capital Punishment in New Zealand: An Experiment that Failed'. *Deviant Behavior*, v.11: 155–174.

Newbold, Greg (1999) 'A Chronology of Correctional History'. *Journal of Criminal Justice Education*, v.10 (1): 87–100.

Oliver, William H. (1990) 'Maketu, Wiremu Kingi'. In William H. Oliver (ed), *Dictionary of New Zealand Biography, v.1: 1769–1869*. Wellington: Allen and Unwin/Department of Internal Affairs.

Peters, Edward M. (1995) 'The Prison Before the Prison: The Ancient and Medieval Worlds'. In Norval Morris and David J. Rothman (eds), *The Oxford History of the Prison*. New York: Oxford University Press.

Page, Kirk (1982) *A Tangled Web*. Auckland: Hodder and Stoughton.

Robson, John L. (1987) *Sacred Cows and Rogue Elephants: Policy Development in the New Zealand Justice Department*.

Royal Commission on Capital Punishment 1949–1953 (1953) *Report*. London: Her Majesty's Stationery Office.

Silverman, Ira J. (2001) *Corrections: A Comprehensive Review*. Belmont, CA: Wadsworth Thomson.

Spierenburg, Pieter (1995) 'The Body and the State: Early Modern Europe'. In Norval Morris and David J. Rothman (eds), *The Oxford History of the Prison*. New York: Oxford University Press.

Yallop, David (1978) *Beyond a Reasonable Doubt? An Inquiry into the Thomas Case*. Auckland: Hodder and Stoughton.

Young, Sherwood (1998) *Guilty on the Gallows: Famous Capital Crimes of New Zealand*. Wellington: Grantham House.

Zimring, Franklin E. and Hawkins, Gordon J. (1973) *Deterrence: The Legal Threat in Crime Control*. Chicago: Chicago University Press.

Zimring, Franklin E. and Hawkins, Gordon J. (1989) *Capital Punishment and the American Agenda*. Cambridge: Cambridge University Press.

CHAPTER 12
CORRECTIONS IN THE COMMUNITY

Although imprisonment remains the primary sanction for serious offenders in New Zealand as in other parts of the world, this country has a number of non-custodial options as well. Often known as 'intermediate' measures, some of these sanctions function as alternatives to imprisonment, and others as a form of controlled supervision after release from custody. The main purposes of intermediate measures are:

1. To provide courts with an alternative to short-term imprisonment that allows an offender to remain in the community while still subject to punitive/reformative control and supervision.

2. To provide parole authorities with an avenue for partial release of offenders deemed in need of control and supervision as they readjust to freedom.

3. To reduce prison populations and relieve some of the costs associated with incarceration.

New Zealand, with its proportionately large numbers of inmates in minimum security, has also been something of a leader in community corrections. Over the last 100 years or so, but particularly since the 1960s, the number of community sanctions has multiplied and the proportion of people awarded community-based measures relative to those imprisoned has grown. The first experiment with community corrections began in 1886 and options have continued to expand and diversify since.

Probation

Deriving from the Latin noun *probatio* (testing), probation in various guises has existed for centuries, for example in the forms of reprieve and suspended sentencing. In more modern understanding of the practice, the earliest probation system is known from Warwickshire in England, where in 1820 courts adopted the practice of sentencing minor youth offenders to one day in prison, followed by a return to supervision by a parent or master. In 1841 the same practice was adopted by the city of Birmingham, but probation lacked specific statutory provision in England until it followed New Zealand with the passage of the Probation of First Offenders Act in 1887.[1]

The term 'probation' was coined in 1841 in Boston, Massachusetts, where John Augustus established an *ad hoc* system by which offenders could be released pre-trial into the custody of an approved person, who might subsequently recommend that the charges be dropped if warranted by an accused's conduct. Over the next few decades a number of states followed Massachusetts' example,[2] although the practice did not receive federal recognition until 1925.

New Zealand was an early starter in probation. Nineteenth-century Inspector-General of Prisons Arthur Hume, in spite of his authoritarian approach to prisons, was a strong supporter of probation and recommended it for naïve offenders as a means of avoiding the contaminating influences of incarceration.[3] In 1886, six years after Hume took office and a year ahead of England, New Zealand passed the First Offenders Probation Act, making it the first country in the world to adopt a national probation system. Nineteenth-century probation was different to what it is now, and required all arrested first offenders to be assessed with a view, if convicted, to being released on probation as an alternative to imprisonment. The offender could be given probation for a period not exceeding the maximum prison sentence available on the charges concerned. Statutory conditions included monthly reporting to a probation officer (normally a serving police officer), keeping the officer informed about one's residential address and having one's form of employment approved. Special conditions could also be imposed. Offenders who failed to comply with probation requirements could be returned to court and imprisoned for the original offence.

The first significant amendment to the 1886 act came in 1903, when the maximum possible term of probation was limited to three years. Probationary assessment was also restricted now to 'convicted' offenders, as opposed to the 'arrested' offenders specified in the original law. The scope of probationary power reverted back to arrested offenders in 1920, and returned to convicted offenders again in 1954.

In 1906 probation was made available to some prison inmates after release. Under the provisions of the Habitual Criminals and Offenders Act 1906, released habitual offenders could be subject to two years' probationary supervision. Post-release supervision became compulsory for habitual criminals and reformative detainees in 1910, for other inmates released on parole in 1917 and for borstal trainees in 1924.

Between 1906 and 1954 changes to the way probation operated were few. The

Figure 12.1: Probationers Received 1890–1950

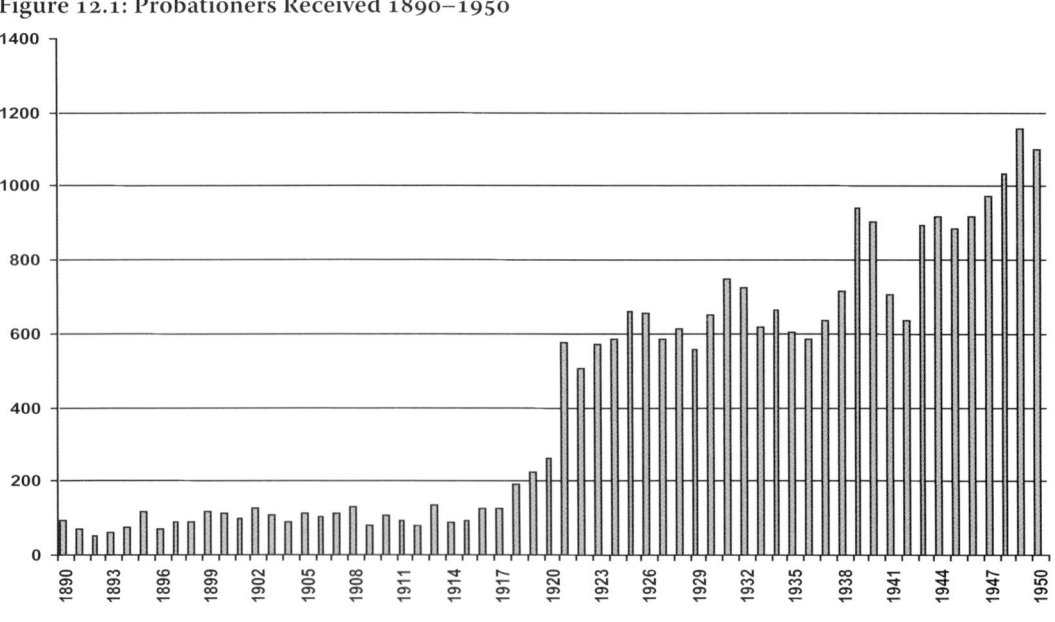

first part-time civilian probation officers were appointed in 1915, followed by four full-time officers in 1926. However, a large volume of probationary work remained in the hands of the police, with 170 police officers also acting as probation officers. By 1949 there were still only seven full-time probation officers for the whole of New Zealand.[4]

At first probation was not popular with the courts. Between 1890 and 1915 only about 100 offenders were given probation each year.[5] However, after the First World War the use of probation grew, with 226 orders made in 1919. In 1920, following dissatisfaction among magistrates,[6] the Offenders Probation Act made probation available to all offenders – not just first offenders – and extended the maximum available probationary term from three years to five. An immediate effect of the 1920 legislation was a further increase in probation orders. In 1920, 264 orders were made. By 1924 this figure had more than doubled, to 572, and they continued to grow, with 650 orders in 1930, 902 in 1940 and about 1,100 a year between 1949 and 1953.[7]

Notwithstanding this expansion, in his annual report to parliament in 1954, outspoken Secretary for Justice Sam Barnett criticised the scope of the current probation system, which he felt had been stagnating for 34 years. He accused the system of being under-developed and under-resourced for the tasks it should be performing. Despite the appointment of some full-time probation officers in 1926, most probationary work had remained in the hands of the police, supported by court bailiffs. A fully developed probation service, Barnett argued, would more than pay its way by diverting offenders from the costly alternative of imprisonment.[8]

That same year, the Criminal Justice Act 1954 made significant changes to the probation system. Coming into effect on 1 January 1955, the act strengthened the original provision whereby probation officers provided reports for courts prior to sentencing. Officers were now to report whenever required by the court (which became almost automatic when imprisonment was contemplated). The 1954 act also confined the use of probation to persons convicted of an offence punishable by imprisonment and restricted the term of probation to between one and three years – a reduction from the five years that had been allowed since 1920.

The standard conditions of probation stayed much the same as those imposed in 1886: an offender was required to report regularly and to have his place of residence and work recorded and approved by his probation officer. And, as amended in 1920, the offender might also be forbidden to associate with any person or class of persons and ordered to be of good behaviour. Special conditions might also be imposed; for example, to abstain from drinking alcohol. A breach of probation could result in further probation and a fine and/or imprisonment of up to three months. Theoretically, a probationer who breached conditions could also be brought back before the court for resentencing on the original charges, although in practice this happened extremely rarely, if at all.[9]

The 1954 act had a dramatic impact on the way probation was used. By 1955 there were 30 full-time probation officers, a figure which had increased to 90 by 1964.[10] In 1969 there were 130 officers, although these were still supplemented by 70 police and three court staff.[11] By the early 1980s, use of part-time probation officers ceased altogether.[12] There was a big jump in numbers sentenced to probation as well. These grew from 1,325 in 1954 to over 2,000 in 1963. In 1970 there were 4,737 probation orders, and more than 7,000 in 1980, but by 1985, when the definition of probation changed, probation orders had dropped to 6,000.

In 1963, in co-operation with various churches, the first of a number of hostels for probationers was set up. By the early 1980s, however, administrative and financial problems caused the use of these hostels to decline. Other than this, use of probation altered little until 1985 when a new Criminal Justice Act became law.

Under the Criminal Justice Act 1985 the term 'probation' was replaced by 'supervision'. Somewhat confusingly, however, the term 'probation officer' was retained and the service continued to be known as the 'probation division' until the Department of Justice split in 1995 and the Department of Corrections was created. Thereafter supervision was handled by a section within Corrections known as the 'Community Corrections Service', which was renamed the 'Community Probation Service' in 1998.

The sentence of supervision was similar to that of probation – with the maximum of two years unchanged – but the minimum term was reduced to six months. Standard conditions also stayed the same but special conditions could not now be imposed without the consent of the offender. And the power of the court to sentence an offender to imprisonment or re-sentence on the original offence when a supervision order was breached, was removed.

Figure 12.2: Probationers Received 1945–2005

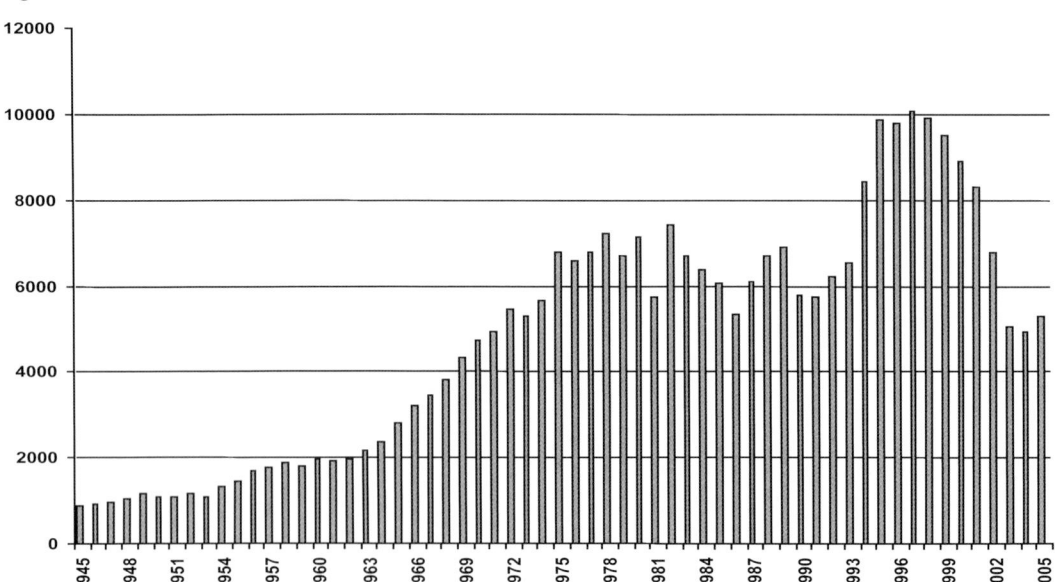

The 1985 act was a liberal experiment, which came under significant criticism and amendment as offending rates escalated and public attitudes toward crime, particularly violent crime, hardened. The major changes to probation came in in 1993. Under the 1985 act, probation and other forms of community sentence could only be awarded as alternatives to imprisonment but from 1993, supervision became available cumulatively on sentences of 12 months' imprisonment or less.

The Criminal Justice Act 1985 and its 1993 amendment impacted significantly on the work of the probation division. After 1985 the number of people sentenced to probation remained steady at about 6,000 per year, but numbers boomed from 6,561 to over 10,000 between 1993 and 1997, and began to fall thereafter. Rises in supervision between 1982 and 1997 were caused by the greater use of supervision for offences involving violence and increases in convictions for violence (in particular domestic violence) for which supervision sentences were common.[13]

Current Use of Supervision

The latest major changes to criminal justice law in New Zealand came in 2002 with the Sentencing Act and the Parole Act. Under the Sentencing Act, supervision remains available from six months to two years, with standard conditions requiring a probationer to report regularly to his probation officer, live at an approved address, work at an approved occupation (if employed) and not to associate with persons or classes of persons specified by the probation officer. Probationers may also be subjected to a wide range of special conditions. Failure to comply with conditions may result in cancellation of the sentence and a return to court for re-sentencing on the original charge, and/or up to three months' imprisonment and a fine of up to $1,000.

After reaching a peak of 10,000 in 1997, use of the sentence of supervision fell year by year, most dramatically after the passage of the 2002 acts. In 2001, 8,300 offenders received supervision and in 2004 there were only 4,928 – less than in 1986.

According to government sources,[14] this downward trend was caused by falling crime rates (convictions declined from 182,000 in 1992 to 173,000 in 2001), combined with a drop in the percentage of cases receiving community-based sentences after 1997.[15] In 2004 the Department of Corrections operated 56 centres throughout three regional precincts and employed approximately 1,200 staff. Although supervision is relatively cheap, about $8,000 per client per year, and is given mainly to minor offenders, about two-thirds of probationers are convicted of another offence within two years of being sentenced.[16]

Parole, Early Release and Post-Release Supervision

Provision has been made for the early release of inmates for good behaviour since the advent of the first penitentiaries. In 1817 America's first 'good time law' was passed at Auburn, New York, allowing first-time inmates serving five years or less to be granted remission of up to one-quarter of their sentences for good behaviour. In England, informal and semi-formal early release provisions have been active since the days of transportation, and in 1898 a formal system of fixed remission was installed, varying from a third to a sixth of the sentence depending on the type of inmate and the sentence being served.[17]

The use of parole, which is less fixed than remission, comes from the French *'parole d'honneur'* (word of honour), and its modern origins lie in the 19th century. As noted in chapter 2, the idea relates back to the liberal experiments of Alexander Maconochie in Norfolk Island in the early 1840s and Sir Walter Crofton in Ireland in the 1850s. In each case, good behaviour among inmates led to increasing liberty, culminating in conditional freedom under 'ticket of leave'. Maconochie's regime was short-lived and he was relieved of his post and returned to England in 1844. Crofton's system, however, supported by the Penal Servitude Act 1853 which recognised parole, was well received and graduated release became officially adopted by the Home Office in 1877. The two systems also received support from the United States, birthplace of the penitentiary, where in 1876 the Elmira Reformatory was established. Here a three-step progressive-release system was commenced that was similar to and directly influenced by those of Maconochie and Crofton.[18]

The period 1876 to 1910 is generally known as the 'reformatory era' in American corrections; between 1877 and 1913 reformatories were established in 17 states. Reformatories were designed to re-socialise offenders before they reached their 30s through work programmes, graduated privilege and eventually, parole. However, maladministration and a failure to achieve their primary objective of reduced recidivism led to disillusionment with reformatories and to their gradual decline from about 1910.[19] Thereafter, although the instrument of parole remained, American prisons increasingly tended toward the functions of confinement and control.

New Zealand was influenced, both directly and indirectly, by developments in the United States and England. Early release and remission were carried out *ad hoc* for most of the 19th century, when vice-regal governors initially used the discretion granted under their letters patent to release prisoners early for a variety of reasons. In 1864 the system was formalised somewhat, with the issuing of a set of rules to define early release for good behaviour.[20] It was not until 1875 that a formal system of release with one-quarter sentence remission for hard-labour inmates was enacted and gazetted in the regulations.

In 1906 the Habitual Criminals and Offenders Act allowed indeterminate sentencing of repeat offenders, whose release could only be ordered by the governor on recommendation of the Supreme Court. In 1910, just as reformatories were proving a failure in the United States, New Zealand attempted to replicate them. That year the government created the sentence of reformative detention as an indeterminate sentence of 0–3 years or 0–10 years, depending on whether the sentence was passed by the lower or the higher court. The following year, in order to consider the release of reformative detainees, a prisons board of three to seven members, one of whom was a Supreme Court judge, was established, also having jurisdiction over habitual criminals. This was New Zealand's first parole authority and it remained active until 1954. As noted, upon release, early habitual offenders could be placed on probation for up to two years, but after 1910 all reformative detainees and habituals were released on a 'probationary licence' that applied until expiry of the full sentence in the case of reformative detainees and for life in the case of habituals. Breach of probationary conditions was punishable by up to three months' imprisonment and a fine, but any inmate released on probation could be recalled to prison for any reason by the governor on recommendation of the Supreme Court.

In 1917 parole eligibility was broadened. Under the Statute Law Amendment Act lifers, who previously could only be released by way of the Royal Prerogative of Mercy, now became paroleable on probation after eight years. This was reduced to five years in the Crimes Amendment Act 1920. At the same time, in 1917, the act made all offenders serving more than two years paroleable at half sentence. In 1920 all offenders serving finite terms became eligible for parole after serving six months or half sentence, whichever was the longest. At the same time release on remission, which had been introduced in 1875, was abolished in favour of this universal system of parole. In 1924, when borstal detention was introduced, borstal detainees came under the umbrella of the prisons board as well.

The next major adjustment to parole conditions did not come until 1954 when the Criminal Justice Act 1954 abolished parole for all finite sentences. At the same time the Penal Institutions Act 1954 introduced a system of one-quarter fixed remission. The principal differences between remission and parole are that remission is awarded automatically as a statutory right and does not always have a probationary period attached to it, whereas parole is discretionary and always carries conditions. Remission is normally granted as a reward for good behaviour in prison; parole is based on an assumption that an inmate has 'reformed' and is unlikely to reoffend. In 1954 all inmates sentenced to at least 12 months' imprisonment were subject to probation until expiry of their full terms and for at least a year. Temporary parole for special purposes was also created in 1954. In 1965 under this provision, 72-hour home leaves were allowed for (suitable) married men every four months. In 1974 home leaves were generally available for minimum-security prisoners and in 1975 the interval between leaves was reduced to two months.

In 1954 reformative detention was substituted with a semi-determinate sentence of 1–3 years for offenders aged 21–30, called corrective training. This was abolished in 1963. At the same time the Habitual Criminals and Offenders Act was repealed and replaced with an indeterminate sentence, for certain repeat offenders, of 3–14 years or 3–life (depending on the offence), called preventive detention. The Criminal Justice Act 1954 also reconstituted the prisons board as the parole board, which had jurisdiction over lifers, preventive detainees and borstal trainees. These are discussed in the next chapter. Lifers continued to be paroleable at five years until 1962 when, partially as a sop to supporters of capital punishment, the non-parole period for murder was raised to 10 years following the abolition of the death penalty for murder in 1961. In 1955 there were 677 post-release probationers received – an increase of 28 per cent over 1953.

In 1961 all inmates became eligible for release on work parole prior to the expiry of their sentences, and in 1964 special remission amounting to an extra one-twelfth was made available to inmates for exemplary behaviour. This increased the maximum amount of remission available from a quarter to a third, and grew increasingly common as time went on. One third remission became general for minimum-security prisoners doing finite terms and others on application in 1975, and automatic for all inmates serving finite terms not released on parole between 1985 and 2002.

After the 1950s there were several changes to parole as well. In 1961 the parole board ceased to adjudicate in borstals, and dedicated borstal parole boards were set up instead. In 1967 the first in a number of moves to reintroduce parole for finite sentences was made, with an amendment to the Criminal Justice Act permitting the parole board to review finite sentences of six years and over, after three-and-a-half years or half sentence, whichever was the longer. In 1975, under the administration of Labour's Minister of Justice Martyn Finlay, parole was liberalised further. By 1980 parole was extended to all prisoners serving at least five years at half sentence or seven years, whichever was the shorter, and the non-parole period for lifers was reduced from 10 to seven years. In reality, parole for finite sentences was hardly given at all.

These changes, combined with rising prison populations, dramatically affected the numbers of offenders on post-release probation. In 1959 nearly 1,000 were received on probationary release, up from 677 four years before. By 1965 the number received had exceeded 1,500, reaching 2,400 in 1974. For the next 20 years, annual post-release probation receptions fluctuated between 2,400 and 3,000.

The final liberalisation arrived in Labour Justice Minister Geoffrey Palmer's Criminal Justice Act 1985, where all prisoners became eligible for parole at half sentence or seven years, whichever was the shorter; those not released on parole were automatically released on remission at two-thirds of sentence. Borstal training and its associated boards had ended in 1981, leaving just the national parole board in operation. In the 1985 act, however, the power to grant parole was again divided between two authorities: the national parole board, chaired by a High Court judge, heard cases involving sentences of seven years and over; and a number of district prisons boards, chaired by a District Court judge, heard other cases. Prisoners serving 12 months or less were discharged without probationary conditions. The length of supervision for prisoners released on remission or parole was cut to six months, except in the case of lifers, who remained on probation for the rest of their lives. These changes, combined with increasing prison populations, caused a rise in annual parole receptions of 24 per cent between 1984 and 1989.

Palmer soon realised that his liberalisations ran against the tide of public opinion. Convictions for violence leapt by 46 per cent between 1981 and 1990, with serious violence growing disproportionately and gangs taking a high profile. The child murder-abduction of six-year-old Louisa Damodran in Christchurch in October 1986, just a year after her killer, Peter Joseph Holdem, had been released on parole, increased pressure on Palmer which was added to in June 1987, when another six-year-old, Teresa Cormack, was abducted and murdered on her way to school in Whirinaki. Thus 1987 saw the first alterations to parole law with non-parole minimums for life and preventive detention increasing from seven to 10 years, and the end parole eligibility for serious violent offenders sentenced to more than two years 'imprisonment. Although still eligible for automatic release at two-thirds of sentence, violent offenders could be empowered to serve their entire sentences if they were judged likely to reoffend.

In 1989 prisoners sentenced to less than 12 months' imprisonment lost their parole eligibility, but they were released automatically at half sentence. This caused a 22 per cent drop in parole receptions the following year. However, the toughening measures had no apparent effect on violence rates, with violent crime convictions growing by another 23 per cent between 1987 and 1992. In Auckland robberies became so frequent that in 1988 the *New Zealand Herald* began publishing a regular column titled, "Today's Armed Robberies". In mid-1989 Karla Cardno (13) was abducted, raped and beaten to death by Paul Dally. That same year David Wayne Tamihere, previously imprisoned for killing a prostitute and currently on bail for rape, murdered two young Swedish tourists, Heidi Paakkonen and Urban Hoglen. The long investigation and eventual conviction of Tamihere in December 1990, followed by a failed appeal and the discovery of Hoglen's body two and a half years later, ensured that this case remained in the public eye for many months.

In 1992 there were 73 reported murders in New Zealand – more than in any year previously. In January alone there had been nine, including the rape and strangulation of eight-year-old Sarah Curry, increasing pressure for further action to combat violent crime. A 300-strong rally in Wellington in February 1993, led by Bevan Smith, father of 15-year-old Kylie Smith who had been raped and shot in Southland in November 1991, presented a petition with 265,000 signatures calling for harsher penalties for violent criminals.

The National Government was quick to respond. By mid-1992 Minister of Justice Doug Graham was promising to toughen sentences and restrict parole further for violent offences, and these changes came in election year 1993. Early that year an internal report by parole board secretary John Meek on parole re-offending between 1985 and 1992, had found that almost half the 249 parolees released during the study period had re-offended. The worst risks were sexual and violent offenders, almost two-thirds of whom had been reconvicted since release. All four periodic detainees had re-offended as well.

Figure 12.3: Parolees Received

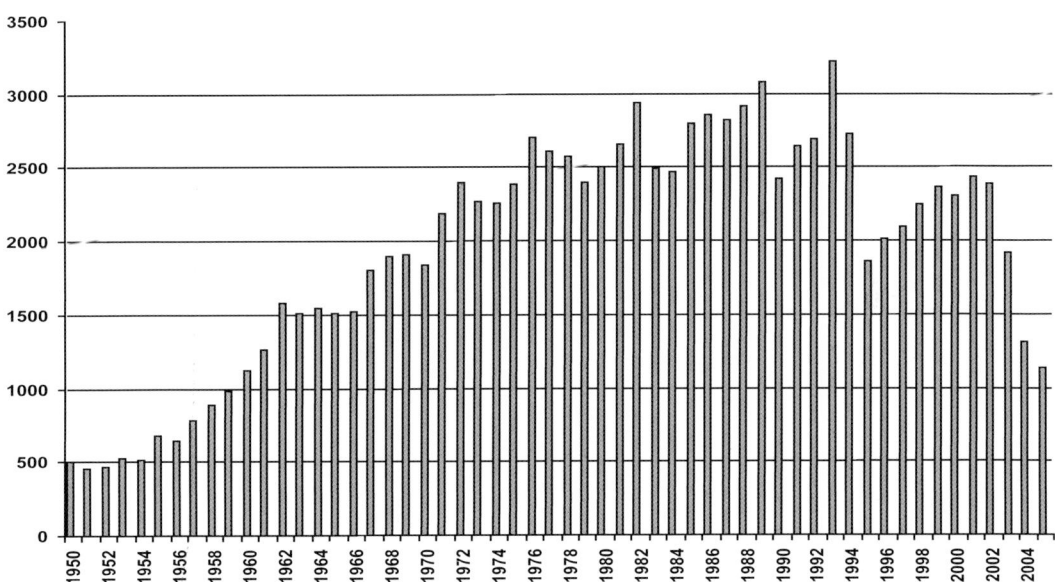

Although most of the reoffending was minor, the picture looked bad. Later in 1993, amendments to the Criminal Justice Act allowed courts to impose non-parole periods in excess of those defined in existing statute, and in order to bring parity with life and preventive detention, violent offenders serving finite terms of 15 years or more and who had not been sentenced to a minimum were given access to parole after 10 years. The 1993 amendment made standard conditions mandatory for all released prisoners. Moreover, where the 1985 act had stipulated that released inmates could be subject to conditions for no more no more than six months, the 1993 amendment extended the conditions right to the end of sentence, and in any case for a minimum of six months. At the same time, release conditions became more stringent, grounds for recall were widened and the recall process was made simpler by passing it from the courts to the parole authorities. Breaching conditions could result in recall to prison until up to three months before the end of a sentence. In an attempt to relieve the pressure that the law might have on prison numbers, conditions for non-violent offenders were made easier, with parole now available at one-third of sentence rather than a half as before. As a result of these measures, there was a sudden 20 per cent spike in post-release receptions in 1993, but numbers soon stabilised at between about 2,000 and 2,300 for the rest of the decade.

During the 1990s, again notwithstanding the latest round of changes, violent crime rates continued to rise. Between 1990 and 1998, when violent crime peaked, violence convictions grew by another 67 per cent. Once more some significant incidents fired public opinion. The killing of housewife Tania Furlan at her home in 1996, followed by the fatal bludgeoning of Joanne McCarthy in her Whangaparaoa house and the robbery-murder of Reporoa farmer Beverly Bouma at her home, both in November 1998, led to an amendment to the Crimes Act in 1999 mandating an automatic three-year add-on to the parole eligibility date of any person convicted of a murder committed during a home invasion. As seen in chapter 6, other events such as the bashing of Nan Withers in 1997 and furore over the parole application of Carla Cardno's killer, Paul Dally, in 1999, led to Nan Withers' son, Norm, organising the highly successful referendum on violent crime that accompanied the 1999 General Election.

Although the wording of the referendum made its detail worthless, high support for a no-nonsense approach to violent crime was clear. As has been seen, the incoming Labour-led government was initially resistant to pressure, but the sex murder of Kylie Jones by newly released career criminal Taffy Hotene just a few months later, forced its hand. Formation of the highly active Sensible Sentencing Trust in February 2001 ensured that pressure did not abate. The government's response was the major revisions to criminal justice law in the Parole Act and the Sentencing Act, which came into force, on 1 July 2002.

Current Use of Parole

The Parole Act removed remission entirely for sentences over two years, returning New Zealand to a system almost identical to what had existed between 1920 and 1954. Persons sentenced to two years or less are now exempt from parole but eligible for remission at half sentence; however, all other prisoners are subject to parole consideration from a re-vamped parole authority known as the New Zealand parole board. The old parole board and the 17 district prisons boards have been replaced by a board of 19 judges and 17 non-judicial members operating in panels of three or five in three regions. The panels of three meet monthly at each prison around the country to hear the cases of less serious offenders. Every three months, extended panels of five members convene in each of the regions to consider the petitions of lifers, preventive detainees and those serving determinate sentences of more than seven years.

All prisoners doing more than two years, including those convicted of crimes of serious violence, are now eligible for parole at one-third of sentence, provided a longer non-parole minimum has not been set. The standard non-parole period for murder is still 10 years unless certain specified aggravating circumstances – such as extreme cruelty, home invasion or death of more than one victim – are involved. In such cases the standard non-parole period is 17 years. Grounds for receiving preventive detention have been broadened and its standard non-parole period has been cut from 10 to five years. Once they attain parole eligibility, inmates are generally entitled to appear before the board at least once a year. Where the board considers an inmate to not be eligible for release within a year it may make a postponement order, which can defer the inmate's next appearance for up to three years. By 30 June 2004, this had been used only 12 times in the two years since the act came into force. The parole board also hears applications for early release on special grounds and all applications for home detention.

According to section 7 of the Parole Act, "the paramount consideration for the board in every case is the safety of the community", and the act states that an offender should not be detained any longer than is consistent with this principle. Theoretically at least, this means that offenders assessed as unlikely to reoffend, or likely to reoffend but in a way that does not endanger the safety of the community (whatever that means), are entitled to release at their first parole board hearing. In practice, it seems that very few inmates fall into the 'unlikely to reoffend' category since Ministry of Justice statistics indicate that 86 per cent of released prisoners will commit another criminal offence within five years of release.[21]

Bad publicity about parole breaches in the time leading up to 2002 act affected both its format and application. It was revealed that Taffy Hotene had breached his parole conditions persistently and with impunity since being set free a few weeks before. The following month, just two months after release on probation from a sentence for armed robbery, William Holz robbed and murdered a Mangere liquor-store worker. Another man who was on parole without proper monitoring was William Bell, who beat three RSA workers to death in 2001. And in 2002 Barry Allan Ryder was on parole for trying to rape an 11-year-old boy, when he sexually assaulted three more boys a year after his release. On 24 February 2002, the *Sunday Star Times* revealed that 422 parolees had breached their conditions in 2001, a 40 per cent jump on the previous year.

Possibly as a result of this new conservatism, between 2001 and 2003 there was a 21 per cent drop in the number of people released from prison into the care of Community Probation, followed by a drop of 32 per cent in 2003–2004. The percentage of parole applications approvals fell from 49 per cent in 2003 to 41 per cent the following year. Moreover, in the two years after the Parole Act came into force, the board had had to consider a total of 756 applications for recall arising from breached conditions – almost half the total number of paroles granted in that period. By 2006, paroled offenders were serving 62 per cent of their entire sentences – almost as much as they would have under the discarded remission system.

Where the 1993 amendment had required all inmates to be released on conditions, from 2002 conditions have not applied to sentences of two years or less unless ordered by the sentencing court. For those serving more than two years, conditions must apply for at least six months and may continue until up to six months after expiry of the full sentence. Lifers and preventive detainees are on parole for life.

If he is deemed a risk to the community or has breached the conditions of his parole, a parolee may be recalled by the parole board to serve his sentence to full expiry. Recall occurs frequently but to date has received little publicity. There has been comment, however, about the problem of high-risk sex offenders being discharged into the community. To deal with the issue, in 2004 the Parole (Extended Supervision) Amendment Act was passed, allowing the High Court to subject high-risk sex offenders to special conditions, such as home detention and/or 24-hour supervision for up to a year after the completion of their full sentences, and to supervision and other conditions for up to 10 years. Serial paedophile Lloyd McIntosh, who in December 2004 was given 10 years' supervision following his release in April 2005, was the first person given such an order.

Periodic Detention

When Secretary for Justice Sam Barnett retired in July 1960 he was replaced by his energetic deputy Dr John Robson (see chapter 3). Four months later Labour was ousted in a general election and National's Ralph Hanan became Minister of Justice. In coalition with one another, Robson and Hanan began a decade-long era of criminal justice reform, remembered as among the most progressive in New Zealand's history. One of the most enduring components of the Hanan-Robson era is periodic detention.

The idea of an intermediate sanction such as weekend detention had been contemplated by Barnett in 1959, and schemes in South Africa, West Germany, and Boston, Massachusetts had been looked at.[22] In May 1962 Robson established a committee to work out a template for such a scheme, and this finally came to fruition in an amendment to the Criminal Justice Act in November 1962. Known as periodic detention, the measure was designed as an alternative to imprisonment for young criminals aged 15–21. The sentence could be given for up to 12 months and after the first centre opened in Auckland in July 1963, involved attendance between 6pm on Friday and 10am Sunday, with reporting required to a Wednesday night lecture as well. Breach of a periodic detention order was punishable by up to three months' imprisonment. Approximately a dozen boys attended the Parnell centre at any one time. They had group counselling on Friday or Saturday night and worked at the centre or in the community on Saturday. The experiment was soon deemed a success and in 1964 a second centre was opened in Christchurch, followed by Lower Hutt in 1965, Invercargill in 1965 and Otahuhu in 1970.[23]

In 1966 the law was amended to include adults and a non-residential adult centre for 25, which required attendance on Saturday only, was opened in Auckland the following year. This too was successful, and by 1970 day-reporting centres had been established in Hamilton, Wellington, Christchurch and Dunedin.[24] In 1974, periodic detention was extended to females.

From almost the beginning periodic detention was popular with the courts. Before 1965 fewer than 50 offenders were awarded the sentence each year, but by 1969 this had grown to 286. From here, increases were exponential, with the greatest growth coming from adult non-residential periodic detention. In 1970 the sentenced figure was more than double this (647), and in 1977 there were more than 5,000. Non-residential centres were soon available for juveniles, and a 1975 amendment restricted use of residential centres to relatively naïve offenders. As a result, after 1976 residential centres became under-utilised and this, combined with their high running costs, caused their decline. By 1985 all residential centres had closed.[25] Non-residential numbers continued to increase. In 1984 more than 10,000 offenders got periodic detention, and sentences peaked in 1992 with over 27,000 sentences given. Periodic detention now operated on weekdays as well as Saturdays, with offenders usually arranging with the centre's warden as to which day or days they would attend.

Unemployment, which grew from two per cent of the labour force in 1976 to 11 per cent at its peak in 1991, was one of the reasons periodic detention became so important during the 1980s and early 1990s. Although periodic detention was intended to be an alternative to imprisonment, in practice courts began to use it in lieu of fining when they knew an offender was unemployed or had defaulted on a fine. After 1992 the use of periodic detention fell gradually to around 20,000 the year before it was abolished in 2002. Part of this was because of falling overall crime rates, part was due to the rising use of imprisonment and part was caused by the use of alternative intermediate sanctions such as community service and community care.

Figure 12.4: Periodic Detainees Received (2003– Community Work)

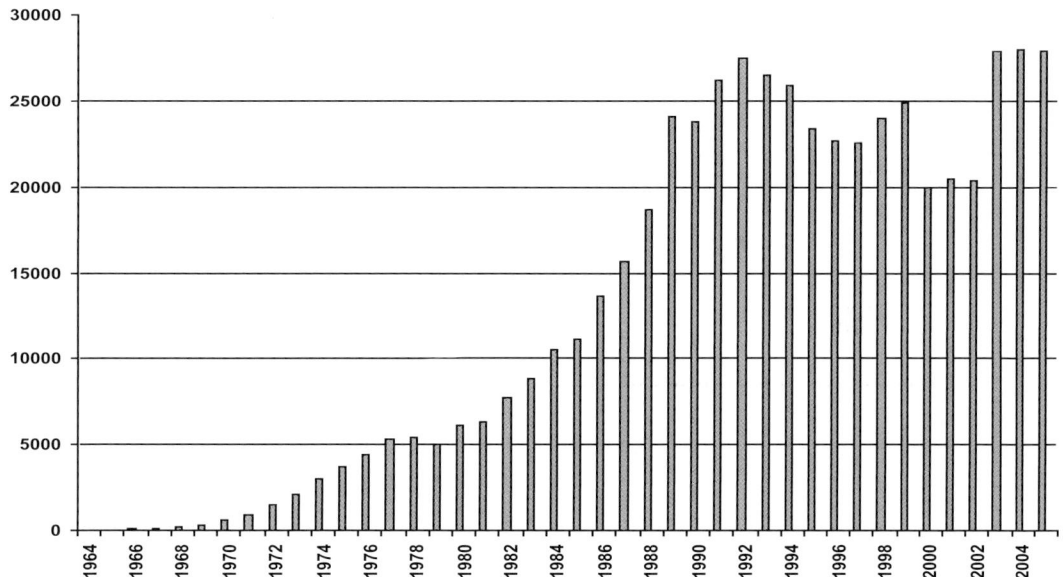

Community Service

The alternative sentence of community service appeared in 1980. Periodic detention provided manual employment, primarily on public works and reserves. Community service was designed to supplement periodic detention by providing a community work alternative for offenders with specific abilities and skills. Unlike periodic detention, community service required the consent of the offender and could be ordered for terms of between 20 and 200 hours within a period of 12 months. Normally the offender organised the type of work he or she would engage in (for example, service to some public or charitable organisation), which was approved but not supervised by a probation officer. Penalties for breaching conditions were lighter than for periodic detention – a fine rather than imprisonment. This made it wide open to abuse.

Community service was never as popular with the courts as periodic detention

Figure 12.5: Community Service Orders

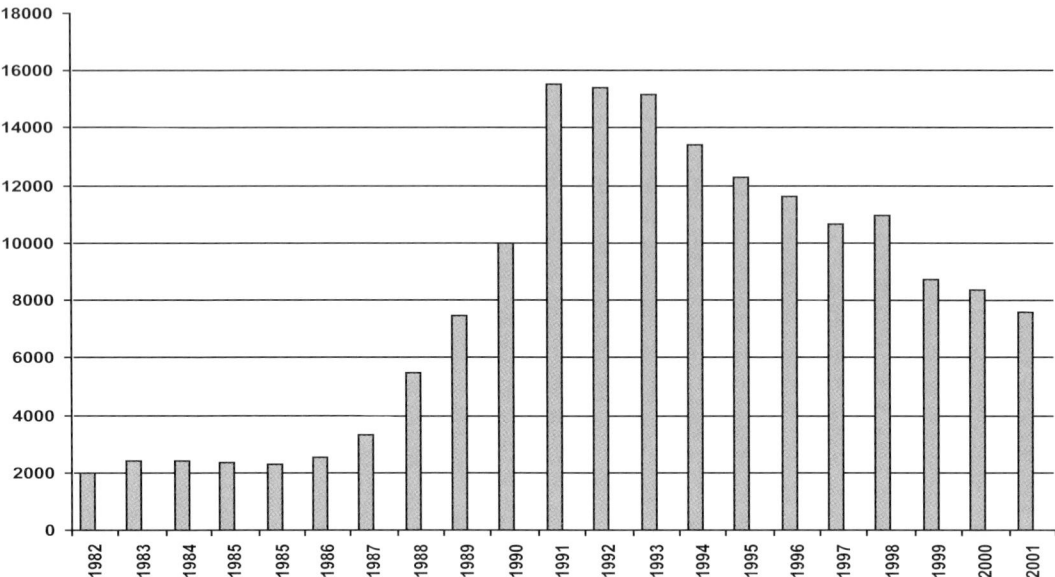

because of its limited applicability and perceived 'softness'. Between 1982 and 1987 fewer than 3,000 offenders got the sentence each year, then numbers expanded rapidly, reaching 15,500 in 1992 – the same year that periodic detention peaked. Thereafter, usage of community service fell, but by even greater margins than periodic detention, and had almost halved by 2001.

In 2002, community service was abolished by the Sentencing Act.

Community Care/Community Programme

In the liberal shake-up of criminal justice law that accompanied the 1985 Criminal Justice Act, a sentence called community care was created. Community care was an alternative to imprisonment, which would allow an offender to be sentenced to the care of a community agency such as a marae, a halfway house, or some other approved organisation. The sentence could be given for up to 12 months, up to six months of which could be residential. The sentence required the consent of the offender, and if conditions were breached the offender could be returned to court for re-sentencing on the original charge. In 1993 community care was renamed 'community programme', although the sentence itself remained unchanged.

Like community service, community care/programme appeared to be a 'soft' option and had a high potential for abuse, so it was not imposed frequently by the courts. Usage grew steadily and peaked at 1,330 sentences in 1992, but like other intermediate measures, fell thereafter. Publicity over misapplication of the sentence caused its falls to be more spectacular than any other community sentence, and only 230 persons received a sentence of community care in 2001. It was abolished in 2002, although provision for treatment in a community centre still exists within the special conditions that may accompany a sentence of probation.

Figure 12.6: Community Care/Programme Orders

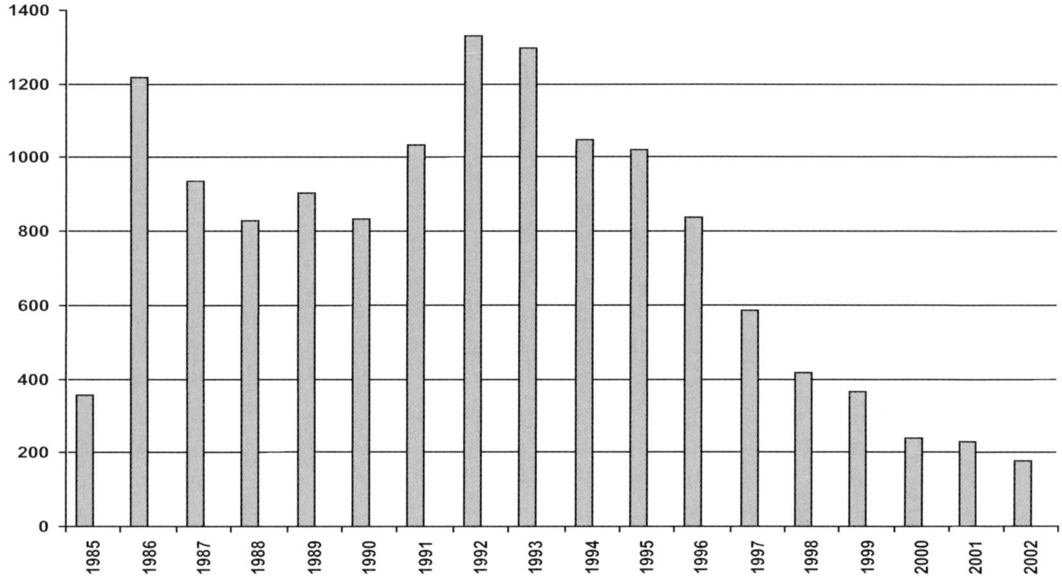

Community Work

The logic of abolishing periodic detention, community service and community programmes in 2002 was to simplify their applications and definitions, which had become confusingly similar. A new sentence called 'community work', which combined the provisions of periodic detention and community care into one, was created. Community work is an alternative to imprisonment that can be imposed for between 40 and 400 hours within a period of 12 months if the sentence is 200 hours or less, and 24 months if it is over 200 hours. The sentence may be served at a community work centre (in the same establishments as the old periodic detention centres), or in some form of independent community service, depending on the judgement of the offender's probation officer. Remission of up to 10 per cent of sentence is available for good conduct. Breach of community work conditions can result in a return to court for re-sentencing on the original charge and/or a sentence of up to three months' imprisonment and/or a fine. The sentence is by far the most popular of all custodial or supervisory options, with about 28,000 offenders given it in 2003 and a similar number in 2004. By contrast, in each of those years approximately 5,000 offenders received supervision and 7,000 were sent to prison.

Home Detention

For a number of years before it was finally enacted in its current form in 1999, home detention was trialled within the Department of Justice. Electronic monitoring had commenced in the United States in 1980, at a time when rising prison populations forced some states to devise a cheaper alternative.[26] By 1998 there were at least 50,000 electronic monitoring devices in use in America.[27] These developments were noted in New Zealand, but there was no public discussion on monitoring until 1987 when the

Associate Minister of Justice reported on a plan in use in British Columbia.[28] Minister of Justice Geoffrey Palmer also advocated the introduction of such a system in June 1988, citing programmes introduced to Australia the previous year.[29] In 1987 and 1988 the Ministerial Committee of Inquiry into the Prisons System considered the matter and recommended the establishment of some form of electronically controlled home detention in 1989.

In early 1989 Palmer announced firm plans for a scheme of home detention which, he said, would allow inmates to spend the last three months of their sentences at home under surveillance. Apart from easing an inmate's transition back into the community, the scheme was also expected to relieve prison populations, which had grown by 27 per cent since 1987. By August 1989 the necessary amendments to the Criminal Justice Act were drafted, but it took another four years for the amendments to become law.

Although Labour opposed having home detainees electronically monitored, National saw it as essential, and when it came to power in 1990 it adopted the new policy with monitoring in mind. This made the scheme more expensive and difficult to organise, and little further progress was made. In September 1993, however, the long-awaited changes to the Criminal Justice Act came into effect, allowing parole authorities to release non-serious violent offenders serving determinate terms of more than 12 months to home detention as a condition of parole. A two-year pilot was planned for Hamilton, but it was soon switched to Auckland. Contracted privately to the firm Wanganui Security, the scheme initially involved video telephones and random calls to establish that offenders were at their approved locations. The estimated cost of the programme was $22,000 per person per year, compared to $30,000 a year to keep an offender in jail. Although projected to commence in December 1994, the scheme ran into difficulties with equipment and organisation delays and the first detainees were not received until February 1995.

Home detention got off to a shaky start. Few inmates applied for it and because of the strict eligibility criteria, only five of the 16 who applied in the first few months actually took part. Thirty-seven inmates had participated in the pilot by the time it ended in 1997, but this was judged too small a number to determine its value. Because of the low numbers the cost of the programme was higher than expected – $44,000 per inmate per year – and although all but one had complied with order requirements, 11 had already been charged with new offences.[30] These modest results notwithstanding, the government decided to expand the programme, but eligibility criteria continued to keep numbers down. In 1997 18 home detention orders were made; the following year there were only 11. In 1999 the figure dropped to five. One unusual example of home detention in 1999 was given to Anita Faisandier, who was bailed to home detention in February 1999 while awaiting trial for writing $40.6 million in bad cheques. In December 1999 her bail conditions were altered and her bracelet removed, and in October 2000 she was sentenced to three years' imprisonment.

On 1 October 1999 a re-vamped home detention scheme with relaxed eligibility criteria and broad application was launched. Previously home detention had been used primarily as a condition of release from prison. Under the 1999 amendment, home detention was divided into two categories: 'front-end' home detention, which could be granted at the commencement of prison sentences of two years or less, and 'back-end' home detention, which came at the end of longer sentences as a release condition. The 'passive' telephone checking system was now abandoned in favour of an 'active' one using a security ankle bracelet with continuous electronic emissions. It was decided to make home detention as broadly applicable as possible, and to implement it nationally. As a result home detention started to become widely used by the courts, the parole board and the district prisons boards. In 2000, 302 orders were made; the following year there were 772. Department of Corrections figures at the time indicated that 27 per cent of home detainees had re-offended within 12 months of release.

Figure 12.7: Home Detention Orders

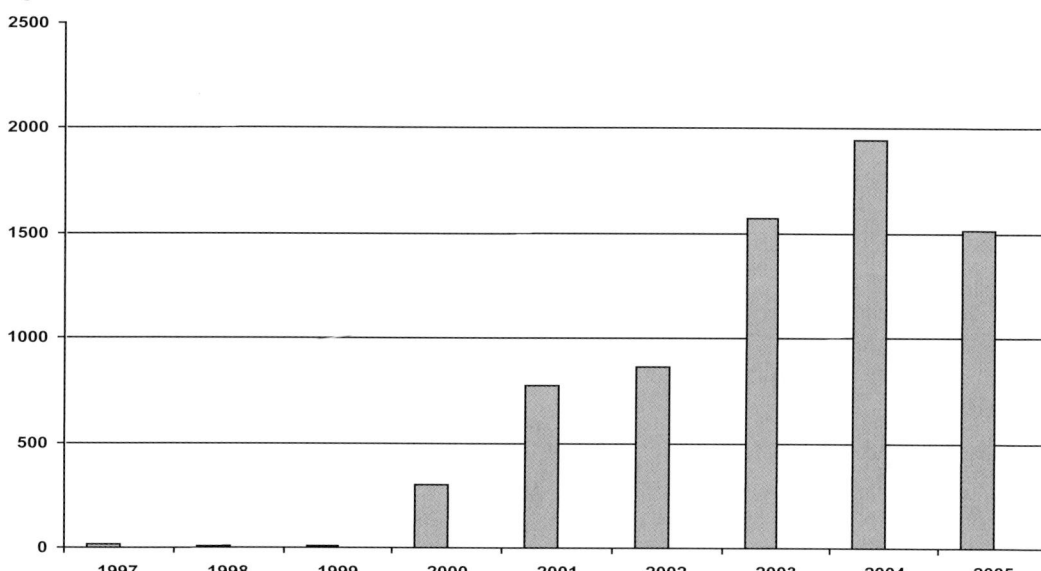

Current Use of Home Detention

In 2001 the number of 'home d' orders more than doubled to nearly 800, and they increased again the following year. In 2002 the Sentencing Act and the Parole Act reiterated the 'front-end'/'back-end' application of the law, with the Sentencing Act allowing offenders serving two years or less to apply for home detention instead of going to jail, and the Parole Act allowing home detention as a condition of parole.

Where a sentence is of two years or less, the presumption is in favour of home detention, and a court is now required to give the offender leave to apply for home detention unless certain extraordinary circumstances exist. The decision about whether or not to grant the measure is made by the parole board. As before, back-end home detention applies to all offenders serving finite sentences of more than two years. These inmates are eligible to apply within five months of their parole eligibility dates and may be granted home detention by the board three months before they become eligible for parole. Technically, therefore, an offender sentenced to six years' imprisonment could be serving his sentence at home within 21 months. Conditions of front-end home detention continue until the point of half sentence, while in the case of back-end they continue until discharge by the parole board. Those who breach the conditions of their orders can be returned to prison to complete their terms or be penalised by the imposition of tougher conditions.

Since October 1999 home detainees have been managed by private contract to Chubb New Zealand Ltd which, under the oversight of the Community Probation Service, supplies electronic ankle bracelets and other equipment, and administers the system. Offenders are monitored 24 hours a day, and have general conditions such as regular visits with a probation officer and restrictions on where they can live and with whom. The sentence is normally divided into four phases, which vary depending on the length and type of sentence and the conduct of the detainee. Phase one is for a minimum of one month and requires the offender to remain at home except for approved outings for shopping, work, training, programmes, medical purposes and funerals. Phase two increases freedoms, allowing the detainee to attend church and to take educational courses more freely. Phase three permits attendance at restricted family functions and sport and recreational activities, and phase four, which occurs near completion of sentence, broadens the previously granted freedoms.

The new form of home detention resulted in an explosion in usage. In 2003 nearly 1,600 offenders received terms of home detention; the following year there were nearly 2,000. In November 2003, of 5,600 sentenced inmates nearly 600 were serving their sentences at home. After this, however, there was a drop in the use of home detention as the parole board became more discriminatory in giving it. Where in 2003 55 per cent of home detention applications had been successful, by 2006 the figure had fallen to 42 per cent. The number of home detention 'new starts' fell from about 1,800 in 2004 to 1,250 in 2006, and the number of offenders serving their time at home fell by a third, to 400.[31] According to the Department of Corrections, approximately 8.5 per cent of home detainees breach their conditions and 18.5 per cent reoffend within 12 months of completion. This compares favourably with prisoners, nearly 58 per cent of whom are reconvicted in a year. This does not mean, as the Community Probation Service has claimed,[32] that home detention is more effective than imprisonment, since high-risk and serious offenders are unlikely to be granted home detention. This is borne out in the figures: whereas in November 2001 about 61 per cent of prison inmates were doing time for violence, 22 per cent for property crimes and eight per cent for drugs; 35 per cent of home detainees were locked up for property offences, 24 per cent for drugs and only 21 per cent for violence. Compared with prison inmates, home detainees were six times as likely to be female (who are low-risk reoffenders) and half as likely to be Maori (who are high risk).[33]

Although home detention is cheap – less than a third of what it costs to keep someone in jail – one of its major criticisms is that, although technically part of a prison sentence, living at home offers more comfort and freedom than living in custody. Moreover, there is almost no way of preventing home detainees from continuing to engage in some forms of crime, such as drug offending and fraud. Detainees without jobs are entitled to unemployment and other benefits. According to Corrections figures, about 8.6 per cent of home detainees breach their conditions, and there have been a few high-profile cases of re-offending. However, it seems probable that home detention, in its current or some altered form, will remain a part of the nation's criminal justice landscape.

Figure 12.8: Community Sentences per Custodial (excluding probation)

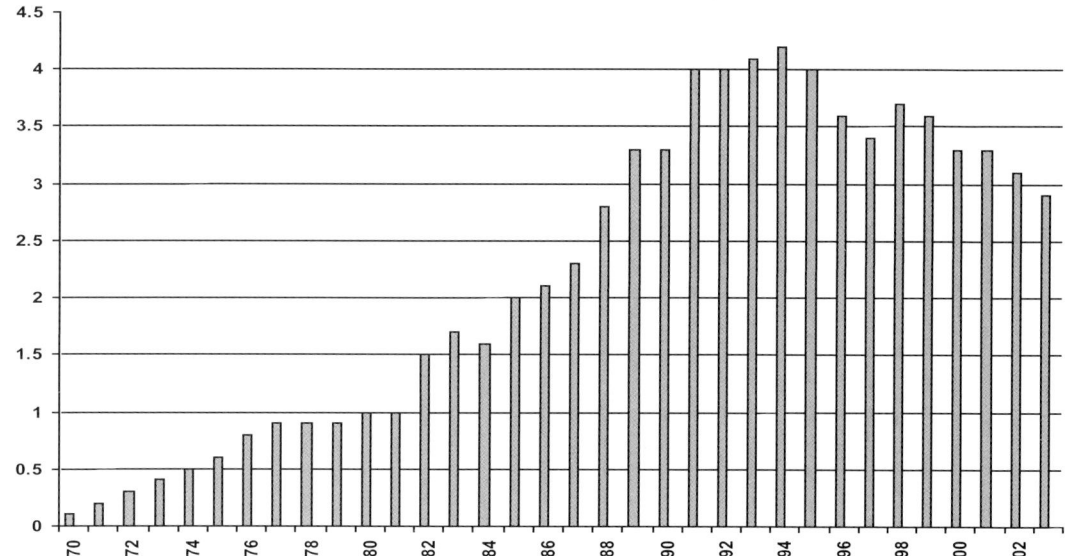

Overview

Since their introduction in 1886, community sentences in New Zealand have undergone significant expansion and change. For most of the 20th century, probation was the only community alternative, but from 1960 community-based sentences became increasingly diverse. Although the use of imprisonment has grown, both relatively and in relation to population, semi-custodial sentences have expanded even faster. In 1960 there were 2.74 people serving community terms for every person in prison. This had this had increased to 3.42 by 1970, to 4.25 by 1975, and in 1980 there were five people on community sentences for each prisoner. Use of community sentences peaked in 1992, when the ratio of prisoners to those on community sentences exceeded 1:6. Thereafter imprisonment relative to semi-custodial measures has increased, causing the ratio to drop to 1:4 by 2004.

Although prison numbers have risen and New Zealand's imprisonment ratio is higher than most Western countries except the United States,[34] the existence of community measures has kept the prison population and the costs of incarceration far lower than they would otherwise have been. In practical terms it would appear that this is their primary value.

Notes

1 Hall Williams, 1970: 251–253.
2 Mays and Winfree, 2002: 208–209.
3 AJHR H.6, 1885: 4; H.20, 1954: 15.
4 Department of Justice, 1964: 41.
5 Mayhew, 1959: 115.
6 Webb, 1982: 164.
7 Mayhew, 1959: 115.
8 AJHR H.20, 1954: 15.
9 Webb, 1982: 180.
10 Department of Justice, 1964: 42.
11 Department of Justice, 1970: 5.
12 Webb, 1982: 167.
13 Triggs 1999: 102–106
14 AJHR E.61, 2002: 78; Spier, 2002a: xxiii–xxiv.
15 Spier, 2002a: 36.
16 Triggs, 1999: 139.
17 Hall Williams, 1970: 180–181.
18 Mays and Winfree, 2002: 43–47.
19 Silverman, 2001: 96–97.
20 Webb, 1982: 133.
21 Spier, 2002b.
22 Robson, 1987: 61; 171–172.
23 Department of Justice, 1970: 6.
24 Department of Justice, 1970: 6–7.
25 Webb, 1982: 189.
26 Baker, 2005; Ministerial Committee of Inquiry, 1989: 62.
27 Allen and Simonsen, 2001: 221.
28 *NZ Herald*, 15 September 1987.
29 *The Press*, 8 June 1988.
30 Ministry of Justice, 1997.
31 *Corrections News*, August 2006.
32 *Judges' Update*, August 2003.
33 Department of Corrections, 2003: 18, 50.
34 See Walmsley, 2006.

References

Allen, Harry and Simonsen, Clifford (2001) *Corrections in America: An Introduction*. Upper Saddle River, NJ: Prentice Hall.
Baker, Melissa (2005) 'Electronic Monitoring'. In Mary Bosworth (ed), *Encyclopedia of Prisons and Correctional Facilities*. Thousand Oaks, CA: Sage.
Department of Corrections (2003) *Census of Prison Inmates and Home Detainees*. Wellington: Department of Corrections.
Department of Justice (1964) *Crime and the Community*. Wellington: Government Printer.
Department of Justice (1970) *Penal Policy in New Zealand*. Wellington: Government Printer.
Hall Williams, J.E. (1970) *The English Penal System in Transition*. London: Butterworths.
Mayhew, P.K. (1959) *The Penal System of New Zealand 1840–1924*. Wellington: Department of Justice.
Mays, Larry and Winfree, Tom (2002) *Contemporary Corrections*. Belmont, CA: Wadsworth.

Meek, John (1993) *Reoffending by Parolees: Reconviction of Persons Released on Parole by the Parole Board October 1985–August 1992.* Unpublished paper, Department of Justice.

Ministerial Committee of Inquiry into the Prisons System (1989) *Te Ara Hou: The New Way.* Wellington: Government Printer.

Ministry of Justice (1987) *Evaluation of the Home Detention Pilot Programme.* Wellington: Ministry of Justice.

Robson, John (1987) *Sacred Cows and Rogue Elephants: Policy Development in the New Zealand Justice Department.* Wellington: Government Printing Office.

Silverman, Ira (2001) *Corrections: A Comprehensive View.* Belmont, CA: Wadsworth.

Spier, Philip (2002a) *Conviction and Sentencing of Offenders in New Zealand.* Wellington: Ministry of Justice.

Spier, Philip (2002b) *Reconviction and Reimprisonment Rates for Released Prisoners.* Wellington: Ministry of Justice.

Triggs, Sue (1999) *Sentencing in New Zealand: A Statistical Analysis.* Wellington: Ministry of Justice.

Walmsley, Roy (2006) *World Prison Population List* (6th ed). London: King's College London.

Webb, Patricia (1982) *A History of Custodial and Related Penalties in New Zealand.* Wellington: Government Printer.

CHAPTER 13
SPECIALISED CUSTODIAL SENTENCES

Throughout New Zealand's criminal justice history custodial alternatives have been available to sentencing courts for dealing with specific types of offender. Although most have proven failures, in the faddish way that corrections tend to develop, many have reflected the trends of the day and, as with parole in the previous chapter, sometimes discarded strategies have been remodelled and resurrected. This chapter looks at sentencing alternatives tried in New Zealand over the last 160 years and comments on why, in the end, most of them disappeared.

Penal Servitude, Imprisonment and Hard Labour (1854–1954)

In 1846, before New Zealand began complete administration of its own prisons, the Legislative Council Ordinance for the Regulation of Prisons made reference to a practice, apparently already in place, of sentencing prisoners to confinement with or without hard labour. In the early days of the colony, most serious offenders were transported to Van Diemen's Land. In 1854, however, when New Zealand established its own criminal justice system under the Secondary Punishment Act, transportation was replaced with penal servitude with hard labour in provincially administered jails. Apart from those sentenced to imprisonment for life (who until 1863 were kept at hard labour under separate confinement), penal servitude inmates were given hard labour, usually in irons, on roading and public works.

In 1893 the Criminal Code Act abolished the sentencing of prisoners to solitary confinement and scrapped penal servitude, leaving only imprisonment with or without hard labour. Most crimes carried a hard labour requirement; only a small number – for example, causing public nuisance and criminal libel – did not. What hard labour actually consisted of was not properly defined until 1918 – in practice it probably meant simply that such prisoners were required to work. Hard-labour prisoners were given more food than those who did not work, and when sentence remission was legislated in 1875 it applied only to hard-labour inmates. To avail themselves of these advantages, non-hard-labour prisoners could volunteer for hard labour.[1] Thus, although there are no data, it is likely that even the few prisoners not given hard labour opted for it, as much to relieve the tedium of unemployment as to qualify for the extra benefits.

The distinction between hard labour and non-hard labour was probably always tenuous, given that the types of employment in a prison are ultimately dependent on the availability of work, the cost of supplying it, the size and location of the institution, the security risk of the individual prisoner and his or her physical capacity. As early as

1916, in fact, the annual report of justice and prisons noted that there was no difference between hard labour and the sentence of reformative detention and recommended the distinction be removed.[2] Nothing was done for 38 years[3] when, recognising that hard labour had been meaningless for decades, the Criminal Justice Act 1954 abolished the distinction between it and standard imprisonment. Even now, from time to time calls are made for a return to hard labour, but history demonstrates that the expense and practicalities of administering the sentence would almost certainly result in its failure. Today all prisoners are expected to work, although practical difficulties and the cost of providing jobs mean that 38 per cent of prisoners are unemployed and large numbers of the remainder are under-employed.

Life Imprisonment (1840–present)

In New Zealand the mandatory sentence for murder has always been death or life imprisonment, but over the years other offences have also qualified for these extreme sanctions. In their purest forms, the rationales for death and life imprisonment are largely the same. Their logic rests upon one or more of the following assumptions:

1. The offender is such a threat to public safety that he/she needs to be eliminated from it (social sanitation).
2. The crime committed is so heinous that the offender has forfeited his/her right to life/freedom (retribution).
3. The crime itself represents such a danger to society that severe measures are necessary to discourage others from taking a similar path (general deterrence).
4. The crime itself is so terrible that severe measures are necessary to underline its gravity (symbolic denunciation).

In practice, before abolition most death sentences were commuted to life imprisonment, and in the 20th century lifers became eligible for parole after a relatively brief statutory non-parole period. The life sentence thus inevitably came to require the same sort of reformative components as any other form of sentence, and aside from security concerns, for most of the 20th century lifers have been treated little differently from other inmates. Apart from being ineligible for parole to home detention, that is still the situation.

When the colony of New Zealand began administering its own criminal justice system, a number of offences, including murder, treason and piracy, carried the death penalty. However, all sentences could be commuted to life imprisonment with hard labour under the royal prerogative of mercy and, in fact, only one person has ever been executed for a crime other than murder: Te Kooti associate Hamiora Peri, hanged for treason in 1869. Most, if not all, lifers in the 19th century were reprieved murderers who, unless pardoned under royal prerogative, were expected to serve the rest of their natural lives in prison. Under the Criminal Code Act 1893, New Zealand's first criminal law statute, a range of other crimes – manslaughter, attempted murder, assisting suicide, procuring abortion, preventing escape from a wreck, endangering people on railways, rape, having sex with a girl under 10 years and wounding with intent to cause grievous bodily harm – also carried discretionary maximums of life imprisonment, although the sentence was used sparingly.

From the inception of the colony all lifers could expect to be incarcerated at hard labour for the rest of their lives. The only chance of relief came from the royal pardon. In 1917, however, the possibility of parole after eight years was introduced, and reduced to five years in 1920. At the time murders were few and a large percentage of capital sentences were commuted to life. Of the 105 people convicted of murder between 1920 and 1966,[4] only 21 were hanged, although this includes two periods when the death penalty for murder was in abeyance. After 1920 most convicted murderers, who had either had their death sentences commuted to life imprisonment or had been automatically sentenced to life on conviction, were eligible for release after a five-year non-parole period. In the mid-20th century this normally meant release on parole after eight or more years, although life parolees could be and still are, liable to recall at any time for the rest of their lives.[5]

Between 1935 and 1941 death sentences were automatically commuted to life. In 1941 the death penalty for murder was replaced with mandatory life imprisonment, but the death sentence was resurrected in 1950. Of the 22 people sentenced to death between 1950 and 1957, eight were hanged.[6] At the end of 1957 the death penalty was shelved again and finally abolished in the Crimes Act 1961. Murder, along with certain acts of treason and piracy, now carried a mandatory life sentence. Today discretionary life sentences also exist for manslaughter and, from 1978, for dealing in Class A drugs, but seldom has the maximum been used. Life for manslaughter was given in two cases in 1915 and 1916, and in 1986 Dean Wickliffe was imprisoned for life for a robbery-manslaughter committed in 1972. Life has also been sustained twice for heroin dealing (to Wayne Beri in 1985 and to Alan King in 1996.)[7]

In 1962 the non-parole period of life for murder was raised, from the five years set in 1920 to 10 years, but dropped again to seven years in 1975. All other life sentences remained subject to parole after five years. However, in 1978 the Misuse of Drugs Amendment Act gave judges the power to impose a seven-year minimum for persons jailed for life for selling Class A drugs, and two years later the non-parole period for all life terms was standardised at seven years. It was returned to 10 years in 1987, and from 1993 the courts could impose discretionary non-parole minimums that were longer than the statutory periods. In 1999 a mandatory three-year provision was added for murders committed during a home invasion. This was repealed in 2002 when a mandatory minimum of 17 years was stipulated for murder committed with certain aggravating features (see chapter 6).

The number of life sentences given, and consequently the number of lifers held in New Zealand prisons, has increased considerably over the last century, but particularly in recent decades. Between 1900 and 1909 only five sentences of death were delivered, of which two were carried out. In the next decade there were nine death sentences, followed by 16 in the 1920s. Before the 1970s there were never more than 30 sentences of death/life imprisonment given in any decade.

After the 1960s murder convictions increased dramatically, with consequent leaps in life sentence numbers. In the 1970s 86 life terms were given; this rose to 283 in the 1990s.

At the same time, sentences got longer. In the 1960s and 1970s, lifers normally gained parole after 12–13 years although a few served more. Edward Raymond Horton, for example, who raped and killed Kitty Cranston under particularly brutal

Figure 13.1: Sentences of Life Imprisonment or Death 1896–1970

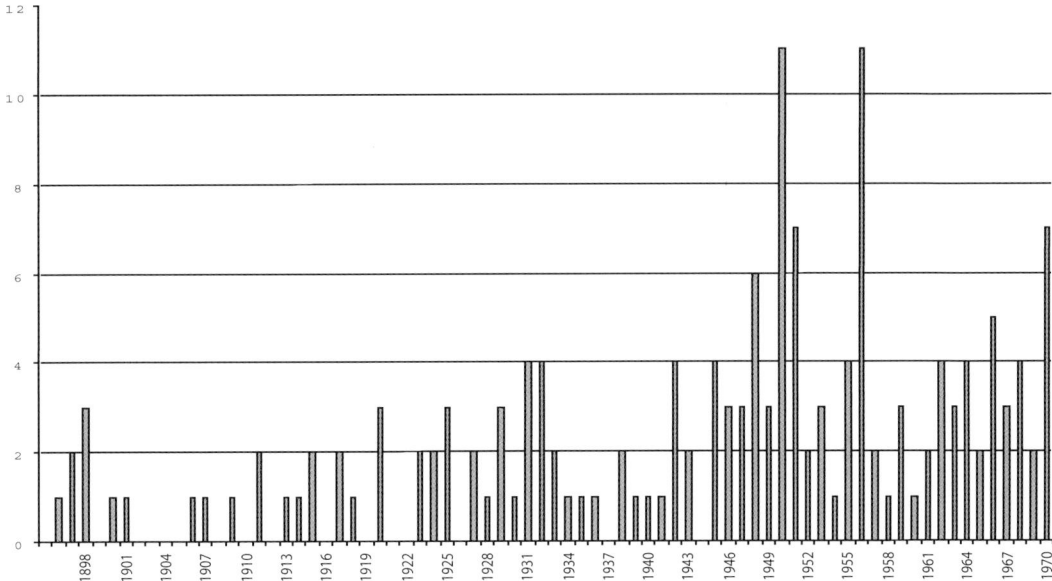

Figure 13.2: Sentences of Life Imprisonment 1965–2003

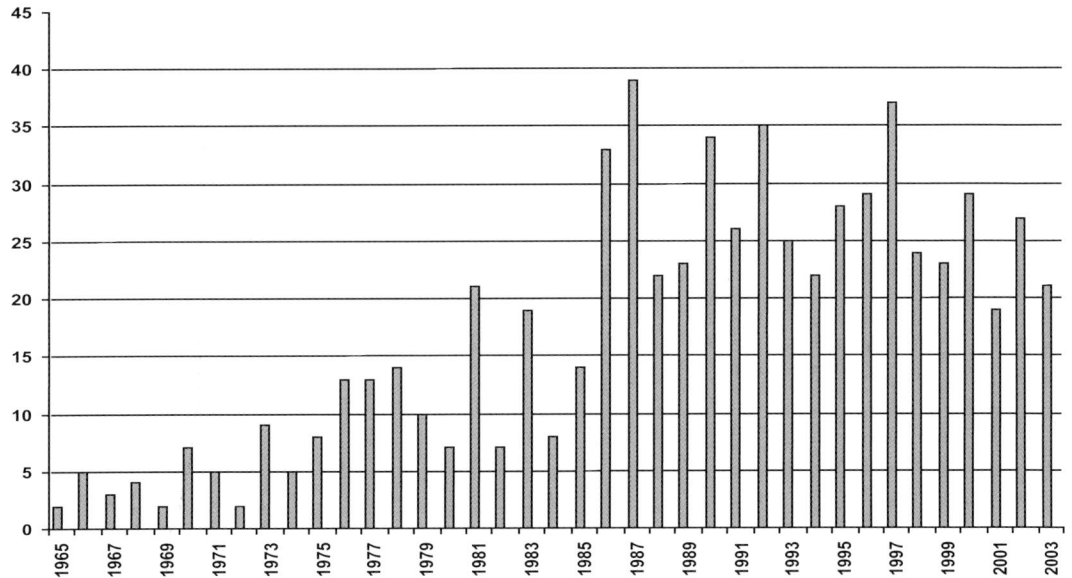

circumstances in Wellington in 1948, served 22. Stanley McKissock Reid, who cut the throat of a woman whose family he was boarding with in Auckland in 1945, served almost 41 years of his life sentence – the longest on record.

Since the introduction of judicial non-parole minimums in 1993, extended non-parole periods for murderers have become quite common. The first non-parole minimum was given to Turoa Hapi who, in 1994, received life with 15 years non parole for raping and murdering a woman in Hawke's Bay. A growing number have

Figure 13.3: Lifers in Prison

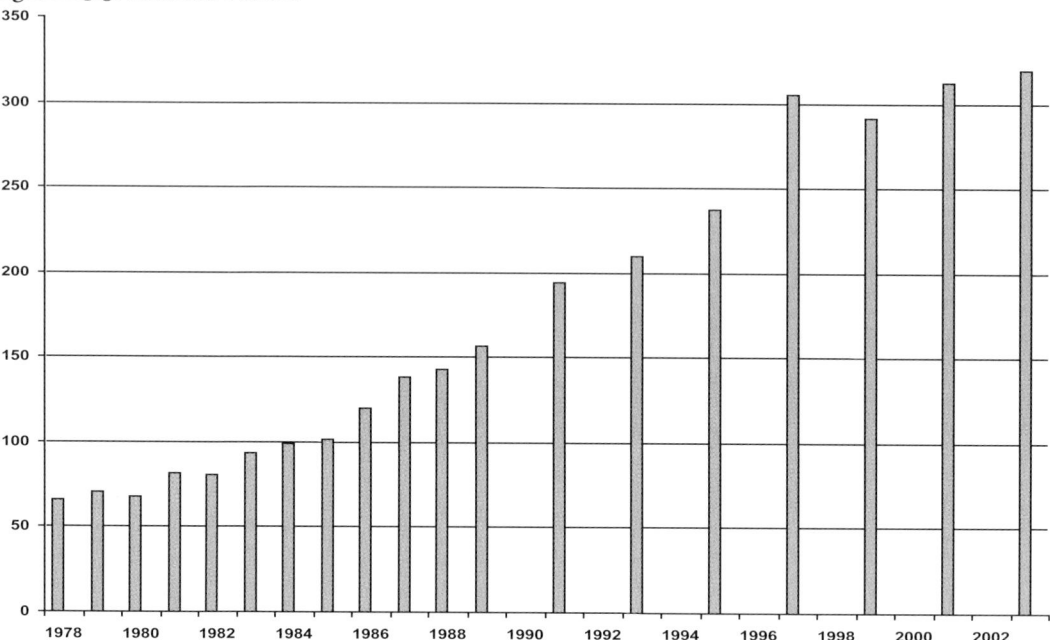

since exceeded this, including Mark Lundy, sentenced to 17 years' minimum in 2002 for killing his wife and daughter (increased to 20 years on appeal) and Bruce Howse, given 28 years in 2002 (reduced to 25 years on appeal) for murdering his two stepdaughters. The longest non-parole period ever given is life with 33 years (reduced to 30 on appeal) imposed on William Bell for bashing three people to death at the Panmure RSA in December 2001. Of the 259 life sentences given between 1994 and 2003, 24 (9.3%) contained extended non-parole minimums.[8] As a result of the increase in murders and the longer non-parole periods, the number of lifers is growing quite dramatically – from 68 in 1980 to 325 in 2003.

Most lifers may expect to be released after less than 15 years – and when they are still relatively young. Because of the length of time they have spent locked up, such inmates usually require special assistance in adjusting to life in the free world. However, there are lifers in prison now, some of them sentenced before the 1993 law change who, because of the new standards, are unlikely to be paroled until they are quite old, if at all. Between 1988 and 2003, for example, the number of inmates in prison aged 50 or over grew from 67 to 462. Such an accumulation of aged inmates will necessitate special facilities to cope with their needs, and specific preparations will have to be made for the aftercare of those who are released.

Habitual Criminals Declaration (1906–1954)

For some time before prisons boss Arthur Hume's retirement in 1909 there had been discussion about the introduction of a custodial sentence that was more than purely punitive. The first of a number of measures specifically aimed at the reformation of offenders was the Habitual Criminals and Offenders Act 1906. The act aimed to give courts the power to contain indefinitely certain offenders whose behaviour was deemed a continuing threat to law and order. Release would be granted once the governor was satisfied that 'reformation' had taken place and reoffending was unlikely.

As noted in previous chapters, the origins of the habitual criminal law, along with reformative detention and borstal detention which followed it, lie in the principle of indeterminate sentencing established by Alexander Maconochie on Norfolk Island in the early 1840s and popularised by the reformatory system at Elmira, New York, after 1876. The Elmira experiment was the subject of favourable comment in the New Zealand Parliament, but it was the Gladstone Committee of England that had the most direct impact. The Gladstone Committee had been set up in 1894 to examine aspects of policy and conditions in English prisons. The 1895 Gladstone Report, described as "a landmark in the history of English penal reform",[9] made sweeping recommendations, many of which flew in the face of the conservative and punitive penal traditions of the day. Apart from promoting general improvements in prison conditions, the committee was instrumental in widening probation in 1907, and creating a borstal system and drafting an indefinite sentence for habitual criminals in 1908.[10]

The idea of indefinite imprisonment for habitual criminals had been discussed internationally since 1900, and England had tried unsuccessfully to legislate for it in 1903 and 1904. In 1905, three years before England finally succeeded, New South Wales passed a habitual criminals law,[11] and New Zealand followed in 1906.

The emphasis of the New Zealand law was as much preventive as it was reformative, and it allowed the Supreme Court to declare any person a habitual criminal who had multiple previous convictions for certain classes of crime. The number of offences required to qualify depended on the class of offence. Class I offences, which were all of a sexual nature, required only two previous convictions. Class II offences, which included both violent and property crimes, required four. There was also provision for repeat offending of a less serious nature such as being idle and disorderly. Habitual criminals would complete a normal prison sentence (known informally as the 'head sentence'), before being transferred indefinitely to a 'reformatory' where they would be treated under more relaxed conditions at the pleasure of the governor. Habituals could apply to a Supreme Court Judge for a release recommendation on the grounds that they had reformed, and if granted, the governor had the power to order up to two years' post-release probation. After the formation of the prisons board in 1911, discretion to release passed to this new authority. Upon discharge, a habitual offender was subject to indefinite probationary conditions and could be recalled for any reason.

The habitual criminals legislation was never widely used; the largest number of offenders ever subjected to it was 34 in 1913. The figure was normally much lower. Between 1910 and 1929, an average of about 20 habituals was declared each year. In the 1930s this dropped to 10.9, and to 5.75 in the 1940s. And, although habituals could be held indefinitely, in practice they were normally paroled between one and two years after completion of their head sentence.[12]

The number of habituals in prison remained fairly steady, seldom exceeding 100 and generally hovering around 50. Between 1920 and 1940, habituals amounted to about four per cent of the incarcerated population.

This stability confirms a fairly steady flow of habituals out of prison. The rise in

Figure 13.4: Habitual Criminals Received

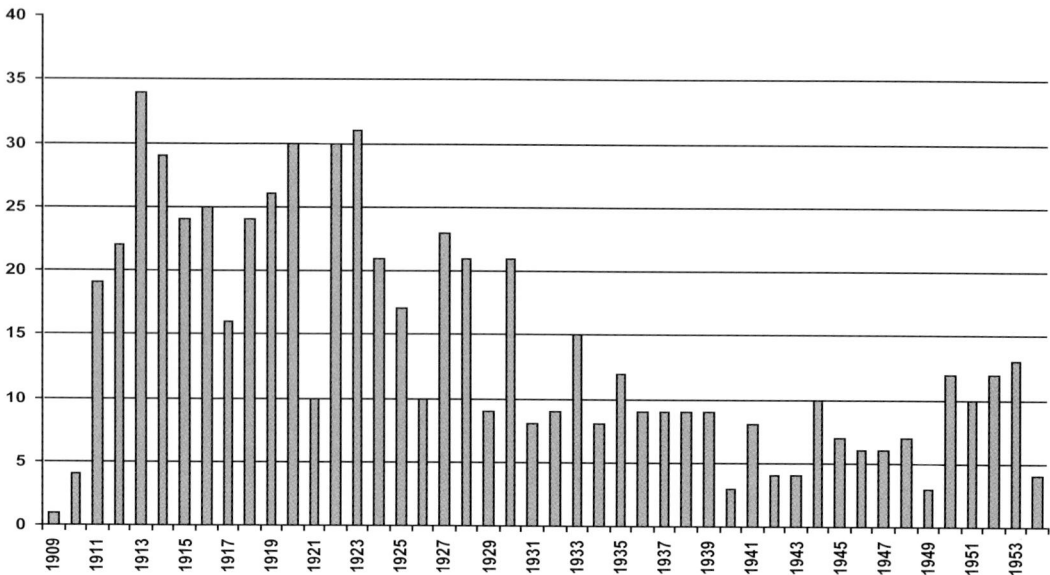

habituals in prison in the late 1940s suggests a toughening attitude from the prisons board after the Second World War.

As noted, the initial intention was for habituals to serve the latter part of their terms in a reformatory, and in 1907 a special wing at New Plymouth prison was set aside for this purpose. But in 1910 New Plymouth was designated for sex offenders, and habituals gradually became dispersed about the country where they were treated no differently from other prisoners. Thus the reformative intentions of the sentence were lost. In his annual report of 1953, Secretary for Justice Sam Barnett declared that approximately 80 per cent of habituals released between 1940 and 1946 had re-offended, and about two-thirds had re-offended seriously or "semi-seriously".[13] The sentence was obviously neither working as intended, nor was it preventing recidivism. Accordingly, the status of habitual criminal was abolished in the major revamping of criminal justice that came with the Criminal Justice Act 1954, and the problem of repeat offending came under a new sentence known as 'preventive detention'.

Reformative Detention (1910–1954)

Another consequence of the move toward indefinite sentences and reformative corrections that came in the tradition of Norfolk Island, Ireland and Elmira was reformative detention, which entered New Zealand legislation in 1910, four years after the Habitual Criminals and Offenders Act. In the debate over the Habitual Criminals and Offenders Bill Minister of Justice Sir John Findlay referred glowingly to the Elmira reformatory, making the mistaken claim that Elmira had a 96 per cent success rate, compared with 53 per cent recidivism in New Zealand. Unaware that Elmira was then on the point of failure, he was convinced that the 'new method' in use at Elmira was the key to reforming criminals.[14]

In New Zealand, the new sentence was part of a stream of activity that followed the retirement of Arthur Hume in 1909, as the country hastened to modernise a system that had been stagnating under Victorian authoritarianism.[15] It was felt that prisons had been rigid and overly punitive, ignoring their primary purpose: the reduction of offending. The new legislation, which came in an amendment to the Crimes Act, would provide magistrates and judges with an indeterminate sentence that would, it was hoped, reform criminals and cut recidivism. A major criticism of fixed remission was that it allowed a prisoner to shorten his sentence simply by staying out of trouble, without any real effort on his part to change. Indeterminate sentences, it was felt, would ensure that early release was granted only to those who showed a commitment to reform. As noted in chapter 3, such was the optimism about this new approach that, introducing the legislation into the House in 1910, Minister of Justice Findlay confidently declared, "when this Bill becomes law we will have a prison system as efficient as any existing anywhere in the world".[16]

Reformative detention could be ordered on a stand-alone basis or as an add-on to a fixed sentence; that is, to commence after a set term had expired. The Magistrates' Court could order reformative detention with a maximum of up to three years; the Supreme Court up to 10 years. The original idea was that the sentence would be served in specially constructed reformatories equipped with schools, trade training and other facilities conducive to offender rehabilitation. The prisons board, which had been created alongside reformative detention, would decide when this had taken place. Once released, reformative detainees were on probation until expiry of their full terms and could be recalled for any reason to serve the remainder.

Reformative detention was thus similar to the habitual criminals law, but with two important differences: first, reformative detention was available to all offenders, not just recidivists and second, the length of reformative detention had both statutory and judicial limits, while a habitual criminals declaration was open ended.

The sentence became immediately popular with the courts. Between 1911 and 1918 about 120 men and women received reformative detention each year, and between 1920 and 1936 the average was over 200. In 1924, when reformative detainees in New Zealand prisons peaked at 454, they represented 38 per cent of the sentenced population. After 1936 the popularity of the option declined dramatically, but picked up again after the Second World War. The largest number of reformative detention sentences ever given was 290 in 1950, and the sentence retained its popularity until it was abolished in 1954.

The problem with reformative detention, as with the treatment of habitual criminals, was that the sentence was never implemented as intended. An early attempt was made to treat reformative detainees in Invercargill prison, but this was soon frustrated as, for various reasons, detainees became dispersed around the country. Just as there were no separate institutions for reformative detainees, there were no separate programmes either. And staff had no training in reformative treatment. In 1917 the Inspector of Prisons informed the Minister of Justice that reformative detainees were being treated no differently from hard-labour prisoners[17] and in 1924 and 1953 the Department of Justice repeated the observation.[18] Moreover, the courts were not familiar with the purposes of the sentence and it was awarded inappropriately and inconsistently.[19] Once they began, criticisms of the meaninglessness of reformative detention continued for years.[20]

These long-recognised flaws were never rectified, and five years after its abolition,

Figure 13.5: Reformative Detainees Received

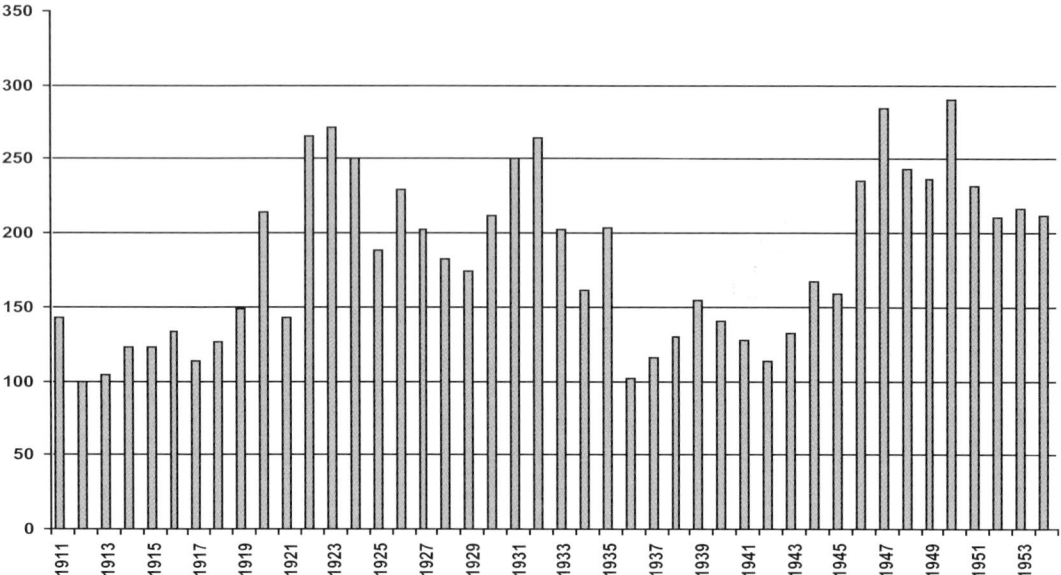

Pat Mayhew, a former chief probation officer who became Director of the Penal Division between 1956 and 1960, summed up the problems:

> … reformative detention was from the first day a sorry farce. The Courts misused the sentence, the prisons system was quite incapable of assimilating this special group, the officers were incompetent to carry out such a radically different regime, the Prisons Board failed to give sufficient consideration to each case, and within a very short time it seems that the senior administrators of the Department had ceased to believe in it. Yet this illusion of reformative training was allowed to continue until 1954.[21]

It was with these difficulties in mind that in the Criminal Justice Act 1954, reformative detention was abolished and replaced by a sentence that proved equally unworkable called 'corrective training'.

Borstal Detention/Training (1924–1981)

The last of the indeterminate sentences introduced in the early 19th century in the quest for criminal reformation was borstal detention. Once again, the idea of borstal in New Zealand was directly influenced by the Elmira experiment and by developments in England.

Like habitual criminality, the concept of borstals came from the Gladstone Committee of 1895, which recommended a 'penal reformatory' for persons in the 16 to 23 age group. As a result, in 1897 Chairman of the Prison Commission Sir Evelyn Ruggles-Brise travelled to the United States, to visit reformatories at Elmira and at Concord in Massachusetts. Elmira, with its system of training and education combined with graded privilege and the possibility of parole after a minimum of

12 months followed by six months' supervision, impressed the English the most. Accordingly, in 1900 a small number of young prisoners from London were transferred to an experimental reformatory in Bedford, and the following year a similar pilot began at a prison in the town of Borstal in Kent. In 1903 the idea was extended to Dartmoor. Discipline and hard work were the methods used at these institutions, but the 'borstal' system itself was not legislated until the Prevention of Crime Act 1908. This provided indeterminate sentences of 0–2 years or 0–3 years borstal detention for young offenders aged 16–21.[22]

New Zealand was directly influenced by these events. The separation of young offenders from adults had begun in 1910 when the newly constructed prison at Invercargill began receiving reformative detainees aged under 25. In 1917 Invercargill was gazetted as 'Invercargill Borstal Institution' under a Statutes Law Amendment, and seven years later the New Zealand Government passed its own Prevention of Crime (Borstal Institutions Establishment) Act. This act created a borstal detention sentence for offenders aged 15–21. As in England, two options were available: a term of 1–3 years if imposed by the Magistrates' Court, and 2–5 years if given by the Supreme Court. Release was authorised by the prisons board, and was followed by 12 months' probation. In 1954 the sentence was renamed 'borstal training' (BT) and the term restricted to 0–3 years (referred to as 'nought-to-three') for boys aged 17–20. In 1961 special borstal parole boards were established, and in 1962 borstal training was reduced to 0–2 years (known as 'nought-to-two').

Data on borstal numbers are fragmentary, but throughout the 1920s musters were relatively high, exceeding 380 in 1927 and in 1928. After this they declined, averaging about 150 through to 1950.

Until 1955 it was rare for the number of detainees sentenced annually to exceed 200. However, just as prison numbers began to rise after 1955 so did the muster of borstal trainees. Between 1955 and 1960 borstal terms jumped 68 per cent, and more

Figure 13.6: Borstal Trainees Received

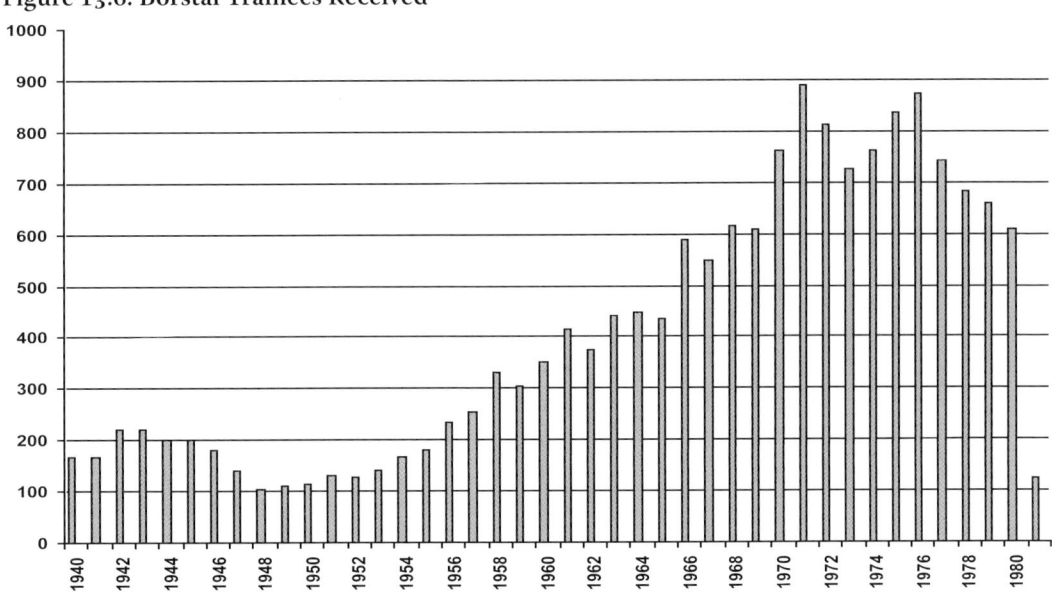

Waikeria borstal trainees, c.1960.

than doubled by 1970. Between 1970 and 1976 borstal sentences averaged 809 per year, but began to fall after legislation to abolish borstals was passed in 1975. This law took effect in 1981.

Unlike reformative detention, borstal detention/training took place in dedicated institutions assisted by instructors with work-skills training. Invercargill and Waikeria became designated as borstals for men, and Point Halswell in Wellington for women before Arohata replaced it in 1944. In 1961 a minimum security borstal for first offenders was opened at Waipiata in Central Otago and in 1969 a smaller but similar one was opened for a short time at Kaitoke near Wanganui.

From the outset, education was offered in borstals and effort invested in providing facilities for sport, recreation, psychological assessment and trade instruction. Invercargill and Waikeria were built on farming estates, with agriculture providing a principal form of employment. However, in spite of all the effort put into them, borstals, like the reformatories on which they were modelled, were unsuccessful. In 1961 the Department of Justice reviewed borstal policy and declared the system was failing, largely because of overcrowding, burgeoning numbers and the contamination effect of having so many recidivists in the programme. The proposed solution was the creation of smaller borstals for low-risk 'star' offenders, who would be removed from the mainstream and subjected to a low-security open borstal regime.

Waipiata was the first borstal used for this purpose. Waipiata was an old sanatorium, taken over from the health department in 1961 for use as an 'open' borstal for 75 trainees, hand-picked because of their assumed high potential for good citizenship. Security was minimal and prisoners had access to education, sport, counselling, vocational instruction, community activity and farm work. It was hoped these conditions would be conducive to producing positive changes in young naïve offenders. However, nine years after the experiment began, the recidivism of Waipiata inmates compared with those of all other borstal trainees was found to be insignificant. Approximately 70 per cent of borstal trainees had re-offended within two years of release whether they had been treated at Waipiata or not.[23] These results were even worse than the English borstals, where 64 per cent had re-offended,[24] and by 1971 it was officially acknowledged that the chances of effecting rehabilitation in young criminals were slim.[25]

The decision to abolish borstals in 1975 was based on the premise that they were no longer working – if they ever had been – and that they had outlived their usefulness. This was accompanied by disenchantment with the notion of indeterminate sentencing and criminal rehabilitation in general, which had been growing internationally since the mid-1960s.[26] The 1969 review of borstal policy noted that most borstal trainees were hardened offenders, resistant to reformative influences, and recommended the indeterminate borstal sentence be phased out. The enabling legislation was carried in 1975, but did not become effective until 1 April 1981 when borstals ceased to exist. Invercargill, Waikeria and Arohata borstals now joined the Manawatu Youth Institution as 'youth prisons' in which young offenders served fixed sentences. Population pressures soon forced adult ingress into these facilities, and under the Penal Institutions Amendment Act 1985 youth prisons were abandoned. Youthful inmates are now kept separate from adults, in closed sections of general prisons.

Corrective Training #1 (1954–1963)

When reformative detention was abandoned in 1954 it was felt that a more controlled alternative could operate effectively. The solution came in the form of a new sentence called corrective training. Two entirely different sentences named 'corrective training' have been used in New Zealand's history so, where there may be confusion, they are referred to as corrective training #1 and corrective training #2. Corrective training #1, like so many of New Zealand's penal developments in the 19th and 20th centuries, was modelled on English precedent. In this case the sentence replicated one conceived by the English Persistent Offenders Committee in 1932 and contained in the Criminal Justice Act 1948.[27] The English law provided a sentence of between two and four years, with the actual term to be decided by the court, for persistent offenders aged over 21 but normally no older than 30.

New Zealand's version of corrective training came with the Criminal Justice Act 1954. The aims were the same as for reformative detention, and the sentence looked remarkably similar to borstal training except it was designed for an older age group. Whereas the maximum term for reformative detention was, within statutory limits, determined by the sentencing court, in corrective training, as with borstal training, the maximum was fixed at three years, with parole eligibility from date of sentencing. Moreover, where reformative detention had no age limits, limits for corrective training were set generally at 21–30 (or 35 in special circumstances), thus overlapping at the lower end with borstal training. And unlike reformative detention, corrective training could be given to specified recidivists only and could not accompany any other prison sentence. Training would take place in a prison, but separate institutions for corrective trainees would be set aside to allow for more intensive treatment.

Early reaction to the sentence was positive. Corrective training was targeted at

Figure 13.7: Corrective Trainees Received

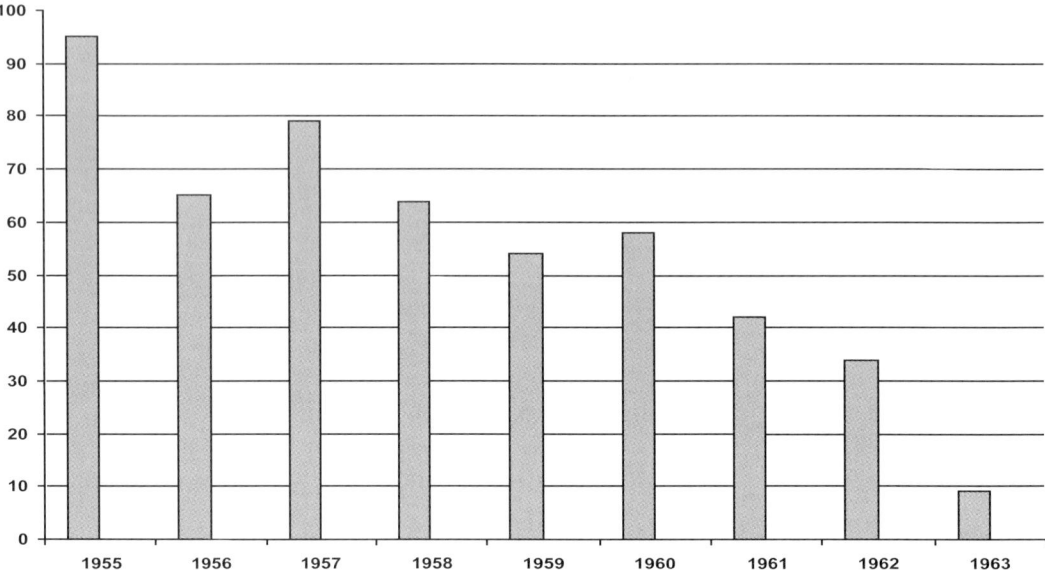

repeat offenders deemed reclaimable, and initially trainees were sent to Waikeria where there was special provision for trade instruction, education, sport, leisure and cultural activity. In his 1956 annual report Secretary for Justice Sam Barnett expressed high confidence in the way the new sentence was working and announced that the first 95 trainees had responded well and that six would be released before serving half of their maximum terms.[28] But optimism did not last and it was soon apparent the sentence was not performing as intended.

There were several reasons. The first was overcrowding. As seen earlier, in the latter half of the 1950s there was a deepening accommodation crisis, with prison musters growing by 57 per cent between 1955 and 1960. Borstal receptions expanded even faster – by 93 per cent in the same period – and soon borstals were bursting at the seams. Every year after 1956 the Secretary for Justice made desperate references to the impossibility of the looming situation. By 1958, with Waikeria full, some corrective trainees were held at Wi Tako, and within 12 months they had all been transferred there.

The courts never favoured corrective training, which was fortunate, Barnett wryly observed, because if they had, the trainees could never have been accommodated.[29]

Barnett knew by 1959 that corrective training was failing. He commented in his report that year that not only were the courts ignoring the sentence, but some were giving it to unsuitable offenders. The penal division's response, when it disagreed with the sentence of the court, was to refuse to apply it and to simply place the offender in the mainstream. Barnett retired, frustrated, in 1960 and his replacement, Dr John Robson, wasted no time getting rid of corrective training. His reasons were first, that no separate institution had been (or was likely to be) made available for it; second, that the courts were awarding it inappropriately; and third, that he disagreed with indeterminate sentences anyhow because of their unsettling effect on inmates.[30] As a result, in 1963 corrective training was abolished.

Detention in a Detention Centre/Corrective Training #2 (1954–2002)

Another sentence in 1954 based on English precedent was detention in a detention centre. Often known in America as 'boot camps' or 'shock incarceration', detention centres originated in the Criminal Justice Act 1948, reflecting a perceived need for more punitive measures after the Second World War. Although, they did not make an appearance in the United States until 1983, the first English centre was opened at Campsfield House in Oxfordshire in 1952.[31]

In New Zealand, as in other parts of the world, the early 1950s were associated with high levels of concern about juvenile delinquency. Although statistics show that the number of children placed under compulsory supervision had fallen since the war (as had complaints against youth aged 10–17), from a low of 105 in 1948 the number of cases brought before the Children's Courts had grown by 28 per cent by 1953. Borstal training sentences grew by 35 per cent in the same period. There was also an apparent increase in premarital sexual activity and this, combined with general fears about changing patterns of youth culture and its possible consequences, led to the formation of a Special Committee on Moral Delinquency in 1954.[32]

It was in this atmosphere of moral panic, with the major redrafting of criminal justice law in 1954, that the National Government created the sentence of detention in a detention centre (DC) as a punitive deterrent for undisciplined youthful offenders. The sentence was similar to its English namesake, but in New Zealand the term was originally four months rather than three, and referred to offenders aged 17–23. It was never applied in this form. For seven years the sentence lay dormant and in 1960, still unused, the term of detention was cut to three months and its application restricted to young offenders aged 16–21. Release was to be followed by 12 months' probation.

Rises in criminal offending, both adult and youth, were now a matter of national concern. Between 1950 and 1960 the number of cases before the Magistrates' Courts grew by 114 per cent and cases before Children's Courts by 190 per cent. Borstal sentences trebled. The phenomenon of youth gangs had commenced and in September 1960, just before the election which ousted the second Labour Government, an unprecedented youth riot at the Hastings Blossom Festival convinced many that juvenile delinquency was out of control and that it was the Labour administration's fault.[33] Thus, when National came to power in November, it wasted no time activating the legislation that had been gathering dust for six years. On 1 June 1961 the first detention centre opened next to the borstal at Waikeria.

The objective of the detention centre was to combat 'hooliganism and larrikinism' by giving criminally naïve young offenders a 'short, sharp shock' of 'boot camp'-style discipline. The sentence was three months, reducible to two for good behaviour, and applied only to young men who had never been incarcerated. At Waikeria, detainees had their heads shaven upon entry, were issued kit which was often ill-fitting or torn, and were subjected to abuse and humiliation from staff. Most movement took place at the march and in squad formation, rations were meagre and work, usually agricultural, was demeaning and pointless. Verbal communication between inmates was forbidden most of the time, but bullying of weaker prisoners by the stronger sometimes continued without staff interference. Staff themelves often slapped, kicked and swore at inmates. Detainees worked six days a week and were locked up in double cells between 7pm and 6am. Talking after lockup was prohibited.[34]

Detention-centre prisoners were constantly reminded that future offending would result in borstal training, which would be longer and harder. This belief was enhanced by borstal inmates, who verbally abused the DC squads, calling detainees "fucking DC wonks" and worse. The primary objective of the detention centre, then, was to terrify the young first offender out of further crime.

The concept of shock incarceration appealed to magistrates and the sentence got off to a healthy start. In 1962, 170 DC sentences were given, and this rose steadily to a peak of 600 in 1976. By 1970, with numbers sentenced exceeding 400 for the first time, it was clear that more centres were needed. New facilities were opened at Tongariro prison farm in September 1970 and at Rolleston in Canterbury in June 1972.

Departmental statements about the effectiveness of detention centre outcomes were initially optimistic, albeit misleading. In 1970, for example, a justice department publication[35] stated that half of DC releases would not be convicted of a serious offence within five years of release. What was not said was that *overall* reconviction rates were high. As early as 1966 a recidivism study found that 68 per cent of detainees had been reconvicted within three years of release. This outcome was backed by subsequent research: a 1971 study found that 71 per cent were reconvicted within two years and another in 1979 revealed a 68 per cent recidivism rate within two years.[36]

Obviously the sentence was having little effect. Recognising this, the department's next response was strange. Instead of scrapping the detention centre sentence altogether, it made a few minor adjustments, renamed it 'corrective training' (CT) and expanded it. Legislation abolishing DC and replacing it with CT was passed in 1975. The Criminal Justice Amendment Act 1975 originally created corrective training with two alternatives: a term of three months (almost the same as the detention centre) and one of six months which involved treatment and an adventure programme.[37] But the law was never applied in this form, and the six-month option was abolished in 1980, before corrective training became operative in April 1981. Corrective training now applied to young women as well as young men aged between 15 and 19. The new sentence could be given more than once, and to those who had previously been incarcerated. Apart from that the CT sentence, and the attached deterrent regime, were all but indistinguishable from DC. In the case of young women, there were seldom more than three or four serving the sentence at any one time, and providing a separate programme for them was virtually impossible.

How the department imagined that such minor qualifying alterations could change the outcomes of a method that had proven so consummately ineffective is a mystery. Nevertheless, it was in a spirit of such faith that corrective training was expanded. The old detention centres at Rolleston and Tongariro were renamed correctional training centres, and new centres were established at Rangipo and Arohata women's prison, and soon after at Invercargill. The new sentence was used immediately, with 622 receiving corrective training in its first year, rising to a peak of 766 in 1984. By now, however, what should have been obvious from the start had been proven: corrective training was no more useful than its predecessor. In fact it was worse. A 1983 departmental study found that 71 per cent of corrective trainees were reconvicted within 12 months of release.[38]

From this point corrective training was doomed. Use of the sentence dropped by almost 80 per cent between 1983 and 2000. With declining demand, centres began to close. Rolleston CT shut in August 1982 and trainees were transferred to Invercargill.

Six years later only Tongariro and Arohata remained, although due to tiny numbers corrective training at Arohata existed in name only. In 2001 only 147 offenders got the sentence and in 2002 there were just 27. In July 2002, with the passage of the Sentencing Act, corrective training came to an end.

Figure 13.8: Detention Centre Trainees Received (CT 1981–)

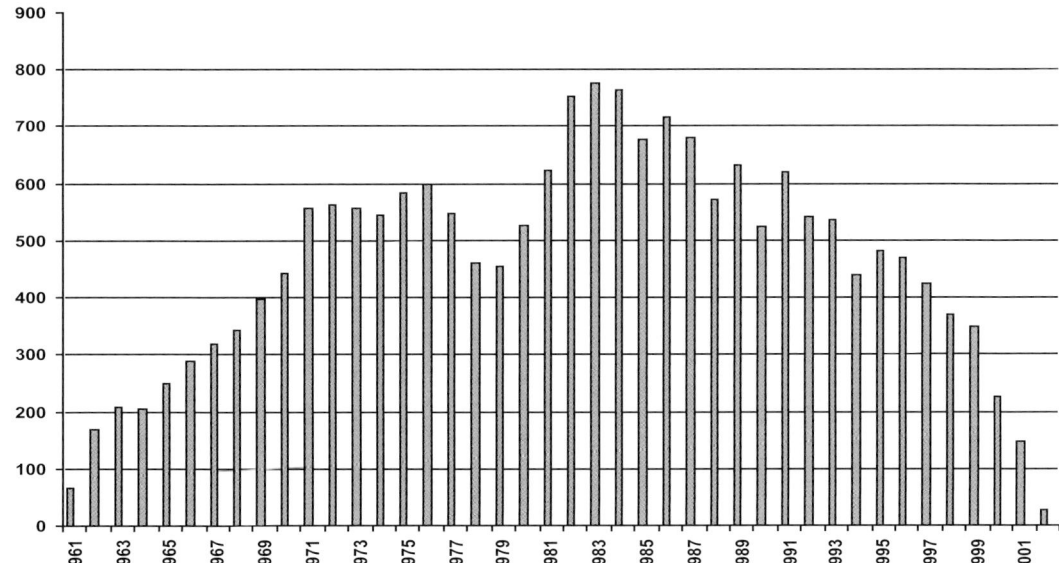

Preventive Detention (1954–present)

The final new sentence that appeared in the Criminal Justice Act 1954 was preventive detention (PD). Just as corrective training replaced reformative detention, so preventive detention was intended as a replacement for the under-used habitual criminal declaration: that is, it was aimed at the persistent recidivist. As with previous sentencing types, the origins of preventive detention lay in English law.

The English Prevention of Crime Act 1908 carried a form of preventive detention very similar to New Zealand's habitual criminals provision, but the version that influenced New Zealand's legislators most was one which, like corrective training #1, was conceived of by the Persistent Offenders Committee in 1932 and which eventually came into being under the English Criminal Justice Act 1948. This act brought a sentence of between five and 14 years' imprisonment – the upper limit to be fixed by the court – for offenders aged over 30 who had at least three previous convictions for serious offences.[39]

New Zealand's conception of the sentence was different from England's in several respects. As it appeared in 1954, preventive detention had fixed upper and lower limits, with release determined by the parole board. In order to qualify for PD an offender had to be at least 25 years of age. The sentence applied under three different sets of conditions:

1. When the offender was convicted of a child sexual offence, having previously been convicted of another such offence since age 17.

2. When the offender was convicted of an offence punishable by at least three years' imprisonment, having on at least three separate occasions since age 17 been convicted of similar offences and been sent to prison for at least a year on two occasions.

3. When the offender was convicted of an offence punishable by imprisonment of more than three months, having on at least seven previous occasions since age 17 been convicted of similar offences and incarcerated on at least four occasions.

Preventive detention was an indeterminate sentence of three–14 years or, in the case of child sex offenders, three years–life. After release the detainee could be recalled at any time to serve the remainder of his term. As the title suggests, the provision was meant to be protective rather than reformative, although preventive detainees were held in the mainstream prison population and had access to the same employment and welfare opportunities as other inmates. Release was contingent on a parole board prediction that a detainee was no longer likely to offend.

The sentence, restricted as it was in its original form, was rarely used. The largest number of sentences ever given was 29 in 1956, and between 1955 and 1961 about 18 individuals received it each year. Thereafter it fell significantly; the average number of sentences given between 1962 and 1967 was only 4.7. Moreover, the parole board was liberal in its deliberations and detainees were normally released after serving no more than six years, often substantially less.[40] Use of the sentence for sex offences was rare: of the 152 terms of preventive detention given between 1955 and 1967, only 32 were for sex crimes. Nearly three-quarters of the sentences were for property crimes. All preventive detainees were male.

In England, preventive detention was pronounced ineffective and was finally abolished in 1967.[41] In his annual report of 1965 Secretary for Justice John Robson commented on the English moves and noted that the sentence in New Zealand (once more) had been misapplied by judges.[42] The following year Minister of Justice Ralph Hanan also criticised the sentence, on the basis that: it was too severe for repeat petty offenders (some of whom had received the penalty); no parole board could reasonably predict whether or not an inmate was likely to reoffend; and that the uncertainty inherent in indeterminate sentences was unsettling and unfair to inmates.[43]

As a result, in 1967 preventive detention was limited solely to repeat child-sex offenders and its term increased to seven years–life, with recall from a parole order possible at any time.

Now more restricted, the sentence was used even less frequently. In the 19 years between 1967 and 1987 when the law changed again, it was imposed only 26 times, and in at least five of these cases the sentence was quashed by the Court of Appeal.[44] In 1972 there were 16 preventive detainees in prisons out of a total muster of 1,800[45] and in 1981 just 15 in a muster of 2,800. The average term served by preventive detainees was 10.25 years[46] – slightly longer than lifers.

By the end of the 1970s the efficacy of preventive detention was seriously in question. Between 1975 and 1981 it was imposed just six times, and on at least one of these occasions the sentence was modified on appeal. The Penal Policy Review Committee in 1981 recommended the abolition of preventive detention on the basis that its use was "arbitrary, selective and inequitable", that no parole board could accurately predict the post-release behaviour of an inmate, and that long finite sentences (of 14 years maximum) were already available.[47]

The major review of criminal justice in the Criminal Justice Act 1985 relied heavily on the committee's recommendations, but the government declined to strike the sentence out. Presumably it thought preventive detention should remain available for the worst cases. This reasoning proved sound because, as seen earlier, a number of high-profiled crimes involving extreme sexual violence followed. The first occurred in March 1986 when, only six weeks after being released from prison from a 10-year sentence for abduction and attempted rape, John Douglas Bennett (31) kidnapped a woman at knife point from a sex shop in Christchurch. Taking her to a remote location he forced her to undress and perform oral sex on him before attempting to rape and strangle her and dumping her unconscious body in the boot of his car. She was saved when the car rolled and she was thrown from the boot, sustaining multiple injuries in the process. Bennett, who had a string of convictions against women from age 15, was sentenced to preventive detention.[48]

The incident drew extensive media coverage and with polls showing public concern over crime rising to a peak,[49] Minister of Justice Geoffrey Palmer ordered a Committee of Inquiry into Violence, which reported in March 1987. In the meantime, in October 1986, Peter Joseph Holdem (30), with a history of sex crimes against young girls, abducted and murdered six-year-old Louisa Damodran as she was walking home from school. Although he received life imprisonment, Holdem was not eligible for preventive detention because it could not be proven that he had sexually assaulted Louisa. A month later and two weeks after Bennett's sentencing, Palmer announced changes to the law relating to crimes of violence, including amendments to preventive detention. Thus, from August 1987, preventive detention was extended to include all persons aged 21 and over convicted of a crime of serious violence who, on at least one previous occasion since age 17, had been convicted of a similar offence. The non-parole period for preventive detainees was increased from seven to 10 years.

Following the law change the number of sentences of preventive detention jumped sharply. The change, however, seems to have had much less to do with the widening of eligibility than with a greater willingness among judges to award the sentence, along with other lengthy terms for violence.[50] For example, where between 1980 and 1986 reluctant courts gave a total of just eight sentences of PD, in the next six years there were 39. A higher acceptance of the sentence was echoed by the Court of Appeal although this resulted in:

> … a disturbing lack of consistency and gross unfairness to many of those who have been sentenced to preventive detention while others whose cases are indistinguishable both in terms of the offender's history and the present offence receive finite sentences of varying severity. On occasion the reasons cited for not imposing preventive detention have been previously rejected by the Court of Appeal as adequate grounds for quashing the sentence in other cases. [51]

Violent and sexual crimes continued to surge. Between 1987 and 1993 police-reported serious violence grew by 141 per cent. Reported sexual attacks grew by 69 per cent. Sensational crimes contributed to rising public outrage. The abduction-murder of six-year-old Teresa Cormack in June 1987, just before a general election, for example,

Figure 13.9: Preventive Detainees Received

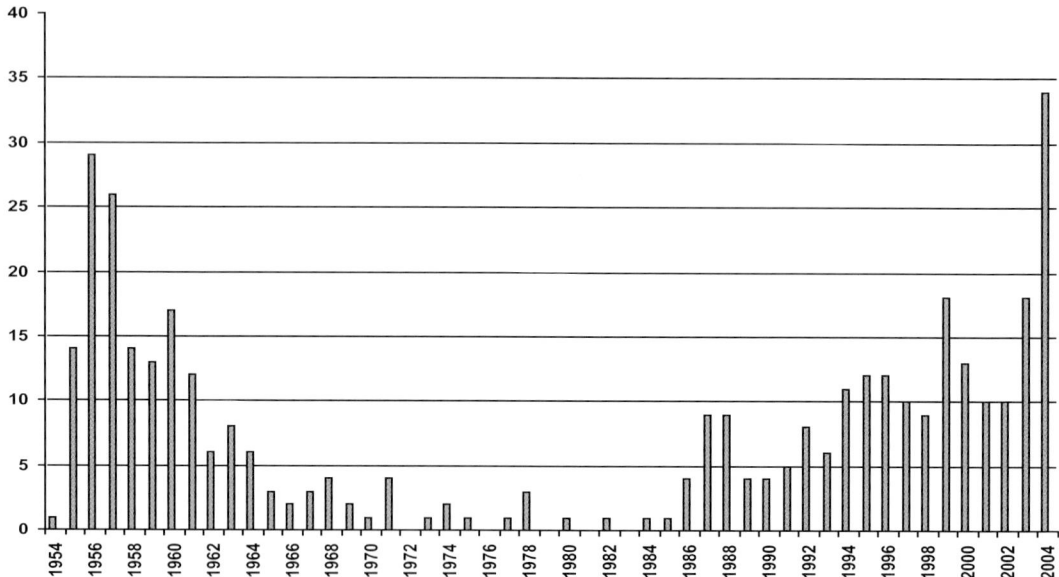

resulted in calls for the restoration of capital punishment and promises from opposition leader Jim Bolger for a referendum on the matter. The sexually-motivated homicides of Tamihere and Dally in 1989, followed by the rape and murder of English tourist Monica Cantwell on Mt Maunganui that November, added fuel to the fire. In November 1991 came the sex killing of Kylie Smith, and in the first month of 1992 there were 10 more reported homicides, including the stabbing of English tourist Margery Hopegood in Hamilton and the rape and strangling of eight-year-old Sarah Curry in Invercargill.

Prime Minister Jim Bolger announced to an outraged public that stronger measures would be taken to combat the problem of serious violence, particularly against women.[52] In February 1992 public furore over the impending release on parole of suspected serial rapist and woman beater Mark Stephens caused his discharge to be delayed, and by June, draft legislation toughening penalties for serious violent offenders, including changes to preventive detention, were in the pipeline. In February 1993, 300 protesters marched to parliament demanding tougher sentences for violent crime and natural life for murder. Organised by family and friends of Kylie Smith (see chapter 5), a petition containing 265,000 signatures was presented.

This was election year and amendments to the Criminal Justice Act were central to the National Government's campaign. When the changes came in June 1993, the maximum penalty for sexual violation was extended to 20 years and preventive detention became available to serious sexual offenders on a first offence. Courts were empowered to order discretionary non-parole minimums longer than those stipulated in law. Release conditions were made more rigorous, grounds for recall were widened and the recall process was simplified.

The 1993 amendments were followed by another leap in the use of preventive detention, but once more these were likely to have been caused by judicial attitudes

Figure 13.10: Preventive Detainees in Custody

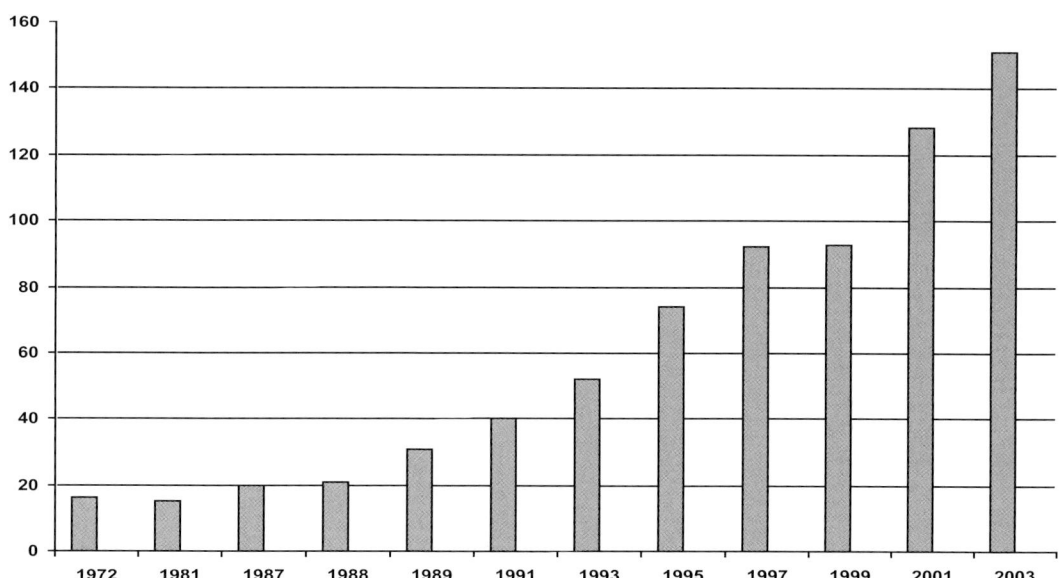

rather than the legal changes themselves. Up to this time, for example, preventive detention for non-sexual violence, as permitted by the 1987 amendment, had never been used. Between 1995 and the next law change in 2002, however, two instances appeared. The first was in 1995 when the Court of Appeal awarded the sentence to Bob McGee (43) for serious domestic assaults in Wellington; the next was given three years later to Tony Albert (41) for serious assaults involving home invasions.[53]

The increased usage of preventive detention is reflected in sentencing figures. Since 1962 the provision had not been used more than nine times in any one year, with an annual average of 6.4 sentences. After 1993, preventive detention was imposed on 10 or more occasions almost every year, with an average of 11.9.

At the same time, as a result of increasing usage, discretionary non-parole periods and more stringent parole procedures, the numbers of preventive detainees in prison rocketed from just 20 in 1987 to 151 in 2003.

Although only three extended non-parole periods for PD were given between 1993 and the 2002 law change, they involved some of the longest terms ever imposed under this sentence. All recipients were serial sex offenders. The first two were 25 years each, imposed on serial rapist Joseph Thompson in 1995 and Sunday School paedophile John Fleming in 1996; the third was 22 years, given to serial rapist Malcolm Rewa in 1998. In 2003, after the law change, Nicholas Reekie got PD with a 25-year minimum for a series of rapes and other offences.

Changes in police recording methods make year-by-year comparisons of reported crime during the 1990s impossible. Ministry of Justice figures, however, show that convictions for violence (including sexual) rose by 94 per cent between 1990 and the peak year of 1995. Numbers then stabilised before dropping by about 12 per cent after 2000.[54] In spite of this, concern about violent offending remained high, driven more by sensational cases than by the crime rates themselves. In the late 1990s, several incidents resurrected calls for harsher penalties. As noted earlier, the first was the death of kindergarten teacher Joanne McCarthy, battered in her Whangaparaoa home in November 1998, followed by the robbery-murder of Reporoa farmer Beverly Bouma at her home less than three weeks later (see chapters 5, 6 and 12). These offences led to the Crimes Amendment Act in 1999, mandating, *inter alia*, automatic three-year add-ons to the non-parole periods for life imprisonment and preventive detention if the crime had been committed during a home invasion.

At the same time, as discussed, Christchurch store owner Norm Withers, whose 71-year-old mother was savagely beaten in a random attack in 1997, organised a petition calling for a referendum on strategies to combat violent crime. The 285,000-signature petition resulted in the referendum at the 1999 General Election, which received almost 92 per cent support for tougher measures. The Withers campaign was supported by Mark Middleton, stepfather of Carla Cardno, the 13-year-old who was raped and murdered by Paul Dally. Middleton's long and highly public stand against Dally's possible release in 1999 resulted in another petition for tougher sentences in 2001, signed by 16,000 people. The organiser of the petition, Garth McVicar, also formed the Sensible Sentencing Trust, in pursuit of stronger violent crime measures.

Withers, Middleton and McVicar were powerful voices in the early 2000s and the Labour-led coalition's reluctance to act soon dissolved as further outrages took place. The most significant was the case of young journalist Kylie Jones (23) who, as recalled, was raped and murdered on her way home from work in mid-2000. Justice minister Phil Goff was quick to respond to the outcry that followed the murder and promised a redrafting of the country's parole and sentencing laws. These finally came in the Parole Act 2002 and the Sentencing Act 2002.

As noted in chapters 6 and 12, these acts changed parole and sentencing law significantly. The age limit for preventive detention was reduced from 21 to 18 and PD was made available on a first offence for a wider range of serious violent or sexual crimes (known as 'qualifying' offences). The statutory non-parole minimum was cut from 10 to five years – distinguishing it from the life sentence for the first time since 1975. The court's discretion to order a longer non-parole minimum remained, as did the non-finite power of recall. With the extension of the definition of preventive detention to its broadest margins in history, courts showed greater readiness than ever to impose it. In 2001 and 2002, 20 men received the sentence, and in the following two years 52 preventive detention terms were given.

The lower statutory non-parole period of five years also encouraged greater use of the extended minimum. Whereas before the Sentencing Act, discretionary extensions had only been ordered on three occasions, in the 24 months after the act came into force on 1 July 2002, minimums accompanied 26 of the 37 cases where the sentence was imposed. In two of these cases the minimum was longer than 10 years.[55]

There was also a noticeable increase in use of PD for non-sexual violence. Before 2003 preventive detention had only been used twice in this way. However, of the 37 sentences imposed in the 24 months after the passage of the 2002 act, eight were for non-sexual violence: five for wounding and one sentence each for the offences of aggravated robbery, kidnapping and using a firearm against a law enforcement officer.[56] The youngest person ever given preventive detention is Mark Hoggart (20) in February 2004, after choking his girlfriend until she gave a false confession of infidelity and stabbing another person with a pair of scissors. In March 2006 Kino Hoki Matete (25) became the first woman ever to get preventive detention. Matete, who had a list of 13 violence convictions dating back to 1994, was given PD with a six-year minimum for throwing boiling water over another inmate while in prison, and breaking a prison officer's arm. The longest-serving preventive detainee is Alfred Thomas Vincent, convicted of indecent assault on boys in September 1968 and still serving his term.

Of all the sentencing alternatives created in the Criminal Justice Act 1954, preventive detention is the only one that has survived. Although it came close to extinction in the 1980s, it has been remodelled as a powerful protective device against the threat of the dangerous violent offender.

Conclusion

The ultimate objective of any correctional system is the reduction of offending, and the history of sentencing alternatives in New Zealand has been a succession of failed attempts to achieve this purpose. The 19th century was characterised by a bludgeoning approach to corrections, with the early sentences of penal servitude and imprisonment at hard labour essentially aimed at deterrence through the infliction of misery. The Habitual Criminals Act 1906 was the first to break with the pattern and this legislation, followed by that which brought in the non-finite terms of reformative detention in 1910 and borstal detention in 1924, combined with parole for all finite sentences in 1920, was the beginning of an era committed to the belief that errant personalities could be corrected through salutary influences in prison. Indeterminate sentences and liberal parole systems are founded upon this assumption.

For practical reasons neither the habitual criminal designation nor reformative detention operated properly, and by the early 1950s scepticism about the corrective potential of the prison had begun. In 1954 the declaration of habitual criminality was replaced by the prophylactic sentence of preventive detention and (as seen in the last chapter) universal parole for finite sentences replaced by fixed remission. But the vestiges of correctionalism still remained, in the restructured sentence of borstal training and the new one of corrective training.

Corrective training #1 was misapplied and proved impracticable, and reformative training in borstals – even when applied to naïve low-risk offenders as it was at Waipiata – was incapable of preventing very high levels of recidivism. John Robson, who ran the justice department between 1960 and 1970, an early critic of the non-determinate sentence, moved swiftly to have corrective training abolished. His scepticism was echoed in the Penal Policy Review Committee's 1981 report. This committee questioned the ability of any prison system to rehabilitate criminals and opposed indeterminate sentences on this ground, as well as on the ground that no parole authority could accurately predict the post-release behaviour of an inmate. Moreover, as Robson had also noted, indeterminate sentences had a very unsettling effect on prisoners. By now, attempts to reform criminals through borstal training had been abandoned, along with the later experiment in punitive deterrence that came with shock incarceration. In the 1970s the parole board gave early release sparingly for finite sentences, and the only non-determinate sentences that remained were life and preventive detention, neither of which had rehabilitation as its primary purpose.

Today the case remains the same, although the scope of parole has recently been expanded back to its 1920 dimensions and the cadaver of correctionalism has been resurrected with the concept of Integrated Offender Management. This has occurred in the face of almost a century of failed experiments in criminal reformation. Corrections has described a full circle, recalling George Hegel's observation that governments learn little from history. The final chapter of this book is dedicated to a brief review of discarded reformative experiments, followed by an examination of why the task of rehabilitating criminals is so difficult.

Notes

1 Webb, 1982: 13–15.
2 AJHR H.20, 1916: 15.
3 AJHR H.20, 1954; NZPD v.304, 1954: 1932.
4 Department of Justice, 1974: 24.
5 Department of Justice, 1974: 26.
6 Young, 1998: 9.
7 See *R v Wickliffe* [1987] 1 NZLR 55, and *R v Beri* [1987] 1 NZLR 46.
8 Spier, 2005: 107.
9 Rose, 1961: 61.
10 Rose, 1961: 61–63, 76–82.
11 Rose, 1961: 79–80.
12 AJHR H.20, 1953: 7.
13 AJHR H.20, 1953.
14 NZPD v.150, 1910: 349–352.
15 See Mayhew, 1959: 94.
16 NZPD v.150, 1910: 360.
17 See Mayhew, 1959: 117.
18 AJHR H.20, 1953.
19 AJHR H.20a, 1913: 2.
20 See Webb, 1982: 59.
21 Mayhew, 1959: 115–116.
22 Hood, 1965: Ch 1.
23 Department of Justice, 1971.
24 Hood, 1965: 212.
25 Department of Social Welfare, 1971: 25–28.
26 See, e.g., Martinson, 1974; Morris and Hawkins 1970: 118; Penal Policy Review Committee, 1981: 196–199; 205–208.
27 Rose, 1961: 226.
28 AJHR H.20, 1956: 15–16.
29 AJHR H.20, 1959.
30 AJHR H.20, 1962: 10.
31 Hall Williams, 1970: 330–331.
32 AJHR H.47, 1954: 15, 16. See also Yska, 1993.
33 See Newbold, 1989: 118–119.
34 The author was an inmate of Waikeria DC in 1971.
35 Department of Justice, 1970: 7.
36 Walker and Brown, 1983: 40.

37 Department of Justice, 1998: 30.
38 Walker and Brown, 1983: 40.
39 Rose, 1961: 226.
40 Webb, 1982: 72.
41 Hall Williams, 1970: 207.
42 AJHR H.20, 1965: 5.
43 Meek, 1995: 232.
44 Meek, 1995: 233.
45 Department of Justice, 1975: 39.
46 Meek, 1995: 236.
47 Penal Policy Review Committee, 1981: 59.
48 Meek, 1995.
49 Pratt and Treacher, 1988: 256.
50 Meek, 1995: 243.
51 Meek, 1995: 246–247.
52 *The Dominion*, 23 Jan 1992; 28 Feb 1992.
53 See Newbold, 2000: 118.
54 Spier, 2001: 14.
55 Spier, 2004.
56 Spier, 2004.

References

Committee of Inquiry into Violence (1986) *Report*. Chair: Clinton Roper. Wellington: Government Printer.

Department of Justice (1969) *Review of Borstal Policy in New Zealand*. Wellington: Government Printer.

Department of Justice (1970) *Penal Policy in New Zealand*. Wellington: Government Printer.

Department of Justice (1971) *Waipiata: A Study of Trainees in an Open Borstal Institution*. Wellington: Government Printer.

Department of Justice (1974) *Crime in New Zealand*. Wellington: Department of Justice.

Department of Justice (1975) *Justice Department Penal Census 1972*. Wellington: Department of Justice.

Department of Justice (1988) *Prisons in Change: The Submission of the Department of Justice to the Ministerial Committee of Inquiry into the Prisons System*. Wellington: Department of Justice.

Department of Social Welfare (1971) *Juvenile Crime in New Zealand*. Wellington: Government Printer.

Hood, Roger (1965) *Borstal Reassessed*. London: Heinemann.

Martinson, Robert (1974) 'What Works? Questions and Answers about Prison Reform'. *The Public Interest*, v.35: 22–54.

Meek, John (1985) 'The Revival of Preventive Detention in New Zealand 1986–93'. *Australian and New Zealand Journal of Criminology*, v.28: 225–227.

Morris, Norval and Hawkins, Gordon (1970) *The Honest Politician's Guide to Crime Control*. Chicago: University of Chicago Press.

Newbold, Greg (2000) *Crime in New Zealand*. Palmerston North: Dunmore Press.

Penal Policy Review Committee (1981) *Report*. Wellington: Government Printer.

Pratt, John and Treacher, Phillip (1988) 'Law and Order and the 1987 New Zealand Election'. *Australian and New Zealand Journal of Criminology*, v.21: 253–268.

Rose, Lionel (1961) *The Struggle for Penal Reform*. London: Stevens and Sons.

Special Committee on Moral Delinquency in Children and Adolescents (1954) *Report*. Chair: Dr Oswald Mazengarb. Wellington: Government Printer (AJHR H.47: 1954).

Spier, Philip (2001) *Conviction and Sentencing of Offenders in New Zealand: 1991–2000*. Wellington: Ministry of Justice.

Spier, Philip (2004) *Preventive Detention Statistics to 30 June 2004*. Wellington: Ministry of Justice, Unpublished.

Spier, Philip (2005) *Conviction and Sentencing of Offenders in New Zealand: 1994–2003*. Wellington: Ministry of Justice.

Walker, Walton and Brown, Robert (1983) *Corrective Training: An Evaluation*. Wellington: Department of Justice.

Webb, Patricia (1982) *A History of Custodial and Related Penalties in New Zealand*. Wellington: Government Printer.

Young, Sherwood (1998) *Guilty on the Gallows: Famous Capital Crimes of New Zealand*. Wellington: Grantham House.

Yska, Redmer (1993) *All Shook Up: The Flash Bodgie and the Rise of the New Zealand Teenager in the 1950s*. Auckland: Penguin.

CHAPTER 14

THE PROBLEM OF REFORMING CRIMINALS

As explained in the first chapter, for more than 200 years criminologists have searched for ways to reform criminals and reduce recidivism. In 1764, Beccaria's famous essay *On Crimes and Punishments* advocated pragmatic rather than vindictive responses to criminality, and it was from this basis that the penitentiary system emerged in the late 18th century. From that point the history of corrections has been a succession of mostly fruitless attempts to find a remedy for crime. After early experiments with silence and social isolation failed, training programmes and early-release incentives were tried. The reformatories and borstals that applied these strategies proved largely unsuccessful and were eventually abandoned. These have been followed by a variety of initiatives, including shock incarceration, life sentences for repeat offenders, chain gangs, halfway houses, weekend detention, 'scared straight' programmes, and restorative justice schemes. New Zealand has been as active as other countries in its quest to cure criminality, but hardly anything has been consistently effective.

Nothing Works?

Scepticism about the value of correctional programmes began to grow in the 1940s after the famous Cambridge–Somerville study showed no variation in the recidivism of boys subjected to different treatment regimes.[1] By the 1960s, discussion about the interchangeability of criminal measures was growing,[2] and probably reached its zenith in 1974 with Martinson's conclusion that 'nothing works'.[3] However, as we know, some criminologists continue to maintain that certain things can work, as long as they are done well.

Other criminologists[4] have recently pointed out that 'effectiveness' can have a range of meanings and manifestations. Raw recidivism rates provide a somewhat crude rubicon. It is clear that there is no universal definition of 'effectiveness', nor is there a generally applicable crime-reducing formula.

Strategies that have reported success make a variety of claims,[5] but in New Zealand it has become accepted that reductions of between 10 and 15 per cent are feasible with certain types of client.[6] In order to achieve even these modest results, however, strategies need to involve careful and professional analysis of an offender's specific problems, followed by well-resourced programmes delivered by dedicated and skilled practitioners. Such requirements are expensive and time consuming, and as seen with Integrated Offender Management, are extremely difficult to apply in an ordinary prison environment. Thus, in spite of the huge amount of money and energy that has been invested in IOM, recidivism levels in New Zealand have remained high and comparable with international rates. In North America, for example, government figures show that within six years of release, more than 70 per cent of inmates are re-arrested and nearly half are re-incarcerated.[7] This is notwithstanding the fact that New Zealand and the USA have quite different systems. In contrast with New Zealand, criminal justice in America is characterised by long sentences, harsh conditions and the frequent abandonment of rehabilitation in favour of warehousing.[8]

Recidivism in New Zealand

Until recently no comprehensive survey of recidivism in New Zealand had been completed, but today there are enough data to give a reasonably clear picture of reoffending and the circumstances surrounding it. The most comprehensive information comes from Bakker and Riley,[9] who considered recidivism in two large groups: 31,985 individuals convicted of an imprisonable criminal offence in 1990 and 4,785 offenders released from prison in 1990. These groups were followed until May 1996 and all who had recorded a criminal conviction before May 1996 were designated as recidivists. Traffic and minor offences were excluded. Bakker and Riley found a 72 per cent recidivist rate among those convicted in 1990 and an 84 per cent rate among the prisoners discharged that year. Of those released in 1990, 53 per cent were back inside by May 1996.

Offence and sentence type were relatively poor predictors of reoffending. Even non-custodial and therapeutic-type sentences, generally given to less serious offenders, had recidivist rates ranging from between 64 and 84 per cent. Apart from sex offenders, whose crimes tend to be specific and whose reoffending rates averaged between 35 and 50 per cent, other types of offenders tended to be generalists and re-offended more than 70 per cent of the time.

The most accurate predictor of reoffending was age, with young offenders far more likely to recidivate than older ones. In the Bakker-Riley study 95 per cent of prison inmates under 20 re-offended, compared with 53 per cent aged 40 or over. Another important correlate of reoffending was previous convictions. Only 20 per cent of first offenders sentenced in 1990 committed another offence. Likelihood of reoffending grew sharply with each subsequent conviction, but began to flatten out after five.

An even stronger relationship was found with previous incarcerations. Those with more than two incarcerations had a very high probability of reconviction. This could be expected: those who were imprisoned would have been the more serious offenders. Another predictor was ethnicity: Maori were reconvicted 80 per cent of the time, Pakeha 70 per cent, and other groups (principally Asian) 30 per cent. A less important predictor was sex, with men slightly more likely to reoffend than women.

These results have been replicated in later work published by Spier in 2002. This study, based on 22,340 offenders released from prison between 1995 and 1998, found that 37 per cent were reconvicted within six months and 86 per cent within five years. More than half were re-imprisoned within five years. Sex offenders (including rapists) had low recidivist rates, with 47 per cent reoffending generally, but only 6.7 per cent reoffending *in a sexual way*, within five years of release. Spier also indicates a relationship between recidivism and length of sentence: as length of sentence increases, reoffending progressively declines; of those sentenced to less than a year in prison, 88.5 per cent were reconvicted within five years of release, compared with 66.5 per cent of those sentenced to more than five years. Among lifers, 57.1 per cent recorded new convictions.

The large size of the samples in these two studies and the similarity of their findings lend them great credibility and hint strongly as to why reforming criminals is so difficult: that is, the principal predictors of reoffending involve factors that are unrelated to prison programmes. What is also interesting is how remarkably the study data correspond to American results in spite of the huge differences between the two systems. The figures suggest strongly that the quite dissimilar approaches taken to corrections in the two countries have little effect on recidivism, and that a person's chances of reoffending bear little or no relation to correctional treatment. It also suggests that the most important predictors of recidivism are factors fixed before the offending takes place: age, offending history, ethnicity and, to a lesser extent, sex.

Why do Correctional Methods Fail?

The reasons that correctional attempts usually fail are manifold. A major part of the explanation is simply procedural: if prisoners are released on restrictive parole conditions and the authorities are quick to revoke even for minor violations, then failure rates will inevitably be high. In California, for example, due largely to compulsory urine testing and rigorous policing of parolees, 62 per cent of all offenders admitted to the state's prisons in 1992 were parole violators.[10] New Zealand parole authorities are far less aggressive. But here, among the 14 per cent who are not reconvicted within five years of release there must be many who reoffend but do not get caught. So, one reason that younger offenders recidivate more often than older is probably that older offenders are smarter and more likely to get away with it.

Human Rationality

The explanation for high recidivist rates is more complex than this. Part of the answer lies in the human condition. Eighteenth-century rationalists believed human beings were logical and driven to seek pleasure and avoid pain. A reasonable person, therefore, should not be tempted to commit crime because the 'pain' of imprisonment would exceed any pleasure that might be derived. In other words, a rational person would realise that 'crime does not pay'.

There are two major and related flaws in this argument. First, not all offenders get caught. In many crimes the chances of detection are slim. Illegal drug taking, for example, is seldom reported and only a small proportion of the large numbers of users are ever prosecuted. Though profits can be substantial, drug-dealing is a relatively low-risk occupation. The higher a person is on the drug-dealing scale the greater the profits, and because the big-time dealer normally distances himself from the crime itself and can often pay off corrupt officials, his chances of being captured are especially low.

Other offences are similar. In New Zealand only about 16 per cent of burglaries are cleared, and the better the burglar the more money he makes and the less likely he is to get caught. So it is with fraud. Sophisticated fraudsters make millions, are difficult to catch and get relatively small penalties if convicted.[11] Former Equiticorp chief executive Allan Hawkins, for example, convicted in 1992 of stealing $87 million (although suspected of stealing up to half a billion), was sentenced to six years' imprisonment but was released on parole after just 28 months. In other words, he served about 10 days in prison for every million dollars he was proven to have stolen.[12]

If a person is unqualified and unable to get a decent job, the rewards of crime – financial, social and psychological – may seem attractive. The 'pains' of possible imprisonment may be little worse than the loathsome drudgery of a boring, low-paying and low-prestige job. Crime might 'pay' after all, and be a truly reasonable choice.

But people are not always logical; this is the second flaw to the rationality argument. Social observers[13] have noted that people behave non-rationally a lot of the time. For much of their lives, people are driven by whim or emotion. Often they make critical life decisions when their minds are befuddled by drugs, alcohol, excitement, love or lust. Rational considerations may play very little part in these decisions.

If people were by nature rational they would not smoke cigarettes, drive when they were drunk, have unprotected casual sex, or risk life and limb volunteering to fight for abstract ideals such as duty, justice or patriotism. And they would almost certainly never get married and have children. But high risk and the associated thrill are what attract many people to certain activities. If sports like boxing, mountain climbing, white-water kayaking and big-wave surfing did not have adrenaline-pumping risks, they would have little appeal. Similarly, many career criminals are drawn to offending as much by the danger and the thrill of getting away with it, as by the potential profits.[14] For many, crime has an emotional appeal that transcends conventional morality and logic. And like rock climbers who seek steeper and tougher routes up the same face of a cliff, some burglars, robbers and thieves become increasingly audacious in the crimes they commit. They love the exhilaration of the act, and the escape, and the kudos they get from their peers. The career criminal is no more deterred by the fear of imprisonment than the boxer is by the fear of concussion, for example, or the climber by the fear of falling, frostbite and avalanche. All these dangers do is encourage him to take greater precautions.

Criminal Subculture

Social control theorists like Travis Hirschi[15] argue that one reason criminals offend is that they have weak social bonds, often due to under-socialisation. Because of this they are thought to lack the inhibitions against offending that a socially bonded person has. Similarly John Braithwaite[16] suggests that a principal explanation for predatory offending is that criminals are not adequately integrated in society, and so do not feel 'ashamed' of the crimes they commit. These theorists say the solution is to instil strong community values in criminals, so the shame they feel on committing an offence would be a deterrent in itself. The problem with such theories, similar to those of 18th-century philosopher Jeremy Bentham, is that they tend to be tautological: offending is evidence that under-socialisation has occurred.

Criminals may in fact not be under-socialised at all; they may simply be differentially socialised. Social values are not homogeneous.[17] Modern society consists of numerous subcultures, and what may be morally condemned in one may be approved in another. A person raised in a criminal subculture is likely to have different values from the mainstream. An ability to steal cleverly, con plausibly and fight bravely may add to, rather than detract from, his social value.[18] And in the cultural milieu of the prison, where criminals are sent for 'correction', such ideals as these are not weakened but reinforced.

Certainly, one of the goals of prison programmes is to change those values and teach cognitive, coping, and job skills that might assist social reintegration. Prisoners may work hard in efforts to reform their lives, but achieving long-term effectiveness is difficult. Overcoming subcultural identities and affiliations, including those learned in prison, remains a major obstacle.

A number of authors have identified factors that impede post-release chances. Clemmer[19] coined the term 'prisonisation' which, he said, depending on length of sentence and conditions of confinement, may "make a man characteristic of the penal community and so direct his personality that a happy adjustment in any community becomes next to impossible". Richards[20] speaks of the 'joint mentality' in describing how a person assumes the walk and talk of the convict, living day to day in prison, unable to foresee a future beyond. In a similar vein, Austin and Irwin[21] have demonstrated how profound alienation and bitterness result from a perception of injustice and note the psychological and social impairment that long-term confinement brings. Richards and Jones[22] have discussed the problems ex-cons face when they are released, with little money and poor job prospects. Rideau[23] remarks that because many prisons offer so little in the way of programmes, prisoners are released unskilled and unprepared to succeed on the outside, just as when they went in. Thus, when they get out of prison they return to the occupations and the value systems with which they are most familiar.

Family Circumstances

Apart from the fact that many convicts have been raised with criminal thinking patterns, most have also had childhoods that were far from ideal. The old Jesuit adage that once a child is seven years old, his or her personality, intellect, values and temperament are fairly well set, seems to bear out. In the first years of a child's life, factors such as parental contact or lack of it, peer group affiliation, mass media input and trauma establish the path of the emerging adult. A person's character becomes more rigid and difficult to change as he or she gets older. By the time a person first goes to prison he or she may have experienced a lifetime of academic failure and unemployment, and violent, alcoholic role models accompanied by deviant values, parental neglect and possibly abuse. The family backgrounds of a large proportion of people in prison have these characteristics.

The prison population makeup in New Zealand was profiled in a 1986 census that asked questions about prisoners' backgrounds. All 120 females in prison at the time, plus a random sample of 879 males (a third of the total male, sentenced, population) completed the questionnaire. The survey found that 11 per cent of prisoners either did not know their parents or their parents' marital status. Thirty-eight per cent had parents they knew were married. The remaining parents were unmarried as a result of death, divorce, separation or their parents never having lived together.

In over 56 per cent of cases where the parents were known, there was an official record of family tension. Major problems identified were marital discord, alcohol abuse and violence toward children. In almost a quarter of cases, family strife had been sufficient to require intervention from state welfare agencies and/or the police. About a third of the prisoners had been placed under the care of the Department of Social Welfare before age 15. Over 70 per cent had come to the notice of police or welfare officials by the time they were 19. Almost a quarter had been taken into pre-prison custodial care.[24] It is not possible to match these figures precisely with the general population, but they seem high.

The family backgrounds of prisoners are reflected in their personal biographies, and some national comparisons can be made here. Eighty-eight per cent of the prisoners sampled had left school without qualifications and only 11 per cent had undertaken any training after leaving school. Only about three per cent had any trade or professional certification. In comparison, in the general New Zealand population that year, only 37 per cent had left school with no qualifications and 36 per cent had post-school credentials.[25]

Approximately 44 per cent of prisoners had required psychological assessment at some time in their lives – in many cases as a result of drug or alcohol abuse, and about half had experienced difficulties with personal alcohol abuse. About 44 per cent had problems with drug abuse. In comparison, a 1998 survey of drug use among New Zealanders aged 15–45 found fewer than 10 per cent used alcohol to the point where it threatened their health. Only 15 per cent were regular cannabis users, and use of other drugs was relatively uncommon.[26] The incidence of drug and alcohol problems among prisoners was thus very high relative to the general population.

Sixty-five per cent of convicts had been unemployed at the time they were sentenced and almost half had been unemployed for over a year.[27] Nationwide, the unemployment rate at the time was about seven per cent. The 1986 prison census provides a useful snapshot. It shows that prisoners come largely from disadvantaged backgrounds and are less educated, demonstrate much higher substance abuse and are less likely to be employed than the general population, all of which means they may have difficulty adjusting in the free world.

Not all people with bad family backgrounds become criminals and not all criminals have bad family backgrounds, but a history of parental neglect is highly predictive of maladjustment in later life.[28] Prisoners are usually in their late teens or early 20s by the time they get a prison term substantial enough for 'rehabilitative' efforts to be potentially effective; by this time the years of psychological and social conditioning make real chances of success remote. Some prisoners, haunted by family dysfunctions and trauma, may never be able to overcome the effect of past history even with significant help from professional services.

The Reality of Life Outside

An added burden to changing people is the harsh reality of life on the outside. It may be very well, through programmes such as anger management, Straight Thinking, Alcoholics Anonymous and so on to get a commitment from prisoners to control their anger, think carefully and drink sensibly.[29] In the sterile and controlled atmosphere of maximum security, such resolutions may be made with absolute sincerity and resolve.

On the outside, things are different. Here the therapist or social worker is not the primary influence. There is the added problem of peer pressure and the temptations of alcohol, drugs, sex and consumer advertising. And, of course, food has to be bought and bills have to be paid. When a person who has been 'reformed' in prison is cast back into the same impoverished, crime-dominated world they came from, where drugs and drink are easy temptations, resolutions made in another world at another time can easily lose their relevance.

When the author was in prison in the 1970s there were many young, middle-class kids doing relatively long periods for dealing drugs. This was a new phenomenon in the 1970s, but apart from being better educated, Pakeha, and not tattooed, the drug dealers were largely undifferentiated from other prisoners. Long-termers tended to mix together, irrespective of race or background. They all subscribed to the inmate value system and were part of the general culture of the prison. Like everyone, the middle-class offenders got drunk and stoned from time to time, and they participated fully in the political life of the jail. The major difference between the middle-class men and the rank and file was that the former were more likely to study or do craft work in their spare time, and they tended to have ongoing support from their families. Career criminals, by contrast, spent a lot of time gambling, talking and listening to music, and many did not get visits.

It was these differences that showed after release. Almost without exception the middle-class offenders went straight from jail into the workforce. Today the majority known to the author are successful, ordinary people with jobs, wives and families. The men from criminal backgrounds, who already had adolescent histories of violence, drunkenness and criminality, moved back to what they always did: living unpredictable, hedonistic lives and surviving from day to day from what they could hustle through drugs, theft, gambling and pulling rorts.[30]

The Allure of the Prison

Among career criminals, prison is a hazard that many accept, albeit with less tolerance as they get older. Apart from their freedom, they may have little to lose by going to jail. For example, they may have no career, reputation, mortgage, marriage or dependent children. Recidivists do not like prison: ask anyone and they will tell you they hate it. But they are used to it and they adjust quickly. In prison they have friends, among staff as well as inmates. Initially a sort of reunion takes place, as the recidivist shakes hands with old acquaintances and trades the latest gossip. If he is older he will normally have a degree of immediate prestige, will not have to prove his 'credentials' to people he does not know and will move directly into one of the jail's respectable cliques. In doing so he is likely to have immediate access to prison perks, including pressed clothes, a better job, access to drugs and the odd drop of brew to keep him warm on a cold night. For the old 'boobhead' the 'pains of imprisonment'[31] will not be as sharp as they are for the hapless first timer.

So for the recidivist, prison offers a number of attractions.[32] It provides friendship and status within a tight primary group that are often absent in life outside. It gives predictability, comfort and freedom from many of the stresses of everyday life. Meals appear ready-cooked, three times a day. There are no dirty dishes to worry about. Laundry is done free of charge, every week. When clothing gets shabby, it is replaced.

The power is always on, the showers are hot, the cells are warm. There are no bills to pay, landlords to appease, long hours of work, or nagging wife and screaming kids. For women in particular, imprisonment may also offer respite from an abusive partner. Due to unemployment or under-employment, the inmate is free to socialise, read, watch TV, do crossword puzzles or engage in gambling or hobbies. The principal enemies are not fear or homesickness, but chronic boredom, which can be alleviated by the intrigues of prison gossip and politics, or by gambling or engagement with the cellblock's underground economy.

While few if any would exchange liberty for life inside, men and women with long histories of incarceration, who find the pressures of the outside world difficult, who often go without food or a roof over their head, the quality of freedom may not be much better than that of captivity. Consciously or unconsciously, therefore, some released prisoners, who struggle with life at large, are drawn back to the prison's protective womb.

So Why Have Prison Programmes?

If the foregoing is true and the chances of achieving statistically significant results are so small, then why spend money on programmes? Why not follow the example of many areas in the United States,[33] and concentrate instead on just locking criminals up?

There are a number of reasons why correctional and welfare programmes are essential components of any well-managed prison system. Perhaps surprisingly, the first has to do with recidivism. Some recidivism measures can discriminate between serious offending and minor offending, others cannot – although the definition of 'serious' and 'non serious' is subjective. For example, drug offending is considered much more serious in America than in New Zealand where violence draws the heaviest penalties. Also, recidivist figures often fail to show intensity of offending. A person convicted for 20 offences within a two-year period usually appears just once in the recidivist figures, alongside others who have offended only once or twice.[34] The problem with measuring recidivism in terms of reconviction rates is that it gives only a crude indication of reoffending.[35]

Moreover, some types of crime have much higher detection rates than others. For example, a bank robber who becomes a drug dealer after release is much less likely to appear as a recidivist statistic than a drug dealer who becomes a bank robber. Likewise, a person who studies law inside might be less likely to be reconvicted than one who does, say, anger management because, although both may reoffend, the former may be less likely to leave incriminating clues.

So, the effectiveness of prison rehabilitation programmes might be confused, rather than revealed, by recidivist data. For example, the ex-convict may reoffend but do so less often. Or he may reoffend less seriously. Or he may offend just as often and just as seriously, but will not be caught. Or maybe although still offending, he now looks after his wife and kids properly – no longer beats up his wife, takes his kids to football and is helpful to his neighbours. Perhaps an active criminal will a better person because of the humane treatment he got in prison.

The second good reason for rehabilitation programmes is that they humanise people, or they at least reduce the deleterious effects of long terms of imprisonment. One thing that most chronic offenders have in common is terrible childhoods. Many have experienced years of suffering from abusive, uncaring parents. Never having known compassion as children, they are likely to have little conception of empathy. As adults, abused children often become merciless, violent and predatory. The classic New Zealand example is Joseph Thompson who, although softly spoken and intelligent, had his childhood punctuated by violence from his father and sexual abuse by a neighbour. When he grew up, Thompson followed the lessons of his youth, bashing and exploiting the weak and vulnerable. Over a 12-year period he raped and terrorised dozens of women in working-class suburbs in Auckland. In 1995 he received what was then the longest term ever given by a New Zealand court: preventive detention with a 25-year minimum.

Prison is the one chance the state has to repair some of the damage done to a prisoner before he was incarcerated. Perhaps, for the first time in his life, he will be shown fair treatment, respect and humanity – treatment he never experienced in his youth. To continue the familiar pattern of brutality and dehumanisation in prison would be to perpetuate the processes by which dangerous criminals are made. Some day, most of these men and women will be released and if their violent inclinations are not curbed, innocent people will suffer.

A third reason for having rehabilitative programmes in prison is that, irrespective of whether the results are statistically visible, some convicts will make use of them, to their own advantage and to the overall benefit of society. There is a time in most prisoners' lives when they get sick of crime and are ready to make a change. Often that point is reached in jail. It is essential that prisons are prepared for such occasions and are equipped with facilities to help sincere prisoners looking for a way out of crime.

The author's own case illustrates the point. Aged 23 when arrested in 1975 and subsequently sentenced to seven-and-a-half years' imprisonment for selling heroin, he knew his 20s would be over by the time he got out. He started thinking about how he could salvage what was left of his life and took advantage of study facilities inside the prison. Had he not been able to study he would not have been released with an MA, completed a PhD, become a university professor, or written this book. He says:

> In all likelihood I would have returned to a life of crime and would be either dead or locked up at this moment. The fact that I am not, and am able now to contribute in a unique way to the understanding of criminality and corrections, is a tribute to the senior management at Paremoremo maximum-security prison and to the floor staff, the inmates and many others outside the wire, who supported me along the way.

The final reason for including programmes in the routine of a prison is that it is sound management practice. For not only is fair and humane treatment likely to create compassionate ex-prisoners, but its presence makes prisons easier to control. Convicts who perceive prison staff to have a real and active concern for their welfare are far more likely to be compliant than those who do not. Studies of prison riots show that in a large number of cases the underlying cause of disturbance is bored, resentful dissatisfied and overcrowded prisoners combined with inconsistent, careless, incompetent and arbitrary management.[36] Well-organised prisons have fewer escapes, strikes, fights and suicides than those that are not.[37] One of the reasons that homosexual rape in prisons in this country is rare is that prisoners, treated with a measure of respect from staff, treat one another with certain respect as well. The social environment in New Zealand prisons simply will not tolerate the abomination of homosexual rape.[38] For this reason, some men who are predatory and recalcitrant in other contexts behave completely differently when they get to prison.

Conclusion

When the prison was first conceived of as a tool for the reformation of criminals, it was because of a belief that something could really be done to address the problem of lawlessness. Early prisons were designed to remedy the crime problem by subjecting offenders to reformative influences. Although this has remained their objective, nearly 200 years of experimentation has been at pains to find a prison programme that is effective in a consistent, significant and generally applicable way. Irrespective of what treatment convicts receive, recidivist rates remain high. Even New Zealand, with its liberal and progressive tradition, has reoffending patterns that differ little from the United States.

Part of this may be due to the crude measures of effectiveness. Most studies use recidivist data that are not sensitive enough to pick up many of the subtle changes that occur while a person is in prison. However, the majority of released prisoners do reoffend after they are discharged – even more than official figures indicate. The reasons that rehabilitation programmes have so much difficulty reducing reoffending are various, but they reflect the complex nature of the human organism itself. Personality is usually well established by the time a person enters prison and the characters of criminals have often been moulded by years of youthful neglect and abuse. This makes achieving radical change very difficult. Moreover, when a prisoner is returned to the realities of a free society, situational factors often impel him or her to discard lessons learned or commitments made in the artificial environment of a cell block.

This does not deny the value of prison programmes. Prisons are agencies of the state, funded by the taxpayer, and as such are bound to serve the interests of all citizens, including prisoners, staff and the general public. The interests of convicts are served by programmes because they soften the impact of incarceration and the hardening effect which years in jail may produce. Moreover, they provide opportunities for inmates who are committed to change to take the steps necessary to become productive citizens. Likewise, the interests of prison officers are served, because programmes make inmates easier to manage and improve the quality of the working environment. Hostility and the threat of violence are reduced in a good prison, and the caustic effects of daily subjection to hatred and threat are removed.

Finally, and most important, humane treatment and prison programmes are of direct benefit to the community. Discontented prisoners riot, and this type of violence is expensive. Property is destroyed and people are often injured. So, well-run prisons which avoid the expense of strikes, riots and sabotage, ease the burden on the taxpayer. In addition, humanely administered penal institutions reduce the threat to the public of violent post-release behaviour. Nearly all inmates will some day be returned to mainstream society. If a prisoner has been brutally or callously treated for years in prison there is every possibility that he or she will be a desperate or dangerous individual when released. This person will be somebody's next door neighbour. Such a situation is to be avoided and it is the duty of the state to protect its citizens as cheaply and effectively as possible from this type of hazard. Thus, one of the primary tasks of corrections must be to devote at least a portion of its resources to programmes that are designed to mellow, moderate and perhaps even rehabilitate the people it takes into its care.

Notes

1 Powers and Witmer, 1970.
2 See Morris and Hawkins, 1969: 116–118.
3 Martinson, 1974: 25.
4 Israel and Chui, 2006.
5 See, e.g., Andrews *et al.*, 1990; Bonta *et al.*, 2000; Bourgon and Armstrong, 2005; Gendreau and Ross. 1986; Gendreau and Ross, 1987; Latessa, Cullen and Gendreau, 2002; Lipsey, 1992; McLaren, 1996; Palmer, 1986; Palmer, 1991; Wilson, 1986.
6 Department of Corrections, 2001; McLaren, 1996; Ward, 2006.
7 Cited in Schmalleger, 2001: 426.
8 See, e.g., Austin and Irwin, 2001: 9–12.
9 Bakker and Riley, 1999.
10 Allen and Simonsen, 1998: 244.
11 See Newbold and Ivory, 1993.
12 See Sturt, 1998: ch 9.
13 See, e.g., Hoffer, 1951/1980; Michels, 1911/1962; Pareto, 1916/1935.
14 Katz, 1988.
15 See, e.g., Hirschi, 1969.
16 Braithwaite, 1989.
17 Sutherland, Cressey and Luckenbill, 1992: 88–90.
18 See also Shover, 1996: ch 4; Sutherland, 1937.
19 Clemmer, 1940/1965: 300.
20 Richards, 1998: 140.
21 Austin and Irwin, 2001: 100–112.
22 Richards and Jones, 1997.
23 Rideau, 1994.
24 Braybrook and O'Neill, 1998: 119–169.
25 Statistics NZ, 1997: 55–56.
26 Field and Casswell, 1999: 14, 21, 40.
27 Braybrook and O'Neill, 1998: 119–169.
28 Fergusson, 1998; Fergusson and Horwood, 1997.
29 See, e.g., Terry, 2002.
30 See also Shover, 1996; Tunnell, 2000.
31 See Sykes, 1970.
32 Duncan, 1988.
33 See, e.g., Schmalleger, 2001: 457–463.
34 Israel and Chui, 2005.
35 See also Austin 2002; Tromhauser, 2002.
36 See Colvin, 1982; Fox, 1956; MacCormick, 1954; Schrag, 1960; Useem and Kimball, 1991.
37 DiIulio, 1987; McLellan, Newbold and Saville-Smith, 1996; Newbold, 1989.
38 Winfree, Newbold and Tubb, 2002.

References

Allen, Harry and Simonsen, Clifford (1998) *Corrections in America: An Introduction*. Upper Saddle River, NJ: Prentice-Hall.

Andrews, D.A., Zinger, I., Hodge, R.A., Bonta, J., Gendreau, P. and Cullen, F.T. (1990) 'Does Correctional Treatment Work? A Clinically Relevant and Psychologically Informed Meta-Analysis'. *Criminology*, v.28 (3): 369–404.

Austin, James (2002) 'The Use of Science to Justify the Imprisonment Binge'. In Jeffrey Ross and Stephen Richards (eds), *Convict Criminology*. Belmont, CA Wadsworth.

Austin, James and Irwin, John (2001) *It's About Time: America's Imprisonment Binge*. Belmont, CA: Wadsworth.

Bakker, Leon and Riley, David (1999) *Recidivism: How to Measure a Fall from Grace*. Wellington: Department of Corrections.

Beccaria, Cesare (1963/1764) *On Crimes and Punishments*. New York: Macmillan.

Bonta, J., Wallace-Capretta, S. and Rooney, J. (2000) 'A Quasi-Experimental Evaluation of an Intensive Rehabilitation Supervision Program'. *Criminal Justice and Behavior*, v.27: 312–319.

Bourgon, G. and Armstrong, B. (2005) 'Transferring the Principles of Effective Treatment into a "Real World" Prison Setting'. *Criminal Justice and Behavior*, v.32: 3–25.

Braithwaite, John (1989) *Crime, Shame and Reintegration*. Cambridge: Cambridge University Press.

Braybrook, Beverley and O'Neill, Rose (1988) *A Census of Prison Inmates*. Wellington: Department of Justice.

Clemmer, Donald (1940/1965) *The Prison Community*. New York: Holt, Rinehart and Winston.

Colvin, Mark (1982) 'The New Mexico Prison Riot'. *Social Problems*, 29(5): 449–463.

Department of Corrections (2001) *About Time: Turning People Away from a Life of Crime and Reducing Reoffending*. Wellington: Department of Corrections.

DiIulio, John (1987) *Governing Prisons: A Comparative Study of Correctional Management*. New York: Free Press.

Du Cane, Edmund (1885) *The Punishment and Prevention of Crime*. London: Macmillan.

Duncan, Martha Grace (1988) 'Cradled on the Sea: Positive Images of Prison and Theories of Punishment'. *California Law Review* v.76(6): 1202–1247.

Fergusson, David (1998) 'The Christchurch Health and Development Study: An Overview of Findings'. *Social Policy Journal of New Zealand* v.10: 154–176.

Fergusson, David and Horwood, John (1997) 'Physical Punishment/Maltreatment during Childhood and Adjustment in Young Adulthood'. *Child Abuse and Neglect* v.21 (7): 617–630.

Field, Adrian and Casswell, Sally (1999) *Drugs in New Zealand: National Survey, 1998*. Auckland: Alcohol and Public Health Research Unit.

Fox, Vernon (1956) *Violence Behind Bars: An Explosive Report on Prison Violence in the United States*. Westport, CT: Greenwood.

Gendreau, Paul and Ross, Robert R. (1986) 'Correctional Treatment: Some Recommendations for Effective Intervention'. In Kenneth C. Haas and Geoffrey P. Alpert (eds), *The Dilemmas of Punishment: Readings in Contemporary Corrections*. Prospect Heights, IL: Waveland.

Gendreau, Paul and Ross, Robert (1987) 'Revivification of Rehabilitation: Evidence from the 1980s'. *Justice Quarterly*, v.4 (3): 349–408.

Hirschi, Travis (1969) *Causes of Delinquency*. Berkeley: University of California Press.

Hoffer, Eric (1951/1980) *The True Believer: Thoughts on the Nature of Mass Movements*. Alexandria VA: Time-Life Books.

Israel, Mark and Chui, Wing Hong (2006) 'If "Something Works" Is the Answer, What Is the Question? Supporting Pluralist Evaluation in Community Corrections in the United Kingdom' *European Journal of Criminology*, v.3 (2): 181–200.

Katz, Jack (1988) *Seductions of Crime: Moral and Sensual Attractions in Doing Evil*. New York: Basic Books.

Latessa, Edward; Cullen, Francis and Gendreau, Paul (2002) 'Beyond Correctional Quackery – Professionalism and the Possibility of Effective Treatment'. *Federal Probation*, v.66 (2): 43–49.

Lipsey, Mark W. (1992) 'Juvenile Delinquency Treatment: A Meta-Analytic Inquiry into the Variability of Effects'. In Thomas Cook, Harris Cooper, David Cordray, Heidi Hartmann, Larry Hedges, Richard Light, Thomas Louis, and Frederick Mostetter (eds), *Meta-Analysis for Explanation: A Casebook*. New York: Russell Sage.

MacCormick, Austin (1954) 'Behind the Prison Riots'. *Annals of the American Academy of Political and Social Science*, v.293: 17–27.

Martinson, Robert (1974) 'What Works? Questions and Answers about Prison Reform'. *The Public Interest*, v.35: 22–54.

McLaren, Kaye (1996) 'Dazed and Confused: New Evidence on What Works in Reducing Offending'. Unpublished paper presented to the Criminology Conference, Victoria University of Wellington.

McLellan, Velma, Newbold, Greg, and Saville-Smith, Kay (1996) *Escape Pressures: Inside Views of the Reasons for Prison Escapes*. Wellington: Ministry of Justice.

Michels, Roberto (1911/1962) *Political Parties: A Sociological Study of Oligarchical Tendencies in Modern Democracy*. New York: Macmillan.

Morris, Norval and Hawkins, Gordon (1970) *The Honest Politician's Guide to Crime Control*. Chicago: University of Chicago Press.

Newbold, Greg (1989) *Punishment and Politics: The Maximum Security Prison in New Zealand*. Auckland: Oxford University Press.

Newbold, Greg and Ivory, Robert (1993) 'Policing Serious Fraud in New Zealand'. *Crime, Law and Social Change*, v.20: 233–248.

Palmer, Ted (1986) 'The "Effectiveness" Issue Today'. In Kenneth C. Haas and Geoffrey P. Alpert (eds), *The Dilemmas of Punishment: Readings in Contemporary Corrections*. Prospect Heights, IL: Waveland.

Palmer, Ted (1991) 'The Effectiveness of Intervention: Recent Trends and Current Issues'. *Crime and Delinquency*, v.37 (3): 330–346.

Pareto, Vilfredo (1916/1935) *The Mind and Society*. Tr. A. Bongiorno and A. Livingston. New York: Harcourt, Brace, Jovanovich.

Penal Policy Review Committee (1981) *Report*. Chair: M.E. Casey J. Wellington: Government Printer.

Powers, E. and Witmer, Helen (1970) 'The Cambridge-Somerville Study'. In Norman Johnston, Leonard Savitz and Marvin E. Wolfgang (eds), *The Sociology of Punishment and Correction*. New York: Wiley.

Richards, Stephen (1998) 'Critical and Radical Perspectives on Community Punishment: Lessons from the Darkness'. In Jeffrey Ross (ed), *Cutting the Edge: Current Perspectives in Radical/Critical Criminology and Criminal Justice*. Westport, CT: Praeger.

Richards, Stephen and Jones, Richard (1997) 'Perpetual Incarceration Machine: Structural Impediments to Postprison Success'. *Journal of Contemporary Criminal Justice*, v.13 (1): 4–22.

Rideau, Wilbert (1994) 'Why Prisons Don't Work'. *New York Times*, 21 March.

Schmalleger, Frank (2001) *Criminal Justice Today: An Introductory Text for the 21st Century*. Upper Saddle River, NJ: Prentice-Hall.

Schrag, Clarence (1960) 'The Sociology of Prison Riots'. *Proceedings of the American Correctional Association*, v.90: 136–145.

Shover, Neal (1996) *Great Pretenders: Pursuits and Careers of Persistent Thieves*. Boulder: Westview Press.

Spier, Philip (2002) *Reconviction and Reimprisonment Rates for Released Prisoners*. Wellington: Ministry of Justice.

Statistics New Zealand (1997) *New Zealand Official Yearbook 1997*. Wellington: Statistics New Zealand.

Sturt, Charles (1998) *Dirty Collars*. Auckland: Reed.

Sutherland, Edwin (1937) *The Professional Thief*. Chicago: Chicago University Press.

Sutherland, Edwin, Cressey, Donald and Luckenbill, David (1992) *Principles of Criminology*. New York: General Hall.

Sykes, Gresham (1970) 'The Pains of Imprisonment'. In Norman Johnston, Leonard Savitz, and Marvin Wolfgang (eds), *The Sociology of Punishment and Correction*. New York: Wiley.

Terry, Charles (2002) 'From C-Block to Academia: You Can't Get There from Here'. In Jeffrey Ross and Stephen Richards (eds), *Convict Criminology*. Belmont, CA: Wadsworth.

Tromhauser, Edward (2002) 'Comments and Reflections on Forty Years in the American Criminal Justice System'. In Jeffrey Ross and Stephen Richards, *Convict Criminology*. Belmont, CA: Wadsworth.

Tunnell, Kenneth (2000) *Living off Crime*. Chicago: Burnham.

Useem, Bert and Kimball, Peter (1991) *States of Siege: US Prison Riots 1971–1986*. New York: Oxford University Press.

Ward, Tony (2006) 'What Works?' Unpublished paper presented to the Prison Fellowship of New Zealand National Conference, Silverstream, Wellington, 12–14 May, 2006.

Wilson, James Q. (1986) '"What Works" Revisited: New Findings on Criminal Rehabilitation'. In Kenneth C. Haas and Geoffrey P. Alpert (eds), *The Dilemmas of Punishment: Readings in Contemporary Corrections*. Prospect Heights, IL: Waveland.

Winfree, Tom; Newbold, Greg and Tubb, Houston (2002) 'Prisoner Perspectives on Inmate Culture in New Mexico and New Zealand: A Descriptive Case Study'. *The Prison Journal*, v.82 (1): 213–233.

Wooton, Barbara (1959) *Social Science and Social Pathology*. London: Allen and Unwin.

APPENDIX 1

CHRONOLOGY OF SENTENCING VARIATIONS

Capital Punishment

1817 The Murders Abroad Act gives the Imperial Parliament the right to treat murders in NZ as if they have been committed on the high seas.

1840 Until 1893 English common law applies in NZ, with crimes carrying the death penalty including murder, treason and piracy.

1858 The Execution of Criminals Act abolishes public executions in NZ.

1935 Capital punishment for murder is placed in abeyance by the 1st Labour Government.

1941 Under the Crimes Amendment Act, capital punishment for murder is abolished.

1950 Under the Capital Punishment Act, capital punishment for murder is reinstated by the 1st National Government.

1957 Capital punishment for murder is again placed in abeyance by the 2nd Labour Government.

1961 Under the Crimes Act, capital punishment for murder is again abolished.

1989 Under the Abolition of the Death Penalty Act, capital punishment is abolished entirely for all remaining capital offences: treason, mutiny and treachery in the armed forces.

Corporal Punishment

1840 Until the Secondary Punishment Act 1854, English common law allows public flogging of criminal offenders.

1846 The Ordinance for the Regulation of Prisons provides for unspecified amounts of 'personal correction' (flogging) of inmates who have committed disciplinary infractions.

1854 The Secondary Punishment Act allows unspecified discretionary punishments for disciplinary infractions of penal servitude inmates.

1863 An amendment to the Secondary Punishment Act specifically limits the whipping of prisoners to 50 lashes, for disciplinary offences.

1867 The Offences Against the Person Act introduces unspecified amounts of whipping for boys under 16 who injure people with explosives, interfere with railway tracks, or steal children. These are to be inflicted in private.

The Act also allows private whipping of males aged 16 and over who choke people in order to commit an indictable offence. Up to 50 strokes are allowed on up to 3 occasions each, within 6 months.

1868　The Offences Against the Person Amendment allows whipping for any person who commits a sex offence upon a female. Up to 50 lashes are allowed on up to 3 occasions each, within 6 months.

1873　The Prisons Act allows up to 50 lashes to be inflicted on prisoners for disciplinary offences.

1874　The range of offences for which corporal punishment can be imposed is expanded.

1883　The Prisons Act abolishes corporal punishment of prisoners.

1893　Flogging for males over 16 (up to 50 lashes) and whipping for males 16 or under (up to 25 strokes) is introduced for a range of offences under the Criminal Code Act. Homosexual offences are included.

1936　Corporal punishment for young offenders dealt with in Children's Courts is abolished. At this time, flogging had been available for 13 types of offence and whipping for 20 types of offence.

1941　The Crimes Amendment Act abolishes corporal punishment entirely.

Parole, Remission and Early Release (finite sentences)

1841　Prisoners serve their entire sentences unless given a royal pardon.

1864　*De facto* rules are created to govern early release of prisoners.

1875　One quarter remission on accumulated work marks for hard labour prisoners is gazetted in new Regulations. Inmates must serve 3 months before qualifying for any remission.

1911　Following the creation of the sentence of reformative detention in 1910, the Prisons Board is established, providing NZ with its first parole system.

1917　The Statute Law Amendment Act allows inmates serving finite sentences of more than 2 years to be paroled at half sentence.

1920　The Crimes Amendment Act makes all offenders serving finite terms eligible for parole after 6 months or half sentence (whichever is longer).
Release on remission is abolished.

1954　The Criminal Justice Act abolishes parole for all finite sentences.
One-quarter remission is reintroduced under the Penal Institutions Act.

1961　Separate borstal and prisons parole boards are established.

1964　Special remission of 1/12 for exemplary conduct is introduced. This special remission increases the maximum available remission from 1/4 to 1/3.
Separate parole boards for prisons and borstals are established.

1967　An amendment to the Criminal Justice Act permits the Parole Board to review finite sentences of 6 years and over, after 3 1/2 years or half sentence, whichever is the longer.

1975　Parole is extended to apply to finite sentences of 5 years and over at 1/2 sentence or 3 1/2 years, whichever is the longer.
An amendment to the Penal Institutions Act makes 1/3 remission generally available to minimum-security prisoners and to other categories on application to the Department of Justice.

1978   Under the Misuse of Drugs Amendment Act, drug dealers sent to prison may be ordered to serve at least 7/10 of their full sentences, up to a maximum of 7 years, by a sentencing judge.

1980   An amendment to the Criminal Justice Act makes parole available to all prisoners serving at least 5 years at 7 years or half sentence, whichever is the shorter.

1985   Parole eligibility is extended to all prisoners at half sentence or 7 years, whichever is the shorter. District prisons boards are established to hear cases involving sentences of less than seven years. Other cases are heard by the parole board.
Prisoners who fail to get parole become eligible for automatic release on remission at 2/3 sentence.

1987   Parole eligibility ceases for violent offenders sentenced to more than 2 years imprisonment. These offenders still remain eligible for automatic remission at 2/3 sentence, but if it is felt likely that they may reoffend, the Secretary for Justice may order that they serve their full terms.

1989   Those sentenced to less than 12 months imprisonment become ineligible for parole but are released automatically on remission at half sentence.

1993   Courts gain power to award non-parole periods longer than those normally available at law.
Violent offenders serving 15 years or more gain parole eligibility at 10 years, provided a longer non-parole minimum has not been set.
Parole becomes available to all non-violent offenders serving more than 12-month determinate sentences, at 1/3 of sentence.

2002   Under the Parole Act, automatic release on remission is abolished for all offenders serving more than 2 years imprisonment.
Those serving 2 years or less are released on remission at half sentence.
All offenders serving finite terms of more than 2 years imprisonment become eligible for release on parole after serving 1/3 of sentence, unless a longer period has been set by the court.
In the case of finite sentences, the non-parole period cannot exceed 2/3 of sentence or 10 years. There is no limit on the non-parole maximums for non-finite sentences.

Non-Parole Periods for Life Imprisonment

1841   Life means life, with release only possible by Royal Pardon.

1917   Under the Statute Law Amendment Act, a non-parole period of 8 years is set for lifers.

1920   The Crimes Amendment Act reduces the non-parole period for lifers to 5 years.

1962   A Criminal Justice amendment increases the non-parole period for murder to 10 years.
All other life sentences remain paroleable after 5 years.

1975   The non-parole period for lifers convicted of murder is reduced to 7 years.
All other life sentences remain paroleable after 5 years.

1978   Under the Misuse of Drugs Amendment Act, persons sentenced to life imprisonment for drug dealing may be ordered by the sentencing judge to serve at least 7 years before becoming eligible for parole.

1980   The non-parole period for all life sentences becomes 7 years.

1987   The non-parole period for all life sentences is increased to 10 years.

1993   Courts gain power to award non-parole periods longer than those set at law.

1999   An amendment to the Criminal Justice Act mandates 3-year add-ons to the standard 10-year non-parole period, for murders committed during the course of a home invasion.

2002   The Sentencing Act mandates 17-year minimums for murders committed with certain aggravating circumstances.

Habitual Criminals and Preventive Detention

1906   The Habitual Criminals and Offenders Act makes prisoners with multiple previous convictions for various offences eligible to be declared Habitual Criminals and held indefinitely.

1954   The habitual criminals legislation is abolished and replaced with preventive detention of 3–14 years for certain repeat adult offenders, and 3–life for repeat adult child sex offenders aged at least 25.

1967   Preventive detention is restricted to repeat sex offenders aged at least 25, and the term is increased to 7–life.

1987   The non-parole period for preventive detainees is increased to 10 years.
        The minimum age of eligibility for preventive detention is reduced from 25 to 21.
        Preventive detention becomes available to serious violence recidivists.

1993   Preventive detention becomes available to serious sex offenders on a first offence.
        Courts gain power to award non-parole periods longer than those set at law.

2002   The Sentencing Act makes preventive detention available on a first offence for all offenders aged 18 and over, who commit a serious violent or sexual offence.
        The minimum non-parole period for preventive detention is reduced to 5 years, unless a longer non-parole minimum is set.

Borstal Detention/Borstal Training

1917   Invercargill prison is gazetted as a borstal, without accompanying legislation.

1924   The Prevention of Crime Act creates borstal detention for boys aged 15–21. Two sentences are available: 1–3 years if imposed by the Magistrates' Court; 2–5 years if imposed by the Supreme Court.

1954   Borstal detention is renamed 'borstal training' and becomes a single sentence of 0–3 years for boys aged 17–20.

1962   Borstal training is reduced to 0–2 years.

1975   Borstal training is abolished, but the law is not effective immediately.

1981   The 1975 law becomes effective and borstals are abolished.

Reformative Detention/Corrective Training (#1)

1910 The Crimes Amendment Act creates an indeterminate term known as 'reformative detention' for persons who the court thinks may benefit from it. The permissible terms are 0–10 years if imposed by the Supreme Court; 0–3 years if imposed by the Magistrates' Court.

1954 Reformative detention is abolished and replaced by corrective training (#1) of 0–3 years for offenders aged 21–30.

1963 Corrective training (#1) is abolished.

Detention Centre Training/Corrective Training (#2)

1954 The Criminal Justice Act introduces the sentence of detention in a detention centre (DC) for 4 months, with 1 month remission, for offenders aged 17–23. It is never used in this form.

1960 An amendment to the Criminal Justice Act reduces the DC sentence from 4 months to 3 months, with 1 month remittable, for 16–21 year-olds. The first DC opens in 1961.

1975 DC is abolished in the 1975 Criminal Justice Amendment Act but the law is not brought into force until 1981.
       DC is replaced by a new form of corrective training, which originally consists of a fixed sentence of 3 months or 6 months, for offenders aged 15–19. The sentence in this form is never implemented.

1980 Corrective training (#2) is restricted to a single sentence of 3 months with 1 month remission, for offenders aged 15–19. The law becomes effective in April 1981.
       Corrective training becomes available for females.

2002 Corrective training (#2) is abolished.

Home Leave

1954 The statutory authority for temporary release is created in the Penal Institutions Act.

1965 72-hour home leaves are made generally available for married men every 4 months.

1974 Home leaves are made generally available to minimum-security prisoners.

1975 The interval between home leaves is reduced to 2 months.

Work Parole

1961 Work parole for up to 12 months is created in an amendment to the Penal Institutions Act.

1963 The first pre-release hostel for male borstal trainees is opened, in Auckland. Others follow in Hamilton in 1964 and in Wellington in 1965.

1964 The first pre-release hostel is opened for adult male prisoners, in Christchurch. Another follows in Auckland in 1969.

1966 The first pre-release hostel is opened for female borstal trainees, in Wellington.

Periodic Detention/Community Work

1962   In an amendment to the Criminal Justice Act, periodic (weekend) detention of up to 12 months is created for offenders aged 15–21. The first (residential) centre opens in 1963.

1966   Periodic detention (PD) becomes available to adult males. The first adult centre (non-residential) opens in Auckland in 1967.

1974:   PD is extended to females.

1976   Residential (overnight) periodic detention begins to decline, and by the early 1980s all periodic detention centres are for day-reporting only.

2002   Under the Sentencing Act, periodic detention and community service become merged into a single sentence called community work. Community work can be served either at a CW centre (as PD was), or unsupervised in the community (as community service was). The duration of CW is 40–400 hours, served within 12 months or 24 months, depending on length of sentence.

Community Service

1980   An amendment to the Criminal Justice Act creates the sentence of community service, which involves between 8 and 200 hours of community work over a 12-month period.
An offender must consent to this sentence.

2002   Under the Sentencing Act, community service is abolished and becomes merged with periodic detention into a single sentence called 'community work'. (See periodic detention above.)

Community Care/Community Programme

1985   The new Criminal Justice Act creates the sentence of community care. With the consent of the offender, a court may pass a sentence of community care. Community-care programmes are administered by recognised public or private agencies – such as halfway houses.
The sentence may be for up to 12 months, with up to 6 months residential.

1993   Community care becomes renamed 'community programme'.

2002   Under the Sentencing Act, the sentence of community programme is abolished.

Probation/Supervision

1886   Under the First Offenders Probation Act, the world's first national probation system is created, requiring all first offenders to be assessed with a view to being released on probation as an alternative to imprisonment. The sentence involves monthly reporting, normally to police acting as probation officers, and any other conditions imposed by the court. Probation may continue for as long as the sentence available on the extant charges.

1903   Probation is limited to 3 years.

1906   2 years probation becomes available to all habitual criminal releases.

1915   Civilian probation officers are first appointed.

1920 The Offenders Probation Act makes probation available to all offenders, not only first offenders.

The maximum period of probation is increased from 3 to 5 years.

1926 The first full time probation appointments are made.

1930 A minor amendment to the Offenders Probation Act introduces the possibility payment of compensation for losses caused by an offence.

1954 Under the Criminal Justice Act, probation may be given as a substitute to imprisonment for between 1 and 3 years.

Compulsory probation is introduced for all released prisoners sentenced to at least 12 months until the expiry of their full terms and in any case for at least a year. Corrective trainees and borstal trainees are also subject to a year's post-release probation.

1960 12 months probation becomes mandatory for all detention centre releases.

1963 The first probation hostel is opened, in co-operation with the Presbyterian Social Services Association.

1985 Under the new Criminal Justice Act the sentence of probation becomes called 'supervision'.

Courts may order supervision for between 6 months and 2 years.

Persons released on parole become subject to supervision with conditions for 6 months in the case of finite sentences; 12 months in the case of life and preventive detention.

Persons serving sentences of 12 months or more who are released on remission become subject to supervision on conditions for 6 months.

1993 All released offenders sentenced to more than 12 months imprisonment become subject to supervision for whatever period is deemed appropriate up to the end of sentence, but in any case for at least 6 months.

2002 Under the Sentencing Act, the sentence of supervision may given for periods of between 6 months and 2 years.

Under the Parole Act, all offenders sentenced to more than 2 years imprisonment become subject to post-release supervision and conditions for at least 6 months, but the Parole Board may order post-release supervision and conditions to continue until up to 6 months after full sentence expiry date.

Persons sentenced to 2 years or less may also be ordered by the sentencing court to be subject to post-release supervision and conditions.

2004 The Parole (Extended Supervision) Amendment Act allows high-risk sex offenders to be held in home detention for up to a year after the completion of their sentences and be subject to supervision and other conditions for up to 10 years.

Home Detention

1993 An amendment to the Criminal Justice Act allows parole authorities to release certain offenders to home detention.

1995 A 2-year pilot begins under the above legislation.

1999 'Front end' home detention for sentences of 2 years or less and 'back end' home detention for prison parolees begin.

2006 The government announces that front end home detention will cease in 2007 and be replaced by home detention as a community-based sentence in itself.

APPENDIX 2

CHRONOLOGY OF WOMEN IN CORRECTIONS

1840–1854
  During the period of transportation, one woman was transported to Tasmania (and about 100 men).

1844 Gov. FitzRoy orders delivery of oakum to Auckland gaol to provide work for female prisoners.

Pre-1845
  Drunken women could be placed in the stocks. The practice is banned in 1845.

1850 Secure separate accommodation is supplied to women at Auckland gaol.

1851 The first female attendant is appointed at Auckland gaol. A Matron is appointed in 1863. Matrons are generally appointed to prisons in the 1860s.

1863 Secure separate accommodation is supplied to women at Dunedin.

1868 Special provision is made for supplying clothing to women at Wellington prison.

1870 Planning begins for a women's prison at Addington. It is completed in 1876 but becomes primarily used for males.

1895 Minnie Dean is hanged for killing babies, at Invercargill prison.

1900 Te Oranga Reformatory opens exclusively for delinquent young women, run by the Education department (closes 1918).

Pre-1913
  Women are held in sections of local prisons about New Zealand. In December 1884, for example, female prisoners were held at Addington, Auckland, Dunedin Hokitika, Invercargill, Timaru Wanganui, and the Terrace gaol in Wellington. Accommodation for females often meant solitary confinement. All prisons contain males and females until the first all-male open work camps commence operation in 1890.

1913 Following a decision made in 1910, Addington becomes NZ's first prison exclusively catering for females it becomes a women's reformatory in 1917. Auckland, Wellington, Napier, Invercargill, Hokitika and other institutions continue to receive women too.

1920 Pt Halswell prison, which opened for men in 1915, is converted for sole use of women (until 1944). The women from Wellington's Terrace gaol are transferred here as a first step to closing the Terrace gaol down. Pt Halswell also receives older women from Addington in 1920. Serious attempts at the 'rehabilitation' of women commence from this date.

1924   By 1924, only Addington, Mt Eden and Pt Halswell routinely cater for women prisoners. A wooden unit for women prisoners is built at Mt Eden in 1924 and others are held in the North Wing Extension.

1925   A borstal unit for young women aged 17–21 is opened at Pt Halswell.

1944   Pt Halswell is taken over by the Defence Dept, and the women are transferred to a new Borstal at Arohata.

1950   A riot takes place at the Arohata Women's Reformatory.

1950   Addington Women's Reformatory ceases to operate and is demolished. In June the site is taken over by the army. Women are transferred to a small, specially constructed unit at Paparua, Christchurch. The Nth Wing Extension at Mt Eden prison becomes expanded for women, supplemented by the old wooden structure outside (cf 1924).

1954   Dressmaking classes begin for women at Mt Eden.

1959   As a result of the 1958 escapes of Maori Mac and general population pressure, women prisoners housed in the Nth Wing Extension at Mt Eden are transferred to Arohata and Dunedin, and the wing is taken over by men. The separate wooden women's division continues to operate. Dunedin prison, used by the Police Department since 1916 and later, partially by Defence, is reclaimed by Justice to become the country's primary institution for women. The 1st floor (Defence) is taken over by women prisoners, while the ground floor remains in the possession of the police. Soon afterward, in November, the women at Dunedin riot. As a result, a decision is made to build a women's prison in Christchurch.

1960   Equal pay for women prison officers comes with the equal pay legislation for the public service, gradually phased in and fully operational by 1965.

1961   A decision (unfulfilled) is made to build two new women's prisons, one of them in the South Island.

1963   The Annual Report of the Justice Department recommends closing down the women's division at Mt Eden in order to build a secure unit for men. This occurs in 1965.

1964   A riot takes place at Dunedin Prison for Women. This prioritises plans for a new facility at Christchurch.

1965   Following the escape of Evans, Gillies and Wilder in Feb 1965, the wooden women's division at Mt Eden, built about 1925, is demolished and women are transferred to the old superintendent's quarters outside the wall. A new security block for men is built on the site (opens 1966).

1967   In September, there is a 6-hour strike at Dunedin Women's prison.

1974   Paparua Women's prison opens in Christchurch, and Dunedin reverts to being a short-sentence/remand men's prison. Paparua was NZ's second purpose-built female institution.

The first periodic detention centre for women opens in Epsom, Auckland, late 1974.

1980   The Minister of Justice announces the intention to build a new women's prison at Papakura, as a high priority. In 1982, the idea is dropped.

1983   The Minister of Justice announces the intention to build five new periodic detention centres for women.

1985   Celia Lashlie becomes the first woman prison officer to be employed in a men's prison (Wi Tako).

1991   Three women officers are appointed to Paremoremo Maximum.

1992   Heather Colby becomes the first woman appointed to run a men's prison (Tongariro Prison Farm).

1998   The first self-care unit opens at Paparua Women's prison.

2001   Belinda Clark becomes NZ's first female Secretary for Justice.

2003   After three years searching, a site for a new women's prison is found at Manukau, Auckland. Originally planned for 150 beds, this is later revised to 286.

2003   A temporary unit for females, Nikau Unit, is opened at Waikeria.

2006   Auckland Region Women's Corrections Facility (ARWCF) opens in Manukau, with capacity for 286. The women's prison at Mt Eden closes and becomes a male reintegration unit.

KEY DATES OF NEW ZEALAND'S MAJOR PRISONS

Addington prison: Construction begins 1874; completed 1876; is used as a 'lunatics' asylum from 1889; becomes a Samaritan Home for indigents from 1896; becomes a dedicated women's prison in 1913 with transfers from Lyttelton; a women's reformatory in 1917, and becomes used for younger women in 1920 with the transfer of older inmates to Pt Halswell. Addington is taken over as an army detention barracks 1950; reverts back to Justice Dept 1959 and reopens as a prison; closes 1999.

Arohata Girls' Borstal/Women's prison: Opens 1944.

Auckland 'City' gaol: Built 1841 Cnr Victoria St/Queen St; closes 1865; inmates transferred to the Stockade, Mt Eden.

Auckland Central Remand prison: Opens 2000 as a private prison; reverts to state management 2005.

Auckland Region Women's Correctional Facility: Opens 2006.

Dunedin prison: Construction begins 1895; completed 1898. Is handed over to Police and Defence Depts 1915; becomes a women's prison 1959; reverts to a men's prison 1974.

Hokitika prison: opens 1865; closes 1909.

Humeville prison camp: opens 1890; closes 1892.

Invercargill prison: Completed 1910; becomes a borstal 1917.

Kaitoke prison: Opens 1978.

Linton prison: Opens 1979.

Lyttelton gaol: Construction begins 1860; completed 1861; closes 1920.

Mangaroa prison: Opens 1989.

Mt Cook prison: Originally gazetted as a prison 1879 from converted immigration barracks. Building begins 1882; completed 1897; closes 1900 and is handed over to Defence Dept and renamed Alexandra Barracks; demolished 1924.

Mt Crawford prison: Construction begins 1923; completed 1927.

Mt Eden prison: Site commences usage as 'The Stockade', which opens 1856. Becomes Auckland's primary prison on closure of the Auckland 'City' gaol 1865. Construction on existing buildings begins 1882; occupied 1888; completed 1917.

Napier prison: Site established 1862; new buildings completed 1906; closes 1993.

Ngawha prison: Opens 2005.

New Plymouth prison: Tenders called 1876; completed 1886; serves as a sex offenders' institution 1910–1952.

Ohura prison: Purchased 1971; opens 1972; closes 2005.

Paparua Men's prison: Land purchased 1914; land occupied 1915; buildings completed 1924.

Paparua Women's prison: Site occupied temporarily 1950; existing prison opens 1974.

Paremoremo Maximum Security prison: Opens 1969.

Paremoremo Medium Security prison: Opens 1981.

Point Halswell prison: Work begins on a male prison at Pt Halswell 1915; opens as a women's reformatory 1920; a girls' borstal opens on the site 1925; closes 1944.

Rolleston prison: Taken over from the army 1957; opens 1958.

The Terrace gaol: Predates 1850; demolished 1923 and replaced by Mt Crawford.

Tongariro (Hautu/Rangipo) Land purchased 1921 (10,000 acres); first buildings erected at Hautu 1922; at Rangipo 1925.

Wanganui prison: Original buildings constructed out of demolition timber from the disused Rutland Stockade, 1867. New prison opens 1924; closes 2000.

Waipiata Borstal: Opens 1961; closes 1979.

Waikeria: Land purchased 1910; work on buildings begins 1912; opens 1912. Becomes a borstal 1925; a youth prison 1981.

Waikune: Established 1914 at Rotoaira as a road-building camp; shifts to Erua 1920 and is re-named Waikune. Rebuilt 1963; closes 1986.

Wi Tako/Rimutaka prison: Originally built 1919; rebuilt 1967; renamed 'Rimutaka prison' 1990.

Tree-planting Camps

Dumgree: Opens 1904; closes 1908.

Hanmer: Opens 1903; closes 1913.

Kaingaroa: Opens 1913; closes 1920.

Waiotapu: Opens 1901 (the first tree-planting camp in NZ); closes 1913.

Waipa Valley: Opens 1904; closes 1916.

APPENDIX 4
NEW ZEALAND PRISON HOMICIDES

1.　　1979, 16 July. Keith Ross Hall (22) is stabbed in the throat and killed in the basement of A. Block at Paremoremo prison. Hall had been convicted in March 1978 of raping, torturing and killing 10-year-old Delphine Phillips at Ohakune in November 1977. On 18 July 1979, Cedric James is charged with Hall's murder but is acquitted. In December 2005 James starves to death in a life raft, after the Nelson-based trawler he is working on sinks in rough seas.

2.　　1985, 6 January. Darcy Te Hira (40) dies after being beaten over the head with a long-handled porridge stirrer in the kitchen at Mt Eden prison. He is within three days of his release date. On 25 July Ross Gary Appelgren (33), serving 2.5 years for receiving stolen car parts, is convicted of Te Hira's murder. Protesting his innocence, on 15 November 1987 Appelgren escapes from Kaitoke prison to advertise his cause. He is recaptured on 20 January 1988. Granted a retrial and released on bail in 1990, on 28 May 1992 Appelgren is reconvicted of murder and returned to serve his life sentence. During his time on bail he lives with one of the jurors in his original trial, Julie Whittaker, who had begun writing to him in 1989 and who is by now convinced of his innocence. They are married in prison on 23 December 1995.

3.　　1993, March. Double Kaiaua murderer Stephen Christopher Matchitt (22) is stabbed to death in Paremoremo's A.Block. Arthur Alexander Gray (32) is charged with Matchitt's murder. He is acquitted on the grounds of self-defence.

4.　　1997, 11 March. James Elliott Tyson (52) dies at Palmerston North Hospital. Tyson had been seriously assaulted in an exercise yard at Manawatu prison, Linton, on 30 January, after asking Christopher Holland to turn his radio down. Holland (23) is charged with his murder but is acquitted and receives seven years for manslaughter. Holland had been serving 6 1/2 years for armed robbery.

5.　　1998, 12 September, at Waikato Hospital, prison, Nga Trego (35) dies of burns after having been doused with accelerant three weeks earlier while in his cell at Tongariro prison, and set alight. Three inmates are charged in relation to his death. In February 1999 John Tuivaga and Visi Taliau are convicted of murder, while Tangata Pahulu is convicted of manslaughter.

6.　　2001, 19 May, Justin Gene Kaa (27) is stabbed to death with a carving chisel in the low security unit (unit 4) at Manawatu prison. In April 02 Michael Kerins is acquitted on the ground of self-defence.

7.   2003, 29 March, Christopher Hereora (30) is beaten in a shower block at Kaitoke prison, just 24 hours after being transferred from Mangaroa. He dies in hospital next day. Hereora had been serving 14 years for taking part in the contracted beating of 53 year-old Robert Rogers with a car jack in a home invasion in 1999 (aggravated burglary and GBH).

8.   2004, 4 March. Rex Leonard Hopper (51), sentenced to life in 1995 for murdering his fiancée shortly before their wedding and attempting suicide (but only succeeded on blowing half his face off), is found dead at Rimutaka prison. Hopper had been in a gardening party outside the Christian faith unit, and had sustained serious head injuries and a stab wound in the throat from a gardening fork. The argument had started over a screwdriver. Emani Seu (46) is convicted of murder.

9.   2006, 28 March. Sonny John Keremete (25) is stabbed to death at Mangaroa prison. Keremete, a senior member of Black Power, had been at the prison since November after assaulting a prison officer at Rimutaka. Nine other inmates are in the unit at the time of the stabbing. Dartelle Alder (28) is charged with Keremete's murder (proceeding). Alder is serving life with a 17-year minimum for raping and murdering a female jogger near Flaxmere in 2001.

10.   2006, 24 August. Liam Ashley (17) is beaten and strangled to death in a Chubb escort van en route to Mt Eden prison on remand for sentencing. Ashley had just been convicted of 10 minor charges – e.g. burglary, breaching bail, trespass, possession of a cannabis pipe. Many of the charges relate to crimes committed against his family. George Charlie Baker (25) confesses to Ashley's murder and is sentenced to life with an 18-year minimum in December.

INDEX

THE AUTHOR

Greg Newbold is an associate professor in the School of Sociology and Anthropology at Canterbury University. Having commenced his criminological training in 1975 while serving seven and a half years in New Zealand's maximum-security prison at Paremoremo, Newbold is a leading criminologist who writes with both academic knowledge and first-hand experience. This is his seventh book.